Praise for *Test-Driven Development with Python*

In this book, Harry takes us on an adventure of discovery with Python and testing. It's an excellent book, fun to read and full of vital information. It has my highest recommendations for anyone interested in testing with Python, learning Django, or wanting to use Selenium. Testing is essential for developer sanity and it's a notoriously difficult field, full of trade-offs. Harry does a fantastic job of holding our attention whilst exploring real-world testing practices.

—*Michael Foord, Python Core Developer and Maintainer of unittest*

This book is far more than an introduction to test-driven development—it's a complete best-practices crash course, from start to finish, into modern web application development with Python. Every web developer needs this book.

—*Kenneth Reitz, Fellow at Python Software Foundation*

Harry's book is what we wish existed when we were learning Django. At a pace that's achievable and yet delightfully challenging, it provides excellent instruction for Django and various test practices. The material on Selenium alone makes the book worth purchasing, but there's so much more!

—*Daniel and Audrey Roy Greenfeld, authors of* Two Scoops of Django *(Two Scoops Press)*

SECOND EDITION

Test-Driven Development with Python

Obey the Testing Goat: Using Django,
Selenium, and JavaScript

Harry J.W. Percival

Beijing · Boston · Farnham · Sebastopol · Tokyo

Test-Driven Development with Python

by Harry J.W. Percival

Copyright © 2017 Harry Percival. All rights reserved.

Printed in the United States of America.

Published by O'Reilly Media, Inc., 1005 Gravenstein Highway North, Sebastopol, CA 95472.

O'Reilly books may be purchased for educational, business, or sales promotional use. Online editions are also available for most titles (*http://oreilly.com/safari*). For more information, contact our corporate/institutional sales department: 800-998-9938 or *corporate@oreilly.com*.

Editor: Nan Barber
Production Editor: Kristen Brown
Copyeditor: Kim Cofer
Proofreader: Rachel Monaghan

Indexer: Judith McConville
Interior Designer: David Futato
Cover Designer: Karen Montgomery
Illustrator: Rebecca Demarest

August 2017:   Second Edition

Revision History for the Second Edition

2017-08-02:   First Release
2018-03-02:   Second Release

See *http://oreilly.com/catalog/errata.csp?isbn=9781491958704* for release details.

The O'Reilly logo is a registered trademark of O'Reilly Media, Inc. *Test-Driven Development with Python*, the cover image, and related trade dress are trademarks of O'Reilly Media, Inc.

978-1-491-95870-4

[LSI]

Table of Contents

Part I.   The Basics of TDD and Django

Part II.   Web Development *Sine Qua Nons*

Part III. More Advanced Topics in Testing

Preface

This book is my attempt to share with the world the journey I've taken from "hacking" to "software engineering". It's mainly about testing, but there's a lot more to it, as you'll soon see.

I want to thank you for reading it.

If you bought a copy, then I'm very grateful. If you're reading the free online version, then I'm *still* grateful that you've decided it's worth spending some of your time on. Who knows, perhaps once you get to the end, you'll decide it's good enough to buy a real copy for yourself or for a friend.

If you have any comments, questions, or suggestions, I'd love to hear from you. You can reach me directly via *obeythetestinggoat@gmail.com*, or on Twitter @hjwp (*https://www.twitter.com/hjwp*). You can also check out the website and my blog (*http://www.obeythetestinggoat.com*), and there's a mailing list (*https://groups.google.com/forum/#!forum/obey-the-testing-goat-book*).

I hope you'll enjoy reading this book as much as I enjoyed writing it.

Why I Wrote a Book About Test-Driven Development

"Who are you, why are you writing this book, and why should I read it?" I hear you ask.

I'm still quite early on in my programming career. They say that in any discipline, you go from apprentice, to journeyman, and eventually, sometimes, on to master. I'd say that I'm—at best—a journeyman programmer. But I was lucky enough, early on in my career, to fall in with a bunch of TDD fanatics, and it made such a big impact on my programming that I'm burning to share it with everyone. You might say I have the enthusiasm of a recent convert, and the learning experience is still a recent memory for me, so I hope I can still empathise with beginners.

When I first learned Python (from Mark Pilgrim's excellent *Dive Into Python*), I came across the concept of TDD, and thought "Yes. I can definitely see the sense in that."

Perhaps you had a similar reaction when you first heard about TDD? It sounds like a really sensible approach, a really good habit to get into—like regularly flossing your teeth.

Then came my first big project, and you can guess what happened—there was a client, there were deadlines, there was lots to do, and any good intentions about TDD went straight out of the window.

And, actually, it was fine. I was fine.

At first.

At first I knew I didn't really need TDD because it was a small website, and I could easily test whether things worked by just manually checking it out. Click this link *here*, choose that drop-down item *there*, and *this* should happen. Easy. This whole writing tests thing sounded like it would have taken *ages*, and besides, I fancied myself, from the full height of my three weeks of adult coding experience, as being a pretty good programmer. I could handle it. Easy.

Then came the fearful goddess Complexity. She soon showed me the limits of my experience.

The project grew. Parts of the system started to depend on other parts. I did my best to follow good principles like DRY (Don't Repeat Yourself), but that just led to some pretty dangerous territory. Soon I was playing with multiple inheritance. Class hierarchies eight levels deep. eval statements.

I became scared of making changes to my code. I was no longer sure what depended on what, and what might happen if I changed this code *over here*, oh gosh, I think that bit over there inherits from it—no, it doesn't, it's overriden. Oh, but it depends on that class variable. Right, well, as long as I override the override it should be fine. I'll just check—but checking was getting much harder. There were lots of sections to the site now, and clicking through them all manually was starting to get impractical. Better to leave well enough alone, forget refactoring, just make do.

Soon I had a hideous, ugly mess of code. New development became painful.

Not too long after this, I was lucky enough to get a job with a company called Resolver Systems (now PythonAnywhere (*https://www.pythonanywhere.com*)), where Extreme Programming (XP) was the norm. They introduced me to rigorous TDD.

Although my previous experience had certainly opened my mind to the possible benefits of automated testing, I still dragged my feet at every stage. "I mean, testing in general might be a good idea, but *really*? All these tests? Some of them seem like a total waste of time... What? Functional tests *as well as* unit tests? Come on, that's overdoing it! And this TDD test/minimal-code-change/test cycle? This is just silly!

We don't need all these baby steps! Come on, we can see what the right answer is, why don't we just skip to the end?"

Believe me, I second-guessed every rule, I suggested every shortcut, I demanded justifications for every seemingly pointless aspect of TDD, and I came out seeing the wisdom of it all. I've lost count of the number of times I've thought "Thanks, tests", as a functional test uncovers a regression we would never have predicted, or a unit test saves me from making a really silly logic error. Psychologically, it's made development a much less stressful process. It produces code that's a pleasure to work with.

So, let me tell you *all* about it!

Aims of This Book

My main aim is to impart a methodology—a way of doing web development, which I think makes for better web apps and happier developers. There's not much point in a book that just covers material you could find by Googling, so this book isn't a guide to Python syntax, or a tutorial on web development *per se*. Instead, I hope to teach you how to use TDD to get more reliably to our shared, holy goal: *clean code that works*.

With that said: I will constantly refer to a real practical example, by building a web app from scratch using tools like Django, Selenium, jQuery, and Mocks. I'm not assuming any prior knowledge of any of these, so you should come out of the other end of this book with a decent introduction to those tools, as well as the discipline of TDD.

In Extreme Programming we always pair-program, so I've imagined writing this book as if I was pairing with my previous self, having to explain how the tools work and answer questions about why we code in this particular way. So, if I ever take a bit of a patronising tone, it's because I'm not all that smart, and I have to be very patient with myself. And if I ever sound defensive, it's because I'm the kind of annoying person that systematically disagrees with whatever anyone else says, so sometimes it takes a lot of justifying to convince myself of anything.

Outline

I've split this book into three parts.

Part I (Chapters 1–7): The basics
Dives straight into building a simple web app using TDD. We start by writing a functional test (with Selenium), and then we go through the basics of Django—models, views, templates—with rigorous unit testing at every stage. I also introduce the Testing Goat.

Part II (Chapters 8–17): Web development essentials

> Covers some of the trickier but unavoidable aspects of web development, and shows how testing can help us with them: static files, deployment to production, form data validation, database migrations, and the dreaded JavaScript.

Part III (Chapters 18–26): More advanced testing topics

> Mocking, integrating a third-party system, test fixtures, Outside-In TDD, and Continuous Integration (CI).

On to a little housekeeping...

Conventions Used in This Book

The following typographical conventions are used in this book:

Italic

> Indicates new terms, URLs, email addresses, filenames, and file extensions.

`Constant width`

> Used for program listings, as well as within paragraphs to refer to program elements such as variable or function names, databases, data types, environment variables, statements, and keywords.

`Constant width bold`

> Shows commands or other text that should be typed literally by the user.

Occasionally I will use the symbol:

> `[...]`

to signify that some of the content has been skipped, to shorten long bits of output, or to skip down to a relevant section.

 This element signifies a tip or suggestion.

 This element signifies a general note or aside.

This element indicates a warning or caution.

Submitting Errata

Spotted a mistake or a typo? The sources for this book are available on GitHub, and I'm always very happy to receive issues and pull requests: *https://github.com/hjwp/Book-TDD-Web-Dev-Python/*.

Using Code Examples

Code examples are available at *https://github.com/hjwp/book-example/*; you'll find branches for each chapter there (e.g., *https://github.com/hjwp/book-example/tree/chapter_unit_test_first_view*). You'll find a full list, and some suggestions on ways of working with this repository, in Appendix J.

This book is here to help you get your job done. In general, if example code is offered with this book, you may use it in your programs and documentation. You do not need to contact us for permission unless you're reproducing a significant portion of the code. For example, writing a program that uses several chunks of code from this book does not require permission. Selling or distributing a CD-ROM of examples from O'Reilly books does require permission. Answering a question by citing this book and quoting example code does not require permission. Incorporating a significant amount of example code from this book into your product's documentation does require permission.

We appreciate, but do not require, attribution. An attribution usually includes the title, author, publisher, and ISBN. For example: "*Test-Driven Development with Python*, 2nd edition, by Harry J.W. Percival (O'Reilly). Copyright 2017 Harry Percival, 978-1-491-95870-4."

If you feel your use of code examples falls outside fair use or the permission given above, feel free to contact us at *permissions@oreilly.com*.

O'Reilly Safari

 *Safari* (formerly Safari Books Online) is a membership-based training and reference platform for enterprise, government, educators, and individuals.

Members have access to thousands of books, training videos, Learning Paths, interactive tutorials, and curated playlists from over 250 publishers, including O'Reilly Media, Harvard Business Review, Prentice Hall Professional, Addison-Wesley Professional, Microsoft Press, Sams, Que, Peachpit Press, Adobe, Focal Press, Cisco Press, John Wiley & Sons, Syngress, Morgan Kaufmann, IBM Redbooks, Packt, Adobe Press, FT Press, Apress, Manning, New Riders, McGraw-Hill, Jones & Bartlett, and Course Technology, among others.

For more information, please visit *http://oreilly.com/safari*.

Contacting O'Reilly

If you'd like to get in touch with my beloved publisher with any questions about this book, contact details follow:

O'Reilly Media, Inc.
1005 Gravenstein Highway North
Sebastopol, CA 95472
800-998-9938 (in the United States or Canada)
707-829-0515 (international or local)
707-829-0104 (fax)

We have a web page for this book, where we list errata, examples, and any additional information. You can access this page at *http://bit.ly/tdd_py_2e*.

To comment or ask technical questions about this book, send email to *bookquestions@oreilly.com*.

For more information about books, courses, conferences, and news, see O'Reilly's website at *http://www.oreilly.com*.

Facebook: *http://facebook.com/oreilly*

Twitter: *http://twitter.com/oreillymedia*

YouTube: *http://www.youtube.com/oreillymedia*

Prerequisites and Assumptions

Here's an outline of what I'm assuming about you and what you already know, as well as what software you'll need ready and installed on your computer.

Python 3 and Programming

I've tried to write this book with beginners in mind, but if you're new to programming, I'm assuming that you've already learned the basics of Python. So if you haven't already, do run through a Python beginner's tutorial or get an introductory book like *Dive Into Python* (*http://www.diveintopython.net/*) or *Learn Python the Hard Way* (*http://learnpythonthehardway.org/*), or, just for fun, *Invent Your Own Computer Games with Python* (*http://inventwithpython.com/*), all of which are excellent introductions.

If you're an experienced programmer but new to Python, you should get along just fine. Python is joyously simple to understand.

I'm using *Python 3* for this book. When I wrote the first edition in 2013–14, Python 3 had been around for several years, and the world was just about on the tipping point at which it was the preferred choice. You should be able to follow this book on Mac, Windows, or Linux. Detailed installation instructions for each OS follow.

 This book was tested against Python 3.6. If you're on an earlier version, you will find minor differences (the f-string syntax, for example), so you're best off upgrading if you can.

I wouldn't recommend trying to use Python 2, as the differences are more substantial. You'll still be able to carry across all the lessons you learn in this book if your next project happens to be in Python 2. But spending time figuring out whether the reason your program output looks different from mine is because of Python 2, or because you made an actual mistake, won't be time spent productively.

If you are thinking of using PythonAnywhere (*http://www.pythonanywhere.com*) (the PaaS startup I work for), rather than a locally installed Python, you should go and take a quick look at Appendix A before you get started.

In any case, I expect you to have access to Python, to know how to launch it from a command line, and to know how to edit a Python file and run it. Again, have a look at the three books I recommended previously if you're in any doubt.

 If you already have Python 2 installed, and you're worried that installing Python 3 will break it in some way, don't! Python 3 and 2 can coexist peacefully on the same system, particularly if you're using a virtualenv, which we will be.

How HTML Works

I'm also assuming you have a basic grasp of how the web works—what HTML is, what a POST request is, and so on. If you're not sure about those, you'll need to find a basic HTML tutorial; there are a few at *http://www.webplatform.org/*. If you can figure out how to create an HTML page on your PC and look at it in your browser, and understand what a form is and how it might work, then you're probably OK.

Django

The book uses the Django framework, which is (probably) the most well-established web framework in the Python world. I've written the book assuming that the reader has no prior knowledge of Django, but if you're new to Python *and* new to web development *and* new to testing, you may occasionally find that there's just one too many topics and sets of concepts to try and take on board. If that's the case, I recommend taking a break from the book, and taking a look at a Django tutorial. DjangoGirls (*https://tutorial.djangogirls.org/*) is the best, most beginner-friendly tutorial I know of. The official tutorial (*https://docs.djangoproject.com/en/1.11/intro/tutorial01/*) is also excellent for more experienced programmers (make sure you follow the 1.11 tutorial rather than a 2.x one though).

This book was published before Django 2.0 came out, and as such is written for Django v1.11 (which is an "long-term-support" or LTS edition). If you're keen to use Django 2, I strongly recommend doing so *after* you've read this book, in your own projects, rather than installing it now and trying to adapt as you go along. Django hasn't changed that much, but when things look different on your own PC from what the book says should happen, you'll waste time trying to figure out whether it's because Django has changed, or because you've made a mistake.

Read on for instructions on installing Django.

JavaScript

There's a little bit of JavaScript in the second half of the book. If you don't know Java-Script, don't worry about it until then, and if you find yourself a little confused, I'll recommend a couple of guides at that point.

A Note on IDEs

If you've come from the world of Java or .NET, you may be keen to use an IDE for your Python coding. They have all sorts of useful tools, including VCS integration, and there are some excellent ones out there for Python. I used one myself when I was starting out, and I found it very useful for my first couple of projects.

Can I suggest (and it's only a suggestion) that you *don't* use an IDE, at least for the duration of this tutorial? IDEs are much less necessary in the Python world, and I've written this whole book with the assumption that you're just using a basic text editor and a command line. Sometimes, that's all you have—when you're working on a server, for example—so it's always worth learning how to use the basic tools first and understanding how they work. It'll be something you always have, even if you decide to go back to your IDE and all its helpful tools, after you've finished this book.

Required Software Installations

Aside from Python, you'll need:

The Firefox web browser
Selenium can actually drive any of the major browsers, but Firefox is the best to use as an example because it's reliably cross-platform and, as a bonus, is less sold out to corporate interests.

The Git version control system

This is available for any platform, at *http://git-scm.com/*. On Windows, this comes with the *Bash* command line, which is needed for the book.

A virtualenv with Python 3, Django 1.11, and Selenium 3 in it

Python's virtualenv and pip tools now come bundled with Python 3.4+ (they didn't always used to, so this is a big hooray). Detailed instructions for preparing your virtualenv follow.

Geckodriver

This is the driver that will let us remotely control Firefox via Selenium. I'll point to a download link in "Installing Firefox and Geckodriver" on page xxix.

Windows Notes

Windows users can sometimes feel a little neglected in the open source world, since macOS and Linux are so prevalent, making it easy to forget there's a world outside the Unix paradigm. Backslashes as directory separators? Drive letters? What? Still, it is absolutely possible to follow along with this book on Windows. Here are a few tips:

1. When you install Git for Windows, make sure you choose **"Run Git and included Unix tools from the Windows command prompt"**. You'll then get access to a program called "Git Bash". Use this as your main command prompt and you'll get all the useful GNU command-line tools like `ls`, `touch`, and `grep`, plus forward-slash directory separators.

2. Also in the Git installer, choose **"Use Windows' default console"**; otherwise, Python won't work properly in the Git-Bash window.

3. When you install Python 3, unless you already have Python 2 and want to keep it as your default, tick the option that says **"Add Python 3.6 to PATH"** as in Figure P-1, so that you can easily run Python from the command line.

Figure P-1. Add Python to the system path from the installer

The test for all this is that you should be able to go to a Git-Bash command prompt and just run `python` or `pip` from any folder.

MacOS Notes

MacOS is a bit more sane than Windows, although getting `pip` installed was still fairly challenging up until recently. Since the arrival of 3.4, things are now quite straightforward:

- Python 3.6 should install without a fuss from its downloadable installer (*http://www.python.org*). It will automatically install `pip`, too.
- Git's installer should also "just work".

Similarly to Windows, the test for all this is that you should be able to open a terminal and just run `git`, `python3`, or `pip` from anywhere. If you run into any trouble, the search terms "system path" and "command not found" should provide good troubleshooting resources.

You might also want to check out Homebrew (*http://brew.sh//*). It used to be the only reliable way of installing lots of Unixy tools (including Python 3) on a Mac.[1] Although the normal Python installer is now fine, you may find Homebrew useful in future. It does require you to download all 1.1 GB of Xcode, but that also gives you a C compiler, which is a useful side effect.

---

1 I wouldn't recommend installing Firefox via Homebrew though: `brew` puts the Firefox binary in a strange location, and it confuses Selenium. You can work around it, but it's simpler to just install Firefox in the normal way.

Git's Default Editor, and Other Basic Git Config

I'll provide step-by-step instructions for Git, but it may be a good idea to get a bit of configuration done now. For example, when you do your first commit, by default *vi* will pop up, at which point you may have no idea what to do with it. Well, much as vi has two modes, you then have two choices. One is to learn some minimal vi com- mands *(press the i key to go into insert mode, type your text, press `<Esc>` to go back to normal mode, then write the file and quit with `:wq<Enter>`)*. You'll then have joined the great fraternity of people who know this ancient, revered text editor.

Or you can point-blank refuse to be involved in such a ridiculous throwback to the 1970s, and configure Git to use an editor of your choice. Quit vi using `<Esc>` followed by `:q!`, then change your Git default editor. See the Git documentation on basic Git configuration (*http://git-scm.com/book/en/Customizing-Git-Git-Configuration*).

Installing Firefox and Geckodriver

Firefox is available as a download for Windows and macOS from *https:// www.mozilla.org/firefox/*. On Linux, you probably already have it installed, but other- wise your package manager will have it.

Geckodriver is available from *https://github.com/mozilla/geckodriver/releases*. You need to download and extract it and put it somewhere on your system path.

- For Windows, you can just put it in the same folder as your code for this book— or if you put it in your Python *Scripts* folder, it'll be available for other projects.

- For macOS or Linux, one convenient place to put it is */usr/local/bin* (you'll need `sudo` for this).

To test that you've got this working, open up a Bash console and you should be able to run:

```
$ geckodriver --version
geckodriver 0.19.1

The source code of this program is available at
https://github.com/mozilla/geckodriver.

This program is subject to the terms of the Mozilla Public License 2.0.
You can obtain a copy of the license at https://mozilla.org/MPL/2.0/.
```

Setting Up Your Virtualenv

A Python virtualenv (short for virtual environment) is how you set up your environment for different Python projects. It allows you to use different packages (e.g., different versions of Django, and even different versions of Python) in each project. And because you're not installing things system-wide, it means you don't need root permissions.

Let's create a Python 3 virtualenv called "superlists".[2] I'm assuming you're working in a folder called *python-tdd-book*, but you can name your work folder whatever you like. Stick to the name "virtualenv" for the virtualenv, though.

```
$ cd python-tdd-book
$ py -3.6 -m venv virtualenv
```

On Windows, the py executable is a shortcut for different Python versions. On Mac or Linux, we use python3.6:

```
$ cd python-tdd-book
$ python3.6 -m venv virtualenv
```

Activating and Deactivating the Virtualenv

Whenever you work on the book, you'll want to make sure your virtualenv has been "activated". You can always tell when your virtualenv is active because you'll see (vir tualenv) in parentheses, in your prompt. But you can also check by running which python to check whether Python is currently the system-installed one, or the virtualenv one.

The command to activate the virtualenv is source virtualenv/Scripts/activate on Windows and source virtualenv/bin/activate on Mac/Linux. The command to deactivate is just deactivate.

Try it out like this:

---

2 Why superlists, I hear you ask? No spoilers! You'll find out in the next chapter.

```
$ source virtualenv/Scripts/activate
(virtualenv)$
(virtualenv)$ which python
/C/Users/harry/python-tdd-book/virtualenv/Scripts/python
(virtualenv)$ deactivate
$
$ which python
/c/Users/harry/AppData/Local/Programs/Python/Python36-32/python

$ source virtualenv/bin/activate
(virtualenv)$
(virtualenv)$ which python
/home/myusername/python-tdd-book/virtualenv/bin/python
(virtualenv)$ deactivate
$
$ which python
/usr/bin/python
```

 Always make sure your virtualenv is active when working on the book. Look out for the (virtualenv) in your prompt, or run which python to check.

Activate Not Working on Windows?

If you see an error like this:

```
bash: virtualenv/Scripts/activate: No such file or directory
```

First, double-check you're in the right folder. Assuming you are, or if you see an error like this:

```
bash: @echo: command not found
bash: virtualenv/Scripts/activate.bat: line 4:
    syntax error near unexpected token `(
bash: virtualenv/Scripts/activate.bat: line 4: `if not defined PROMPT ('
```

Then you've probably run into a old bug where Python wouldn't install an activate script that was compatible with Git-Bash. Reinstall the latest Python 3, making sure you have 3.6.3 or later, then delete and re-create your virtualenv.

Installing Django and Selenium

We'll install Django 1.11 and the latest Selenium, Selenium 3.

Remember to make sure your virtualenv is active first!

```
(virtualenv) $ pip install "django<1.12" "selenium<4"
Collecting django==1.11.8
  Using cached Django-1.11.8-py2.py3-none-any.whl
Collecting selenium<4
  Using cached selenium-3.9.0-py2.py3-none-any.whl
Installing collected packages: django, selenium
Successfully installed django-1.11.8 selenium-3.9.0
```

Some Error Messages You're Likely to See When You *Inevitably* Fail to Activate Your Virtualenv

If you're new to virtualenvs—or even if you're not, to be honest—at some point you're *guaranteed* to forget to activate it, and then you'll be staring at an error message. Happens to me all the time. Here are some of the things to look out for:

```
ImportError: No module named selenium
```

Or:

```
ImportError: No module named django.core.management
```

As always, look out for that (virtualenv) in your command prompt, and a quick source virtualenv/Scripts/activate or source virtualenv/bin/activate is probably what you need to get it working again.

Here's a couple more, for good measure:

```
bash: virtualenv/Scripts/activate: No such file or directory
```

This means you're not currently in the right directory for working on the project. Try a cd tdd-python-book, or similar.

Alternatively, if you're sure you're in the right place, you may have run into a bug from an older version of Python, where it wouldn't install an activate script that was compatible with Git-Bash. Reinstall Python 3, and make sure you have version 3.6.3 or later, and then delete and re-create your virtualenv.

If you see something like this, it's probably the same issue, you need to upgrade Python:

```
bash: @echo: command not found
bash: virtualenv/Scripts/activate.bat: line 4:
    syntax error near unexpected token `(
bash: virtualenv/Scripts/activate.bat: line 4: `if not defined PROMPT ('
```

Final one! If you see this:

```
'source' is not recognized as an internal or external command,
operable program or batch file.
```

It's because you've launched the default Windows command prompt, cmd, instead of Git-Bash. Close it and open the latter.

On Anaconda

Anaconda is another tool for managing different Python environments. It's particularly popular on Windows and for scientific computing, where it can be hard to get some of the compiled libraries to install.

In the world of web programming it's much less necessary, so *I recommend you do not use Anaconda for this book.*

Apart from anything else I don't know enough about it to help you debug any problems with it if they occur!

Happy coding!

 Did these instructions not work for you? Or have you got better ones? Get in touch: *obeythetestinggoat@gmail.com*!

Companion Video

I've recorded a 10-part video series to accompany this book (*http://oreil.ly/1svTFqB*).[1] It covers the content of Part I. If you find you learn well from video-based material, then I encourage you to check it out. Over and above what's in the book, it should give you a feel for what the "flow" of TDD is like, flicking between tests and code, explaining the thought process as we go.

Plus I'm wearing a delightful yellow T-shirt.

---

1 The video has not been updated for the second edition, but the content is all mostly the same.

Acknowledgments

Lots of people to thank, without whom this book would never have happened, and/or would have been even worse than it is.

Thanks first to "Greg" at $OTHER_PUBLISHER, who was the first person to encourage me to believe it really could be done. Even though your employers turned out to have overly regressive views on copyright, I'm forever grateful that you believed in me.

Thanks to Michael Foord, another ex-employee of Resolver Systems, for providing the original inspiration by writing a book himself, and thanks for his ongoing support for the project. Thanks also to my boss Giles Thomas, for foolishly allowing another one of his employees to write a book (although I believe he's now changed the standard employment contract to say "no books"). Thanks also for your ongoing wisdom and for setting me off on the testing path.

Thanks to my other colleagues, Glenn Jones and Hansel Dunlop, for being invaluable sounding boards, and for your patience with my one-track record conversation over the last year.

Thanks to my wife Clementine, and to both my families, without whose support and patience I would never have made it. I apologise for all the time spent with nose in computer on what should have been memorable family occasions. I had no idea when I set out what the book would do to my life ("Write it in my spare time, you say? That sounds reasonable…"). I couldn't have done it without you.

Thanks to my tech reviewers, Jonathan Hartley, Nicholas Tollervey, and Emily Bache, for your encouragements and invaluable feedback. Especially Emily, who actually conscientiously read every single chapter. Partial credit to Nick and Jon, but that should still be read as eternal gratitude. Having y'all around made the whole thing less of a lonely endeavour. Without all of you the book would have been little more than the nonsensical ramblings of an idiot.

Thanks to everyone else who's given up some of their time to give some feedback on the book, out of nothing more than the goodness of their heart: Gary Bernhardt, Mark Lavin, Matt O'Donnell, Michael Foord, Hynek Schlawack, Russell Keith-Magee, Andrew Godwin, Kenneth Reitz, and Nathan Stocks. Thanks for being much smarter than I am, and for preventing me from saying several stupid things. Naturally, there are still plenty of stupid things left in the book, for which y'all can absolutely not be held responsible.

Thanks to my editor Meghan Blanchette, for being a very friendly and likeable slave driver, and for keeping the book on track, both in terms of timescales and by restraining my sillier ideas. Thanks to all the others at O'Reilly for your help, including Sarah Schneider, Kara Ebrahim, and Dan Fauxsmith for letting me keep British English. Thanks to Charles Roumeliotis for your help with style and grammar. We may never see eye-to-eye on the merits of Chicago School quotation/punctuation rules, but I sure am glad you were around. And thanks to the design department for giving us a goat for the cover!

And thanks most especially to all my Early Release readers, for all your help picking out typos, for your feedback and suggestions, for all the ways in which you helped to smooth out the learning curve in the book, and most of all for your kind words of encouragement and support that kept me going. Thank you Jason Wirth, Dave Pawson, Jeff Orr, Kevin De Baere, crainbf, dsisson, Galeran, Michael Allan, James O'Donnell, Marek Turnovec, SoonerBourne, julz, Cody Farmer, William Vincent, Trey Hunner, David Souther, Tom Perkin, Sorcha Bowler, Jon Poler, Charles Quast, Siddhartha Naithani, Steve Young, Roger Camargo, Wesley Hansen, Johansen Christian Vermeer, Ian Laurain, Sean Robertson, Hari Jayaram, Bayard Randel, Konrad Korżel, Matthew Waller, Julian Harley, Barry McClendon, Simon Jakobi, Angelo Cordon, Jyrki Kajala, Manish Jain, Mahadevan Sreenivasan, Konrad Korżel, Deric Crago, Cosmo Smith, Markus Kemmerling, Andrea Costantini, Daniel Patrick, Ryan Allen, Jason Selby, Greg Vaughan, Jonathan Sundqvist, Richard Bailey, Diane Soini, Dale Stewart, Mark Keaton, Johan Wärlander, Simon Scarfe, Eric Grannan, Marc-Anthony Taylor, Maria McKinley, John McKenna, Rafał Szymański, Roel van der Goot, Ignacio Reguero, TJ Tolton, Jonathan Means, Theodor Nolte, Jungsoo Moon, Craig Cook, Gabriel Ewilazarus, Vincenzo Pandolfo, David "farbish2", Nico Coetzee, Daniel Gonzalez, Jared Contrascere, Zhao 赵亮, and many, many more. If I've missed your name, you have an absolute right to be aggrieved; I am incredibly grateful to you too, so write to me and I will try and make it up to you in any way I can.

And finally thanks to you, the latest reader, for deciding to check out the book! I hope you enjoy it.

Additional Thanks for the Second Edition

Thanks to my wonderful editor for the second edition, Nan Barber, and to Susan Conant, Kristen Brown, and the whole team at O'Reilly. Thanks once again to Emily and Jonathan for tech reviewing, as well as to Edward Wong for his very thorough notes. Any remaining errors and inadequacies are all my own.

Thanks also to the readers of the free edition who contributed comments, suggestions, and even some pull requests. I have definitely missed some of you on this list, so apologies if your name isn't here, but thanks to Emre Gonulates, Jésus Gómez, Jordon Birk, James Evans, Iain Houston, Jason DeWitt, Ronnie Raney, Spencer Ogden, Suresh Nimbalkar, Darius, Caco, LeBodro, Jeff, Duncan Betts, wasabigeek, joegnis, Lars, Mustafa, Jared, Craig, Sorcha, TJ, Ignacio, Roel, Justyna, Nathan, Andrea, Alexandr, bilyanhadzhi, mosegontar, sfarzy, henziger, hunterji, das-g, juanriaza, GeoWill, Windsooon, gonulate, Margie Roswell, Ben Elliott, Ramsay Mayka, peterj, 1hx, Wi, Duncan Betts, Matthew Senko, Neric "Kasu" Kaz, and many, many more.

The Basics of TDD and Django

In this first part, I'm going to introduce the basics of *Test-Driven Development* (TDD). We'll build a real web application from scratch, writing tests first at every stage.

We'll cover functional testing with Selenium, as well as unit testing, and see the difference between the two. I'll introduce the TDD workflow, what I call the unit-test/code cycle. We'll also do some refactoring, and see how that fits with TDD. Since it's absolutely essential to serious software engineering, I'll also be using a version control system (Git). We'll discuss how and when to do commits and integrate them with the TDD and web development workflow.

We'll be using Django, the Python world's most popular web framework (probably). I've tried to introduce the Django concepts slowly and one at a time, and provide lots of links to further reading. If you're a total beginner to Django, I thoroughly recommend taking the time to read them. If you find yourself feeling a bit lost, take a couple of hours to go through the official Django tutorial (make sure to use the 1.11 version (*https://docs.djangoproject.com/en/1.11/intro/tutorial01/*)), and then come back to the book.

You'll also get to meet the Testing Goat…

Be Careful with Copy and Paste

If you're working from a digital version of the book, it's natural to want to copy and paste code listings from the book as you're working through it. It's much better if you don't: typing things in by hand gets them into your muscle memory, and just feels much more real. You also inevitably make the occasional typo, and debugging them is an important thing to learn.

Quite apart from that, you'll find that the quirks of the PDF format mean that weird stuff often happens when you try to copy/paste from it…

## CHAPTER 1

Getting Django Set Up Using a Functional Test

TDD isn't something that comes naturally. It's a discipline, like a martial art, and just like in a Kung Fu movie, you need a bad-tempered and unreasonable master to force you to learn the discipline. Ours is the Testing Goat.

Obey the Testing Goat! Do Nothing Until You Have a Test

The Testing Goat is the unofficial mascot of TDD in the Python testing community. It probably means different things to different people, but, to me, the Testing Goat is a voice inside my head that keeps me on the True Path of Testing—like one of those little angels or demons that pop up above your shoulder in the cartoons, but with a very niche set of concerns. I hope, with this book, to install the Testing Goat inside your head too.

We've decided to build a website, even if we're not quite sure what it's going to do yet. Normally the first step in web development is getting your web framework installed and configured. *Download this, install that, configure the other, run the script…*but TDD requires a different mindset. When you're doing TDD, you always have the Testing Goat inside you—single-minded as goats are—bleating "Test first, test first!"

In TDD the first step is always the same: *write a test*.

First we write the test; *then* we run it and check that it fails as expected. *Only then* do we go ahead and build some of our app. Repeat that to yourself in a goat-like voice. I know I do.

Another thing about goats is that they take one step at a time. That's why they seldom fall off mountains, see, no matter how steep they are. As you can see in Figure 1-1.

Figure 1-1. Goats are more agile than you think (source: Caitlin Stewart, on Flickr (http://www.flickr.com/photos/caitlinstewart/2846642630/))

We'll proceed with nice small steps; we're going to use *Django*, which is a popular Python web framework, to build our app.

The first thing we want to do is check that we've got Django installed, and that it's ready for us to work with. The *way* we'll check is by confirming that we can spin up Django's development server and actually see it serving up a web page, in our web browser, on our local PC. We'll use the *Selenium* browser automation tool for this.

Create a new Python file called *functional_tests.py*, wherever you want to keep the code for your project, and enter the following code. If you feel like making a few little goat noises as you do it, it may help:

```
from selenium import webdriver

browser = webdriver.Firefox()
browser.get('http://localhost:8000')

assert 'Django' in browser.title
```

That's our first *functional test* (FT); I'll talk more about what I mean by functional tests, and how they contrast with unit tests, in a bit. For now, it's enough to assure ourselves that we understand what it's doing:

- Starting a Selenium "webdriver" to pop up a real Firefox browser window
- Using it to open up a web page which we're expecting to be served from the local PC
- Checking (making a test assertion) that the page has the word "Django" in its title

Let's try running it:

```
$ python functional_tests.py
  File ".../selenium/webdriver/remote/webdriver.py", line 324, in get
    self.execute(Command.GET, {'url': url})
  File ".../selenium/webdriver/remote/webdriver.py", line 312, in execute
    self.error_handler.check_response(response)
  File ".../selenium/webdriver/remote/errorhandler.py", line 242, in
check_response
    raise exception_class(message, screen, stacktrace)
selenium.common.exceptions.WebDriverException: Message: Reached error page: abo
ut:neterror?e=connectionFailure&u=http%3A//localhost%3A8000/[...]
```

You should see a browser window pop up and try to open *localhost:8000*, and show the "Unable to connect" error page. If you switch back to your console, you'll see the big ugly error message, telling us that Selenium hit an error page. And then, you will probably be irritated at the fact that it left the Firefox window lying around your desktop for you to tidy up. We'll fix that later!

If, instead, you see an error trying to import Selenium, or an error trying to find "geckodriver", you might need to go back and have another look at the "Prerequisites and Assumptions" section.

For now though, we have a *failing test*, so that means we're allowed to start building our app.

Getting Django Up and Running

Since you've definitely read "Prerequisites and Assumptions" by now, you've already got Django installed. The first step in getting Django up and running is to create a *project*, which will be the main container for our site. Django provides a little command-line tool for this:

```
$ django-admin.py startproject superlists .
```

Don't forget that "." at the end; it's important!

That will create a file called *manage.py* in your current folder, and a subfolder called *superlists*, with more stuff inside it:

```
├── functional_tests.py
├── geckodriver.log
├── manage.py
├── superlists
│   ├── __init__.py
│   ├── settings.py
│   ├── urls.py
│   └── wsgi.py
└── virtualenv
    ├── [...]
```

 Make sure your project folder looks exactly like this! If you see two nested folders called superlists, it's because you forgot the "." above. Delete them and try again.

The *superlists* folder is intended for stuff that applies to the whole project—like *settings.py*, for example, which is used to store global configuration information for the site.

But the main thing to notice is *manage.py*. That's Django's Swiss Army knife, and one of the things it can do is run a development server. Let's try that now:

```
$ python manage.py runserver
Performing system checks...

System check identified no issues (0 silenced).

You have 13 unapplied migration(s). Your project may not work properly until
you apply the migrations for app(s): admin, auth, contenttypes, sessions.
Run 'python manage.py migrate' to apply them.

Django version 1.11.3, using settings 'superlists.settings'
Starting development server at http://127.0.0.1:8000/
Quit the server with CONTROL-C.
```

It's safe to ignore that message about "unapplied migrations" for now. We'll look at migrations in Chapter 5.

That's Django's development server now up and running on our machine.

Leave it there and open another command shell. Navigate to your project folder, activate your virtualenv, and then try running our test again:

```
$ python functional_tests.py
$
```

If you see an error saying "no module named selenium", you've forgotten to activate your virtualenv. Check the Prerequisites and Assumptions section again if you need to.

Not much action on the command line, but you should notice two things: firstly, there was no ugly AssertionError and secondly, the Firefox window that Selenium popped up had a different-looking page on it.

Well, it may not look like much, but that was our first ever passing test! Hooray!

If it all feels a bit too much like magic, like it wasn't quite real, why not go and take a look at the dev server manually, by opening a web browser yourself and visiting *http://localhost:8000*? You should see something like Figure 1-2.

You can quit the development server now if you like, back in the original shell, using Ctrl-C.

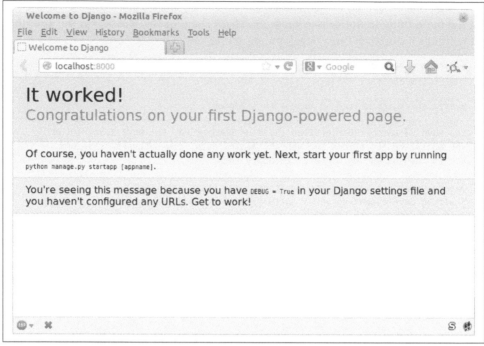

Figure 1-2. It worked!

Starting a Git Repository

There's one last thing to do before we finish the chapter: start to commit our work to a *version control system* (VCS). If you're an experienced programmer you don't need to hear me preaching about version control, but if you're new to it please believe me when I say that VCS is a must-have. As soon as your project gets to be more than a few weeks old and a few lines of code, having a tool available to look back over old versions of code, revert changes, explore new ideas safely, even just as a backup...boy. TDD goes hand in hand with version control, so I want to make sure I impart how it fits into the workflow.

So, our first commit! If anything it's a bit late; shame on us. We're using *Git* as our VCS, 'cos it's the best.

Let's start by doing the `git init` to start the repository:

```
$ ls
db.sqlite3
functional_tests.py
geckodriver.log
manage.py
superlists
virtualenv

$ git init .
Initialised empty Git repository in ...python-tdd-book/.git/
```

Our Working Directory Is Always the Folder that Contains *manage.py*

We'll be using this same folder throughout the book as our working directory—if in doubt, it's the one that contains *manage.py*.

(For simplicity, in my command listings, I'll always show it as *...python-tdd-book/*, although it will probably actually be something like */home/kind-reader-username/my-python-projects/python-tdd-book/.*)

Whenever I show a command to type in, it will assume we're in this directory. Similarly, if I mention a path to a file, it will be relative to this directory. So for example, *superlists/settings.py* means the *settings.py* inside the *superlists* folder.

Now let's take a look and see what files we want to commit:

```
$ ls
db.sqlite3
functional_tests.py
geckodriver.log
manage.py
superlists
virtualenv
```

There are a few things in here that we *don't* want under version control: *db.sqlite3* is the database file, *geckodriver.log* contains Selenium debug output, and finally our virtualenv shouldn't be in git either. We'll add all of them to a special file called *.gitignore* which, um, tells Git what to ignore:

```
$ echo "db.sqlite3" >> .gitignore
$ echo "geckodriver.log" >> .gitignore
$ echo "virtualenv" >> .gitignore
```

Next we can add the rest of the contents of the current folder, ".":

```
$ git add .
$ git status
On branch master

Initial commit

Changes to be committed:
  (use "git rm --cached <file>..." to unstage)

        new file:   .gitignore
        new file:   functional_tests.py
        new file:   manage.py
        new file:   superlists/__init__.py
        new file:   superlists/__pycache__/__init__.cpython-36.pyc
        new file:   superlists/__pycache__/settings.cpython-36.pyc
        new file:   superlists/__pycache__/urls.cpython-36.pyc
        new file:   superlists/__pycache__/wsgi.cpython-36.pyc
        new file:   superlists/settings.py
        new file:   superlists/urls.py
        new file:   superlists/wsgi.py
```

Oops! We've got a bunch of *.pyc* files in there; it's pointless to commit those. Let's remove them from Git and add them to *.gitignore* too:

```
$ git rm -r --cached superlists/__pycache__
rm 'superlists/__pycache__/__init__.cpython-36.pyc'
rm 'superlists/__pycache__/settings.cpython-36.pyc'
rm 'superlists/__pycache__/urls.cpython-36.pyc'
rm 'superlists/__pycache__/wsgi.cpython-36.pyc'
$ echo "__pycache__" >> .gitignore
$ echo "*.pyc" >> .gitignore
```

Now let's see where we are... (You'll see I'm using `git status` a lot—so much so that I often alias it to `git st`...I'm not telling you how to do that though; I leave you to discover the secrets of Git aliases on your own!):

```
$ git status
On branch master

Initial commit

Changes to be committed:
  (use "git rm --cached <file>..." to unstage)

        new file:   .gitignore
        new file:   functional_tests.py
        new file:   manage.py
        new file:   superlists/__init__.py
        new file:   superlists/settings.py
        new file:   superlists/urls.py
        new file:   superlists/wsgi.py

Changes not staged for commit:
  (use "git add <file>..." to update what will be committed)
  (use "git checkout -- <file>..." to discard changes in working directory)

        modified:   .gitignore
```

Looking good—we're ready to do our first commit!

```
$ git add .gitignore
$ git commit
```

When you type git commit, it will pop up an editor window for you to write your commit message in. Mine looked like Figure 1-3.[1]

---

[1] Did vi pop up and you had no idea what to do? Or did you see a message about account identity and git config --global user.username? Go and take another look at "Prerequisites and Assumptions"; there are some brief instructions.

```
COMMIT_EDITMSG + (/workspace/superlists/.git) - VIM
File  Edit  View  Search  Terminal  Help
  1 First commit: First FT and basic Django config
  2 # Please enter the commit message for your changes. Lines starting
  3 # with '#' will be ignored, and an empty message aborts the commit.
  4 # On branch master
  5 #
  6 # Initial commit
  7 #
  8 # Changes to be committed:
  9 #    (use "git rm --cached <file>..." to unstage)
 10 #
 11 #       new file:   .gitignore
 12 #       new file:   functional_tests.py
 13 #       new file:   manage.py
 14 #       new file:   superlists/__init__.py
 15 #       new file:   superlists/settings.py
 16 #       new file:   superlists/urls.py
 17 #       new file:   superlists/wsgi.py
 18 #
~
~
~
~
.git/COMMIT_EDITMSG [+][tabs]                        gitcommit 103,0x67 46,1/18
```

Figure 1-3. First Git commit

 If you want to really go to town on Git, this is the time to also learn about how to push your work to a cloud-based VCS hosting service, like GitHub or Bitbucket. They'll be useful if you think you want to follow along with this book on different PCs. I leave it to you to find out how they work; they have excellent documentation. Alternatively, you can wait until Chapter 9 when we'll be using one for deployment.

That's it for the VCS lecture. Congratulations! You've written a functional test using Selenium, and you've gotten Django installed and running, in a certifiable, test-first, goat-approved TDD way. Give yourself a well-deserved pat on the back before moving on to Chapter 2.

Extending Our Functional Test Using the unittest Module

Let's adapt our test, which currently checks for the default Django "it worked" page, and check instead for some of the things we want to see on the real front page of our site.

Time to reveal what kind of web app we're building: a to-do lists site! In doing so we're very much following fashion: a few years ago all web tutorials were about building a blog. Then it was forums and polls; nowadays it's all to-do lists.

The reason is that a to-do list is a really nice example. At its most basic it is very simple indeed—just a list of text strings—so it's easy to get a "minimum viable" list app up and running. But it can be extended in all sorts of ways—different persistence models, adding deadlines, reminders, sharing with other users, and improving the client-side UI. There's no reason to be limited to just "to-do" lists either; they could be any kind of lists. But the point is that it should allow me to demonstrate all of the main aspects of web programming, and how you apply TDD to them.

Using a Functional Test to Scope Out a Minimum Viable App

Tests that use Selenium let us drive a real web browser, so they really let us see how the application *functions* from the user's point of view. That's why they're called *functional tests*.

This means that an FT can be a sort of specification for your application. It tends to track what you might call a *User Story*, and follows how the user might work with a particular feature and how the app should respond to them.

Terminology:
Functional Test == Acceptance Test == End-to-End Test

What I call functional tests, some people prefer to call *acceptance tests*, or *end-to-end tests*. The main point is that these kinds of tests look at how the whole application functions, from the outside. Another term is *black box test*, because the test doesn't know anything about the internals of the system under test.

FTs should have a human-readable story that we can follow. We make it explicit using comments that accompany the test code. When creating a new FT, we can write the comments first, to capture the key points of the User Story. Being human-readable, you could even share them with nonprogrammers, as a way of discussing the requirements and features of your app.

TDD and agile software development methodologies often go together, and one of the things we often talk about is the minimum viable app; what is the simplest thing we can build that is still useful? Let's start by building that, so that we can test the water as quickly as possible.

A minimum viable to-do list really only needs to let the user enter some to-do items, and remember them for their next visit.

Open up *functional_tests.py* and write a story a bit like this one:

```python
from selenium import webdriver

browser = webdriver.Firefox()

# Edith has heard about a cool new online to-do app. She goes
# to check out its homepage
browser.get('http://localhost:8000')

# She notices the page title and header mention to-do lists
assert 'To-Do' in browser.title

# She is invited to enter a to-do item straight away

# She types "Buy peacock feathers" into a text box (Edith's hobby
# is tying fly-fishing lures)

# When she hits enter, the page updates, and now the page lists
# "1: Buy peacock feathers" as an item in a to-do list

# There is still a text box inviting her to add another item. She
# enters "Use peacock feathers to make a fly" (Edith is very methodical)

# The page updates again, and now shows both items on her list

# Edith wonders whether the site will remember her list. Then she sees
# that the site has generated a unique URL for her -- there is some
# explanatory text to that effect.

# She visits that URL - her to-do list is still there.

# Satisfied, she goes back to sleep

browser.quit()
```

We Have a Word for Comments...

When I first started at Resolver, I used to virtuously pepper my code with nice descriptive comments. My colleagues said to me: "Harry, we have a word for comments. We call them lies." I was shocked! But I learned in school that comments are good practice?

They were exaggerating for effect. There is definitely a place for comments that add context and intention. But their point was that it's pointless to write a comment that just repeats what you're doing with the code:

```python
# increment wibble by 1
wibble += 1
```

Not only is it pointless, but there's a danger that you'll forget to update the comments when you update the code, and they end up being misleading. The ideal is to strive to make your code so readable, to use such good variable names and function names, and to structure it so well that you no longer need any comments to explain *what* the code is doing. Just a few here and there to explain *why*.

There are other places where comments are very useful. We'll see that Django uses them a lot in the files it generates for us to use as a way of suggesting helpful bits of its API. And, of course, we use comments to explain the User Story in our functional tests—by forcing us to make a coherent story out of the test, it makes sure we're always testing from the point of view of the user.

There is more fun to be had in this area, things like *Behaviour-Driven Development* (see Appendix E) and testing DSLs, but they're topics for other books.

You'll notice that, apart from writing the test out as comments, I've updated the `assert` to look for the word "To-Do" instead of "Django". That means we expect the test to fail now. Let's try running it.

First, start up the server:

```
$ python manage.py runserver
```

And then, in another shell, run the tests:

```
$ python functional_tests.py
Traceback (most recent call last):
  File "functional_tests.py", line 10, in <module>
    assert 'To-Do' in browser.title
AssertionError
```

That's what we call an *expected fail*, which is actually good news—not quite as good as a test that passes, but at least it's failing for the right reason; we can have some confidence we've written the test correctly.

The Python Standard Library's unittest Module

There are a couple of little annoyances we should probably deal with. Firstly, the message "AssertionError" isn't very helpful—it would be nice if the test told us what it actually found as the browser title. Also, it's left a Firefox window hanging around the desktop, so it would be nice if that got cleared up for us automatically.

One option would be to use the second parameter to the `assert` keyword, something like:

```
assert 'To-Do' in browser.title, "Browser title was " + browser.title
```

And we could also use a `try/finally` to clean up the old Firefox window. But these sorts of problems are quite common in testing, and there are some ready-made solutions for us in the standard library's unittest module. Let's use that! In *functional_tests.py*:

```python
from selenium import webdriver
import unittest

class NewVisitorTest(unittest.TestCase):  ❶

    def setUp(self):  ❸
        self.browser = webdriver.Firefox()

    def tearDown(self):  ❸
        self.browser.quit()

    def test_can_start_a_list_and_retrieve_it_later(self):  ❷
        # Edith has heard about a cool new online to-do app. She goes
        # to check out its homepage
        self.browser.get('http://localhost:8000')

        # She notices the page title and header mention to-do lists
        self.assertIn('To-Do', self.browser.title)  ❹
        self.fail('Finish the test!')  ❺

        # She is invited to enter a to-do item straight away
        [...rest of comments as before]

if __name__ == '__main__':  ❻
    unittest.main(warnings='ignore')  ❼
```

You'll probably notice a few things here:

❶   Tests are organised into classes, which inherit from unittest.TestCase.

❷   The main body of the test is in a method called test_can_start_ a_list_and_retrieve_it_later. Any method whose name starts with test is a test method, and will be run by the test runner. You can have more than one test_ method per class. Nice descriptive names for our test methods are a good idea too.

❸   setUp and tearDown are special methods which get run before and after each test. I'm using them to start and stop our browser—note that they're a bit like a try/ except, in that tearDown will run even if there's an error during the test itself.[1] No more Firefox windows left lying around!

---

1 The only exception is if you have an exception inside setUp, then tearDown doesn't run.

❹ We use `self.assertIn` instead of just `assert` to make our test assertions. `uni ttest` provides lots of helper functions like this to make test assertions, like `assertEqual`, `assertTrue`, `assertFalse`, and so on. You can find more in the `unittest` documentation (*http://docs.python.org/3/library/unittest.html*).

❺ `self.fail` just fails no matter what, producing the error message given. I'm using it as a reminder to finish the test.

❻ Finally, we have the `if __name__ == '__main__'` clause (if you've not seen it before, that's how a Python script checks if it's been executed from the command line, rather than just imported by another script). We call `unittest.main()`, which launches the `unittest` test runner, which will automatically find test classes and methods in the file and run them.

❼ `warnings='ignore'` suppresses a superfluous `ResourceWarning` which was being emitted at the time of writing. It may have disappeared by the time you read this; feel free to try removing it!

 If you've read the Django testing documentation, you might have seen something called `LiveServerTestCase`, and are wondering whether we should use it now. Full points to you for reading the friendly manual! `LiveServerTestCase` is a bit too complicated for now, but I promise I'll use it in a later chapter...

Let's try it!

```
$ python functional_tests.py
F
======================================================================
FAIL: test_can_start_a_list_and_retrieve_it_later (__main__.NewVisitorTest)
----------------------------------------------------------------------
Traceback (most recent call last):
  File "functional_tests.py", line 18, in
test_can_start_a_list_and_retrieve_it_later
    self.assertIn('To-Do', self.browser.title)
AssertionError: 'To-Do' not found in 'Welcome to Django'

----------------------------------------------------------------------
Ran 1 test in 1.747s

FAILED (failures=1)
```

That's a bit nicer, isn't it? It tidied up our Firefox window, it gives us a nicely format-ted report of how many tests were run and how many failed, and the `assertIn` has given us a helpful error message with useful debugging info. Bonzer!

Commit

This is a good point to do a commit; it's a nicely self-contained change. We've expanded our functional test to include comments that describe the task we're setting ourselves, our minimum viable to-do list. We've also rewritten it to use the Python unittest module and its various testing helper functions.

Do a `git status`—that should assure you that the only file that has changed is *functional_tests.py*. Then do a `git diff`, which shows you the difference between the last commit and what's currently on disk. That should tell you that *functional_tests.py* has changed quite substantially:

```
$ git diff
diff --git a/functional_tests.py b/functional_tests.py
index d333591..b0f22dc 100644
--- a/functional_tests.py
+++ b/functional_tests.py
@@ -1,6 +1,45 @@
 from selenium import webdriver
+import unittest

-browser = webdriver.Firefox()
-browser.get('http://localhost:8000')
+class NewVisitorTest(unittest.TestCase):

-assert 'Django' in browser.title
+    def setUp(self):
+        self.browser = webdriver.Firefox()
+
+    def tearDown(self):
+        self.browser.quit()
[...]
```

Now let's do a:

```
$ git commit -a
```

The `-a` means "automatically add any changes to tracked files" (i.e., any files that we've committed before). It won't add any brand new files (you have to explicitly `git add` them yourself), but often, as in this case, there aren't any new files, so it's a useful shortcut.

When the editor pops up, add a descriptive commit message, like "First FT specced out in comments, and now uses unittest."

Now we're in an excellent position to start writing some real code for our lists app. Read on!

Useful TDD Concepts

User Story
> A description of how the application will work from the point of view of the user. Used to structure a functional test.

Expected failure
> When a test fails in the way that we expected it to.

## CHAPTER 3

Testing a Simple Home Page with Unit Tests

We finished the last chapter with a functional test failing, telling us that it wanted the home page for our site to have "To-Do" in its title. It's time to start working on our application.

Warning: Things Are About to Get Real

The first two chapters were intentionally nice and light. From now on, we get into some more meaty coding. Here's a prediction: at some point, things are going to go wrong. You're going to see different results from what I say you should see. This is a Good Thing, because it will be a genuine character-building Learning Experience™.

One possibility is that I've given some ambiguous explanations, and you've done something different from what I intended. Step back and have a think about what we're trying to achieve at this point in the book. Which file are we editing, what do we want the user to be able to do, what are we testing and why? It may be that you've edited the wrong file or function, or are running the wrong tests. I reckon you'll learn more about TDD from these "stop and think" moments than you do from all the times when following instructions and copy-pasting goes smoothly.

Or it may be a real bug. Be tenacious, read the error message carefully (see "Reading Tracebacks" on page 27 a little later on in the chapter), and you'll get to the bottom of it. It's probably just a missing comma, or trailing slash, or maybe a missing *s* in one of the Selenium find methods. But, as Zed Shaw put it so well, this kind of debugging is also an absolutely vital part of learning, so do stick it out!

You can always drop me an email (or try the Google Group (*https:// groups.google.com/forum/#!forum/obey-the-testing-goat-book*)) if you get really stuck. Happy debugging!

Our First Django App, and Our First Unit Test

Django encourages you to structure your code into *apps*: the theory is that one project can have many apps, you can use third-party apps developed by other people, and you might even reuse one of your own apps in a different project…although I admit I've never actually managed it myself! Still, apps are a good way to keep your code organised.

Let's start an app for our to-do lists:

```
$ python manage.py startapp lists
```

That will create a folder called *lists*, next to *manage.py* and the existing *superlists* folder , and within it a number of placeholder files for things like models, views, and, of immediate interest to us, tests:

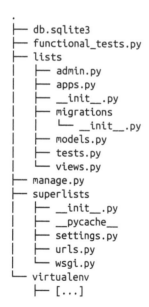

```
.
├── db.sqlite3
├── functional_tests.py
├── lists
│   ├── admin.py
│   ├── apps.py
│   ├── __init__.py
│   ├── migrations
│   │   └── __init__.py
│   ├── models.py
│   ├── tests.py
│   └── views.py
├── manage.py
├── superlists
│   ├── __init__.py
│   ├── __pycache__
│   ├── settings.py
│   ├── urls.py
│   └── wsgi.py
└── virtualenv
    ├── [...]
```

Unit Tests, and How They Differ from Functional Tests

As with so many of the labels we put on things, the line between unit tests and functional tests can become a little blurry at times. The basic distinction, though, is that functional tests test the application from the outside, from the point of view of the user. Unit tests test the application from the inside, from the point of view of the programmer.

The TDD approach I'm following wants our application to be covered by both types of test. Our workflow will look a bit like this:

1. We start by writing a *functional test*, describing the new functionality from the user's point of view.

2. Once we have a functional test that fails, we start to think about how to write code that can get it to pass (or at least to get past its current failure). We now use one or more *unit tests* to define how we want our code to behave—the idea is that each line of production code we write should be tested by (at least) one of our unit tests.

3. Once we have a failing unit test, we write the smallest amount of *application code* we can, just enough to get the unit test to pass. We may iterate between steps 2 and 3 a few times, until we think the functional test will get a little further.

4. Now we can rerun our functional tests and see if they pass, or get a little further. That may prompt us to write some new unit tests, and some new code, and so on.

You can see that, all the way through, the functional tests are driving what development we do from a high level, while the unit tests drive what we do at a low level.

Does that seem slightly redundant? Sometimes it can feel that way, but functional tests and unit tests do really have very different objectives, and they will usually end up looking quite different.

 Functional tests should help you build an application with the right functionality, and guarantee you never accidentally break it. Unit tests should help you to write code that's clean and bug free.

Enough theory for now—let's see how it looks in practice.

Unit Testing in Django

Let's see how to write a unit test for our home page view. Open up the new file at *lists/tests.py*, and you'll see something like this:

lists/tests.py

```
from django.test import TestCase

# Create your tests here.
```

Django has helpfully suggested we use a special version of TestCase, which it provides. It's an augmented version of the standard unittest.TestCase, with some additional Django-specific features, which we'll discover over the next few chapters.

You've already seen that the TDD cycle involves starting with a test that fails, then writing code to get it to pass. Well, before we can even get that far, we want to know that the unit test we're writing will definitely be run by our automated test runner, whatever it is. In the case of *functional_tests.py*, we're running it directly, but this file made by Django is a bit more like magic. So, just to make sure, let's make a deliberately silly failing test:

lists/tests.py

```python
from django.test import TestCase

class SmokeTest(TestCase):

    def test_bad_maths(self):
        self.assertEqual(1 + 1, 3)
```

Now let's invoke this mysterious Django test runner. As usual, it's a *manage.py* command:

```
$ python manage.py test
Creating test database for alias 'default'...
F
======================================================================
FAIL: test_bad_maths (lists.tests.SmokeTest)
----------------------------------------------------------------------
Traceback (most recent call last):
  File "...python-tdd-book/lists/tests.py", line 6, in test_bad_maths
    self.assertEqual(1 + 1, 3)
AssertionError: 2 != 3


----------------------------------------------------------------------
Ran 1 test in 0.001s

FAILED (failures=1)
System check identified no issues (0 silenced).
Destroying test database for alias 'default'...
```

Excellent. The machinery seems to be working. This is a good point for a commit:

```
$ git status  # should show you lists/ is untracked
$ git add lists
$ git diff --staged  # will show you the diff that you're about to commit
$ git commit -m "Add app for lists, with deliberately failing unit test"
```

As you've no doubt guessed, the -m flag lets you pass in a commit message at the command line, so you don't need to use an editor. It's up to you to pick the way you like to use the Git command line; I'll just show you the main ones I've seen used. The key rule is: *make sure you always review what you're about to commit before you do it.*

Django's MVC, URLs, and View Functions

Django is structured along a classic *Model-View-Controller* (MVC) pattern. Well, *broadly*. It definitely does have models, but its views are more like a controller, and it's the templates that are actually the view part, but the general idea is there. If you're interested, you can look up the finer points of the discussion in the Django FAQs (*https://docs.djangoproject.com/en/1.11/faq/general/*).

Irrespective of any of that, as with any web server, Django's main job is to decide what to do when a user asks for a particular URL on our site. Django's workflow goes something like this:

1. An HTTP *request* comes in for a particular *URL*.
2. Django uses some rules to decide which *view* function should deal with the request (this is referred to as *resolving* the URL).
3. The view function processes the request and returns an HTTP *response*.

So we want to test two things:

- Can we resolve the URL for the root of the site ("/") to a particular view function we've made?
- Can we make this view function return some HTML which will get the functional test to pass?

Let's start with the first. Open up *lists/tests.py*, and change our silly test to something like this:

lists/tests.py

```
from django.urls import resolve
from django.test import TestCase
from lists.views import home_page    ❷

class HomePageTest(TestCase):

    def test_root_url_resolves_to_home_page_view(self):
        found = resolve('/')    ❶
        self.assertEqual(found.func, home_page)    ❶
```

What's going on here?

❶ resolve is the function Django uses internally to resolve URLs and find what view function they should map to. We're checking that resolve, when called with "/", the root of the site, finds a function called home_page.

❷ What function is that? It's the view function we're going to write next, which will actually return the HTML we want. You can see from the import that we're planning to store it in *lists/views.py*.

So, what do you think will happen when we run the tests?

```
$ python manage.py test
ImportError: cannot import name 'home_page'
```

It's a very predictable and uninteresting error: we tried to import something we haven't even written yet. But it's still good news—for the purposes of TDD, an exception which was predicted counts as an expected failure. Since we have both a failing functional test and a failing unit test, we have the Testing Goat's full blessing to code away.

At Last! We Actually Write Some Application Code!

It is exciting, isn't it? Be warned, TDD means that long periods of anticipation are only defused very gradually, and by tiny increments. Especially since we're learning and only just starting out, we only allow ourselves to change (or add) one line of code at a time—and each time, we make just the minimal change required to address the current test failure.

I'm being deliberately extreme here, but what's our current test failure? We can't import home_page from lists.views? OK, let's fix that—and only that. In *lists/views.py*:

lists/views.py

```python
from django.shortcuts import render

# Create your views here.
home_page = None
```

"You must be joking!" I can hear you say.

I can hear you because it's what I used to say (with feeling) when my colleagues first demonstrated TDD to me. Well, bear with me, and we'll talk about whether or not this is all taking it too far in a little while. But for now, let yourself follow along, even if it's with some exasperation, and see if our tests can help us write the correct code, one tiny step at a time.

We run the tests again:

```
$ python manage.py test
Creating test database for alias 'default'...
E
=======================================================================
ERROR: test_root_url_resolves_to_home_page_view (lists.tests.HomePageTest)
-----------------------------------------------------------------------
Traceback (most recent call last):
  File "...python-tdd-book/lists/tests.py", line 8, in
test_root_url_resolves_to_home_page_view
    found = resolve('/')
  File ".../django/urls/base.py", line 27, in resolve
    return get_resolver(urlconf).resolve(path)
  File ".../django/urls/resolvers.py", line 392, in resolve
    raise Resolver404({'tried': tried, 'path': new_path})
django.urls.exceptions.Resolver404: {'tried': [[<RegexURLResolver
<RegexURLPattern list> (admin:admin) ^admin/>]], 'path': ''}


-----------------------------------------------------------------------
Ran 1 test in 0.002s

FAILED (errors=1)
System check identified no issues (0 silenced).
Destroying test database for alias 'default'...
```

Reading Tracebacks

Let's spend a moment talking about how to read tracebacks, since it's something we have to do a lot in TDD. You soon learn to scan through them and pick up relevant clues:

```
=======================================================================
ERROR: test_root_url_resolves_to_home_page_view (lists.tests.HomePageTest)   ❷
-----------------------------------------------------------------------
Traceback (most recent call last):
  File "...python-tdd-book/lists/tests.py", line 8, in
test_root_url_resolves_to_home_page_view
    found = resolve('/')   ❸
  File ".../django/urls/base.py", line 27, in resolve
    return get_resolver(urlconf).resolve(path)
  File ".../django/urls/resolvers.py", line 392, in resolve
    raise Resolver404({'tried': tried, 'path': new_path})
django.urls.exceptions.Resolver404: {'tried': [[<RegexURLResolver   ❶
<RegexURLPattern list> (admin:admin) ^admin/>]], 'path': ''}   ❶
-----------------------------------------------------------------------
[...]
```

❶ The first place you look is usually *the error itself*. Sometimes that's all you need to see, and it will let you identify the problem immediately. But sometimes, like in this case, it's not quite self-evident.

❷ The next thing to double-check is: *which test is failing?* Is it definitely the one we expected—that is, the one we just wrote? In this case, the answer is yes.

❸ Then we look for the place in *our test code* that kicked off the failure. We work our way down from the top of the traceback, looking for the filename of the tests file, to check which test function, and what line of code, the failure is coming from. In this case it's the line where we call the resolve function for the "/" URL.

There is ordinarily a fourth step, where we look further down for any of *our own application code* which was involved with the problem. In this case it's all Django code, but we'll see plenty of examples of this fourth step later in the book.

Pulling it all together, we interpret the traceback as telling us that, when trying to resolve "/", Django raised a 404 error—in other words, Django can't find a URL mapping for "/". Let's help it out.

urls.py

Our tests are telling us that we need a URL mapping. Django uses a file called *urls.py* to map URLs to view functions. There's a main *urls.py* for the whole site in the *superlists/superlists* folder. Let's go take a look:

superlists/urls.py

```
"""superlists URL Configuration

The `urlpatterns` list routes URLs to views. For more information please see:
    https://docs.djangoproject.com/en/1.11/topics/http/urls/
Examples:
Function views
    1. Add an import:  from my_app import views
    2. Add a URL to urlpatterns:  url(r'^$', views.home, name='home')
Class-based views
    1. Add an import:  from other_app.views import Home
    2. Add a URL to urlpatterns:  url(r'^$', Home.as_view(), name='home')
Including another URLconf
    1. Import the include() function: from django.conf.urls import url, include
    2. Add a URL to urlpatterns:  url(r'^blog/', include('blog.urls'))
"""
from django.conf.urls import url
from django.contrib import admin

urlpatterns = [
    url(r'^admin/', admin.site.urls),
]
```

As usual, lots of helpful comments and default suggestions from Django.

If your *urls.py* looks different or if it mentions a function called `path` instead of `url`, it's because you've got the wrong version of Django. This book is written for Django v1.11. Take another look at the "Prerequisites and Assumptions" section and get the right version before you go any further.

A `url` entry starts with a regular expression that defines which URLs it applies to, and goes on to say where it should send those requests—either to a view function you've imported, or maybe to another *urls.py* file somewhere else.

The first example entry has the regular expression ^$, which means an empty string —could this be the same as the root of our site, which we've been testing with "/"? Let's find out—what happens if we include it?

If you've never come across regular expressions, you can get away with just taking my word for it, for now—but you should make a mental note to go learn about them.

We'll also get rid of the admin URL, because we won't be using the Django admin site for now:

superlists/urls.py

```
from django.conf.urls import url
from lists import views

urlpatterns = [
    url(r'^$', views.home_page, name='home'),
]
```

Run the unit tests again, with **python manage.py test**:

```
[...]
TypeError: view must be a callable or a list/tuple in the case of include().
```

That's progress! We're no longer getting a 404.

The traceback is messy, but the message at the end is telling us what's going on: the unit tests have actually made the link between the URL "/" and the `home_page` = `None` in *lists/views.py*, and are now complaining that the `home_page` view is not callable. And that gives us a justification for changing it from being `None` to being an actual function. Every single code change is driven by the tests!

Back in *lists/views.py*:

```
from django.shortcuts import render

# Create your views here.
def home_page():
    pass
```

And now?

```
$ python manage.py test
Creating test database for alias 'default'...
.
----------------------------------------------------------------------
Ran 1 test in 0.003s

OK
System check identified no issues (0 silenced).
Destroying test database for alias 'default'...
```

Hooray! Our first ever unit test pass! That's so momentous that I think it's worthy of a commit:

```
$ git diff   # should show changes to urls.py, tests.py, and views.py
$ git commit -am "First unit test and url mapping, dummy view"
```

That was the last variation on `git commit` I'll show, the a and m flags together, which adds all changes to tracked files and uses the commit message from the command line.

`git commit -am` is the quickest formulation, but also gives you the least feedback about what's being committed, so make sure you've done a `git status` and a `git diff` beforehand, and are clear on what changes are about to go in.

Unit Testing a View

On to writing a test for our view, so that it can be something more than a do-nothing function, and instead be a function that returns a real response with HTML to the browser. Open up *lists/tests.py*, and add a new *test method*. I'll explain each bit:

```
from django.urls import resolve
from django.test import TestCase
from django.http import HttpRequest

from lists.views import home_page


class HomePageTest(TestCase):

    def test_root_url_resolves_to_home_page_view(self):
        found = resolve('/')
        self.assertEqual(found.func, home_page)


    def test_home_page_returns_correct_html(self):
        request = HttpRequest()                                    ❶
        response = home_page(request)                              ❷
        html = response.content.decode('utf8')                    ❸
        self.assertTrue(html.startswith('<html>'))                ❹
        self.assertIn('<title>To-Do lists</title>', html)         ❺
        self.assertTrue(html.endswith('</html>'))                 ❹
```

What's going on in this new test?

❶ We create an HttpRequest object, which is what Django will see when a user's browser asks for a page.

❷ We pass it to our home_page view, which gives us a response. You won't be surprised to hear that this object is an instance of a class called HttpResponse.

❸ Then, we extract the .content of the response. These are the raw bytes, the ones and zeros that would be sent down the wire to the user's browser. We call .decode() to convert them into the string of HTML that's being sent to the user.

❹ We want it to start with an <html> tag which gets closed at the end.

❺ And we want a <title> tag somewhere in the middle, with the words "To-Do lists" in it—because that's what we specified in our functional test.

Once again, the unit test is driven by the functional test, but it's also much closer to the actual code—we're thinking like programmers now.

Let's run the unit tests now and see how we get on:

```
TypeError: home_page() takes 0 positional arguments but 1 was given
```

The Unit-Test/Code Cycle

We can start to settle into the TDD *unit-test/code cycle* now:

1. In the terminal, run the unit tests and see how they fail.
2. In the editor, make a minimal code change to address the current test failure.

And repeat!

The more nervous we are about getting our code right, the smaller and more minimal we make each code change—the idea is to be absolutely sure that each bit of code is justified by a test.

This may seem laborious, and at first, it will be. But once you get into the swing of things, you'll find yourself coding quickly even if you take microscopic steps—this is how we write all of our production code at work.

Let's see how fast we can get this cycle going:

- Minimal code change:

lists/views.py

```
def home_page(request):
    pass
```

- Tests:

```
html = response.content.decode('utf8')
AttributeError: 'NoneType' object has no attribute 'content'
```

- Code—we use `django.http.HttpResponse`, as predicted:

lists/views.py

```
from django.http import HttpResponse

# Create your views here.
def home_page(request):
    return HttpResponse()
```

- Tests again:

```
self.assertTrue(html.startswith('<html>'))
AssertionError: False is not true
```

- Code again:

lists/views.py

```python
def home_page(request):
    return HttpResponse('<html>')
```

- Tests:

```
AssertionError: '<title>To-Do lists</title>' not found in '<html>'
```

- Code:

lists/views.py

```python
def home_page(request):
    return HttpResponse('<html><title>To-Do lists</title>')
```

- Tests—almost there?

```
    self.assertTrue(html.endswith('</html>'))
AssertionError: False is not true
```

- Come on, one last effort:

lists/views.py

```python
def home_page(request):
    return HttpResponse('<html><title>To-Do lists</title></html>')
```

- Surely?

```
$ python manage.py test
Creating test database for alias 'default'...
..
----------------------------------------------------------------
Ran 2 tests in 0.001s

OK
System check identified no issues (0 silenced).
Destroying test database for alias 'default'...
```

Yes! Now, let's run our functional tests. Don't forget to spin up the dev server again, if it's not still running. It feels like the final heat of the race here; surely this is it…could it be?

```
$ python functional_tests.py
F
======================================================================
FAIL: test_can_start_a_list_and_retrieve_it_later (__main__.NewVisitorTest)
----------------------------------------------------------------------
Traceback (most recent call last):
  File "functional_tests.py", line 19, in
test_can_start_a_list_and_retrieve_it_later
    self.fail('Finish the test!')
AssertionError: Finish the test!


----------------------------------------------------------------------
Ran 1 test in 1.609s

FAILED (failures=1)
```

Failed? What? Oh, it's just our little reminder? Yes? Yes! We have a web page!

Ahem. Well, *I* thought it was a thrilling end to the chapter. You may still be a little baffled, perhaps keen to hear a justification for all these tests, and don't worry, all that will come, but I hope you felt just a tinge of excitement near the end there.

Just a little commit to calm down, and reflect on what we've covered:

```
$ git diff   # should show our new test in tests.py, and the view in views.py
$ git commit -am "Basic view now returns minimal HTML"
```

That was quite a chapter! Why not try typing git log, possibly using the --oneline flag, for a reminder of what we got up to:

```
$ git log --oneline
a6e6cc9 Basic view now returns minimal HTML
450c0f3 First unit test and url mapping, dummy view
ea2b037 Add app for lists, with deliberately failing unit test
[...]
```

Not bad—we covered:

- Starting a Django app
- The Django unit test runner
- The difference between FTs and unit tests
- Django URL resolving and *urls.py*
- Django view functions, request and response objects
- And returning basic HTML

Useful Commands and Concepts

Running the Django dev server
```
python manage.py runserver
```

Running the functional tests
```
python functional_tests.py
```

Running the unit tests
```
python manage.py test
```

The unit-test/code cycle
1. Run the unit tests in the terminal.

2. Make a minimal code change in the editor.

3. Repeat!

## CHAPTER 4

What Are We Doing with All These Tests? (And, Refactoring)

Now that we've seen the basics of TDD in action, it's time to pause and talk about why we're doing it.

I'm imagining several of you, dear readers, have been holding back some seething frustration—perhaps some of you have done a bit of unit testing before, and perhaps some of you are just in a hurry. You've been biting back questions like:

- Aren't all these tests a bit excessive?
- Surely some of them are redundant? There's duplication between the functional tests and the unit tests.
- I mean, what are you doing importing `django.urls.resolve` in your unit tests? Isn't that testing Django—that is, testing third-party code? I thought that was a no-no?
- Those unit tests seemed way too trivial—testing one line of declaration, and a one-line function that returns a constant! Isn't that just a waste of time? Shouldn't we save our tests for more complex things?
- What about all those tiny changes during the unit-test/code cycle? Surely we could have just skipped to the end? I mean, `home_page = None!`? Really?
- You're not telling me you *actually* code like this in real life?

Ah, young grasshopper. I too was once full of questions like these. But only because they're perfectly good questions. In fact, I still ask myself questions like these, all the time. Does all this stuff really have value? Is this a bit of a cargo cult?

Programming Is Like Pulling a Bucket of Water Up from a Well

Ultimately, programming is hard. Often, we are smart, so we succeed. TDD is there to help us out when we're not so smart. Kent Beck (who basically invented TDD) uses the metaphor of lifting a bucket of water out of a well with a rope: when the well isn't too deep, and the bucket isn't very full, it's easy. And even lifting a full bucket is pretty easy at first. But after a while, you're going to get tired. TDD is like having a ratchet that lets you save your progress, take a break, and make sure you never slip backwards. That way you don't have to be smart *all* the time.

Figure 4-1. Test ALL the things (original illustration source: Allie Brosh, Hyperbole and a Half (http://bit.ly/1iXxdYp))

OK, perhaps *in general*, you're prepared to concede that TDD is a good idea, but maybe you still think I'm overdoing it? Testing the tiniest thing, and taking ridiculously many small steps?

TDD is a *discipline*, and that means it's not something that comes naturally; because many of the payoffs aren't immediate but only come in the longer term, you have to force yourself to do it in the moment. That's what the image of the Testing Goat is supposed to illustrate—you need to be a bit bloody-minded about it.

On the Merits of Trivial Tests for Trivial Functions

In the short term it may feel a bit silly to write tests for simple functions and constants.

It's perfectly possible to imagine still doing "mostly" TDD, but following more relaxed rules where you don't unit test *absolutely* everything. But in this book my aim is to demonstrate full, rigorous TDD. Like a kata in a martial art, the idea is to learn the motions in a controlled context, when there is no adversity, so that the techniques are part of your muscle memory. It seems trivial now, because we've started with a very simple example. The problem comes when your application gets complex—that's when you really need your tests. And the danger is that complexity tends to sneak up on you, gradually. You may not notice it happening, but quite soon you're a boiled frog.

There are two other things to say in favour of tiny, simple tests for simple functions.

Firstly, if they're really trivial tests, then they won't take you that long to write them. So stop moaning and just write them already.

Secondly, it's always good to have a placeholder. Having a test *there* for a simple function means it's that much less of a psychological barrier to overcome when the simple function gets a tiny bit more complex—perhaps it grows an if. Then a few weeks later it grows a for loop. Before you know it, it's a recursive metaclass-based polymorphic tree parser factory. But because it's had tests from the very beginning, adding a new test each time has felt quite natural, and it's well tested. The alternative involves trying to decide when a function becomes "complicated enough", which is highly subjective, but worse, because there's no placeholder, it seems like that much more effort, and you're tempted each time to put it off a little longer, and pretty soon—frog soup!

Instead of trying to figure out some hand-wavy subjective rules for when you should write tests, and when you can get away with not bothering, I suggest following the discipline for now—as with any discipline, you have to take the time to learn the rules before you can break them.

Now, back to our onions.

Using Selenium to Test User Interactions

Where were we at the end of the last chapter? Let's rerun the test and find out:

```
$ python functional_tests.py
F
======================================================================
FAIL: test_can_start_a_list_and_retrieve_it_later (__main__.NewVisitorTest)
----------------------------------------------------------------------
Traceback (most recent call last):
  File "functional_tests.py", line 19, in
test_can_start_a_list_and_retrieve_it_later
    self.fail('Finish the test!')
AssertionError: Finish the test!

----------------------------------------------------------------------
Ran 1 test in 1.609s

FAILED (failures=1)
```

Did you try it, and get an error saying *Problem loading page* or *Unable to connect*? So did I. It's because we forgot to spin up the dev server first using `manage.py runserver`. Do that, and you'll get the failure message we're after.

> One of the great things about TDD is that you never have to worry about forgetting what to do next—just rerun your tests and they will tell you what you need to work on.

"Finish the test", it says, so let's do just that! Open up *functional_tests.py* and we'll extend our FT:

```
from selenium import webdriver
from selenium.webdriver.common.keys import Keys
import time
import unittest

class NewVisitorTest(unittest.TestCase):

    def setUp(self):
        self.browser = webdriver.Firefox()

    def tearDown(self):
        self.browser.quit()

    def test_can_start_a_list_and_retrieve_it_later(self):
        # Edith has heard about a cool new online to-do app. She goes
        # to check out its homepage
        self.browser.get('http://localhost:8000')

        # She notices the page title and header mention to-do lists
        self.assertIn('To-Do', self.browser.title)
        header_text = self.browser.find_element_by_tag_name('h1').text  ❶
        self.assertIn('To-Do', header_text)

        # She is invited to enter a to-do item straight away
        inputbox = self.browser.find_element_by_id('id_new_item')  ❶
        self.assertEqual(
            inputbox.get_attribute('placeholder'),
            'Enter a to-do item'
        )

        # She types "Buy peacock feathers" into a text box (Edith's hobby
        # is tying fly-fishing lures)
        inputbox.send_keys('Buy peacock feathers')  ❷

        # When she hits enter, the page updates, and now the page lists
        # "1: Buy peacock feathers" as an item in a to-do list table
        inputbox.send_keys(Keys.ENTER)  ❸
        time.sleep(1)  ❹

        table = self.browser.find_element_by_id('id_list_table')
        rows = table.find_elements_by_tag_name('tr')  ❶
        self.assertTrue(
            any(row.text == '1: Buy peacock feathers' for row in rows)
        )

        # There is still a text box inviting her to add another item. She
        # enters "Use peacock feathers to make a fly" (Edith is very
        # methodical)
        self.fail('Finish the test!')

        # The page updates again, and now shows both items on her list
        [...]
```

❶ We're using several of the methods that Selenium provides to examine web pages: `find_element_by_tag_name`, `find_element_by_id`, and `find_elements_by_tag_name` (notice the extra `s`, which means it will return several elements rather than just one).

❷ We also use `send_keys`, which is Selenium's way of typing into input elements.

❸ The `Keys` class (don't forget to import it) lets us send special keys like Enter.[1]

❹ When we hit Enter, the page will refresh. The `time.sleep` is there to make sure the browser has finished loading before we make any assertions about the new page. This is called an "explicit wait" (a very simple one; we'll improve it in Chapter 6).

 Watch out for the difference between the Selenium `find_element_...` and `find_elements_...` functions. One returns an element and raises an exception if it can't find it, whereas the other returns a list, which may be empty.

Also, just look at that `any` function. It's a little-known Python built-in. I don't even need to explain it, do I? Python is such a joy.

Although, if you're one of my readers who doesn't know Python, what's happening inside the `any` is a *generator expression*, which is like a *list comprehension* but awesomer. You need to read up on this. If you Google it, you'll find Guido himself explaining it nicely (*http://bit.ly/1iXxD18*). Come back and tell me that's not pure joy!

Let's see how it gets on:

```
$ python functional_tests.py
[...]
selenium.common.exceptions.NoSuchElementException: Message: Unable to locate
element: h1
```

Decoding that, the test is saying it can't find an `<h1>` element on the page. Let's see what we can do to add that to the HTML of our home page.

Big changes to a functional test are usually a good thing to commit on their own. I failed to do so in my first draft, and I regretted it later when I changed my mind and had the change mixed up with a bunch of others. The more atomic your commits, the better:

---

1 You could also just use the string `"\n"`, but Keys also lets you send special keys like Ctrl so I thought I'd show it.

```
$ git diff  # should show changes to functional_tests.py
$ git commit -am "Functional test now checks we can input a to-do item"
```

The "Don't Test Constants" Rule, and Templates to the Rescue

Let's take a look at our unit tests, *lists/tests.py*. Currently we're looking for specific HTML strings, but that's not a particularly efficient way of testing HTML. In general, one of the rules of unit testing is *Don't test constants*, and testing HTML as text is a lot like testing a constant.

In other words, if you have some code that says:

```
wibble = 3
```

There's not much point in a test that says:

```
from myprogram import wibble
assert wibble == 3
```

Unit tests are really about testing logic, flow control, and configuration. Making assertions about exactly what sequence of characters we have in our HTML strings isn't doing that.

What's more, mangling raw strings in Python really isn't a great way of dealing with HTML. There's a much better solution, which is to use templates. Quite apart from anything else, if we can keep HTML to one side in a file whose name ends in *.html*, we'll get better syntax highlighting! There are lots of Python templating frameworks out there, and Django has its own which works very well. Let's use that.

Refactoring to Use a Template

What we want to do now is make our view function return exactly the same HTML, but just using a different process. That's a refactor—when we try to improve the code *without changing its functionality*.

That last bit is really important. If you try to add new functionality at the same time as refactoring, you're much more likely to run into trouble. Refactoring is actually a whole discipline in itself, and it even has a reference book: Martin Fowler's *Refactoring* (*http://refactoring.com/*).

The first rule is that you can't refactor without tests. Thankfully, we're doing TDD, so we're way ahead of the game. Let's check that our tests pass; they will be what makes sure that our refactoring is behaviour preserving:

```
$ python manage.py test
[...]
OK
```

Great! We'll start by taking our HTML string and putting it into its own file. Create a directory called *lists/templates* to keep templates in, and then open a file at *lists/templates/home.html*, to which we'll transfer our HTML:[2]

lists/templates/home.html

```
<html>
    <title>To-Do lists</title>
</html>
```

Mmmh, syntax-highlighted…much nicer! Now to change our view function:

lists/views.py

```
from django.shortcuts import render

def home_page(request):
    return render(request, 'home.html')
```

Instead of building our own HttpResponse, we now use the Django render function. It takes the request as its first parameter (for reasons we'll go into later) and the name of the template to render. Django will automatically search folders called *templates* inside any of your apps' directories. Then it builds an HttpResponse for you, based on the content of the template.

 Templates are a very powerful feature of Django's, and their main strength consists of substituting Python variables into HTML text. We're not using this feature yet, but we will in future chapters. That's why we use render and (later) render_to_string rather than, say, manually reading the file from disk with the built-in open.

Let's see if it works:

---

2 Some people like to use another subfolder named after the app (i.e., *lists/templates/lists*) and then refer to the template as *lists/home.html*. This is called "template namespacing". I figured it was overcomplicated for this small project, but it may be worth it on larger projects. There's more in the Django tutorial (*https://docs.djangoproject.com/en/1.11/intro/tutorial03/#write-views-that-actually-do-something*).

```
$ python manage.py test
[...]
======================================================================
ERROR: test_home_page_returns_correct_html (lists.tests.HomePageTest)❷
----------------------------------------------------------------------
Traceback (most recent call last):
  File "...python-tdd-book/lists/tests.py", line 17, in
test_home_page_returns_correct_html
    response = home_page(request)❸
  File "...python-tdd-book/lists/views.py", line 5, in home_page
    return render(request, 'home.html')❹
  File "/usr/local/lib/python3.6/dist-packages/django/shortcuts.py", line 48,
in render
    return HttpResponse(loader.render_to_string(*args, **kwargs),
  File "/usr/local/lib/python3.6/dist-packages/django/template/loader.py", line
170, in render_to_string
    t = get_template(template_name, dirs)
  File "/usr/local/lib/python3.6/dist-packages/django/template/loader.py", line
144, in get_template
    template, origin = find_template(template_name, dirs)
  File "/usr/local/lib/python3.6/dist-packages/django/template/loader.py", line
136, in find_template
    raise TemplateDoesNotExist(name)
django.template.base.TemplateDoesNotExist: home.html❶


----------------------------------------------------------------------
Ran 2 tests in 0.004s
```

Another chance to analyse a traceback:

❶ We start with the error: it can't find the template.

❷ Then we double-check what test is failing: sure enough, it's our test of the view HTML.

❸ Then we find the line in our tests that caused the failure: it's when we call the home_page function.

❹ Finally, we look for the part of our own application code that caused the failure: it's when we try to call render.

So why can't Django find the template? It's right where it's supposed to be, in the *lists/ templates* folder.

The thing is that we haven't yet *officially* registered our lists app with Django. Unfortunately, just running the startapp command and having what is obviously an app in your project folder isn't quite enough. You have to tell Django that you *really* mean it, and add it to *settings.py* as well. Belt and braces. Open it up and look for a variable called INSTALLED_APPS, to which we'll add lists:

```
# Application definition

INSTALLED_APPS = [
    'django.contrib.admin',
    'django.contrib.auth',
    'django.contrib.contenttypes',
    'django.contrib.sessions',
    'django.contrib.messages',
    'django.contrib.staticfiles',
    'lists',
]
```

You can see there's lots of apps already in there by default. We just need to add ours, lists, to the bottom of the list. Don't forget the trailing comma—it may not be required, but one day you'll be really annoyed when you forget it and Python concatenates two strings on different lines...

Now we can try running the tests again:

```
$ python manage.py test
    [...]
    self.assertTrue(html.endswith('</html>'))
AssertionError: False is not true
```

Darn, not quite.

 Depending on whether your text editor insists on adding newlines to the end of files, you may not even see this error. If so, you can safely ignore the next bit, and skip straight to where you can see the listing says OK.

But it did get further! It seems it managed to find our template, but the last of the three assertions is failing. Apparently there's something wrong at the end of the output. I had to do a little print(repr(html)) to debug this, but it turns out that the switch to templates has introduced an additional newline (\n) at the end. We can get them to pass like this:

```
    self.assertTrue(html.strip().endswith('</html>'))
```

It's a tiny bit of a cheat, but whitespace at the end of an HTML file really shouldn't matter to us. Let's try running the tests again:

```
$ python manage.py test
[...]
OK
```

Our refactor of the code is now complete, and the tests mean we're happy that behaviour is preserved. Now we can change the tests so that they're no longer testing constants; instead, they should just check that we're rendering the right template.

The Django Test Client

One way we could test this is to manually render the template ourselves in the test, and then compare that to what the view returns. Django has a function called `render_to_string` which will let us do that:

lists/tests.py

```python
from django.template.loader import render_to_string
[...]

    def test_home_page_returns_correct_html(self):
        request = HttpRequest()
        response = home_page(request)
        html = response.content.decode('utf8')
        expected_html = render_to_string('home.html')
        self.assertEqual(html, expected_html)
```

But that's a bit of an unwieldy way of testing that we use the right template. And all this faffing about with `.decode()` and `.strip()` is distracting. Instead, Django gives us a tool called the Django Test Client (*https://docs.djangoproject.com/en/1.11/topics/testing/tools/#the-test-client*), which has built-in ways of checking what templates are used. Here's how it looks:

lists/tests.py

```python
    def test_home_page_returns_correct_html(self):
        response = self.client.get('/')   ❶

        html = response.content.decode('utf8')   ❷
        self.assertTrue(html.startswith('<html>'))
        self.assertIn('<title>To-Do lists</title>', html)
        self.assertTrue(html.strip().endswith('</html>'))

        self.assertTemplateUsed(response, 'home.html')   ❸
```

❶ Instead of manually creating an `HttpRequest` object and calling the view function directly, we call `self.client.get`, passing it the URL we want to test.

❷ We'll leave the old tests there for now, just to make sure everything is working the way we think it is.

❸ `.assertTemplateUsed` is the test method that the Django `TestCase` class provides us. It lets us check what template was used to render a response (NB—it will only work for responses that were retrieved by the test client).

And that test will still pass:

```
Ran 2 tests in 0.016s

OK
```

Just because I'm always suspicious of a test I haven't seen fail, let's deliberately break it:

lists/tests.py

```
self.assertTemplateUsed(response, 'wrong.html')
```

That way we'll also learn what its error messages look like:

```
AssertionError: False is not true : Template 'wrong.html' was not a template
used to render the response. Actual template(s) used: home.html
```

That's very helpful! Let's change the assert back to the right thing. While we're at it, we can delete our old assertions. And we can also delete the old `test_root_url_resolves` test, because that's tested implicitly by the Django Test Client. We've combined two long-winded tests into one!

lists/tests.py (ch04l010)

```
from django.test import TestCase

class HomePageTest(TestCase):

    def test_uses_home_template(self):
        response = self.client.get('/')
        self.assertTemplateUsed(response, 'home.html')
```

The main point, though, is that instead of testing constants we're testing our implementation. Great![3]

---

3 Are you unable to move on because you're wondering what those *ch04l0xx* things are, next to some of the code listings? They refer to specific commits (*https://github.com/hjwp/book-example/commits/chapter_philoso phy_and_refactoring*) in the book's example repo. It's all to do with my book's own tests (*https://github.com/ hjwp/Book-TDD-Web-Dev-Python/tree/master/tests*). You know, the tests for the tests in the book about testing. They have tests of their own, naturally.

On Refactoring

That was an absolutely trivial example of refactoring. But, as Kent Beck puts it in *Test-Driven Development: By Example*, "Am I recommending that you actually work this way? No. I'm recommending that you be *able* to work this way".

In fact, as I was writing this my first instinct was to dive in and change the test first—make it use the `assertTemplateUsed` function straight away; delete the three superfluous assertions, leaving just a check of the contents against the expected render; and then go ahead and make the code change. But notice how that actually would have left space for me to break things: I could have defined the template as containing *any* arbitrary string, instead of the string with the right `<html>` and `<title>` tags.

When refactoring, work on either the code or the tests, but not both at once.

There's always a tendency to skip ahead a couple of steps, to make a couple of tweaks to the behaviour while you're refactoring, but pretty soon you've got changes to half a dozen different files, you've totally lost track of where you are, and nothing works any more. If you don't want to end up like Refactoring Cat (*http://bit.ly/1iXyRt4*) (Figure 4-2), stick to small steps; keep refactoring and functionality changes entirely separate.

Figure 4-2. Refactoring Cat—be sure to look up the full animated GIF (source: 4GIFs.com)

We'll come across "Refactoring Cat" again during this book, as an example of what happens when we get carried away and want to change too many things at once. Think of it as the little cartoon demon counterpart to the Testing Goat, popping up over your other shoulder and giving you bad advice…

It's a good idea to do a commit after any refactoring:

```
$ git status # see tests.py, views.py, settings.py, + new templates folder
$ git add .  # will also add the untracked templates folder
$ git diff --staged # review the changes we're about to commit
$ git commit -m "Refactor home page view to use a template"
```

A Little More of Our Front Page

In the meantime, our functional test is still failing. Let's now make an actual code change to get it passing. Because our HTML is now in a template, we can feel free to make changes to it, without needing to write any extra unit tests. We wanted an `<h1>`:

```
<html>
    <head>
        <title>To-Do lists</title>
    </head>
    <body>
        <h1>Your To-Do list</h1>
    </body>
</html>
```

Let's see if our functional test likes it a little better:

```
selenium.common.exceptions.NoSuchElementException: Message: Unable to locate
element: [id="id_new_item"]
```

OK...

```
[...]
        <h1>Your To-Do list</h1>
        <input id="id_new_item" />
    </body>
[...]
```

And now?

```
AssertionError: '' != 'Enter a to-do item'
```

We add our placeholder text...

```
        <input id="id_new_item" placeholder="Enter a to-do item" />
```

Which gives:

```
selenium.common.exceptions.NoSuchElementException: Message: Unable to locate
element: [id="id_list_table"]
```

So we can go ahead and put the table onto the page. At this stage it'll just be empty...

```
        <input id="id_new_item" placeholder="Enter a to-do item" />
        <table id="id_list_table">
        </table>
    </body>
```

Now what does the FT say?

```
    File "functional_tests.py", line 43, in
test_can_start_a_list_and_retrieve_it_later
    any(row.text == '1: Buy peacock feathers' for row in rows)
AssertionError: False is not true
```

Slightly cryptic. We can use the line number to track it down, and it turns out it's that any function I was so smug about earlier—or, more precisely, the assertTrue, which doesn't have a very explicit failure message. We can pass a custom error message as an argument to most assertX methods in unittest:

functional_tests.py

```
self.assertTrue(
    any(row.text == '1: Buy peacock feathers' for row in rows),
    "New to-do item did not appear in table"
)
```

If you run the FT again, you should see our message:

```
AssertionError: False is not true : New to-do item did not appear in table
```

But now, to get this to pass, we will need to actually process the user's form submission. And that's a topic for the next chapter.

For now let's do a commit:

```
$ git diff
$ git commit -am "Front page HTML now generated from a template"
```

Thanks to a bit of refactoring, we've got our view set up to render a template, we've stopped testing constants, and we're now well placed to start processing user input.

Recap: The TDD Process

We've now seen all the main aspects of the TDD process, in practice:

- Functional tests
- Unit tests
- The unit-test/code cycle
- Refactoring

It's time for a little recap, and perhaps even some flowcharts. Forgive me, years misspent as a management consultant have ruined me. On the plus side, it will feature recursion.

What is the overall TDD process? See Figure 4-3.

We write a test. We run the test and see it fail. We write some minimal code to get it a little further. We rerun the test and repeat until it passes. Then, optionally, we might refactor our code, using our tests to make sure we don't break anything.

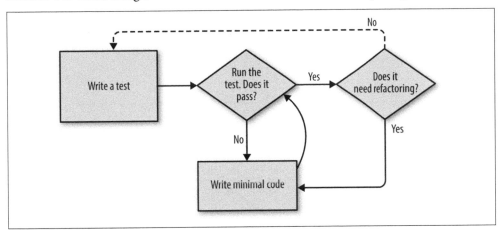

Figure 4-3. Overall TDD process

But how does this apply when we have functional tests *and* unit tests? Well, you can think of the functional test as being a high-level view of the cycle, where "writing the code" to get the functional tests to pass actually involves using another, smaller TDD cycle which uses unit tests. See Figure 4-4.

We write a functional test and see it fail. Then, the process of "writing code" to get it to pass is a mini-TDD cycle of its own: we write one or more unit tests, and go into the unit-test/code cycle until the unit tests pass. Then, we go back to our FT to check that it gets a little further, and we can write a bit more of our application—using more unit tests, and so on.

What about refactoring, in the context of functional tests? Well, that means we use the functional test to check that we've preserved the behaviour of our application, but we can change or add and remove unit tests, and use a unit test cycle to actually change the implementation.

The functional tests are the ultimate judge of whether your application works or not. The unit tests are a tool to help you along the way.

This way of looking at things is sometimes called "Double-Loop TDD". One of my eminent tech reviewers, Emily Bache, wrote a blog post (*http://bit.ly/1iXzoLR*) on the topic, which I recommend for a different perspective.

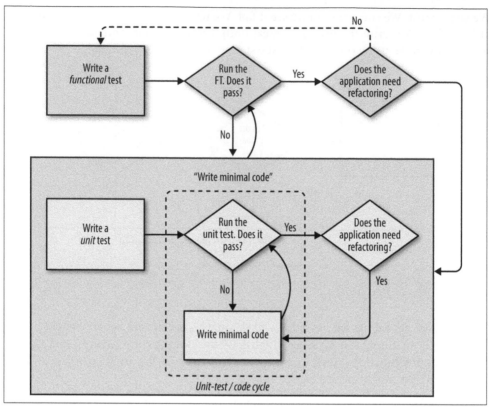

Figure 4-4. The TDD process with functional and unit tests

We'll explore all of the different parts of this workflow in more detail over the coming chapters.

How to "Check" Your Code, or Skip Ahead (If You Must)

All of the code examples I've used in the book are available in my repo (*https://github.com/hjwp/book-example/*) on GitHub. So, if you ever want to compare your code against mine, you can take a look at it there.

Each chapter has its own branch which is named after its short name. The one for this chapter is here (*https://github.com/hjwp/book-example/tree/chapter_philosophy_and_refactoring*), for example. It is a snapshot of the code as it should be at the *end* of the chapter.

You can find a full list of them in Appendix J, as well as instructions on how to download them or use Git to compare your code to mine.

## CHAPTER 5

Saving User Input: Testing the Database

We want to take the to-do item input from the user and send it to the server, so that we can save it somehow and display it back to her later.

As I started writing this chapter, I immediately skipped to what I thought was the right design: multiple models for lists and list items, a bunch of different URLs for adding new lists and items, three new view functions, and about half a dozen new unit tests for all of the above. But I stopped myself. Although I was pretty sure I was smart enough to handle all those problems at once, the point of TDD is to allow you to do one thing at a time, when you need to. So I decided to be deliberately short-sighted, and at any given moment only do what was necessary to get the functional tests a little further.

It's a demonstration of how TDD can support an iterative style of development—it may not be the quickest route, but you do get there in the end. There's a neat side benefit, which is that it allows me to introduce new concepts like models, dealing with POST requests, Django template tags, and so on *one at a time* rather than having to dump them on you all at once.

None of this says that you *shouldn't* try to think ahead, and be clever. In the next chapter we'll use a bit more design and up-front thinking, and show how that fits in with TDD. But for now let's plough on mindlessly and just do what the tests tell us to.

Wiring Up Our Form to Send a POST Request

At the end of the last chapter, the tests were telling us we weren't able to save the user's input. For now, we'll use a standard HTML POST request. A little boring, but also nice and easy to deliver—we can use all sorts of sexy HTML5 and JavaScript later in the book.

To get our browser to send a POST request, we need to do two things:

1. Give the `<input>` element a `name=` attribute.

2. Wrap it in a `<form>` tag with `method="POST"`.

Let's adjust our template at *lists/templates/home.html*:

lists/templates/home.html

```
<h1>Your To-Do list</h1>
<form method="POST">
    <input name="item_text" id="id_new_item" placeholder="Enter a to-do item" />
</form>

<table id="id_list_table">
```

Now, running our FTs gives us a slightly cryptic, unexpected error:

```
$ python functional_tests.py
[...]
Traceback (most recent call last):
  File "functional_tests.py", line 40, in
test_can_start_a_list_and_retrieve_it_later
    table = self.browser.find_element_by_id('id_list_table')
[...]
selenium.common.exceptions.NoSuchElementException: Message: Unable to locate
element: [id="id_list_table"]
```

When a functional test fails with an unexpected failure, there are several things we can do to debug it:

- Add `print` statements, to show, for example, what the current page text is.

- Improve the *error message* to show more info about the current state.

- Manually visit the site yourself.

- Use `time.sleep` to pause the test during execution.[1]

We'll look at all of these over the course of this book, but the `time.sleep` option is one I find myself using very often. Let's try it now.

Conveniently, we've already got a sleep just before the error occurs; let's just extend it a little:

---

1 Lots of people also swear by using `pdb.set_trace()` to be able to drop into a debugger, particularly for unit tests. I'm not enough of a pdb user to be able to give a good intro to it, but you should definitely check it out at some point in your testing career.

```
# When she hits enter, the page updates, and now the page lists
# "1: Buy peacock feathers" as an item in a to-do list table
inputbox.send_keys(Keys.ENTER)
time.sleep(10)

table = self.browser.find_element_by_id('id_list_table')
```

Depending on how fast Selenium runs on your PC, you may have caught a glimpse of this already, but when we run the functional tests again, we've got time to see what's going on: you should see a page that looks like Figure 5-1, with lots of Django debug information.

Figure 5-1. Django DEBUG page showing CSRF error

Security: Surprisingly Fun!

If you've never heard of a *Cross-Site Request Forgery* exploit, why not look it up now? Like all security exploits, it's entertaining to read about, being an ingenious use of a system in unexpected ways...

When I went back to university to get my Computer Science degree, I signed up for the Security module out of a sense of duty: *Oh well, it'll probably be very dry and boring, but I suppose I'd better take it*. It turned out to be one of the most fascinating modules of the whole course—absolutely full of the joy of hacking, of the particular mindset it takes to think about how systems can be used in unintended ways.

I want to recommend the textbook for my course, Ross Anderson's *Security Engineering*. It's quite light on pure crypto, but it's absolutely full of interesting discussions of unexpected topics like lock picking, forging bank notes, inkjet printer cartridge economics, and spoofing South African Air Force jets with replay attacks. It's a huge tome, about three inches thick, and I promise you it's an absolute page-turner.

Django's CSRF protection involves placing a little auto-generated token into each generated form, to be able to identify POST requests as having come from the original site. So far our template has been pure HTML, and in this step we make the first use of Django's template magic. To add the CSRF token we use a *template tag*, which has the curly-bracket/percent syntax, {% ... %}—famous for being the world's most annoying two-key touch-typing combination:

lists/templates/home.html

```
<form method="POST">
    <input name="item_text" id="id_new_item" placeholder="Enter a to-do item" />
    {% csrf_token %}
</form>
```

Django will substitute that during rendering with an `<input type="hidden">` containing the CSRF token. Rerunning the functional test will now give us an expected failure:

```
AssertionError: False is not true : New to-do item did not appear in table
```

Since our long `time.sleep` is still there, the test will pause on the final screen, showing us that the new item text disappears after the form is submitted, and the page refreshes to show an empty form again. That's because we haven't wired up our server to deal with the POST request yet—it just ignores it and displays the normal home page.

We can put our normal short `time.sleep` back now though:

functional_tests.py

```
# "1: Buy peacock feathers" as an item in a to-do list table
inputbox.send_keys(Keys.ENTER)
time.sleep(1)

table = self.browser.find_element_by_id('id_list_table')
```

Processing a POST Request on the Server

Because we haven't specified an action= attribute in the form, it is submitting back to the same URL it was rendered from by default (i.e., /), which is dealt with by our home_page function. Let's adapt the view to be able to deal with a POST request.

That means a new unit test for the home_page view. Open up *lists/tests.py*, and add a new method to HomePageTest:

lists/tests.py (ch05l005)

```python
def test_uses_home_template(self):
    response = self.client.get('/')
    self.assertTemplateUsed(response, 'home.html')


def test_can_save_a_POST_request(self):
    response = self.client.post('/', data={'item_text': 'A new list item'})
    self.assertIn('A new list item', response.content.decode())
```

To do a POST, we call self.client.post, and as you can see it takes a data argument which contains the form data we want to send. Then we check that the text from our POST request ends up in the rendered HTML. That gives us our expected fail:

```
$ python manage.py test
[...]
AssertionError: 'A new list item' not found in '<html>\n     <head>\n
<title>To-Do lists</title>\n     </head>\n     <body>\n          <h1>Your To-Do
list</h1>\n          <form method="POST">\n               <input name="item_text"
[...]
</body>\n</html>\n'
```

We can get the test to pass by adding an if and providing a different code path for POST requests. In typical TDD style, we start with a deliberately silly return value:

lists/views.py

```python
from django.http import HttpResponse
from django.shortcuts import render

def home_page(request):
    if request.method == 'POST':
        return HttpResponse(request.POST['item_text'])
    return render(request, 'home.html')
```

That gets our unit tests passing, but it's not really what we want. What we really want to do is add the POST submission to the table in the home page template.

Passing Python Variables to Be Rendered in the Template

We've already had a hint of it, and now it's time to start to get to know the real power of the Django template syntax, which is to pass variables from our Python view code into HTML templates.

Let's start by seeing how the template syntax lets us include a Python object in our template. The notation is {{ ... }}, which displays the object as a string:

lists/templates/home.html

```
<body>
    <h1>Your To-Do list</h1>
    <form method="POST">
        <input name="item_text" id="id_new_item" placeholder="Enter a to-do item" />
        {% csrf_token %}
    </form>

    <table id="id_list_table">
        <tr><td>{{ new_item_text }}</td></tr>  ❶
    </table>
</body>
```

❶ Here's our template variable. `new_item_text` will be the variable name for the user input we display in the template, to help distinguish it from `item_text`, which is the name of the form field which we use in the POST request. That just reminds us that transforming the one into the other doesn't happen automatically; it's something we do ourselves in the view...

Let's adjust our unit test so that it checks whether we are still using the template:

lists/tests.py

```
def test_can_save_a_POST_request(self):
    response = self.client.post('/', data={'item_text': 'A new list item'})
    self.assertIn('A new list item', response.content.decode())
    self.assertTemplateUsed(response, 'home.html')
```

And that will fail as expected:

```
AssertionError: No templates used to render the response
```

Good, our deliberately silly return value is now no longer fooling our tests, so we are allowed to rewrite our view, and tell it to pass the POST parameter to the template. The `render` function takes, as its third argument, a dictionary which maps template variable names to their values, so we can use it for the POST case as well as the normal case. Let's simplify our view right down to:

```
def home_page(request):
    return render(request, 'home.html', {
        'new_item_text': request.POST['item_text'],
    })
```

Running the unit tests again:

```
ERROR: test_uses_home_template (lists.tests.HomePageTest)
[...]
  File "...python-tdd-book/lists/views.py", line 5, in home_page
    'new_item_text': request.POST['item_text'],
[...]
django.utils.datastructures.MultiValueDictKeyError: "'item_text'"
```

An Unexpected Failure

Oops, an *unexpected failure*.

If you remember the rules for reading tracebacks, you'll spot that it's actually a failure in a *different* test. We got the actual test we were working on to pass, but the unit tests have picked up an unexpected consequence, a regression: we broke the code path where there is no POST request.

This is the whole point of having tests. Yes, we could have predicted this would happen, but imagine if we'd been having a bad day or weren't paying attention: our tests have just saved us from accidentally breaking our application, and, because we're using TDD, we found out immediately. We didn't have to wait for a QA team, or switch to a web browser and click through our site manually, and we can get on with fixing it straight away. Here's how:

```
def home_page(request):
    return render(request, 'home.html', {
        'new_item_text': request.POST.get('item_text', ''),
    })
```

We use `dict.get` (*http://docs.python.org/3/library/stdtypes.html#dict.get*) to supply a default value, for the case where we are doing a normal GET request, so the POST dictionary is empty.

The unit tests should now pass. Let's see what the functional tests say:

```
AssertionError: False is not true : New to-do item did not appear in table
```

If your functional tests show you a different error at this point, or at any point in this chapter, complaining about a StaleElementRe ferenceException, you may need to increase the time.sleep explicit wait—try 2 or 3 seconds instead of 1; then read on to the next chapter for a more robust solution.

Hmm, not a wonderfully helpful error. Let's use another of our FT debugging techniques: improving the error message. This is probably the most constructive technique, because those improved error messages stay around to help debug any future errors:

functional_tests.py (ch05l011)

```
self.assertTrue(
    any(row.text == '1: Buy peacock feathers' for row in rows),
    f"New to-do item did not appear in table. Contents were:\n{table.text}"    ❶
)
```

❶ If you've not seen this syntax before, it's the new Python "f-string" syntax (probably the most exciting new feature from Python 3.6). You just prepend a string with an f, and then you can use the curly-bracket syntax to insert local variables. There's more info in the Python 3.6 release notes (*https://docs.python.org/3/what snew/3.6.html#pep-498-formatted-string-literals*).

That gives us a more helpful error message:

```
AssertionError: False is not true : New to-do item did not appear in table.
Contents were:
Buy peacock feathers
```

You know what could be even better than that? Making that assertion a bit less clever. As you may remember, I was very pleased with myself for using the any function, but one of my Early Release readers (thanks, Jason!) suggested a much simpler implementation. We can replace all four lines of the assertTrue with a single assertIn:

functional_tests.py (ch05l012)

```
self.assertIn('1: Buy peacock feathers', [row.text for row in rows])
```

Much better. You should always be very worried whenever you think you're being clever, because what you're probably being is *overcomplicated*. And we get the error message for free:

```
self.assertIn('1: Buy peacock feathers', [row.text for row in rows])
AssertionError: '1: Buy peacock feathers' not found in ['Buy peacock feathers']
```

Consider me suitably chastened.

If, instead, your FT seems to be saying the table is empty ("not found in []"), check your `<input>` tag—does it have the correct `name="item_text"` attribute? And does it have `method="POST"`? Without them, the user's input won't be in the right place in `request.POST`.

The point is that the FT wants us to enumerate list items with a "1:" at the beginning of the first list item. The fastest way to get that to pass is with a quick "cheating" change to the template:

lists/templates/home.html

```
<tr><td>1: {{ new_item_text }}</td></tr>
```

Red/Green/Refactor and Triangulation

The unit-test/code cycle is sometimes taught as *Red, Green, Refactor*:

- Start by writing a unit test which fails (*Red*).
- Write the simplest possible code to get it to pass (*Green*), *even if that means cheating*.
- *Refactor* to get to better code that makes more sense.

So what do we do during the Refactor stage? What justifies moving from an implementation where we "cheat" to one we're happy with?

One methodology is *eliminate duplication*: if your test uses a magic constant (like the "1:" in front of our list item), and your application code also uses it, that counts as duplication, so it justifies refactoring. Removing the magic constant from the application code usually means you have to stop cheating.

I find that leaves things a little too vague, so I usually like to use a second technique, which is called *triangulation*: if your tests let you get away with writing "cheating" code that you're not happy with, like returning a magic constant, *write another test* that forces you to write some better code. That's what we're doing when we extend the FT to check that we get a "2:" when inputting a *second* list item.

Now we get to the `self.fail('Finish the test!')`. If we extend our FT to check for adding a second item to the table (copy and paste is our friend), we begin to see that our first cut solution really isn't going to, um, cut it:

```
# There is still a text box inviting her to add another item. She
# enters "Use peacock feathers to make a fly" (Edith is very
# methodical)
inputbox = self.browser.find_element_by_id('id_new_item')
inputbox.send_keys('Use peacock feathers to make a fly')
inputbox.send_keys(Keys.ENTER)
time.sleep(1)

# The page updates again, and now shows both items on her list
table = self.browser.find_element_by_id('id_list_table')
rows = table.find_elements_by_tag_name('tr')
self.assertIn('1: Buy peacock feathers', [row.text for row in rows])
self.assertIn(
    '2: Use peacock feathers to make a fly',
    [row.text for row in rows]
)

# Edith wonders whether the site will remember her list. Then she sees
# that the site has generated a unique URL for her -- there is some
# explanatory text to that effect.
self.fail('Finish the test!')

# She visits that URL - her to-do list is still there.
```

Sure enough, the functional tests return an error:

```
AssertionError: '1: Buy peacock feathers' not found in ['1: Use peacock
feathers to make a fly']
```

Three Strikes and Refactor

Before we go further—we've got a bad *code smell*[2] in this FT. We have three almost identical code blocks checking for new items in the list table. There's a principle called *Don't Repeat Yourself* (DRY), which we like to apply by following the mantra *three strikes and refactor*. You can copy and paste code once, and it may be premature to try to remove the duplication it causes, but once you get three occurrences, it's time to remove duplication.

We start by committing what we have so far. Even though we know our site has a major flaw—it can only handle one list item—it's still further ahead than it was. We may have to rewrite it all, and we may not, but the rule is that before you do any refactoring, always do a commit:

---

2 If you've not come across the concept, a "code smell" is something about a piece of code that makes you want to rewrite it. Jeff Atwood has a compilation on his blog Coding Horror (*http://www.codinghorror.com/blog/2006/05/code-smells.html*). The more experience you gain as a programmer, the more fine-tuned your nose becomes to code smells…

```
$ git diff
# should show changes to functional_tests.py, home.html,
# tests.py and views.py
$ git commit -a
```

Back to our functional test refactor: we could use an inline function, but that upsets the flow of the test slightly. Let's use a helper method—remember, only methods that begin with `test_` will get run as tests, so you can use other methods for your own purposes:

functional_tests.py

```python
    def tearDown(self):
        self.browser.quit()


    def check_for_row_in_list_table(self, row_text):
        table = self.browser.find_element_by_id('id_list_table')
        rows = table.find_elements_by_tag_name('tr')
        self.assertIn(row_text, [row.text for row in rows])


    def test_can_start_a_list_and_retrieve_it_later(self):
        [...]
```

I like to put helper methods near the top of the class, between the `tearDown` and the first test. Let's use it in the FT:

functional_tests.py

```python
    # When she hits enter, the page updates, and now the page lists
    # "1: Buy peacock feathers" as an item in a to-do list table
    inputbox.send_keys(Keys.ENTER)
    time.sleep(1)
    self.check_for_row_in_list_table('1: Buy peacock feathers')

    # There is still a text box inviting her to add another item. She
    # enters "Use peacock feathers to make a fly" (Edith is very
    # methodical)
    inputbox = self.browser.find_element_by_id('id_new_item')
    inputbox.send_keys('Use peacock feathers to make a fly')
    inputbox.send_keys(Keys.ENTER)
    time.sleep(1)

    # The page updates again, and now shows both items on her list
    self.check_for_row_in_list_table('1: Buy peacock feathers')
    self.check_for_row_in_list_table('2: Use peacock feathers to make a fly')

    # Edith wonders whether the site will remember her list. Then she sees
    [...]
```

We run the FT again to check that it still behaves in the same way…

```
AssertionError: '1: Buy peacock feathers' not found in ['1: Use peacock
feathers to make a fly']
```

Good. Now we can commit the FT refactor as its own small, atomic change:

```
$ git diff # check the changes to functional_tests.py
$ git commit -a
```

And back to work. If we're ever going to handle more than one list item, we're going to need some kind of persistence, and databases are a stalwart solution in this area.

The Django ORM and Our First Model

An *Object-Relational Mapper* (ORM) is a layer of abstraction for data stored in a database with tables, rows, and columns. It lets us work with databases using familiar object-oriented metaphors which work well with code. Classes map to database tables, attributes map to columns, and an individual instance of the class represents a row of data in the database.

Django comes with an excellent ORM, and writing a unit test that uses it is actually an excellent way of learning it, since it exercises code by specifying how we want it to work.

Let's create a new class in *lists/tests.py*:

lists/tests.py

```python
from lists.models import Item
[...]

class ItemModelTest(TestCase):

    def test_saving_and_retrieving_items(self):
        first_item = Item()
        first_item.text = 'The first (ever) list item'
        first_item.save()

        second_item = Item()
        second_item.text = 'Item the second'
        second_item.save()

        saved_items = Item.objects.all()
        self.assertEqual(saved_items.count(), 2)

        first_saved_item = saved_items[0]
        second_saved_item = saved_items[1]
        self.assertEqual(first_saved_item.text, 'The first (ever) list item')
        self.assertEqual(second_saved_item.text, 'Item the second')
```

You can see that creating a new record in the database is a relatively simple matter of creating an object, assigning some attributes, and calling a `.save()` function. Django also gives us an API for querying the database via a class attribute, `.objects`, and we use the simplest possible query, `.all()`, which retrieves all the records for that table. The results are returned as a list-like object called a `QuerySet`, from which we can extract individual objects, and also call further functions, like `.count()`. We then check the objects as saved to the database, to check whether the right information was saved.

Django's ORM has many other helpful and intuitive features; this might be a good time to skim through the Django tutorial (*https://docs.djangoproject.com/en/1.11/ intro/tutorial01/*), which has an excellent intro to them.

I've written this unit test in a very verbose style, as a way of introducing the Django ORM. I wouldn't recommend writing your model tests like this "in real life". We'll actually rewrite this test to be much more concise later on, in Chapter 15.

Terminology 2: Unit Tests Versus Integrated Tests, and the Database

Purists will tell you that a "real" unit test should never touch the database, and that the test I've just written should be more properly called an integrated test, because it doesn't only test our code, but also relies on an external system—that is, a database.

It's OK to ignore this distinction for now—we have two types of test, the high-level functional tests which test the application from the user's point of view, and these lower-level tests which test it from the programmer's point of view.

We'll come back to this and talk about unit tests and integrated tests in Chapter 23, towards the end of the book.

Let's try running the unit test. Here comes another unit-test/code cycle:

```
ImportError: cannot import name 'Item'
```

Very well, let's give it something to import from *lists/models.py*. We're feeling confident so we'll skip the `Item = None` step, and go straight to creating a class:

lists/models.py

```
from django.db import models

class Item(object):
    pass
```

That gets our test as far as:

```
first_item.save()
AttributeError: 'Item' object has no attribute 'save'
```

To give our Item class a save method, and to make it into a real Django model, we make it inherit from the Model class:

lists/models.py

```
from django.db import models

class Item(models.Model):
    pass
```

Our First Database Migration

The next thing that happens is a database error:

```
django.db.utils.OperationalError: no such table: lists_item
```

In Django, the ORM's job is to model the database, but there's a second system that's in charge of actually building the database called *migrations*. Its job is to give you the ability to add and remove tables and columns, based on changes you make to your *models.py* files.

One way to think of it is as a version control system for your database. As we'll see later, it comes in particularly useful when we need to upgrade a database that's deployed on a live server.

For now all we need to know is how to build our first database migration, which we do using the makemigrations command:[3]

```
$ python manage.py makemigrations
Migrations for 'lists':
  lists/migrations/0001_initial.py
    - Create model Item
$ ls lists/migrations
0001_initial.py  __init__.py  __pycache__
```

If you're curious, you can go and take a look in the migrations file, and you'll see it's a representation of our additions to *models.py*.

In the meantime, we should find our tests get a little further.

---

3 Are you wondering about when we're going to run "migrate" as well as "makemigrations"? Read on; that's coming up later in the chapter.

The Test Gets Surprisingly Far

The test actually gets surprisingly far:

```
$ python manage.py test lists
[...]
    self.assertEqual(first_saved_item.text, 'The first (ever) list item')
AttributeError: 'Item' object has no attribute 'text'
```

That's a full eight lines later than the last failure—we've been all the way through saving the two Items, and we've checked that they're saved in the database, but Django just doesn't seem to have remembered the .text attribute.

Incidentally, if you're new to Python, you might have been surprised we were allowed to assign the .text attribute at all. In a language like Java, you would probably get a compilation error. Python is more relaxed.

Classes that inherit from models.Model map to tables in the database. By default they get an auto-generated id attribute, which will be a primary key column in the database, but you have to define any other columns you want explicitly; here's how we set up a text field:

lists/models.py

```
class Item(models.Model):
    text = models.TextField()
```

Django has many other field types, like IntegerField, CharField, DateField, and so on. I've chosen TextField rather than CharField because the latter requires a length restriction, which seems arbitrary at this point. You can read more on field types in the Django tutorial (*https://docs.djangoproject.com/en/1.11/intro/tutorial01/#creating-models*) and in the documentation (*https://docs.djangoproject.com/en/1.11/ref/models/fields/*).

A New Field Means a New Migration

Running the tests gives us another database error:

```
django.db.utils.OperationalError: no such column: lists_item.text
```

It's because we've added another new field to our database, which means we need to create another migration. Nice of our tests to let us know!

Let's try it:

```
$ python manage.py makemigrations
You are trying to add a non-nullable field 'text' to item without a default; we
can't do that (the database needs something to populate existing rows).
Please select a fix:
 1) Provide a one-off default now (will be set on all existing rows with a null
value for this column)
 2) Quit, and let me add a default in models.py
Select an option:2
```

Ah. It won't let us add the column without a default value. Let's pick option 2 and set a default in *models.py*. I think you'll find the syntax reasonably self-explanatory:

lists/models.py

```python
class Item(models.Model):
    text = models.TextField(default='')
```

And now the migration should complete:

```
$ python manage.py makemigrations
Migrations for 'lists':
  lists/migrations/0002_item_text.py
    - Add field text to item
```

So, two new lines in *models.py*, two database migrations, and as a result, the .text attribute on our model objects is now recognised as a special attribute, so it does get saved to the database, and the tests pass...

```
$ python manage.py test lists
[...]

Ran 3 tests in 0.010s
OK
```

So let's do a commit for our first ever model!

```
$ git status # see tests.py, models.py, and 2 untracked migrations
$ git diff # review changes to tests.py and models.py
$ git add lists
$ git commit -m "Model for list Items and associated migration"
```

Saving the POST to the Database

Let's adjust the test for our home page POST request, and say we want the view to save a new item to the database instead of just passing it through to its response. We can do that by adding three new lines to the existing test called test_can_save_ a_POST_request:

```
def test_can_save_a_POST_request(self):
    response = self.client.post('/', data={'item_text': 'A new list item'})

    self.assertEqual(Item.objects.count(), 1)  ❶
    new_item = Item.objects.first()  ❷
    self.assertEqual(new_item.text, 'A new list item')  ❸

    self.assertIn('A new list item', response.content.decode())
    self.assertTemplateUsed(response, 'home.html')
```

❶ We check that one new `Item` has been saved to the database. `objects.count()` is a shorthand for `objects.all().count()`.

❷ `objects.first()` is the same as doing `objects.all()[0]`.

❸ We check that the item's text is correct.

This test is getting a little long-winded. It seems to be testing lots of different things. That's another *code smell*—a long unit test either needs to be broken into two, or it may be an indication that the thing you're testing is too complicated. Let's add that to a little to-do list of our own, perhaps on a piece of scrap paper:

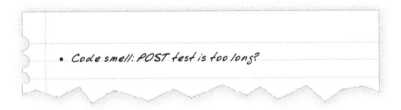

• *Code smell: POST test is too long?*

Writing it down on a scratchpad like this reassures us that we won't forget, so we are comfortable getting back to what we were working on. We rerun the tests and see an expected failure:

```
    self.assertEqual(Item.objects.count(), 1)
AssertionError: 0 != 1
```

Let's adjust our view:

```
from django.shortcuts import render
from lists.models import Item

def home_page(request):
    item = Item()
    item.text = request.POST.get('item_text', '')
    item.save()

    return render(request, 'home.html', {
        'new_item_text': request.POST.get('item_text', ''),
    })
```

I've coded a very naive solution and you can probably spot a very obvious problem, which is that we're going to be saving empty items with every request to the home page. Let's add that to our list of things to fix later. You know, along with the painfully obvious fact that we currently have no way at all of having different lists for different people. That we'll keep ignoring for now.

Remember, I'm not saying you should always ignore glaring problems like this in "real life". Whenever we spot problems in advance, there's a judgement call to make over whether to stop what you're doing and start again, or leave them until later. Sometimes finishing off what you're doing is still worth it, and sometimes the problem may be so major as to warrant a stop and rethink.

Let's see how the unit tests get on…they pass! Good. We can do a bit of refactoring:

```
    return render(request, 'home.html', {
        'new_item_text': item.text
    })
```

Let's have a little look at our scratchpad. I've added a couple of the other things that are on our mind:

- Don't save blank items for every request
- Code smell: POST test is too long?
- Display multiple items in the table
- Support more than one list!

Let's start with the first one. We could tack on an assertion to an existing test, but it's best to keep unit tests to testing one thing at a time, so let's add a new one:

lists/tests.py

```python
class HomePageTest(TestCase):
    [...]

    def test_only_saves_items_when_necessary(self):
        self.client.get('/')
        self.assertEqual(Item.objects.count(), 0)
```

That gives us a 1 != 0 failure. Let's fix it. Watch out; although it's quite a small change to the logic of the view, there are quite a few little tweaks to the implementation in code:

lists/views.py

```python
def home_page(request):
    if request.method == 'POST':
        new_item_text = request.POST['item_text']   ❶
        Item.objects.create(text=new_item_text)   ❷
    else:
        new_item_text = ''   ❶

    return render(request, 'home.html', {
        'new_item_text': new_item_text,   ❶
    })
```

❶ We use a variable called new_item_text, which will either hold the POST contents, or the empty string.

❷ .objects.create is a neat shorthand for creating a new Item, without needing to call .save().

And that gets the test passing:

```
Ran 4 tests in 0.010s

OK
```

Redirect After a POST

But, yuck, that whole `new_item_text = ''` dance is making me pretty unhappy. Thankfully we now have an opportunity to fix it. A view function has two jobs: processing user input, and returning an appropriate response. We've taken care of the first part, which is saving the users' input to the database, so now let's work on the second part.

Always redirect after a POST (*https://en.wikipedia.org/wiki/Post/Redirect/Get*), they say, so let's do that. Once again we change our unit test for saving a POST request to say that, instead of rendering a response with the item in it, it should redirect back to the home page:

lists/tests.py

```python
def test_can_save_a_POST_request(self):
    response = self.client.post('/', data={'item_text': 'A new list item'})

    self.assertEqual(Item.objects.count(), 1)
    new_item = Item.objects.first()
    self.assertEqual(new_item.text, 'A new list item')

    self.assertEqual(response.status_code, 302)
    self.assertEqual(response['location'], '/')
```

We no longer expect a response with a `.content` rendered by a template, so we lose the assertions that look at that. Instead, the response will represent an HTTP *redirect*, which should have status code 302, and points the browser towards a new location.

That gives us the error `200 != 302`. We can now tidy up our view substantially:

lists/views.py (ch05l028)

```python
from django.shortcuts import redirect, render
from lists.models import Item

def home_page(request):
    if request.method == 'POST':
        Item.objects.create(text=request.POST['item_text'])
        return redirect('/')

    return render(request, 'home.html')
```

And the tests should now pass:

```
Ran 4 tests in 0.010s
```

OK

Better Unit Testing Practice: Each Test Should Test One Thing

Our view now does a redirect after a POST, which is good practice, and we've short-ened the unit test somewhat, but we can still do better.

Good unit testing practice says that each test should only test one thing. The reason is that it makes it easier to track down bugs. Having multiple assertions in a test means that, if the test fails on an early assertion, you don't know what the status of the later assertions is. As we'll see in the next chapter, if we ever break this view accidentally, we want to know whether it's the saving of objects that's broken, or the type of response.

You may not always write perfect unit tests with single assertions on your first go, but now feels like a good time to separate out our concerns:

lists/tests.py

```python
def test_can_save_a_POST_request(self):
    self.client.post('/', data={'item_text': 'A new list item'})

    self.assertEqual(Item.objects.count(), 1)
    new_item = Item.objects.first()
    self.assertEqual(new_item.text, 'A new list item')


def test_redirects_after_POST(self):
    response = self.client.post('/', data={'item_text': 'A new list item'})
    self.assertEqual(response.status_code, 302)
    self.assertEqual(response['location'], '/')
```

And we should now see five tests pass instead of four:

```
Ran 5 tests in 0.010s
```

OK

Rendering Items in the Template

Much better! Back to our to-do list:

- ~~Don't save blank items for every request~~
- ~~Code smell: POST test is too long?~~
- Display multiple items in the table
- Support more than one list!

Crossing things off the list is almost as satisfying as seeing tests pass!

The third item is the last of the "easy" ones. Let's have a new unit test that checks that the template can also display multiple list items:

lists/tests.py

```python
class HomePageTest(TestCase):
    [...]

    def test_displays_all_list_items(self):
        Item.objects.create(text='itemey 1')
        Item.objects.create(text='itemey 2')

        response = self.client.get('/')

        self.assertIn('itemey 1', response.content.decode())
        self.assertIn('itemey 2', response.content.decode())
```

 Are you wondering about the line spacing in the test? I'm grouping together two lines at the beginning which set up the test, one line in the middle which actually calls the code under test, and the assertions at the end. This isn't obligatory, but it does help see the structure of the test. Setup, Exercise, Assert is the typical structure for a unit test.

That fails as expected:

```
AssertionError: 'itemey 1' not found in '<html>\n    <head>\n [...]
```

The Django template syntax has a tag for iterating through lists, {% for .. in .. %}; we can use it like this:

lists/templates/home.html

```html
<table id="id_list_table">
    {% for item in items %}
        <tr><td>1: {{ item.text }}</td></tr>
    {% endfor %}
</table>
```

This is one of the major strengths of the templating system. Now the template will render with multiple <tr> rows, one for each item in the variable items. Pretty neat! I'll introduce a few more bits of Django template magic as we go, but at some point you'll want to go and read up on the rest of them in the Django docs (*https:// docs.djangoproject.com/en/1.11/topics/templates/*).

Just changing the template doesn't get our tests to green; we need to actually pass the items to it from our home page view:

lists/views.py

```
def home_page(request):
    if request.method == 'POST':
        Item.objects.create(text=request.POST['item_text'])
        return redirect('/')

    items = Item.objects.all()
    return render(request, 'home.html', {'items': items})
```

That does get the unit tests to pass…moment of truth, will the functional test pass?

```
$ python functional_tests.py
[...]
AssertionError: 'To-Do' not found in 'OperationalError at /'
```

Oops, apparently not. Let's use another functional test debugging technique, and it's one of the most straightforward: manually visiting the site! Open up *http://localhost: 8000* in your web browser, and you'll see a Django debug page saying "no such table: lists_item", as in Figure 5-2.

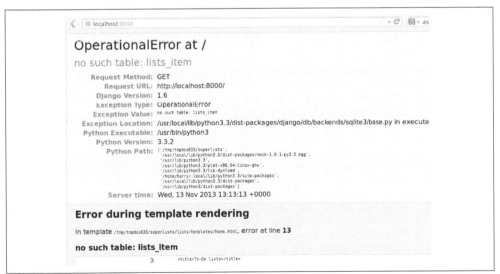

Figure 5-2. Another helpful debug message

Creating Our Production Database with migrate

Another helpful error message from Django, which is basically complaining that we haven't set up the database properly. How come everything worked fine in the unit tests, I hear you ask? Because Django creates a special *test database* for unit tests; it's one of the magical things that Django's TestCase does.

To set up our "real" database, we need to create it. SQLite databases are just a file on disk, and you'll see in *settings.py* that Django, by default, will just put it in a file called *db.sqlite3* in the base project directory:

superlists/settings.py

```
[...]
# Database
# https://docs.djangoproject.com/en/1.11/ref/settings/#databases

DATABASES = {
    'default': {
        'ENGINE': 'django.db.backends.sqlite3',
        'NAME': os.path.join(BASE_DIR, 'db.sqlite3'),
    }
}
```

We've told Django everything it needs to create the database, first via *models.py* and then when we created the migrations file. To actually apply it to creating a real database, we use another Django Swiss Army knife *manage.py* command, migrate:

```
$ python manage.py migrate
Operations to perform:
  Apply all migrations: admin, auth, contenttypes, lists, sessions
Running migrations:
  Applying contenttypes.0001_initial... OK
  Applying auth.0001_initial... OK
  Applying admin.0001_initial... OK
  Applying admin.0002_logentry_remove_auto_add... OK
  Applying contenttypes.0002_remove_content_type_name... OK
  Applying auth.0002_alter_permission_name_max_length... OK
  Applying auth.0003_alter_user_email_max_length... OK
  Applying auth.0004_alter_user_username_opts... OK
  Applying auth.0005_alter_user_last_login_null... OK
  Applying auth.0006_require_contenttypes_0002... OK
  Applying auth.0007_alter_validators_add_error_messages... OK
  Applying auth.0008_alter_user_username_max_length... OK
  Applying lists.0001_initial... OK
  Applying lists.0002_item_text... OK
  Applying sessions.0001_initial... OK
```

Now we can refresh the page on *localhost*, see that our error is gone, and try running the functional tests again:[4]

```
AssertionError: '2: Use peacock feathers to make a fly' not found in ['1: Buy
peacock feathers', '1: Use peacock feathers to make a fly']
```

So close! We just need to get our list numbering right. Another awesome Django template tag, `forloop.counter`, will help here:

lists/templates/home.html

```
{% for item in items %}
    <tr><td>{{ forloop.counter }}: {{ item.text }}</td></tr>
{% endfor %}
```

If you try it again, you should now see the FT get to the end:

```
    self.fail('Finish the test!')
AssertionError: Finish the test!
```

But, as it's running, you may notice something is amiss, like in Figure 5-3.

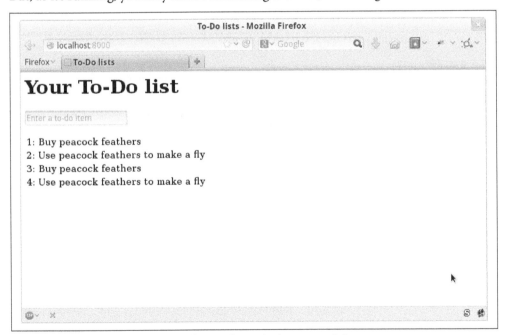

Figure 5-3. There are list items left over from the last run of the test

---

4 If you get a different error at this point, try restarting your dev server—it may have gotten confused by the changes to the database happening under its feet.

Oh dear. It looks like previous runs of the test are leaving stuff lying around in our database. In fact, if you run the tests again, you'll see it gets worse:

```
1: Buy peacock feathers
2: Use peacock feathers to make a fly
3: Buy peacock feathers
4: Use peacock feathers to make a fly
5: Buy peacock feathers
6: Use peacock feathers to make a fly
```

Grrr. We're so close! We're going to need some kind of automated way of tidying up after ourselves. For now, if you feel like it, you can do it manually, by deleting the database and re-creating it fresh with `migrate`:

```
$ rm db.sqlite3
$ python manage.py migrate --noinput
```

And then reassure yourself that the FT still passes.

Apart from that little bug in our functional testing, we've got some code that's more or less working. Let's do a commit.

Start by doing a **git status** and a **git diff**, and you should see changes to *home.html*, *tests.py*, and *views.py*. Let's add them:

```
$ git add lists
$ git commit -m "Redirect after POST, and show all items in template"
```

 You might find it useful to add markers for the end of each chapter, like **git tag end-of-chapter-05**.

Recap

Where are we?

- We've got a form set up to add new items to the list using POST.

- We've set up a simple model in the database to save list items.

- We've learned about creating database migrations, both for the test database (where they're applied automatically) and for the real database (where we have to apply them manually).

- We've used our first couple of Django template tags: {% csrf_token %} and the {% for ... endfor %} loop.

- And we've used at least three different FT debugging techniques: in-line print statements, time.sleeps, and improving the error messages.

But we've got a couple of items on our own to-do list, namely getting the FT to clean up after itself, and perhaps more critically, adding support for more than one list.

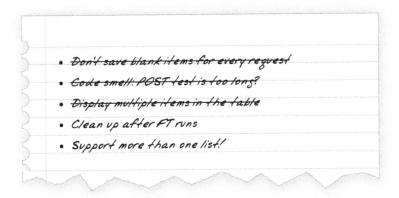

- ~~Don't save blank items for every request~~
- ~~Code smell: POST test is too long?~~
- ~~Display multiple items in the table~~
- Clean up after FT runs
- Support more than one list!

I mean, we *could* ship the site as it is, but people might find it strange that the entire human population has to share a single to-do list. I suppose it might get people to stop and think about how connected we all are to one another, how we all share a common destiny here on Spaceship Earth, and how we must all work together to solve the global problems that we face.

But in practical terms, the site wouldn't be very useful.

Ah well.

Useful TDD Concepts

Regression

When new code breaks some aspect of the application which used to work.

Unexpected failure

When a test fails in a way we weren't expecting. This either means that we've made a mistake in our tests, or that the tests have helped us find a regression, and we need to fix something in our code.

Red/Green/Refactor

Another way of describing the TDD process. Write a test and see it fail (Red), write some code to get it to pass (Green), then Refactor to improve the implementation.

Triangulation

Adding a test case with a new specific example for some existing code, to justify generalising the implementation (which may be a "cheat" until that point).

Three strikes and refactor

A rule of thumb for when to remove duplication from code. When two pieces of code look very similar, it often pays to wait until you see a third use case, so that you're more sure about what part of the code really is the common, re-usable part to refactor out.

The scratchpad to-do list

A place to write down things that occur to us as we're coding, so that we can finish up what we're doing and come back to them later.

Improving Functional Tests: Ensuring Isolation and Removing Voodoo Sleeps

Before we dive in and fix our real problem, let's take care of a couple of housekeeping items. At the end of the last chapter, we made a note that different test runs were interfering with each other, so we'll fix that. I'm also not happy with all these `time.sleep`s peppered through the code; they seem a bit unscientific, so we'll replace them with something more reliable.

Both of these changes will be moving towards testing "best practices", making our tests more deterministic and more reliable.

Ensuring Test Isolation in Functional Tests

We ended the last chapter with a classic testing problem: how to ensure *isolation* between tests. Each run of our functional tests was leaving list items lying around in the database, and that would interfere with the test results when you next ran the tests.

When we run *unit* tests, the Django test runner automatically creates a brand new test database (separate from the real one), which it can safely reset before each individual test is run, and then throw away at the end. But our functional tests currently run against the "real" database, *db.sqlite3*.

One way to tackle this would be to "roll our own" solution, and add some code to *functional_tests.py* which would do the cleaning up. The setUp and tearDown methods are perfect for this sort of thing.

Since Django 1.4 though, there's a new class called LiveServerTestCase which can do this work for you. It will automatically create a test database (just like in a unit test run), and start up a development server for the functional tests to run against. Although as a tool it has some limitations which we'll need to work around later, it's dead useful at this stage, so let's check it out.

LiveServerTestCase expects to be run by the Django test runner using *manage.py*. As of Django 1.6, the test runner will find any files whose name begins with *test*. To keep things neat and tidy, let's make a folder for our functional tests, so that it looks a bit like an app. All Django needs is for it to be a valid Python package directory (i.e., one with a ___*init*___.*py* in it):

```
$ mkdir functional_tests
$ touch functional_tests/__init__.py
```

Then we *move* our functional tests, from being a standalone file called *functional_tests.py*, to being the *tests.py* of the functional_tests app. We use **git mv** so that Git notices that we've moved the file:

```
$ git mv functional_tests.py functional_tests/tests.py
$ git status # shows the rename to functional_tests/tests.py and __init__.py
```

At this point your directory tree should look like this:

```
.
├── db.sqlite3
├── functional_tests
│   ├── __init__.py
│   └── tests.py
├── lists
│   ├── admin.py
│   ├── apps.py
│   ├── __init__.py
│   ├── migrations
│   │   ├── 0001_initial.py
│   │   ├── 0002_item_text.py
│   │   ├── __init__.py
│   │   └── __pycache__
│   ├── models.py
│   ├── __pycache__
│   ├── templates
│   │   └── home.html
│   ├── tests.py
│   └── views.py
├── manage.py
├── superlists
│   ├── __init__.py
│   ├── __pycache__
│   ├── settings.py
│   ├── urls.py
│   └── wsgi.py
└── virtualenv
    ├── [...]
```

functional_tests.py is gone, and has turned into *functional_tests/tests.py*. Now, whenever we want to run our functional tests, instead of running python func
tional_tests.py, we will use python manage.py test functional_tests.

 You could mix your functional tests into the tests for the lists app.
I tend to prefer to keep them separate, because functional tests usually have cross-cutting concerns that run across different apps. FTs are meant to see things from the point of view of your users, and your users don't care about how you've split work between different apps!

Now let's edit *functional_tests/tests.py* and change our NewVisitorTest class to make it use LiveServerTestCase:

```
from django.test import LiveServerTestCase
from selenium import webdriver
from selenium.webdriver.common.keys import Keys
import time


class NewVisitorTest(LiveServerTestCase):

    def setUp(self):
        [...]
```

Next, instead of hardcoding the visit to localhost port 8000, `LiveServerTestCase` gives us an attribute called `live_server_url`:

```
    def test_can_start_a_list_and_retrieve_it_later(self):
        # Edith has heard about a cool new online to-do app. She goes
        # to check out its homepage
        self.browser.get(self.live_server_url)
```

We can also remove the `if __name__ == '__main__'` from the end if we want, since we'll be using the Django test runner to launch the FT.

Now we are able to run our functional tests using the Django test runner, by telling it to run just the tests for our new `functional_tests` app:

```
$ python manage.py test functional_tests
Creating test database for alias 'default'...
F
=======================================================================
FAIL: test_can_start_a_list_and_retrieve_it_later
(functional_tests.tests.NewVisitorTest)
-----------------------------------------------------------------
Traceback (most recent call last):
  File "...python-tdd-book/functional_tests/tests.py", line 65, in
test_can_start_a_list_and_retrieve_it_later
    self.fail('Finish the test!')
AssertionError: Finish the test!

-----------------------------------------------------------------
Ran 1 test in 6.578s

FAILED (failures=1)
System check identified no issues (0 silenced).
Destroying test database for alias 'default'...
```

The FT gets through to the `self.fail`, just like it did before the refactor. You'll also notice that if you run the tests a second time, there aren't any old list items lying around from the previous test—it has cleaned up after itself. Success! We should commit it as an atomic change:

```
$ git status # functional_tests.py renamed + modified, new __init__.py
$ git add functional_tests
$ git diff --staged -M
$ git commit # msg eg "make functional_tests an app, use LiveServerTestCase"
```

The -M flag on the `git diff` is a useful one. It means "detect moves", so it will notice that *functional_tests.py* and *functional_tests/tests.py* are the same file, and show you a more sensible diff (try it without the flag!).

Running Just the Unit Tests

Now if we run `manage.py test`, Django will run both the functional and the unit tests:

```
$ python manage.py test
Creating test database for alias 'default'...
......F
========================================================================
FAIL: test_can_start_a_list_and_retrieve_it_later
[...]
AssertionError: Finish the test!


------------------------------------------------------------------------
Ran 7 tests in 6.732s

FAILED (failures=1)
```

In order to run just the unit tests, we can specify that we want to only run the tests for the `lists` app:

```
$ python manage.py test lists
Creating test database for alias 'default'...
......
------------------------------------------------------------------------
Ran 6 tests in 0.009s

OK
System check identified no issues (0 silenced).
Destroying test database for alias 'default'...
```

Aside: Upgrading Selenium and Geckodriver

As I was running through this chapter again today, I found the FTs hung when I tried to run them.

It turns out that Firefox had auto-updated itself overnight, and my versions of Selenium and Geckodriver needed upgrading too. A quick visit to the geckodriver releases page (*https://github.com/mozilla/geckodriver/releases*) confirmed there was a new version out. So a few downloads and upgrades were in order:

- A quick `pip install --upgrade selenium` first.
- Then a quick download of the new geckodriver.
- I saved a backup copy of the old one somewhere, and put the new one in its place somewhere on the PATH.
- And a quick check with `geckodriver --version` confirms the new one was ready to go.

The FTs were then back to running the way I expected them to.

There was no particular reason that it happened at this point in the book; indeed, it's quite unlikely that it'll happen right now for you, but it may happen at some point, and this seemed as good a place as any to talk about it, since we're doing some housekeeping.

It's one of the things you have to put up with when using Selenium. Although it is possible to pin your browser and Selenium versions (on a CI server, for example), browser versions don't stand still out in the real world, and you need to keep up with what your users have.

If something strange is going on with your FTs, it's always worth trying to upgrade Selenium.

Back to our regular programming now.

On Implicit and Explicit Waits, and Voodoo time.sleeps

Let's talk about the `time.sleep` in our FT:

functional_tests/tests.py

```
# When she hits enter, the page updates, and now the page lists
# "1: Buy peacock feathers" as an item in a to-do list table
inputbox.send_keys(Keys.ENTER)
time.sleep(1)

self.check_for_row_in_list_table('1: Buy peacock feathers')
```

This is what's called an "explicit wait". That's by contrast with "implicit waits": in certain cases, Selenium tries to wait "automatically" for you when it thinks the page is loading. It even provides a method called `implicitly_wait` that lets you control how long it will wait if you ask it for an element that doesn't seem to be on the page yet.

In fact, in the first edition, I was able to rely entirely on implicit waits. The problem is that implicit waits are always a little flakey, and with the release of Selenium 3, implicit waits became even more unreliable. At the same time, the general opinion from the Selenium team was that implicit waits were just a bad idea, and to be avoided.

So this edition has explicit waits from the very beginning. But the problem is that those `time.sleeps` have their own issues. Currently we're waiting for one second, but who's to say that's the right amount of time? For most tests we run against our own machine, one second is way too long, and it's going to really slow down our FT runs. 0.1s would be fine. But the problem is that if you set it that low, every so often you're going to get a spurious failure because, for whatever reason, the laptop was being a bit slow just then. And even at 1s you can never be quite sure you're not going to get random failures that don't indicate a real problem, and false positives in tests are a real annoyance (there's lots more on this in an article by Martin Fowler (*https://martinfowler.com/articles/nonDeterminism.html*)).

Unexpected `NoSuchElementException` and `StaleElementExcep`
`tion` errors are the usual symptoms of forgetting an explicit wait.
Try removing the `time.sleep` and see if you get one.

So let's replace our sleeps with a tool that will wait for just as long as is needed, up to a nice long timeout to catch any glitches. We'll rename `check_for_row_in_list_table` to `wait_for_row_in_list_table`, and add some polling/retry logic to it:

functional_tests/tests.py (ch06l004)

```python
from selenium.common.exceptions import WebDriverException

MAX_WAIT = 10   ❶
[...]

    def wait_for_row_in_list_table(self, row_text):
        start_time = time.time()
        while True:   ❷
            try:
                table = self.browser.find_element_by_id('id_list_table')   ❸
                rows = table.find_elements_by_tag_name('tr')
                self.assertIn(row_text, [row.text for row in rows])
                return   ❹
            except (AssertionError, WebDriverException) as e:   ❺
                if time.time() - start_time > MAX_WAIT:   ❻
                    raise e   ❻
                time.sleep(0.5)   ❺
```

❶ We'll use a constant called `MAX_WAIT` to set the maximum amount of time we're prepared to wait. 10 seconds should be more than enough to catch any glitches or random slowness.

❷ Here's the loop, which will keep going forever, unless we get to one of two possible exit routes.

❸ Here are our three lines of assertions from the old version of the method.

❹ If we get through them and our assertion passes, we return from the function and escape the loop.

❺ But if we catch an exception, we wait a short amount of time and loop around to retry. There are two types of exceptions we want to catch: `WebDriverException` for when the page hasn't loaded and Selenium can't find the table element on the page, and `AssertionError` for when the table is there, but it's perhaps a table from before the page reloads, so it doesn't have our row in yet.

---

❻ Here's our second escape route. If we get to this point, that means our code kept raising exceptions every time we tried it until we exceeded our timeout. So this time, we re-raise the exception and let it bubble up to our test, and most likely end up in our traceback, telling us why the test failed.

Are you thinking this code is a little ugly, and makes it a bit harder to see exactly what we're doing? I agree. Later on, we'll refactor out a general `wait_for` helper, to separate the timing and re-raising logic from the test assertions. But we'll wait until we need it in multiple places.

 If you've used Selenium before, you may know that it has a few helper functions to do waits (*http://www.seleniumhq.org/docs/04_webdriver_advanced.jsp*). I'm not a big fan of them. Over the course of the book we'll build a couple of wait helper tools which I think will make for nice, readable code, but of course you should check out the homegrown Selenium waits in your own time, and see what you think of them.

Now we can rename our method calls, and remove the voodoo `time.sleep`s:

functional_tests/tests.py (ch06l005)

```
[...]
# When she hits enter, the page updates, and now the page lists
# "1: Buy peacock feathers" as an item in a to-do list table
inputbox.send_keys(Keys.ENTER)
self.wait_for_row_in_list_table('1: Buy peacock feathers')

# There is still a text box inviting her to add another item. She
# enters "Use peacock feathers to make a fly" (Edith is very
# methodical)
inputbox = self.browser.find_element_by_id('id_new_item')
inputbox.send_keys('Use peacock feathers to make a fly')
inputbox.send_keys(Keys.ENTER)

# The page updates again, and now shows both items on her list
self.wait_for_row_in_list_table('2: Use peacock feathers to make a fly')
self.wait_for_row_in_list_table('1: Buy peacock feathers')
[...]
```

And rerun the tests:

```
$ python manage.py test
Creating test database for alias 'default'...
......F
======================================================================
FAIL: test_can_start_a_list_and_retrieve_it_later
(functional_tests.tests.NewVisitorTest)
----------------------------------------------------------------------
Traceback (most recent call last):
  File "...python-tdd-book/functional_tests/tests.py", line 73, in
test_can_start_a_list_and_retrieve_it_later
    self.fail('Finish the test!')
AssertionError: Finish the test!


----------------------------------------------------------------------
Ran 7 tests in 4.552s

FAILED (failures=1)
System check identified no issues (0 silenced).
Destroying test database for alias 'default'...
```

We get to the same place, and notice we've shaved a couple of seconds off the execution time too. That might not seem like a lot right now, but it all adds up.

Just to check we've done the right thing, let's deliberately break the test in a couple of ways and see some errors. First let's check that if we look for some row text that will never appear, we get the right error:

functional_tests/tests.py (ch06l006)

```
        rows = table.find_elements_by_tag_name('tr')
        self.assertIn('foo', [row.text for row in rows])
        return
```

We see we still get a nice self-explanatory test failure message:

```
        self.assertIn('foo', [row.text for row in rows])
    AssertionError: 'foo' not found in ['1: Buy peacock feathers']
```

Let's put that back the way it was and break something else:

functional_tests/tests.py (ch06l007)

```
    try:
        table = self.browser.find_element_by_id('id_nothing')
        rows = table.find_elements_by_tag_name('tr')
        self.assertIn(row_text, [row.text for row in rows])
        return
    [...]
```

Sure enough, we get the errors for when the page doesn't contain the element we're looking for too:

```
selenium.common.exceptions.NoSuchElementException: Message: Unable to locate
element: [id="id_nothing"]
```

Everything seems to be in order. Let's put our code back to way it should be, and do one final test run:

```
$ python manage.py test
[...]
AssertionError: Finish the test!
```

Great. With that little interlude over, let's crack on with getting our application actually working for multiple lists.

Testing "Best Practices" Applied in this Chapter

Ensuring test isolation and managing global state
> Different tests shouldn't affect one another. This means we need to reset any permanent state at the end of each test. Django's test runner helps us do this by creating a test database, which it wipes clean in between each test. (See also Chapter 23.)

Avoid "voodoo" sleeps
> Whenever we need to wait for something to load, it's always tempting to throw in a quick-and-dirty time.sleep. But the problem is that the length of time we wait is always a bit of a shot in the dark, either too short and vulnerable to spurious failures, or too long and it'll slow down our test runs. Prefer a retry loop that polls our app and moves on as soon as possible.

Don't rely on Selenium's implicit waits
> Selenium does theoretically do some "implicit" waits, but the implementation varies between browsers, and at the time of writing was highly unreliable in the Selenium 3 Firefox driver. "Explicit is better than implicit", as the Zen of Python says, so prefer explicit waits.

## CHAPTER 7

Working Incrementally

Now let's address our real problem, which is that our design only allows for one global list. In this chapter I'll demonstrate a critical TDD technique: how to adapt existing code using an incremental, step-by-step process which takes you from working state to working state. Testing Goat, not Refactoring Cat.

Small Design When Necessary

Let's have a think about how we want support for multiple lists to work. Currently the FT (which is the closest we have to a design document) says this:

functional_tests/tests.py
```
# Edith wonders whether the site will remember her list. Then she sees
# that the site has generated a unique URL for her -- there is some
# explanatory text to that effect.
self.fail('Finish the test!')

# She visits that URL - her to-do list is still there.

# Satisfied, she goes back to sleep
```

But really we want to expand on this, by saying that different users don't see each other's lists, and each get their own URL as a way of going back to their saved lists. What might a new design look like?

Not Big Design Up Front

TDD is closely associated with the agile movement in software development, which includes a reaction against *Big Design Up Front*, the traditional software engineering practice whereby, after a lengthy requirements gathering exercise, there is an equally lengthy design stage where the software is planned out on paper. The agile philosophy is that you learn more from solving problems in practice than in theory, especially when you confront your application with real users as soon as possible. Instead of a long up-front design phase, we try to put a *minimum viable application* out there early, and let the design evolve gradually based on feedback from real-world usage.

But that doesn't mean that thinking about design is outright banned! In the last big chapter we saw how just blundering ahead without thinking can *eventually* get us to the right answer, but often a little thinking about design can help us get there faster. So, let's think about our minimum viable lists app, and what kind of design we'll need to deliver it:

- We want each user to be able to store their own list—at least one, for now.
- A list is made up of several items, whose primary attribute is a bit of descriptive text.
- We need to save lists from one visit to the next. For now, we can give each user a unique URL for their list. Later on we may want some way of automatically recognising users and showing them their lists.

To deliver the "for now" items, it sounds like we're going to store lists and their items in a database. Each list will have a unique URL, and each list item will be a bit of descriptive text, associated with a particular list.

YAGNI!

Once you start thinking about design, it can be hard to stop. All sorts of other thoughts are occurring to us—we might want to give each list a name or title, we might want to recognise users using usernames and passwords, we might want to add a longer notes field as well as short descriptions to our list, we might want to store some kind of ordering, and so on. But we obey another tenet of the agile gospel: "YAGNI" (pronounced yag-knee), which stands for "You ain't gonna need it!" As software developers, we have fun creating things, and sometimes it's hard to resist the urge to build things just because an idea occurred to us and we *might* need it. The trouble is that more often than not, no matter how cool the idea was, you *won't* end up using it. Instead you have a load of unused code, adding to the complexity of your application. YAGNI is the mantra we use to resist our overenthusiastic creative urges.

REST (ish)

We have an idea of the data structure we want—the Model part of Model-View-Controller (MVC). What about the View and Controller parts? How should the user interact with Lists and their Items using a web browser?

Representational State Transfer (REST) is an approach to web design that's usually used to guide the design of web-based APIs. When designing a user-facing site, it's not possible to stick *strictly* to the REST rules, but they still provide some useful inspiration (skip ahead to Appendix F if you want to see a real REST API).

REST suggests that we have a URL structure that matches our data structure, in this case lists and list items. Each list can have its own URL:

```
/lists/<list identifier>/
```

That will fulfill the requirement we've specified in our FT. To view a list, we use a GET request (a normal browser visit to the page).

To create a brand new list, we'll have a special URL that accepts POST requests:

```
/lists/new
```

To add a new item to an existing list, we'll have a separate URL, to which we can send POST requests:

```
/lists/<list identifier>/add_item
```

(Again, we're not trying to perfectly follow the rules of REST, which would use a PUT request here—we're just using REST for inspiration. Apart from anything else, you can't use PUT in a standard HTML form.)

In summary, our scratchpad for this chapter looks something like this:

- Adjust model so that items are associated with different lists
- Add unique URLs for each list
- Add a URL for creating a new list via POST
- Add URLs for adding a new item to an existing list via POST

Implementing the New Design Incrementally Using TDD

How do we use TDD to implement the new design? Let's take another look at the flowchart for the TDD process in Figure 7-1.

At the top level, we're going to use a combination of adding new functionality (by adding a new FT and writing new application code), and refactoring our application —that is, rewriting some of the existing implementation so that it delivers the same functionality to the user but using aspects of our new design. We'll be able to use the existing functional test to verify we don't break what already works, and the new functional test to drive the new features.

At the unit test level, we'll be adding new tests or modifying existing ones to test for the changes we want, and we'll be able to similarly use the unit tests we don't touch to help make sure we don't break anything in the process.

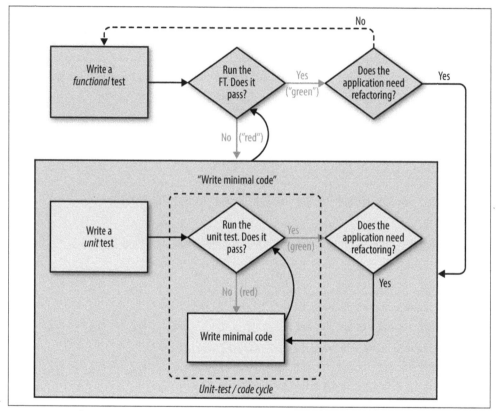

Figure 7-1. The TDD process with functional and unit tests

Ensuring We Have a Regression Test

Let's translate our scratchpad into a new functional test method, which introduces a second user and checks that their to-do list is separate from Edith's.

We'll start out very similarly to the first. Edith adds a first item to create a to-do list, but we introduce our first new assertion—Edith's list should live at its own, unique URL:

functional_tests/tests.py (ch07l005)

```python
def test_can_start_a_list_for_one_user(self):
    # Edith has heard about a cool new online to-do app. She goes
    [...]
    # The page updates again, and now shows both items on her list
    self.wait_for_row_in_list_table('2: Use peacock feathers to make a fly')
    self.wait_for_row_in_list_table('1: Buy peacock feathers')

    # Satisfied, she goes back to sleep


def test_multiple_users_can_start_lists_at_different_urls(self):
    # Edith starts a new to-do list
    self.browser.get(self.live_server_url)
    inputbox = self.browser.find_element_by_id('id_new_item')
    inputbox.send_keys('Buy peacock feathers')
    inputbox.send_keys(Keys.ENTER)
    self.wait_for_row_in_list_table('1: Buy peacock feathers')

    # She notices that her list has a unique URL
    edith_list_url = self.browser.current_url
    self.assertRegex(edith_list_url, '/lists/.+')    ❶
```

❶ assertRegex is a helper function from unittest that checks whether a string matches a regular expression. We use it to check that our new REST-ish design has been implemented. Find out more in the unittest documentation (*http://docs.python.org/3/library/unittest.html*).

Next we imagine a new user coming along. We want to check that they don't see any of Edith's items when they visit the home page, and that they get their own unique URL for their list:

```
[...]
        self.assertRegex(edith_list_url, '/lists/.+')  ❶

        # Now a new user, Francis, comes along to the site.

        ## We use a new browser session to make sure that no information
        ## of Edith's is coming through from cookies etc
        self.browser.quit()
        self.browser = webdriver.Firefox()

        # Francis visits the home page.  There is no sign of Edith's
        # list
        self.browser.get(self.live_server_url)
        page_text = self.browser.find_element_by_tag_name('body').text
        self.assertNotIn('Buy peacock feathers', page_text)
        self.assertNotIn('make a fly', page_text)

        # Francis starts a new list by entering a new item. He
        # is less interesting than Edith...
        inputbox = self.browser.find_element_by_id('id_new_item')
        inputbox.send_keys('Buy milk')
        inputbox.send_keys(Keys.ENTER)
        self.wait_for_row_in_list_table('1: Buy milk')

        # Francis gets his own unique URL
        francis_list_url = self.browser.current_url
        self.assertRegex(francis_list_url, '/lists/.+')
        self.assertNotEqual(francis_list_url, edith_list_url)

        # Again, there is no trace of Edith's list
        page_text = self.browser.find_element_by_tag_name('body').text
        self.assertNotIn('Buy peacock feathers', page_text)
        self.assertIn('Buy milk', page_text)

        # Satisfied, they both go back to sleep
```

❶ I'm using the convention of double-hashes (##) to indicate "meta-comments"—comments about *how* the test is working and why—so that we can distinguish them from regular comments in FTs which explain the User Story. They're a message to our future selves, which might otherwise be wondering why the heck we're quitting the browser and starting a new one...

Other than that, the new test is fairly self-explanatory. Let's see how we do when we run our FTs:

```
$ python manage.py test functional_tests
[...]
.F
======================================================================
FAIL: test_multiple_users_can_start_lists_at_different_urls
(functional_tests.tests.NewVisitorTest)
----------------------------------------------------------------------
Traceback (most recent call last):
  File "...python-tdd-book/functional_tests/tests.py", line 83, in
test_multiple_users_can_start_lists_at_different_urls
    self.assertRegex(edith_list_url, '/lists/.+')
AssertionError: Regex didn't match: '/lists/.+' not found in
'http://localhost:8081/'

----------------------------------------------------------------------
Ran 2 tests in 5.786s

FAILED (failures=1)
```

Good, our first test still passes, and the second one fails where we might expect. Let's do a commit, and then go and build some new models and views:

```
$ git commit -a
```

Iterating Towards the New Design

Being all excited about our new design, I had an overwhelming urge to dive in at this point and start changing *models.py*, which would have broken half the unit tests, and then pile in and change almost every single line of code, all in one go. That's a natural urge, and TDD, as a discipline, is a constant fight against it. Obey the Testing Goat, not Refactoring Cat! We don't need to implement our new, shiny design in a single big bang. Let's make small changes that take us from a working state to a working state, with our design guiding us gently at each stage.

There are four items on our to-do list. The FT, with its `Regexp didn't match`, is telling us that the second item—giving lists their own URL and identifier—is the one we should work on next. Let's have a go at fixing that, and only that.

The URL comes from the redirect after POST. In *lists/tests.py*, find `test_redi rects_after_POST`, and change the expected redirect location:

lists/tests.py

```
    self.assertEqual(response.status_code, 302)
    self.assertEqual(response['location'], '/lists/the-only-list-in-the-world/')
```

Does that seem slightly strange? Clearly, */lists/the-only-list-in-the-world* isn't a URL that's going to feature in the final design of our application. But we're committed to changing one thing at a time. While our application only supports one list, this is the only URL that makes sense. We're still moving forwards, in that we'll have a different URL for our list and our home page, which is a step along the way to a more REST-ful design. Later, when we have multiple lists, it will be easy to change.

 Another way of thinking about it is as a problem-solving technique: our new URL design is currently not implemented, so it works for 0 items. Ultimately, we want to solve for *n* items, but solving for 1 item is a good step along the way.

Running the unit tests gives us an expected fail:

```
$ python manage.py test lists
[...]
AssertionError: '/' != '/lists/the-only-list-in-the-world/'
```

We can go adjust our home_page view in *lists/views.py*:

lists/views.py

```python
def home_page(request):
    if request.method == 'POST':
        Item.objects.create(text=request.POST['item_text'])
        return redirect('/lists/the-only-list-in-the-world/')

    items = Item.objects.all()
    return render(request, 'home.html', {'items': items})
```

Of course, that will now totally break the functional tests, because there is no such URL on our site yet. Sure enough, if you run them, you'll find they fail just after trying to submit the first item, saying that they can't find the list table; it's because the URL */the-only-list-in-the-world/* doesn't exist yet!

```
  File "...python-tdd-book/functional_tests/tests.py", line 57, in
test_can_start_a_list_for_one_user
[...]
selenium.common.exceptions.NoSuchElementException: Message: Unable to locate
element: [id="id_list_table"]

[...]

  File "...python-tdd-book/functional_tests/tests.py", line 79, in
test_multiple_users_can_start_lists_at_different_urls
    self.wait_for_row_in_list_table('1: Buy peacock feathers')
[...]
selenium.common.exceptions.NoSuchElementException: Message: Unable to locate
element: [id="id_list_table"]
```

Not only is our new test failing, but the old one is too. That tells us we've introduced a *regression*. Let's try to get back to a working state as quickly as possible by building a URL for our one and only list.

Taking a First, Self-Contained Step: One New URL

Open up *lists/tests.py*, and add a new test class called `ListViewTest`. Then copy the method called `test_displays_all_list_items` across from `HomePageTest` into our new class, rename it, and adapt it slightly:

lists/tests.py (ch07l009)

```
class ListViewTest(TestCase):

    def test_displays_all_items(self):
        Item.objects.create(text='itemey 1')
        Item.objects.create(text='itemey 2')

        response = self.client.get('/lists/the-only-list-in-the-world/')

        self.assertContains(response, 'itemey 1')  ❶
        self.assertContains(response, 'itemey 2')  ❶
```

❶ Here's a new helper method: instead of using the slightly annoying `assertIn`/`response.content.decode()` dance, Django provides the `assertContains` method, which knows how to deal with responses and the bytes of their content.

Let's try running this test now:

```
    self.assertContains(response, 'itemey 1')
[...]
AssertionError: 404 != 200 : Couldn't retrieve content: Response code was 404
```

Here's a nice side effect of using `assertContains`: it tells us straight away that the test is failing because our new URL doesn't exist yet, and is returning a 404.

A New URL

Our singleton list URL doesn't exist yet. We fix that in *superlists/urls.py*.

 Watch out for trailing slashes in URLs, both here in the tests and in *urls.py*. They're a common source of bugs.

```
urlpatterns = [
    url(r'^$', views.home_page, name='home'),
    url(r'^lists/the-only-list-in-the-world/$', views.view_list, name='view_list'),
]
```

Running the tests again, we get:

```
AttributeError: module 'lists.views' has no attribute 'view_list'
```

A New View Function

Nicely self-explanatory. Let's create a dummy view function in *lists/views.py*:

```
def view_list(request):
    pass
```

Now we get:

```
ValueError: The view lists.views.view_list didn't return an HttpResponse
object. It returned None instead.

[...]
FAILED (errors=1)
```

Down to just one failure, and it's pointing us in the right direction. Let's copy the two last lines from the home_page view and see if they'll do the trick:

```
def view_list(request):
    items = Item.objects.all()
    return render(request, 'home.html', {'items': items})
```

Rerun the unit tests and they should pass:

```
Ran 7 tests in 0.016s
OK
```

Now let's try the FTs again and see what they tell us:

```
FAIL: test_can_start_a_list_for_one_user
[...]
  File "...python-tdd-book/functional_tests/tests.py", line 67, in
test_can_start_a_list_for_one_user
[...]
AssertionError: '2: Use peacock feathers to make a fly' not found in ['1: Buy
peacock feathers']

FAIL: test_multiple_users_can_start_lists_at_different_urls
[...]
AssertionError: 'Buy peacock feathers' unexpectedly found in 'Your To-Do
list\n1: Buy peacock feathers'
[...]
```

Both of them are getting a little further than they were before, but they're still failing. It would be nice to get back to a working state and get that first one passing again. What's it trying to tell us?

It's failing when we try to add the second item. We have to put our debugging hats on here. We know the home page is working, because the test has got all the way down to line 67 in the FT, so we've at least added a first item. And our unit tests are all passing, so we're pretty sure the URLs and views are doing what they should—the home page displays the right template, and can handle POST requests, and the *only-list-in-the-world* view knows how to display all items…but it doesn't know how to handle POST requests. Ah, that gives us a clue.

A second clue is the rule of thumb that, when all the unit tests are passing but the functional tests aren't, it's often pointing at a problem that's not covered by the unit tests, and in our case, that's often a template problem.

The answer is that our *home.html* input form currently doesn't specify an explicit URL to POST to:

lists/templates/home.html

```
<form method="POST">
```

By default the browser sends the POST data back to the same URL it's currently on. When we're on the home page that works fine, but when we're on our *only-list-in-the-world* page, it doesn't.

Now we could dive in and add POST request handling to our new view, but that would involve writing a bunch more tests and code, and at this point we'd like to get back to a working state as quickly as possible. Actually the quickest thing we can do to get things fixed is to just use the existing home page view, which already works, for all POST requests:

lists/templates/home.html

```
<form method="POST" action="/">
```

Try that, and we'll see our FTs get back to a happier place:

```
FAIL: test_multiple_users_can_start_lists_at_different_urls
[...]
AssertionError: 'Buy peacock feathers' unexpectedly found in 'Your To-Do
list\n1: Buy peacock feathers'

Ran 2 tests in 8.541s
FAILED (failures=1)
```

Our original test passes once again, so we know we're back to a working state. The new functionality may not be working yet, but at least the old stuff works as well as it used to.

Green? Refactor

Time for a little tidying up.

In the *Red/Green/Refactor* dance, we've arrived at green, so we should see what needs a refactor. We now have two views, one for the home page, and one for an individual list. Both are currently using the same template, and passing it all the list items currently in the database. If we look through our unit test methods, we can see some stuff we probably want to change:

```
$ grep -E "class|def" lists/tests.py
class HomePageTest(TestCase):
    def test_uses_home_template(self):
    def test_displays_all_list_items(self):
    def test_can_save_a_POST_request(self):
    def test_redirects_after_POST(self):
    def test_only_saves_items_when_necessary(self):
class ListViewTest(TestCase):
    def test_displays_all_items(self):
class ItemModelTest(TestCase):
    def test_saving_and_retrieving_items(self):
```

We can definitely delete the `test_displays_all_list_items` method from `HomePageTest`; it's no longer needed. If you run **manage.py test lists** now, it should say it ran 6 tests instead of 7:

```
Ran 6 tests in 0.016s
OK
```

Next, since we don't actually need the home page template to display all list items any more, it should just show a single input box inviting you to start a new list.

Another Small Step: A Separate Template for Viewing Lists

Since the home page and the list view are now quite distinct pages, they should be using different HTML templates; *home.html* can have the single input box, whereas a new template, *list.html*, can take care of showing the table of existing items.

Let's add a new test to check that it's using a different template:

lists/tests.py

```python
class ListViewTest(TestCase):

    def test_uses_list_template(self):
        response = self.client.get('/lists/the-only-list-in-the-world/')
        self.assertTemplateUsed(response, 'list.html')


    def test_displays_all_items(self):
        [...]
```

assertTemplateUsed is one of the more useful functions that the Django Test Client gives us. Let's see what it says:

```
AssertionError: False is not true : Template 'list.html' was not a template
used to render the response. Actual template(s) used: home.html
```

Great! Let's change the view:

lists/views.py

```python
def view_list(request):
    items = Item.objects.all()
    return render(request, 'list.html', {'items': items})
```

But, obviously, that template doesn't exist yet. If we run the unit tests, we get:

```
django.template.exceptions.TemplateDoesNotExist: list.html
```

Let's create a new file at *lists/templates/list.html*:

```
$ touch lists/templates/list.html
```

A blank template, which gives us this error—good to know the tests are there to make sure we fill it in:

```
AssertionError: False is not true : Couldn't find 'itemey 1' in response
```

The template for an individual list will reuse quite a lot of the stuff we currently have in *home.html*, so we can start by just copying that:

```
$ cp lists/templates/home.html lists/templates/list.html
```

That gets the tests back to passing (green). Now let's do a little more tidying up (refactoring). We said the home page doesn't need to list items, it only needs the new list input field, so we can remove some lines from *lists/templates/home.html*, and maybe slightly tweak the h1 to say "Start a new To-Do list":

lists/templates/home.html

```
<body>
  <h1>Start a new To-Do list</h1>
  <form method="POST">
    <input name="item_text" id="id_new_item" placeholder="Enter a to-do item" />
    {% csrf_token %}
  </form>
</body>
```

We rerun the unit tests to check that hasn't broken anything—good...

There's actually no need to pass all the items to the *home.html* template in our home_page view, so we can simplify that:

lists/views.py

```
def home_page(request):
    if request.method == 'POST':
        Item.objects.create(text=request.POST['item_text'])
        return redirect('/lists/the-only-list-in-the-world/')
    return render(request, 'home.html')
```

Rerun the unit tests once more; they still pass. Time to run the functional tests:

```
AssertionError: '1: Buy milk' not found in ['1: Buy peacock feathers', '2: Buy
milk']
```

Not bad! Our regression test (the first FT) is passing, and our new test is now getting slightly further forwards—it's telling us that Francis isn't getting his own list page (because he still sees some of Edith's list items).

It may feel like we haven't made much headway since, functionally, the site still behaves almost exactly like it did when we started the chapter, but this really is progress. We've started on the road to our new design, and we've implemented a number of stepping stones *without making anything worse than it was before*. Let's commit our progress so far:

```
$ git status # should show 4 changed files and 1 new file, list.html
$ git add lists/templates/list.html
$ git diff # should show we've simplified home.html,
         # moved one test to a new class in lists/tests.py added a new view
         # in views.py, and simplified home_page and made one addition to
         # urls.py
$ git commit -a # add a message summarising the above, maybe something like
             # "new URL, view and template to display lists"
```

A Third Small Step: A URL for Adding List Items

Where are we with our own to-do list?

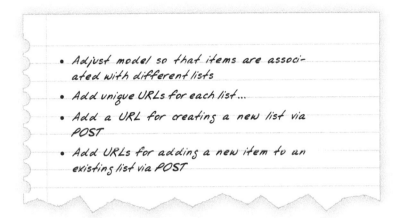

We've *sort of* made progress on the second item, even if there's still only one list in the world. The first item is a bit scary. Can we do something about items 3 or 4?

Let's have a new URL for adding new list items. If nothing else, it'll simplify the home page view.

A Test Class for New List Creation

Open up *lists/tests.py*, and *move* the test_can_save_a_POST_request and test_redi rects_after_POST methods into a new class, then change the URL they POST to:

lists/tests.py (ch07l021-1)

```
class NewListTest(TestCase):

    def test_can_save_a_POST_request(self):
        self.client.post('/lists/new', data={'item_text': 'A new list item'})
        self.assertEqual(Item.objects.count(), 1)
        new_item = Item.objects.first()
        self.assertEqual(new_item.text, 'A new list item')


    def test_redirects_after_POST(self):
        response = self.client.post('/lists/new', data={'item_text': 'A new list item'})
        self.assertEqual(response.status_code, 302)
        self.assertEqual(response['location'], '/lists/the-only-list-in-the-world/')
```

This is another place to pay attention to trailing slashes, incidentally. It's /new, with no trailing slash. The convention I'm using is that URLs without a trailing slash are "action" URLs which modify the database.

While we're at it, let's learn a new Django Test Client method, `assertRedirects`:

lists/tests.py (ch07l021-2)

```python
def test_redirects_after_POST(self):
    response = self.client.post('/lists/new', data={'item_text': 'A new list item'})
    self.assertRedirects(response, '/lists/the-only-list-in-the-world/')
```

There's not much to it, but it just nicely replaces two asserts with a single one...

Try running that:

```
    self.assertEqual(Item.objects.count(), 1)
AssertionError: 0 != 1
[...]
    self.assertRedirects(response, '/lists/the-only-list-in-the-world/')
[...]
AssertionError: 404 != 302 : Response didn't redirect as expected: Response
code was 404 (expected 302)
```

The first failure tells us we're not saving a new item to the database, and the second says that, instead of returning a 302 redirect, our view is returning a 404. That's because we haven't built a URL for */lists/new*, so the `client.post` is just getting a "not found" response.

Do you remember how we split this out into two tests earlier? If we only had one test that checked both the saving and the redirect, it would have failed on the 0 != 1 failure, which would have been much harder to debug. Ask me how I know this.

A URL and View for New List Creation

Let's build our new URL now:

superlists/urls.py

```python
urlpatterns = [
    url(r'^$', views.home_page, name='home'),
    url(r'^lists/new$', views.new_list, name='new_list'),
    url(r'^lists/the-only-list-in-the-world/$', views.view_list, name='view_list'),
]
```

Next we get a `no attribute 'new_list'`, so let's fix that, in *lists/views.py*:

```
def new_list(request):
    pass
```

Then we get "The view lists.views.new_list didn't return an HttpResponse object". (This is getting rather familiar!) We could return a raw `HttpResponse`, but since we know we'll need a redirect, let's borrow a line from `home_page`:

```
def new_list(request):
    return redirect('/lists/the-only-list-in-the-world/')
```

That gives:

```
    self.assertEqual(Item.objects.count(), 1)
AssertionError: 0 != 1
```

Seems reasonably straightforward. We borrow another line from `home_page`:

```
def new_list(request):
    Item.objects.create(text=request.POST['item_text'])
    return redirect('/lists/the-only-list-in-the-world/')
```

And everything now passes:

```
Ran 7 tests in 0.030s

OK
```

And the FTs show me that I'm back to the working state:

```
[...]
AssertionError: '1: Buy milk' not found in ['1: Buy peacock feathers', '2: Buy
milk']
Ran 2 tests in 8.972s
FAILED (failures=1)
```

Removing Now-Redundant Code and Tests

We're looking good. Since our new views are now doing most of the work that `home_page` used to do, we should be able to massively simplify it. Can we remove the whole `if request.method == 'POST'` section, for example?

```
def home_page(request):
    return render(request, 'home.html')
```

Yep!

```
OK
```

And while we're at it, we can remove the now-redundant test_only_saves_items_when_necessary test too!

Doesn't that feel good? The view functions are looking much simpler. We rerun the tests to make sure...

```
Ran 6 tests in 0.016s
OK
```

and the FTs?

A Regression! Pointing Our Forms at the New URL

Oops:

```
ERROR: test_can_start_a_list_for_one_user
[...]
  File "...python-tdd-book/functional_tests/tests.py", line 57, in
test_can_start_a_list_for_one_user
    self.wait_for_row_in_list_table('1: Buy peacock feathers')
  File "...python-tdd-book/functional_tests/tests.py", line 23, in
wait_for_row_in_list_table
    table = self.browser.find_element_by_id('id_list_table')
selenium.common.exceptions.NoSuchElementException: Message: Unable to locate
element: [id="id_list_table"]

ERROR: test_multiple_users_can_start_lists_at_different_urls
[...]
  File "...python-tdd-book/functional_tests/tests.py", line 79, in
test_multiple_users_can_start_lists_at_different_urls
    self.wait_for_row_in_list_table('1: Buy peacock feathers')
selenium.common.exceptions.NoSuchElementException: Message: Unable to locate
element: [id="id_list_table"]
[...]

Ran 2 tests in 11.592s
FAILED (errors=2)
```

It's because our forms are still pointing to the old URL. In *both home.html* and *lists.html*, let's change them to:

lists/templates/home.html, lists/templates/list.html

```
<form method="POST" action="/lists/new">
```

And that should get us back to working again:

```
AssertionError: '1: Buy milk' not found in ['1: Buy peacock feathers', '2: Buy
milk']
[...]
FAILED (failures=1)
```

That's another nicely self-contained commit, in that we've made a bunch of changes
to our URLs, our *views.py* is looking much neater and tidier, and we're sure the application is still working as well as it did before. We're getting good at this working-state-
to-working-state malarkey!

```
$ git status # 5 changed files
$ git diff # URLs for forms x2, moved code in views + tests, new URL
$ git commit -a
```

And we can cross out an item on the to-do list:

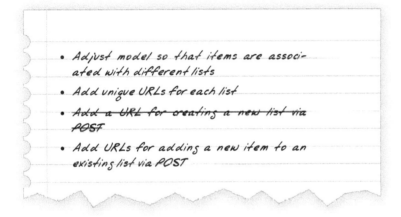

Biting the Bullet: Adjusting Our Models

Enough housekeeping with our URLs. It's time to bite the bullet and change our models. Let's adjust the model unit test. Just for a change, I'll present the changes in the
form of a diff:

```
@@ -1,5 +1,5 @@
 from django.test import TestCase
-from lists.models import Item
+from lists.models import Item, List


 class HomePageTest(TestCase):
@@ -44,22 +44,32 @@ class ListViewTest(TestCase):



-class ItemModelTest(TestCase):
+class ListAndItemModelsTest(TestCase):

     def test_saving_and_retrieving_items(self):
+        list_ = List()
+        list_.save()
+
         first_item = Item()
         first_item.text = 'The first (ever) list item'
+        first_item.list = list_
         first_item.save()

         second_item = Item()
         second_item.text = 'Item the second'
+        second_item.list = list_
         second_item.save()

+        saved_list = List.objects.first()
+        self.assertEqual(saved_list, list_)
+
         saved_items = Item.objects.all()
         self.assertEqual(saved_items.count(), 2)

         first_saved_item = saved_items[0]
         second_saved_item = saved_items[1]
         self.assertEqual(first_saved_item.text, 'The first (ever) list item')
+        self.assertEqual(first_saved_item.list, list_)
         self.assertEqual(second_saved_item.text, 'Item the second')
+        self.assertEqual(second_saved_item.list, list_)
```

We create a new List object, and then we assign each item to it by assigning it as its .list property. We check that the list is properly saved, and we check that the two items have also saved their relationship to the list. You'll also notice that we can compare list objects with each other directly (saved_list and list_)—behind the scenes, these will compare themselves by checking that their primary key (the .id attribute) is the same.

I'm using the variable name `list_` to avoid "shadowing" the Python built-in `list` function. It's ugly, but all the other options I tried were equally ugly or worse (`my_list`, `the_list`, `list1`, `lis tey`...).

Time for another unit-test/code cycle.

For the first couple of iterations, rather than explicitly showing you what code to enter in between every test run, I'm only going to show you the expected error messages from running the tests. I'll let you figure out what each minimal code change should be on your own.

 Need a hint? Go back and take a look at the steps we took to introduce the `Item` model in the chapter before last.

Your first error should be:

```
ImportError: cannot import name 'List'
```

Fix that, and then you should see:

```
AttributeError: 'List' object has no attribute 'save'
```

Next you should see:

```
django.db.utils.OperationalError: no such table: lists_list
```

So we run a `makemigrations`:

```
$ python manage.py makemigrations
Migrations for 'lists':
  lists/migrations/0003_list.py
    - Create model List
```

And then you should see:

```
    self.assertEqual(first_saved_item.list, list_)
AttributeError: 'Item' object has no attribute 'list'
```

A Foreign Key Relationship

How do we give our `Item` a list attribute? Let's just try naively making it like the `text` attribute (and here's your chance to see whether your solution so far looks like mine by the way):

```
from django.db import models

class List(models.Model):
    pass

class Item(models.Model):
    text = models.TextField(default='')
    list = models.TextField(default='')
```

As usual, the tests tell us we need a migration:

```
$ python manage.py test lists
[...]
django.db.utils.OperationalError: no such column: lists_item.list

$ python manage.py makemigrations
Migrations for 'lists':
  lists/migrations/0004_item_list.py
    - Add field list to item
```

Let's see what that gives us:

```
AssertionError: 'List object' != <List: List object>
```

We're not quite there. Look closely at each side of the !=. Django has only saved the string representation of the List object. To save the relationship to the object itself, we tell Django about the relationship between the two classes using a ForeignKey:

```
from django.db import models

class List(models.Model):
    pass


class Item(models.Model):
    text = models.TextField(default='')
    list = models.ForeignKey(List, default=None)
```

That'll need a migration too. Since the last one was a red herring, let's delete it and replace it with a new one:

```
$ rm lists/migrations/0004_item_list.py
$ python manage.py makemigrations
Migrations for 'lists':
  lists/migrations/0004_item_list.py
    - Add field list to item
```

Deleting migrations is dangerous. We do need to do it now and again, because we don't always get our models code right on the first go. But if you delete a migration that's already been applied to a database somewhere, Django will be confused about what state it's in, and how to apply future migrations. You should only do it when you're sure the migration hasn't been used. A good rule of thumb is that you should never delete or modify a migration that's already been committed to your VCS.

Adjusting the Rest of the World to Our New Models

Back in our tests, now what happens?

```
$ python manage.py test lists
[...]
ERROR: test_displays_all_items (lists.tests.ListViewTest)
django.db.utils.IntegrityError: NOT NULL constraint failed: lists_item.list_id
[...]
ERROR: test_redirects_after_POST (lists.tests.NewListTest)
django.db.utils.IntegrityError: NOT NULL constraint failed: lists_item.list_id
[...]
ERROR: test_can_save_a_POST_request (lists.tests.NewListTest)
django.db.utils.IntegrityError: NOT NULL constraint failed: lists_item.list_id

Ran 6 tests in 0.021s

FAILED (errors=3)
```

Oh dear!

There is some good news. Although it's hard to see, our model tests are passing. But three of our view tests are failing nastily.

The reason is because of the new relationship we've introduced between Items and Lists, which requires each item to have a parent list, which our old tests and code aren't prepared for.

Still, this is exactly why we have tests! Let's get them working again. The easiest is the ListViewTest; we just create a parent list for our two test items:

lists/tests.py (ch07l031)

```python
class ListViewTest(TestCase):

    def test_displays_all_items(self):
        list_ = List.objects.create()
        Item.objects.create(text='itemey 1', list=list_)
        Item.objects.create(text='itemey 2', list=list_)
```

That gets us down to two failing tests, both on tests that try to POST to our new_list view. Decoding the tracebacks using our usual technique, working back from error to line of test code to, buried in there somewhere, the line of our own code that caused the failure:

```
File "...python-tdd-book/lists/views.py", line 9, in new_list
Item.objects.create(text=request.POST['item_text'])
```

It's when we try to create an item without a parent list. So we make a similar change in the view:

lists/views.py

```
from lists.models import Item, List
[...]
def new_list(request):
    list_ = List.objects.create()
    Item.objects.create(text=request.POST['item_text'], list=list_)
    return redirect('/lists/the-only-list-in-the-world/')
```

And that gets our tests passing again:

```
Ran 6 tests in 0.030s

OK
```

Are you cringing internally at this point? *Arg! This feels so wrong; we create a new list for every single new item submission, and we're still just displaying all items as if they belong to the same list!* I know, I feel the same. The step-by-step approach, in which you go from working code to working code, is counterintuitive. I always feel like just diving in and trying to fix everything all in one go, instead of going from one weird half-finished state to another. But remember the Testing Goat! When you're up a mountain, you want to think very carefully about where you put each foot, and take one step at a time, checking at each stage that the place you've put it hasn't caused you to fall off a cliff.

So just to reassure ourselves that things have worked, we rerun the FT:

```
AssertionError: '1: Buy milk' not found in ['1: Buy peacock feathers', '2: Buy
milk']
[...]
```

Sure enough, it gets all the way through to where we were before. We haven't broken anything, and we've made a change to the database. That's something to be pleased with! Let's commit:

```
$ git status # 3 changed files, plus 2 migrations
$ git add lists
$ git diff --staged
$ git commit
```

And we can cross out another item on the to-do list:

- ~~Adjust model so that items are associated with different lists~~
- Add unique URLs for each list
- ~~Add a URL for creating a new list via POST~~
- Add URLs for adding a new item to an existing list via POST

Each List Should Have Its Own URL

What shall we use as the unique identifier for our lists? Probably the simplest thing, for now, is just to use the auto generated id field from the database. Let's change List ViewTest so that the two tests point at new URLs.

We'll also change the old test_displays_all_items test and call it test_displays_only_items_for_that_list instead, and make it check that only the items for a specific list are displayed:

```
class ListViewTest(TestCase):

    def test_uses_list_template(self):
        list_ = List.objects.create()
        response = self.client.get(f'/lists/{list_.id}/')
        self.assertTemplateUsed(response, 'list.html')


    def test_displays_only_items_for_that_list(self):
        correct_list = List.objects.create()
        Item.objects.create(text='itemey 1', list=correct_list)
        Item.objects.create(text='itemey 2', list=correct_list)
        other_list = List.objects.create()
        Item.objects.create(text='other list item 1', list=other_list)
        Item.objects.create(text='other list item 2', list=other_list)

        response = self.client.get(f'/lists/{correct_list.id}/')

        self.assertContains(response, 'itemey 1')
        self.assertContains(response, 'itemey 2')
        self.assertNotContains(response, 'other list item 1')
        self.assertNotContains(response, 'other list item 2')
```

A couple more of those lovely f-strings in this listing! If they're still a bit of a mystery, take a look at the docs (*https://docs.python.org/3/ reference/lexical_analysis.html#f-strings*) (although if your formal CS education is as bad as mine, you'll probably skip the formal grammar).

Running the unit tests gives an expected 404, and another related error:

```
FAIL: test_displays_only_items_for_that_list (lists.tests.ListViewTest)
AssertionError: 404 != 200 : Couldn't retrieve content: Response code was 404
(expected 200)
[...]
FAIL: test_uses_list_template (lists.tests.ListViewTest)
AssertionError: No templates used to render the response
```

Capturing Parameters from URLs

It's time to learn how we can pass parameters from URLs to views:

```
urlpatterns = [
    url(r'^$', views.home_page, name='home'),
    url(r'^lists/new$', views.new_list, name='new_list'),
    url(r'^lists/(.+)/$', views.view_list, name='view_list'),
]
```

We adjust the regular expression for our URL to include a *capture group*, (.+), which will match any characters, up to the following /. The captured text will get passed to the view as an argument.

In other words, if we go to the URL */lists/1/*, view_list will get a second argument after the normal request argument, namely the string "1". If we go to */lists/foo/*, we get view_list(request, "foo").

But our view doesn't expect an argument yet! Sure enough, this causes problems:

```
ERROR: test_displays_only_items_for_that_list (lists.tests.ListViewTest)
[...]
TypeError: view_list() takes 1 positional argument but 2 were given
[...]
ERROR: test_uses_list_template (lists.tests.ListViewTest)
[...]
TypeError: view_list() takes 1 positional argument but 2 were given
[...]
ERROR: test_redirects_after_POST (lists.tests.NewListTest)
[...]
TypeError: view_list() takes 1 positional argument but 2 were given
FAILED (errors=3)
```

We can fix that easily with a dummy parameter in *views.py*:

lists/views.py

```python
def view_list(request, list_id):
    [...]
```

Now we're down to our expected failure:

```
FAIL: test_displays_only_items_for_that_list (lists.tests.ListViewTest)
[...]
AssertionError: 1 != 0 : Response should not contain 'other list item 1'
```

Let's make our view discriminate over which items it sends to the template:

lists/views.py

```python
def view_list(request, list_id):
    list_ = List.objects.get(id=list_id)
    items = Item.objects.filter(list=list_)
    return render(request, 'list.html', {'items': items})
```

Adjusting new_list to the New World

Oops, now we get errors in another test:

```
ERROR: test_redirects_after_POST (lists.tests.NewListTest)
ValueError: invalid literal for int() with base 10:
'the-only-list-in-the-world'
```

Let's take a look at this test then, since it's moaning:

lists/tests.py

```python
class NewListTest(TestCase):
    [...]

    def test_redirects_after_POST(self):
        response = self.client.post('/lists/new', data={'item_text': 'A new list item'})
        self.assertRedirects(response, '/lists/the-only-list-in-the-world/')
```

It looks like it hasn't been adjusted to the new world of Lists and Items. The test should be saying that this view redirects to the URL of the specific new list it just created:

lists/tests.py (ch07l036-1)

```python
    def test_redirects_after_POST(self):
        response = self.client.post('/lists/new', data={'item_text': 'A new list item'})
        new_list = List.objects.first()
        self.assertRedirects(response, f'/lists/{new_list.id}/')
```

That still gives us the *invalid literal* error. We take a look at the view itself, and change it so it redirects to a valid place:

lists/views.py (ch07l036-2)

```python
def new_list(request):
    list_ = List.objects.create()
    Item.objects.create(text=request.POST['item_text'], list=list_)
    return redirect(f'/lists/{list_.id}/')
```

That gets us back to passing unit tests:

```
$ python3 manage.py test lists
[...]
......
----------------------------------------------------------------
Ran 6 tests in 0.033s

OK
```

What about the functional tests? We must be almost there?

The Functional Tests Detect Another Regression

Well, almost:

```
F.
========================================================================
FAIL: test_can_start_a_list_for_one_user
(functional_tests.tests.NewVisitorTest)
------------------------------------------------------------------------
Traceback (most recent call last):
  File "...python-tdd-book/functional_tests/tests.py", line 67, in
test_can_start_a_list_for_one_user
    self.wait_for_row_in_list_table('2: Use peacock feathers to make a fly')
[...]
AssertionError: '2: Use peacock feathers to make a fly' not found in ['1: Use
peacock feathers to make a fly']

------------------------------------------------------------------------
Ran 2 tests in 8.617s

FAILED (failures=1)
```

Our new test is actually passing, and different users can get different lists, but the old test is warning us of a regression. It looks like you can't add a second item to a list any more. It's because of our quick-and-dirty hack where we create a new list for every single POST submission. This is exactly what we have functional tests for!

And it correlates nicely with the last item on our to-do list:

- ~~Adjust model so that items are associated with different lists~~
- ~~Add unique URLs for each list~~
- ~~Add a URL for creating a new list via POST~~
- Add URLs for adding a new item to an existing list via POST

One More View to Handle Adding Items to an Existing List

We need a URL and view to handle adding a new item to an existing list (*/lists/<list_id>/add_item*). We're getting pretty good at these now, so let's knock one together quickly:

lists/tests.py

```python
class NewItemTest(TestCase):

    def test_can_save_a_POST_request_to_an_existing_list(self):
        other_list = List.objects.create()
        correct_list = List.objects.create()

        self.client.post(
            f'/lists/{correct_list.id}/add_item',
            data={'item_text': 'A new item for an existing list'}
        )

        self.assertEqual(Item.objects.count(), 1)
        new_item = Item.objects.first()
        self.assertEqual(new_item.text, 'A new item for an existing list')
        self.assertEqual(new_item.list, correct_list)


    def test_redirects_to_list_view(self):
        other_list = List.objects.create()
        correct_list = List.objects.create()

        response = self.client.post(
            f'/lists/{correct_list.id}/add_item',
            data={'item_text': 'A new item for an existing list'}
        )

        self.assertRedirects(response, f'/lists/{correct_list.id}/')
```

 Are you wondering about `other_list`? A bit like in the tests for viewing a specific list, it's important that we add items to a specific list. Adding this second object to the database prevents me from using a hack like `List.objects.first()` in the implementation. That would be a stupid thing to do, and you can go too far down the road of testing for all the stupid things you must not do (there are an infinite number of those, after all). It's a judgement call, but this one feels worth it. There's some more discussion of this in "An Aside on When to Test for Developer Stupidity" on page 268.

We get:

```
AssertionError: 0 != 1
[...]
AssertionError: 301 != 302 : Response didn't redirect as expected: Response
code was 301 (expected 302)
```

Beware of Greedy Regular Expressions!

That's a little strange. We haven't actually specified a URL for *lists/1/add_item* yet, so our expected failure is 404 != 302. Why are we getting a 301?

This was a bit of a puzzler! It's because we've used a very "greedy" regular expression in our URL:

superlists/urls.py

```
url(r'^lists/(.+)/$', views.view_list, name='view_list'),
```

Django has some built-in code to issue a permanent redirect (301) whenever someone asks for a URL which is *almost* right, except for a missing slash. In this case, *lists/1/add_item/* would be a match for `lists/(.+)/`, with the `(.+)` capturing `1/add_item`. So Django "helpfully" guesses that we actually wanted the URL with a trailing slash.

We can fix that by making our URL pattern explicitly capture only numerical digits, by using the regular expression \d:

superlists/urls.py

```
url(r'^lists/(\d+)/$', views.view_list, name='view_list'),
```

That gives us the failure we expected:

```
AssertionError: 0 != 1
[...]
AssertionError: 404 != 302 : Response didn't redirect as expected: Response
code was 404 (expected 302)
```

The Last New URL

Now we've got our expected 404, let's add a new URL for adding new items to existing lists:

superlists/urls.py

```
urlpatterns = [
    url(r'^$', views.home_page, name='home'),
    url(r'^lists/new$', views.new_list, name='new_list'),
    url(r'^lists/(\d+)/$', views.view_list, name='view_list'),
    url(r'^lists/(\d+)/add_item$', views.add_item, name='add_item'),
]
```

Three very similar-looking URLs there. Let's make a note on our to-do list; they look like good candidates for a refactoring:

- ~~Adjust model so that items are associated with different lists~~
- ~~Add unique URLs for each list~~
- ~~Add a URL for creating a new list via POST~~
- Add URLs for adding a new item to an existing list via POST
- Refactor away some duplication in urls.py

Back to the tests, we get the usual missing module view objects:

```
AttributeError: module 'lists.views' has no attribute 'add_item'
```

The Last New View

Let's try:

lists/views.py

```python
def add_item(request):
    pass
```

Aha:

```
TypeError: add_item() takes 1 positional argument but 2 were given
```

lists/views.py

```python
def add_item(request, list_id):
    pass
```

And then:

```
ValueError: The view lists.views.add_item didn't return an HttpResponse object.
It returned None instead.
```

We can copy the redirect from `new_list` and the `List.objects.get` from `view_list`:

lists/views.py

```python
def add_item(request, list_id):
    list_ = List.objects.get(id=list_id)
    return redirect(f'/lists/{list_.id}/')
```

That takes us to:

```
    self.assertEqual(Item.objects.count(), 1)
AssertionError: 0 != 1
```

Finally we make it save our new list item:

lists/views.py

```python
def add_item(request, list_id):
    list_ = List.objects.get(id=list_id)
    Item.objects.create(text=request.POST['item_text'], list=list_)
    return redirect(f'/lists/{list_.id}/')
```

And we're back to passing tests.

```
Ran 8 tests in 0.050s

OK
```

Testing the Response Context Objects Directly

We've got our new view and URL for adding items to existing lists; now we just need to actually use it in our *list.html* template. So we open it up to adjust the form tag…

lists/templates/list.html

```html
<form method="POST" action="but what should we put here?">
```

…oh. To get the URL for adding to the current list, the template needs to know what list it's rendering, as well as what the items are. We want to be able to do something like this:

lists/templates/list.html

```html
<form method="POST" action="/lists/{{ list.id }}/add_item">
```

For that to work, the view will have to pass the list to the template. Let's create a new unit test in `ListViewTest`:

```
def test_passes_correct_list_to_template(self):
    other_list = List.objects.create()
    correct_list = List.objects.create()
    response = self.client.get(f'/lists/{correct_list.id}/')
    self.assertEqual(response.context['list'], correct_list)  ❶
```

❶ `response.context` represents the context we're going to pass into the render function—the Django Test Client puts it on the `response` object for us, to help with testing.

That gives us:

```
KeyError: 'list'
```

because we're not passing `list` into the template. It actually gives us an opportunity to simplify a little:

lists/views.py

```
def view_list(request, list_id):
    list_ = List.objects.get(id=list_id)
    return render(request, 'list.html', {'list': list_})
```

That, of course, will break one of our old tests, because the template needed `items`:

```
FAIL: test_displays_only_items_for_that_list (lists.tests.ListViewTest)
[...]
AssertionError: False is not true : Couldn't find 'itemey 1' in response
```

But we can fix it in *list.html*, as well as adjusting the form's POST action:

lists/templates/list.html (ch07l043)

```
<form method="POST" action="/lists/{{ list.id }}/add_item">  ❶

    [...]

    {% for item in list.item_set.all %}  ❷
      <tr><td>{{ forloop.counter }}: {{ item.text }}</td></tr>
    {% endfor %}
```

❶ There's our new form action.

❷ `.item_set` is called a reverse lookup (*https://docs.djangoproject.com/en/1.11/topics/db/queries/#following-relationships-backward*). It's one of Django's incredibly useful bits of ORM that lets you look up an object's related items from a different table…

So that gets the unit tests to pass:

```
Ran 9 tests in 0.040s

OK
```

How about the FTs?

```
$ python manage.py test functional_tests
[...]
..
---------------------------------------------------------------
Ran 2 tests in 9.771s

OK
```

HOORAY! Oh, and a quick check on our to-do list:

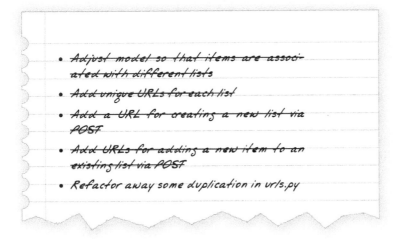

Irritatingly, the Testing Goat is a stickler for tying up loose ends too, so we've got to do this one final thing.

Before we start, we'll do a commit—always make sure you've got a commit of a working state before embarking on a refactor:

```
$ git diff
$ git commit -am "new URL + view for adding to existing lists. FT passes :-)"
```

A Final Refactor Using URL includes

superlists/urls.py is really meant for URLs that apply to your entire site. For URLs that only apply to the `lists` app, Django encourages us to use a separate *lists/urls.py*, to make the app more self-contained. The simplest way to make one is to use a copy of the existing *urls.py*:

```
$ cp superlists/urls.py lists/
```

Then we replace three lines in *superlists/urls.py* with an include:

superlists/urls.py

```
from django.conf.urls import include, url
from lists import views as list_views     ❶
from lists import urls as list_urls       ❶

urlpatterns = [
    url(r'^$', list_views.home_page, name='home'),
    url(r'^lists/', include(list_urls)),   ❷
]
```

❶ While we're at it, we use the import x as y syntax to alias views and urls. This is good practice in your top-level *urls.py*, because it will let us import views and urls from multiple apps if we want—and indeed we will need to later on in the book.

❷ Here's the include. Notice that it can take a part of a URL regex as a prefix, which will be applied to all the included URLs (this is the bit where we reduce duplication, as well as giving our code a better structure).

Back in *lists/urls.py* we can trim down to only include the latter part of our three URLs, and none of the other stuff from the parent *urls.py*:

lists/urls.py (ch07l046)

```
from django.conf.urls import url
from lists import views

urlpatterns = [
    url(r'^new$', views.new_list, name='new_list'),
    url(r'^(\d+)/$', views.view_list, name='view_list'),
    url(r'^(\d+)/add_item$', views.add_item, name='add_item'),
]
```

Rerun the unit tests to check that everything worked.

When I did it, I couldn't quite believe I did it correctly on the first go. It always pays to be skeptical of your own abilities, so I deliberately changed one of the URLs slightly, just to check if it broke a test. It did. We're covered.

Feel free to try it yourself! Remember to change it back, check that the tests all pass again, and then do a final commit:

```
$ git status
$ git add lists/urls.py
$ git add superlists/urls.py
$ git diff --staged
$ git commit
```

Phew. A marathon chapter. But we covered a number of important topics, starting with test isolation, and then some thinking about design. We covered some rules of thumb like "YAGNI" and "three strikes then refactor". But, most importantly, we saw how to adapt an existing site step by step, going from working state to working state, in order to iterate towards a new design.

I'd say we're pretty close to being able to ship this site, as the very first beta of the superlists website that's going to take over the world. Maybe it needs a little prettification first...let's look at what we need to do to deploy it in the next couple of chapters.

Some More TDD Philosophy

Working State to Working State (aka The Testing Goat vs. Refactoring Cat)
> Our natural urge is often to dive in and fix everything at once...but if we're not careful, we'll end up like Refactoring Cat, in a situation with loads of changes to our code and nothing working. The Testing Goat encourages us to take one step at a time, and go from working state to working state.

Split work out into small, achievable tasks
> Sometimes this means starting with "boring" work rather than diving straight in with the fun stuff, but you'll have to trust that YOLO-you in the parallel universe is probably having a bad time, having broken everything, and struggling to get the app working again.

YAGNI
> You ain't gonna need it! Avoid the temptation to write code that you think *might* be useful, just because it suggests itself at the time. Chances are, you won't use it, or you won't have anticipated your future requirements correctly. See Chapter 22 for one methodology that helps us avoid this trap.

## PART II

Web Development *Sine Qua Nons*

Real developers ship.

—Jeff Atwood

If this were just a guide to TDD in a normal programming field, we might be able to congratulate ourselves about now. After all, we've got some solid basics of TDD and Django under our belts; we've got all we need to start building a website.

But, real developers ship, and in order to ship, we're going to have to tackle some of the trickier but unavoidable aspects of web development: static files, form data validation, the dreaded JavaScript, but most hairy of all, deployment to a production server.

At every stage, TDD can help us to get these things right too.

In this section, I'm still trying to keep the learning curve relatively soft, but we will meet several major new concepts and technologies. I'll only be able to dip lightly into each one—I hope to demonstrate enough of each to get you started when you get to your own project, but you will also need to do your own reading around when you start to apply these topics in "real life".

For example, if you weren't familiar with Django before starting on the book, you may find that taking a little time to run through the official Django tutorial (*https:// docs.djangoproject.com/en/1.11/intro/tutorial01/#creating-models*) at this point would complement what you've learned so far nicely, and will leave you more confident with the Django stuff over the next few chapters, so you can focus on the core concepts.

Oh, but there's lots of fun stuff coming up! Just you wait!

## CHAPTER 8

Prettification: Layout and Styling, and What to Test About It

We're starting to think about releasing the first version of our site, but we're a bit embarrassed by how ugly it looks at the moment. In this chapter, we'll cover some of the basics of styling, including integrating an HTML/CSS framework called Bootstrap. We'll learn how static files work in Django, and what we need to do about testing them.

What to Functionally Test About Layout and Style

Our site is undeniably a bit unattractive at the moment (Figure 8-1).

> If you spin up your dev server with `manage.py runserver`, you may run into a database error "table lists_item has no column named list_id". You need to update your local database to reflect the changes we made in *models.py*. Use `manage.py migrate`. If it gives you any grief about `IntegrityErrors`, just delete[1] the database file and try again.

We can't be adding to Python's reputation for being ugly (*http://grokcode.com/746/dear-python-why-are-you-so-ugly/*), so let's do a tiny bit of polishing. Here's a few things we might want:

---

[1] What? Delete the database? Are you crazy? Not completely. The local dev database often gets out of sync with its migrations as we go back and forth in our development, and it doesn't have any important data in it, so it's OK to blow it away now and again. We'll be much more careful once we have a "production" database on the server. More on this in Appendix D.

- A nice large input field for adding new and existing lists

- A large, attention-grabbing, centered box to put it in

How do we apply TDD to these things? Most people will tell you you shouldn't test aesthetics, and they're right. It's a bit like testing a constant, in that tests usually wouldn't add any value.

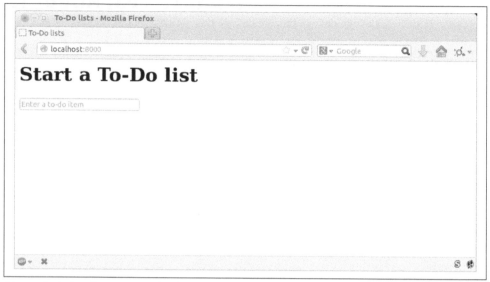

Figure 8-1. Our home page, looking a little ugly...

But we can test the implementation of our aesthetics—just enough to reassure ourselves that things are working. For example, we're going to use Cascading Style Sheets (CSS) for our styling, and they are loaded as static files. Static files can be a bit tricky to configure (especially, as we'll see later, when you move off your own PC and onto a hosting site), so we'll want some kind of simple "smoke test" that the CSS has loaded. We don't have to test fonts and colours and every single pixel, but we can do a quick check that the main input box is aligned the way we want it on each page, and that will give us confidence that the rest of the styling for that page is probably loaded too.

We start with a new test method inside our functional test:

```python
class NewVisitorTest(LiveServerTestCase):
    [...]


    def test_layout_and_styling(self):
        # Edith goes to the home page
        self.browser.get(self.live_server_url)
        self.browser.set_window_size(1024, 768)

        # She notices the input box is nicely centered
        inputbox = self.browser.find_element_by_id('id_new_item')
        self.assertAlmostEqual(
            inputbox.location['x'] + inputbox.size['width'] / 2,
            512,
            delta=10
        )
```

A few new things here. We start by setting the window size to a fixed size. We then find the input element, look at its size and location, and do a little maths to check whether it seems to be positioned in the middle of the page. assertAlmostEqual helps us to deal with rounding errors and the occasional weirdness due to scrollbars and the like, by letting us specify that we want our arithmetic to work to within plus or minus 10 pixels.

If we run the functional tests, we get:

```
$ python manage.py test functional_tests
[...]
.F.
======================================================================
FAIL: test_layout_and_styling (functional_tests.tests.NewVisitorTest)
----------------------------------------------------------------------
Traceback (most recent call last):
  File "...python-tdd-book/functional_tests/tests.py", line 129, in
test_layout_and_styling
    delta=10
AssertionError: 106.5 != 512 within 10 delta


----------------------------------------------------------------------
Ran 3 tests in 9.188s

FAILED (failures=1)
```

That's the expected failure. Still, this kind of FT is easy to get wrong, so let's use a quick-and-dirty "cheat" solution, to check that the FT also passes when the input box is centered. We'll delete this code again almost as soon as we've used it to check the FT:

```
<form method="POST" action="/lists/new">
  <p style="text-align: center;">
    <input name="item_text" id="id_new_item" placeholder="Enter a to-do item" />
  </p>
  {% csrf_token %}
</form>
```

That passes, which means the FT works. Let's extend it to make sure that the input box is also center-aligned on the page for a new list:

functional_tests/tests.py (ch08l003)

```
# She starts a new list and sees the input is nicely
# centered there too
inputbox.send_keys('testing')
inputbox.send_keys(Keys.ENTER)
self.wait_for_row_in_list_table('1: testing')
inputbox = self.browser.find_element_by_id('id_new_item')
self.assertAlmostEqual(
    inputbox.location['x'] + inputbox.size['width'] / 2,
    512,
    delta=10
)
```

That gives us another test failure:

```
File "...python-tdd-book/functional_tests/tests.py", line 141, in
test_layout_and_styling
    delta=10
AssertionError: 106.5 != 512 within 10 delta
```

Let's commit just the FT:

```
$ git add functional_tests/tests.py
$ git commit -m "first steps of FT for layout + styling"
```

Now it feels like we're justified in finding a "proper" solution to our need for some better styling for our site. We can back out our hacky <p style="text-align: center">:

```
$ git reset --hard
```

git reset --hard is the "take off and nuke the site from orbit" Git command, so be careful with it—it blows away all your uncommitted changes. Unlike almost everything else you can do with Git, there's no way of going back after this one.

Prettification: Using a CSS Framework

Design is hard, and doubly so now that we have to deal with mobile, tablets, and so forth. That's why many programmers, particularly lazy ones like me, are turning to CSS frameworks to solve some of those problems for them. There are lots of frameworks out there, but one of the earliest and most popular is Twitter's Bootstrap. Let's use that.

You can find bootstrap at *http://getbootstrap.com/*.

We'll download it and put it in a new folder called *static* inside the lists app:[2]

```
$ wget -O bootstrap.zip https://github.com/twbs/bootstrap/releases/download/\
v3.3.4/bootstrap-3.3.4-dist.zip
$ unzip bootstrap.zip
$ mkdir lists/static
$ mv bootstrap-3.3.4-dist lists/static/bootstrap
$ rm bootstrap.zip
```

Bootstrap comes with a plain, uncustomised installation in the *dist* folder. We're going to use that for now, but you should really never do this for a real site—vanilla Bootstrap is instantly recognisable, and a big signal to anyone in the know that you couldn't be bothered to style your site. Learn how to use LESS and change the font, if nothing else! There is info in Bootstrap's docs, or there's a good guide here (*http://coding.smashingmagazine.com/2013/03/12/customizing-bootstrap/*).

Our *lists* folder will end up looking like this:

---

2 On Windows, you may not have wget and unzip, but I'm sure you can figure out how to download Bootstrap, unzip it, and put the contents of the *dist* folder into the *lists/static/bootstrap* folder.

```
$ tree lists
lists
├── __init__.py
├── __pycache__
│   └── [...]
├── admin.py
├── models.py
├── static
│   └── bootstrap
│       ├── css
│       │   ├── bootstrap.css
│       │   ├── bootstrap.css.map
│       │   ├── bootstrap.min.css
│       │   ├── bootstrap-theme.css
│       │   ├── bootstrap-theme.css.map
│       │   └── bootstrap-theme.min.css
│       ├── fonts
│       │   ├── glyphicons-halflings-regular.eot
│       │   ├── glyphicons-halflings-regular.svg
│       │   ├── glyphicons-halflings-regular.ttf
│       │   ├── glyphicons-halflings-regular.woff
│       │   └── glyphicons-halflings-regular.woff2
│       └── js
│           ├── bootstrap.js
│           ├── bootstrap.min.js
│           └── npm.js
├── templates
│   ├── home.html
│   └── list.html
├── tests.py
├── urls.py
└── views.py
```

Look at the "Getting Started" section of the Bootstrap documentation (*http://bit.ly/2u1lROA*); you'll see it wants our HTML template to include something like this:

```html
<!DOCTYPE html>
<html>
  <head>
    <meta charset="utf-8">
    <meta http-equiv="X-UA-Compatible" content="IE=edge">
    <meta name="viewport" content="width=device-width, initial-scale=1">
    <title>Bootstrap 101 Template</title>
    <!-- Bootstrap -->
    <link href="css/bootstrap.min.css" rel="stylesheet">
  </head>
  <body>
    <h1>Hello, world!</h1>
    <script src="http://code.jquery.com/jquery.js"></script>
    <script src="js/bootstrap.min.js"></script>
  </body>
</html>
```

We already have two HTML templates. We don't want to be adding a whole load of boilerplate code to each, so now feels like the right time to apply the "Don't repeat yourself" rule, and bring all the common parts together. Thankfully, the Django template language makes that easy using something called template inheritance.

Django Template Inheritance

Let's have a little review of what the differences are between *home.html* and *list.html*:

```
$ diff lists/templates/home.html lists/templates/list.html
<       <h1>Start a new To-Do list</h1>
<       <form method="POST" action="/lists/new">
---
>       <h1>Your To-Do list</h1>
>       <form method="POST" action="/lists/{{ list.id }}/add_item">
[...]
>       <table id="id_list_table">
>         {% for item in list.item_set.all %}
>           <tr><td>{{ forloop.counter }}: {{ item.text }}</td></tr>
>         {% endfor %}
>       </table>
```

They have different header texts, and their forms use different URLs. On top of that, *list.html* has the additional <table> element.

Now that we're clear on what's in common and what's not, we can make the two templates inherit from a common "superclass" template. We'll start by making a copy of *home.html*:

```
$ cp lists/templates/home.html lists/templates/base.html
```

We make this into a base template which just contains the common boilerplate, and mark out the "blocks", places where child templates can customise it:

lists/templates/base.html

```
<html>
  <head>
    <title>To-Do lists</title>
  </head>

  <body>
    <h1>{% block header_text %}{% endblock %}</h1>
    <form method="POST" action="{% block form_action %}{% endblock %}">
      <input name="item_text" id="id_new_item" placeholder="Enter a to-do item" />
      {% csrf_token %}
    </form>
    {% block table %}
    {% endblock %}
  </body>
</html>
```

The base template defines a series of areas called "blocks", which will be places that other templates can hook in and add their own content. Let's see how that works in practice, by changing *home.html* so that it "inherits from" *base.html*:

lists/templates/home.html

```
{% extends 'base.html' %}

{% block header_text %}Start a new To-Do list{% endblock %}

{% block form_action %}/lists/new{% endblock %}
```

You can see that lots of the boilerplate HTML disappears, and we just concentrate on the bits we want to customise. We do the same for *list.html*:

lists/templates/list.html

```
{% extends 'base.html' %}

{% block header_text %}Your To-Do list{% endblock %}

{% block form_action %}/lists/{{ list.id }}/add_item{% endblock %}

{% block table %}
  <table id="id_list_table">
    {% for item in list.item_set.all %}
      <tr><td>{{ forloop.counter }}: {{ item.text }}</td></tr>
    {% endfor %}
  </table>
{% endblock %}
```

That's a refactor of the way our templates work. We rerun the FTs to make sure we haven't broken anything...

```
AssertionError: 106.5 != 512 within 10 delta
```

Sure enough, they're still getting to exactly where they were before. That's worthy of a commit:

```
$ git diff -b
# the -b means ignore whitespace, useful since we've changed some html indenting
$ git status
$ git add lists/templates # leave static, for now
$ git commit -m "refactor templates to use a base template"
```

Integrating Bootstrap

Now it's much easier to integrate the boilerplate code that Bootstrap wants—we won't add the JavaScript yet, just the CSS:

```
<!DOCTYPE html>
<html lang="en">

  <head>
    <meta charset="utf-8">
    <meta http-equiv="X-UA-Compatible" content="IE=edge">
    <meta name="viewport" content="width=device-width, initial-scale=1">
    <title>To-Do lists</title>
    <link href="css/bootstrap.min.css" rel="stylesheet">
  </head>
[...]
```

Rows and Columns

Finally, let's actually use some of the Bootstrap magic! You'll have to read the documentation yourself, but we should be able to use a combination of the grid system and the `text-center` class to get what we want:

```
<body>
  <div class="container">

    <div class="row">
      <div class="col-md-6 col-md-offset-3">
        <div class="text-center">
          <h1>{% block header_text %}{% endblock %}</h1>
          <form method="POST" action="{% block form_action %}{% endblock %}">
            <input name="item_text" id="id_new_item"
                   placeholder="Enter a to-do item" />
            {% csrf_token %}
          </form>
        </div>
      </div>
    </div>

    <div class="row">
      <div class="col-md-6 col-md-offset-3">
        {% block table %}
        {% endblock %}
      </div>
    </div>

  </div>
</body>
```

(If you've never seen an HTML tag broken up over several lines, that `<input>` may be a little shocking. It is definitely valid, but you don't have to use it if you find it offensive. ;)

Take the time to browse through the Bootstrap documentation (*http://getbootstrap.com/*), if you've never seen it before. It's a shopping trolley brimming full of useful tools to use in your site.

Does that work?

```
AssertionError: 106.5 != 512 within 10 delta
```

Hmm. No. Why isn't our CSS loading?

Static Files in Django

Django, and indeed any web server, needs to know two things to deal with static files:

1. How to tell when a URL request is for a static file, as opposed to for some HTML that's going to be served via a view function

2. Where to find the static file the user wants

In other words, static files are a mapping from URLs to files on disk.

For item 1, Django lets us define a URL "prefix" to say that any URLs which start with that prefix should be treated as requests for static files. By default, the prefix is */static/*. It's defined in *settings.py*:

superlists/settings.py

```
[...]

# Static files (CSS, JavaScript, Images)
# https://docs.djangoproject.com/en/1.11/howto/static-files/

STATIC_URL = '/static/'
```

The rest of the settings we will add to this section are all to do with item 2: finding the actual static files on disk.

While we're using the Django development server (`manage.py runserver`), we can rely on Django to magically find static files for us—it'll just look in any subfolder of one of our apps called *static*.

You now see why we put all the Bootstrap static files into *lists/static*. So why are they not working at the moment? It's because we're not using the `/static/` URL prefix. Have another look at the link to the CSS in *base.html*:

```
<link href="css/bootstrap.min.css" rel="stylesheet">
```

To get this to work, we need to change it to:

lists/templates/base.html

```
<link href="/static/bootstrap/css/bootstrap.min.css" rel="stylesheet">
```

When `runserver` sees the request, it knows that it's for a static file because it begins with `/static/`. It then tries to find a file called *bootstrap/css/bootstrap.min.css*, looking in each of our app folders for subfolders called *static*, and it should find it at *lists/static/bootstrap/css/bootstrap.min.css*.

So if you take a look manually, you should see it works, as in Figure 8-2.

Figure 8-2. Our site starts to look a little better...

Switching to StaticLiveServerTestCase

If you run the FT though, it won't pass:

```
AssertionError: 106.5 != 512 within 10 delta
```

That's because, although `runserver` automagically finds static files, `LiveServerTest Case` doesn't. Never fear, though: the Django developers have made a more magical test class called `StaticLiveServerTestCase` (see the docs (*http://bit.ly/Suv4Ip*)).

Let's switch to that:

```
@@ -1,14 +1,14 @@
-from django.test import LiveServerTestCase
+from django.contrib.staticfiles.testing import StaticLiveServerTestCase
 from selenium import webdriver
 from selenium.common.exceptions import WebDriverException
 from selenium.webdriver.common.keys import Keys
 import time

 MAX_WAIT = 10


-class NewVisitorTest(LiveServerTestCase):
+class NewVisitorTest(StaticLiveServerTestCase):

     def setUp(self):
```

And now it will find the new CSS, which will get our test to pass:

```
$ python manage.py test functional_tests
Creating test database for alias 'default'...
...
 ----------------------------------------------------------------
Ran 3 tests in 9.764s
```

At this point, Windows users may see some (harmless, but distracting) error messages that say `socket.error: [WinError 10054] An existing connection was forcibly closed by the remote host`. Add a `self.browser.refresh()` just before the `self.browser.quit()` in tearDown to get rid of them. The issue is being tracked in a bug on the Django tracker (*https://code.django project.com/ticket/21227*).

Hooray!

Using Bootstrap Components to Improve the Look of the Site

Let's see if we can do even better, using some of the other tools in Bootstrap's panoply.

Jumbotron!

Bootstrap has a class called `jumbotron` for things that are meant to be particularly prominent on the page. Let's use that to embiggen the main page header and the input form:

```
<div class="col-md-6 col-md-offset-3 jumbotron">
  <div class="text-center">
    <h1>{% block header_text %}{% endblock %}</h1>
    <form method="POST" action="{% block form_action %}{% endblock %}">
      [...]
```

 When hacking about with design and layout, it's best to have a window open that we can hit refresh on, frequently. Use python manage.py runserver to spin up the dev server, and then browse to *http://localhost:8000* to see your work as we go.

Large Inputs

The jumbotron is a good start, but now the input box has tiny text compared to everything else. Thankfully, Bootstrap's form control classes offer an option to set an input to be "large":

```
<input name="item_text" id="id_new_item"
       class="form-control input-lg"
       placeholder="Enter a to-do item" />
```

Table Styling

The table text also looks too small compared to the rest of the page now. Adding the Bootstrap table class improves things:

```
<table id="id_list_table" class="table">
```

Using Our Own CSS

Finally I'd like to just offset the input from the title text slightly. There's no ready-made fix for that in Bootstrap, so we'll make one ourselves. That will require specifying our own CSS file:

```
[...]
  <title>To-Do lists</title>
  <link href="/static/bootstrap/css/bootstrap.min.css" rel="stylesheet">
  <link href="/static/base.css" rel="stylesheet">
</head>
```

We create a new file at *lists/static/base.css*, with our new CSS rule. We'll use the id of the input element, id_new_item, to find it and give it some styling:

lists/static/base.css

```
#id_new_item {
    margin-top: 2ex;
}
```

All that took me a few goes, but I'm reasonably happy with it now (Figure 8-3).

If you want to go further with customising Bootstrap, you need to get into compiling LESS. I *definitely* recommend taking the time to do that some day. LESS and other pseudo-CSS-alikes like Sass are a great improvement on plain old CSS, and a useful tool even if you don't use Bootstrap. I won't cover it in this book, but you can find resources on the internets. Here's one (*http://coding.smashingmagazine.com/2013/03/12/customizing-bootstrap/*), for example.

A last run of the functional tests, to see if everything still works OK:

```
$ python manage.py test functional_tests
[...]
...
----------------------------------------------------------------------
Ran 3 tests in 10.084s

OK
```

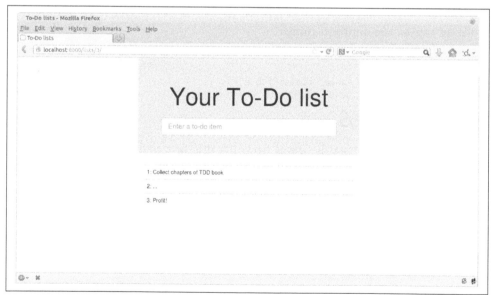

Figure 8-3. The lists page, with all big chunks...

That's it! Definitely time for a commit:

```
$ git status # changes tests.py, base.html, list.html + untracked lists/static
$ git add .
$ git status # will now show all the bootstrap additions
$ git commit -m "Use Bootstrap to improve layout"
```

What We Glossed Over: collectstatic and Other Static Directories

We saw earlier that the Django dev server will magically find all your static files inside app folders, and serve them for you. That's fine during development, but when you're running on a real web server, you don't want Django serving your static content—using Python to serve raw files is slow and inefficient, and a web server like Apache or Nginx can do this all for you. You might even decide to upload all your static files to a CDN, instead of hosting them yourself.

For these reasons, you want to be able to gather up all your static files from inside their various app folders, and copy them into a single location, ready for deployment. This is what the collectstatic command is for.

The destination, the place where the collected static files go, is defined in *settings.py* as STATIC_ROOT. In the next chapter we'll be doing some deployment, so let's actually experiment with that now. A common and straightforward place to put it is in a folder called "static" in the root of our repo:

```
.
├── db.sqlite3
├── functional_tests/
├── lists/
├── manage.py
├── static/
├── superlists/
└── virtualenv/
```

Here's a neat way of specifying that folder, making it relative to the location of the project base directory:

superlists/settings.py (ch08l018)

```python
# Static files (CSS, JavaScript, Images)
# https://docs.djangoproject.com/en/1.11/howto/static-files/

STATIC_URL = '/static/'
STATIC_ROOT = os.path.join(BASE_DIR, 'static')
```

Take a look at the top of the settings file, and you'll see how that `BASE_DIR` variable is helpfully defined for us, using `__file__` (which itself is a really, really useful Python built-in[3]).

Anyway, let's try running `collectstatic`:

```
$ python manage.py collectstatic
[...]
Copying '...python-tdd-book/lists/static/bootstrap/css/bootstrap-theme.css'
Copying '...python-tdd-book/lists/static/bootstrap/css/bootstrap.min.css'

76 static files copied to '...python-tdd-book/static'.
```

And if we look in *./static*, we'll find all our CSS files:

---

3 Notice in the `os.path` wrangling of `BASE_DIR` that the abspath gets done first (i.e., innermost). Always follow this pattern when chaining `os.path` operations, otherwise you can see unpredictable behaviours depending on how the file is imported. Thanks to Green Nathan (*https://github.com/CleanCut/green*) for that tip!

```
$ tree static/
static/
├── admin
│   ├── css
│   │   ├── base.css
[...]
│                   └── xregexp.min.js
├── base.css
└── bootstrap
    ├── css
    │   ├── bootstrap.css
    │   ├── [...]
    │   └── bootstrap-theme.min.css
    ├── fonts
    │   ├── glyphicons-halflings-regular.eot
    │   ├── [...]
    │   └── glyphicons-halflings-regular.woff2
    └── js
        ├── bootstrap.js
        ├── bootstrap.min.js
        └── npm.js


14 directories, 76 files
```

collectstatic has also picked up all the CSS for the admin site. It's one of Django's powerful features, and we'll find out all about it one day, but we're not ready to use that yet, so let's disable it for now:

superlists/settings.py

```
INSTALLED_APPS = [
    #'django.contrib.admin',
    'django.contrib.auth',
    'django.contrib.contenttypes',
    'django.contrib.sessions',
    'django.contrib.messages',
    'django.contrib.staticfiles',
    'lists',
]
```

And we try again:

```
$ rm -rf static/
$ python manage.py collectstatic --noinput
Copying '...python-tdd-book/lists/static/base.css'
[...]
Copying '...python-tdd-book/lists/static/bootstrap/css/bootstrap-theme.css'
Copying '...python-tdd-book/lists/static/bootstrap/css/bootstrap.min.css'


15 static files copied to '...python-tdd-book/static'.
```

Much better.

Now we know how to collect all the static files into a single folder, where it's easy for a web server to find them. We'll find out all about that, including how to test it, in the next chapter!

For now let's save our changes to *settings.py*. We'll also add the top-level static folder to our gitignore, since it will only contain copies of files we actually keep in individual apps' static folders.

```
$ git diff # should show changes in settings.py plus the new directory*
$ echo /static >> .gitignore
$ git commit -am "set STATIC_ROOT in settings and disable admin"
```

A Few Things That Didn't Make It

Inevitably this was only a whirlwind tour of styling and CSS, and there were several topics that I'd considered covering that didn't make it. Here are a few candidates for further study:

- Customising bootstrap with LESS or SASS
- The {% static %} template tag, for more DRY and fewer hardcoded URLs
- Client-side packaging tools, like npm and bower

Recap: On Testing Design and Layout

The short answer is: you shouldn't write tests for design and layout *per se*. It's too much like testing a constant, and the tests you write are often brittle.

With that said, the *implementation* of design and layout involves something quite tricky: CSS and static files. As a result, it is valuable to have some kind of minimal "smoke test" which checks that your static files and CSS are working. As we'll see in the next chapter, it can help pick up problems when you deploy your code to production.

Similarly, if a particular piece of styling required a lot of client-side JavaScript code to get it to work (dynamic resizing is one I've spent a bit of time on), you'll definitely want some tests for that.

Try to write the minimal tests that will give you confidence that your design and layout is working, without testing *what* it actually is. Aim to leave yourself in a position where you can freely make changes to the design and layout, without having to go back and adjust tests all the time.

Testing Deployment Using a Staging Site

Is all fun and game until you are need of put it in production.

—Devops Borat (*http://bit.ly/2uhCXnH*)

It's time to deploy the first version of our site and make it public. They say that if you wait until you feel ready to ship, then you've waited too long.

Is our site usable? Is it better than nothing? Can we make lists on it? Yes, yes, yes.

No, you can't log in yet. No, you can't mark tasks as completed. But do we really need any of that stuff? Not really—and you can never be sure what your users are *actually* going to do with your site once they get their hands on it. We think our users want to use the site for to-do lists, but maybe they actually want to use it to make "top 10 best fly-fishing spots" lists, for which you don't need any kind of "mark completed" function. We won't know until we put it out there.

In this chapter we're going to go through and actually deploy our site to a real, live web server.

You might be tempted to skip this chapter—there's lots of daunting stuff in it, and maybe you think this isn't what you signed up for. But I *strongly* urge you to give it a go. This is one of the sections of the book I'm most pleased with, and it's one that people often write to me saying they were really glad they stuck through it.

If you've never done a server deployment before, it will demystify a whole world for you, and there's nothing like the feeling of seeing your site live on the actual internet. Give it a buzzword name like "DevOps" if that's what it takes to convince you it's worth it.

Why not ping me a note once your site is live on the web, and send me the URL? It always gives me a warm and fuzzy feeling... *obey-thetestinggoat@gmail.com.*

TDD and the Danger Areas of Deployment

Deploying a site to a live web server can be a tricky topic. Oft-heard is the forlorn cry *"but it works on my machine!"*

Some of the danger areas of deployment include:

Networking
> Once we're off our own machine, networking issues come in: making sure the DNS service is routing our domain to the correct IP address for our server, making sure our server is configured to listen to traffic coming in from the world, making sure it's using the right ports, and making sure any firewalls in the way are configured to let traffic through.

Dependencies
> We need to make sure that the packages our software relies on (Python, Django, and so on) are installed on the server, and have the correct versions.

The database
> There can be permissions and path issues, and we need to be careful about preserving data between deploys.

Static files (CSS, JavaScript, images, etc.)
> Web servers usually need special configuration for serving these.

But there are solutions to all of these. In order:

- Using a *staging site*, on the same infrastructure as the production site, can help us test out our deployments and get things right before we go to the "real" site.

- We can also *run our functional tests against the staging site*. That will reassure us that we have the right code and packages on the server, and since we now have a "smoke test" for our site layout, we'll know that the CSS is loaded correctly.

- Just like on our own PC, a *virtualenv* is useful on the server for managing packages and dependencies when you might be running more than one Python application.

- And finally, *automation, automation, automation.* By using an automated script to deploy new versions, and by using the same script to deploy to staging and production, we can reassure ourselves that staging is as much like live as possible.[1]

Over the next few pages I'm going to go through *a* deployment procedure. It isn't meant to be the *perfect* deployment procedure, so please don't take it as being best practice, or a recommendation—it's meant to be an illustration, to show the kinds of issues involved in deployment and where testing fits in.

Deployment Chapters Overview

There's lots of stuff in the next three chapters, so here's an overview to help you keep your bearings:

This chapter: getting a basic manual deployment up and running

- Adapt our FTs so they can run against a staging server.
- Spin up a server, install all the required software on it, and point our staging and live domains at it.
- Upload our code to the server using Git.
- Try and get a quick-and-dirty version of our site running on the staging domain using the Django dev server.
- Set up a virtualenv on the server and make sure the database and static files are working.
- As we go, we'll keep running our FT, to tell us what's working and what's not.

Next chapter: moving to a production-ready config

- Move from our quick-and-dirty version to a production-ready configuration.
- Stop using the Django dev server, use Nginx and Gunicorn as web servers, configure efficient static file serving, set our app to start automatically on boot with Systemd.
- Security: Use environment variables to DEBUG to False, change the SECRET_KEY, and so on

---

1 What I'm calling a "staging" server, some people would call a "development" server, and some others would also like to distinguish "preproduction" servers. Whatever we call it, the point is to have somewhere we can try our code out in an environment that's as similar as possible to the real production server.

> **Third deployment chapter: automating the deployment**
>
> - Once we have a working config, we'll write a script to automate the process we've just been through manually, so that we can deploy our site automatically in future.
>
> - Finally we'll use this script to deploy the production version of our site on its real domain.

As Always, Start with a Test

Let's adapt our functional tests slightly so that it can be run against a staging site, instead of the local dev server. We'll do it by checking for an environment variable called STAGING_SERVER:

functional_tests/tests.py (ch08l001)

```python
import os
[...]

class NewVisitorTest(StaticLiveServerTestCase):

    def setUp(self):
        self.browser = webdriver.Firefox()
        staging_server = os.environ.get('STAGING_SERVER')   ❶
        if staging_server:
            self.live_server_url = 'http://' + staging_server   ❷
```

Do you remember I said that LiveServerTestCase had certain limitations? Well, one is that it always assumes you want to use its own test server, which it makes available at self.live_server_url. I still want to be able to do that sometimes, but I also want to be able to selectively tell it not to bother, and to use a real server instead.

❶ The way I decided to do it is using an environment variable called STAGING_SERVER.

❷ Here's the hack: we replace self.live_server_url with the address of our "real" server.

We test that said hack hasn't broken anything by running the functional tests "normally":

```
$ python manage.py test functional_tests
[...]
Ran 3 tests in 8.544s

OK
```

And now we can try them against our staging server URL. I'm planning to host my staging server at *superlists-staging.ottg.eu*:

 A clarification: in this chapter, we run tests *against* our staging server, not *on* our staging server. So we still run the tests from our own laptop, but they target the site that's running on the server.

```
$ STAGING_SERVER=superlists-staging.ottg.eu python manage.py test functional_tests

EEE
======================================================================
ERROR: test_can_start_a_list_for_one_user
(functional_tests.tests.NewVisitorTest)
----------------------------------------------------------------------
Traceback (most recent call last):
  File "...python-tdd-book/functional_tests/tests.py", line 41, in
test_can_start_a_list_for_one_user
    self.browser.get(self.live_server_url)
[...]
selenium.common.exceptions.WebDriverException: Message: Reached error page: abo
ut:neterror?e=connectionFailure&u=http%3A//superlists-staging.ottg.eu/&c=UTF-8&
f=regular&d=Firefox%20can%27t%20establish%20a%20connection%20to%20the%20server%
20at%20superlists-staging.ottg.eu.


======================================================================
ERROR: test_layout_and_styling (functional_tests.tests.NewVisitorTest)
----------------------------------------------------------------------
Traceback (most recent call last):
  File "...python-tdd-book/functional_tests/tests.py", line 126, in
test_layout_and_styling
[...]
selenium.common.exceptions.WebDriverException: Message: Reached error page: abo
[...]


======================================================================
ERROR: test_multiple_users_can_start_lists_at_different_urls
(functional_tests.tests.NewVisitorTest)
----------------------------------------------------------------------
Traceback (most recent call last):
  File "...python-tdd-book/functional_tests/tests.py", line 80, in
test_multiple_users_can_start_lists_at_different_urls
[...]
selenium.common.exceptions.WebDriverException: Message: Reached error page: abo
[...]

Ran 3 tests in 10.518s

FAILED (errors=3)
```

If, on Windows, you see an error saying something like "STAG-ING_SERVER is not recognized as a command", it's probably because you're not using Git-Bash. Take another look at the "Pre-requisites and Assumptions" section.

You can see that all the tests are failing, as expected, since I haven't actually set up my domain yet. Selenium reports that Firefox is seeing an error and "cannot establish connection to the server" (depending on your registrar, you might see content from its default landing page instead).

The FT seems to be testing the right things though, so let's commit:

```
$ git diff # should show changes to functional_tests.py
$ git commit -am "Hack FT runner to be able to test staging"
```

Don't use export to set the *STAGING_SERVER* environment variable; otherwise, all your subsequent test runs in that terminal will be against staging (and that can be very confusing if you're not expecting it). Setting it explicitly inline each time you run the FTs is best.

Getting a Domain Name

We're going to need a couple of domain names at this point in the book—they can both be subdomains of a single domain. I'm going to use *superlists.ottg.eu* and *superlists-staging.ottg.eu*. If you don't already own a domain, this is the time to register one! Again, this is something I really want you to *actually* do. If you've never registered a domain before, just pick any old registrar and buy a cheap one—it should only cost you $5 or so, and you can even find free ones. I promise seeing your site on a "real" website will be a thrill.

Manually Provisioning a Server to Host Our Site

We can separate out "deployment" into two tasks:

- *Provisioning* a new server to be able to host the code
- *Deploying* a new version of the code to an existing server

Some people like to use a brand new server for every deployment—it's what we do at PythonAnywhere. That's only necessary for larger, more complex sites though, or major changes to an existing site. For a simple site like ours, it makes sense to separate the two tasks. And, although we eventually want both to be completely automated, we can probably live with a manual provisioning system for now.

As you go through this chapter, you should be aware that provisioning is something that varies a lot, and that as a result there are few universal best practices for deployment. So, rather than trying to remember the specifics of what I'm doing here, you should be trying to understand the rationale, so that you can apply the same kind of thinking in the specific future circumstances you encounter.

Choosing Where to Host Our Site

There are loads of different solutions out there these days, but they broadly fall into two camps:

- Running your own (possibly virtual) server
- Using a Platform-As-A-Service (PaaS) offering like Heroku, OpenShift, or PythonAnywhere

Particularly for small sites, a PaaS offers a lot of advantages, and I would definitely recommend looking into them. We're not going to use a PaaS in this book however, for several reasons. Firstly, I have a conflict of interest, in that I think PythonAnywhere is the best, but then again I would say that because I work there. Secondly, all the PaaS offerings are quite different, and the procedures to deploy to each vary a lot —learning about one doesn't necessarily tell you about the others. Any one of them might radically change their process or business model by the time you get to read this book.

Instead, we'll learn just a tiny bit of good old-fashioned server admin, including SSH and web server config. They're unlikely to ever go away, and knowing a bit about them will get you some respect from all the grizzled dinosaurs out there.

What I have done is to try to set up a server in such a way that's a bit like the environment you get from a PaaS, so you should be able to apply the lessons we learn in the deployment section, no matter what provisioning solution you choose.

Spinning Up a Server

I'm not going to dictate how you do this—whether you choose Amazon AWS, Rackspace, Digital Ocean, your own server in your own data centre or a Raspberry Pi in a cupboard under the stairs, any solution should be fine, as long as:

- Your server is running Ubuntu 16.04 (aka "Xenial/LTS").
- You have root access to it.
- It's on the public internet.
- You can SSH into it.

I'm recommending Ubuntu as a distro because it's easy to get Python 3.6 on it and it has some specific ways of configuring Nginx, which I'm going to make use of next. If you know what you're doing, you can probably get away with using something else, but you're on your own.

If you've never started a Linux server before and you have absolutely no idea where to start, I wrote a very brief guide on GitHub (*https://github.com/hjwp/Book-TDD-Web-Dev-Python/blob/master/server-quickstart.md*).

Some people get to this chapter, and are tempted to skip the domain bit, and the "getting a real server" bit, and just use a VM on their own PC. Don't do this. It's *not* the same, and you'll have more difficulty following the instructions, which are complicated enough as it is. If you're worried about cost, have a look at the link above for free options.

User Accounts, SSH, and Privileges

In these instructions, I'm assuming that you have a nonroot user account set up that has "sudo" privileges, so whenever we need to do something that requires root access, we use sudo, and I'm explicit about that in the various instructions that follow.

My user is called "elspeth", but you can call yours whatever you like! Just remember to substitute it in all the places I've hardcoded it below. See the guide linked above if you need tips on creating a sudo user.

Installing Python 3.6

Python 3.6 wasn't available in the standard repositories on Ubuntu at the time of writing, but the user-contributed "Deadsnakes PPA" (*https://launchpad.net/~fkrull/+archive/ubuntu/deadsnakes*) has it. Here's how we install it:

```
elspeth@server:$ sudo add-apt-repository ppa:deadsnakes/ppa
elspeth@server:$ sudo apt update
elspeth@server:$ sudo apt install python3.6 python3.6-venv
```

Look out for that elspeth@server in the command-line listings in this chapter. It indicates commands that must be run on the server, as opposed to commands you run on your own PC.

And while we're at it, we'll just make sure Git is installed too.

```
elspeth@server:$ sudo apt install git
```

Configuring Domains for Staging and Live

We don't want to be messing about with IP addresses all the time, so we should point our staging and live domains to the server. At my registrar, the control screens looked a bit like Figure 9-1.

DNS ENTRY	TYPE	PRIORITY	TTL	DESTINATION/TARGET		
*	A			81.21.76.62	✎	🗑
@	A			81.21.76.62	✎	🗑
@	MX	10		mx0.123-reg.co.uk.	✎	🗑
@	MX	20		mx1.123-reg.co.uk.	✎	🗑
dev	CNAME			harry.pythonanywhere…	✎	🗑
www	CNAME			harry.pythonanywhere…	✎	🗑
book-example	A			82.196.1.70	✎	🗑
book-example-staging	A			82.196.1.70	✎	🗑
Hostname	Type			Destination IPv4 address		Add

Figure 9-1. Domain setup

In the DNS system, pointing a domain at a specific IP address is called an "A-Record". All registrars are slightly different, but a bit of clicking around should get you to the right screen in yours. You'll need two A-records: one for the staging address and one for the live one. No need to worry about any other type of record.

DNS records take some time to "propagate" around the world (it's controlled by a setting called "TTL", Time To Live), so once you've set up your A-record, you can check its progress on a "propagation checking" service like this one: *https://www.what smydns.net/#A/superlists-staging.ottg.eu.*

Deploying Our Code Manually

The next step is to get a basic copy of the staging site up and running. As we do so, we're starting to move into doing "deployment" rather than provisioning, so we should be thinking about how we can automate the process as we go.

One rule of thumb for distinguishing provisioning from deployment is that you tend to need root permissions for the former, but you don't for the latter.

We need a directory for the source to live in. We'll put it somewhere in the home folder of our nonroot user; in my case it would be at */home/elspeth* (this is likely to be the setup on any shared hosting system, but you should always run your web apps as a nonroot user, in any case). I'm going to set up my sites like this:

```
/home/elspeth
├── sites
│   ├── www.live.my-website.com
│   │   ├── db.sqlite3
│   │   ├── manage.py
│   │   ├── [etc...]
│   │   ├── static
│   │   │   ├── base.css
│   │   │   ├── [etc...]
│   │   └── virtualenv
│   │       ├── lib
│   │       ├── [etc...]
│   │
│   ├── www.staging.my-website.com
│   │   ├── db.sqlite3
│   │   ├── [etc...]
```

Each site (staging, live, or any other website) has its own folder, which will contain a checkout of the source code (managed by git), along with the database, static files and virtualenv (managed separately).

To get our code onto the server, we'll use Git and go via one of the code-sharing sites. If you haven't already, push your code up to GitHub, BitBucket, GitLab, or similar. They all have excellent instructions for beginners on how to do that.

Here are some Bash commands that will set this all up.

```
elspeth@server:$ export SITENAME=superlists-staging.ottg.eu
# you should replace the URL in the next line with the URL for your own repo
elspeth@server:$ git clone https://github.com/hjwp/book-example.git ~/sites/$SITENAME
Resolving deltas: 100% [...]
```

- The export command sets up a "local variable" in Bash; a bit like the inline environment variable we used earlier, but it's available to all subsequent commands in that same shell.

- git clone takes your repo URL as its first argument, and an (optional) destination as its second argument. That will create the target folder for us and get our code into the right place in one go.

A Bash variable defined using `export` only lasts as long as that console session. If you log out of the server and log back in again, you'll need to redefine it. It's devious because Bash won't error, it will just substitute the empty string for the variable, which will lead to weird results...if in doubt, do a quick **echo $SITENAME**.

Now we've got the code, let's just try running the dev server, and see how far we get:

```
elspeth@server:$ $ cd ~/sites/$SITENAME
$ python3.6 manage.py runserver
Traceback (most recent call last):
  File "manage.py", line 8, in <module>
    from django.core.management import execute_from_command_line
ImportError: No module named django
[...]
ImportError: Couldn't import Django. Are you sure it's installed and available
on your PYTHONPATH environment variable? Did you forget to activate a virtual
environment?
```

Ah. Django isn't installed on the server.

Creating a Virtualenv on the Server Using requirements.txt

Just like on our own machine, a virtualenv is useful on the server to make sure we have full control over the packages installed for a particular project. It can also let us run different projects with different (or conflicting) dependencies on the same server.

To reproduce our local virtualenv, we can "save" the list of packages we're using by creating a *requirements.txt* file. Back on our own machine:

```
$ echo "django==1.11" > requirements.txt
$ git add requirements.txt
$ git commit -m "Add requirements.txt for virtualenv"
```

You may be wondering why we didn't add our other dependency, Selenium, to our requirements. The reason is that Selenium is only a dependency for the tests, not the application code (we're never going to run the tests on the server itself). Some people like to also create a file called *test-requirements.txt*.

Now we do a `git push` to send our updates up to our code-sharing site:

```
$ git push
```

And we can pull those changes down to the server:

```
elspeth@server:$ git pull  # may ask you to do some git config first
```

We create our virtualenv just like we did on our own machine:

```
elspeth@server:$ pwd
/home/elspeth/sites/superlists-staging.ottg.eu
elspeth@server:$ python3.6 -m venv virtualenv
elspeth@server:$ ls virtualenv/bin
activate        activate.fish  easy_install-3.6  pip3     python   python3.6
activate.csh    easy_install   pip               pip3.6   python3
```

If we wanted to activate the virtualenv, we could do so with `source ./virtualenv/bin/activate` just like we do locally, but on the server we don't need that. We can actually do everything we want to by directly calling the versions of Python, pip, and the other executables in the virtualenv's *bin* directory, as we'll soon see.

For example, to install our requirements into the virtualenv, we use the virtualenv pip:

```
elspeth@server:$ ./virtualenv/bin/pip install -r requirements.txt
Collecting django==1.11 (from -r requirements.txt (line 1))
[...]
Successfully installed django-1.11 pytz-2017.3
```

And to run Python in the virtualenv, we use the virtualenv `python` binary:

```
elspeth@server:$ ./virtualenv/bin/python manage.py runserver
Performing system checks...

System check identified no issues (0 silenced).
[...]
You have 15 unapplied migration(s). Your project may not work [...]
[...]
Starting development server at http://127.0.0.1:8000/
```

If we ignore the ominous message about migrations for now, Django certainly looks a lot happier.

Progress! We've got a system for getting code to and from the server (`git push` and `git pull`), we've got a virtualenv set up to match our local one, and a single file, *requirements.txt*, to keep them in sync.

Using the FT to Check That Our Deployment Works

Let's see what our FTs think about this version of our site running on the server. I'll use the `--failfast` option to exit as soon as a single test fails:

```
$ STAGING_SERVER=superlists-staging.ottg.eu ./manage.py test functional_tests \
    --failfast
[...]
selenium.common.exceptions.WebDriverException: Message: Reached error page: [...]
```

Nope! What's going on here? Time for a little debugging.

Debugging a Deployment That Doesn't Seem to Work at All

You may remember that Django's runserver usually chooses to run on port 8000. But a "normal" web server should run on port 80, and that's where our FTs are currently looking, on *superlists-staging.ottg.eu*.

But we can actually use our STAGING_SERVER variable to point the tests at port 8000. Let's try that:

```
$ STAGING_SERVER=superlists-staging.ottg.eu:8000 ./manage.py test functional_tests \
    --failfast

selenium.common.exceptions.WebDriverException: Message: Reached error page: [...]
```

Nope, that didn't work earlier. Let's try an even lower-level smoke test, the traditional Unix utility "curl" — it's a command-line tool for making web requests. Try it on your own computer first:

```
$ curl superlists-staging.ottg.eu
curl: (7) Failed to connect to superlists-staging.ottg.eu port 80: Connection
refused
```

And maybe just to be sure, we could even open up our web browser and type in *http://superlists-staging.ottg.eu:8000*, and confirm using a familiar tool that things aren't working. Nope.

On Debugging

Let me let you in on a little secret. I'm actually bad at debugging. We all have our psychological strengths and weakness, and one of my weaknesses is that when I run into a problem I can't see an obvious solution to, I want to throw up my hands way too soon and say "well, this is hopeless, it can't be fixed", and give up.

Thankfully I have some good role models at work who are much better at it than me (hi Glenn!). Debugging needs the patience and tenacity of a bloodhound. If at first you don't succeed, you need to systematically rule out options, check your assumptions, eliminate various aspects of the problem and simplify things down, find the parts that do and don't work, until you eventually find the cause.

It always seems hopeless at first! But eventually you get there.

We're pretty sure the server is running and listening on port 8000, but we can't get to it from the outside. What about from the inside? Try running curl on the server itself (you'll need a second SSH shell onto your server, so as not to interrupt the existing runserver process):

```
elspeth@server:$ curl localhost:8000
<!DOCTYPE html>
<html lang="en">
  <head>

    [...]
    <title>To-Do lists</title>
    [...]

  </body>
</html>
```

Ah-ha! That looks like the HTML for our site. So we *can* reach it from the server itself, just not from the outside. What could be going on?

Actually there's clue in the output that Django printed out earlier when we ran run server:

```
Starting development server at http://127.0.0.1:8000/
```

Django's development server is configured to listen on 127.0.0.1, aka the "localhost" IP address. But we're trying to reach it from the outside, via the server's "real" public address.

But Django isn't listening on that address by default. Here's how we tell it to listen on all addresses. Use Ctrl-C to interrupt the runserver process, and restart it like this:

```
elspeth@server:$ ./virtualenv/bin/python manage.py runserver 0.0.0.0:8000
[...]
Starting development server at http://0.0.0.0:8000/
```

And in a second SSH shell, we can confirm it works from the server:

```
elspeth@server:$ curl localhost:8000
<!DOCTYPE html>
[...]
</html>
```

What about from our own laptop?

```
$ curl superlists-staging.ottg.eu:8000
<!DOCTYPE html>
<html lang="en">
[...]
</body>
</html>
```

Looks good at first glance! Let's try our FTs again:

```
$ STAGING_SERVER=superlists-staging.ottg.eu:8000 ./manage.py test functional_tests \
  --failfast

======================================================================
FAIL: test_can_start_a_list_for_one_user
(functional_tests.tests.NewVisitorTest)
----------------------------------------------------------------------
Traceback (most recent call last):
  File "...python-tdd-book/functional_tests/tests.py", line 44, in
test_can_start_a_list_for_one_user
    self.assertIn('To-Do', self.browser.title)
AssertionError: 'To-Do' not found in 'DisallowedHost at /'
----------------------------------------------------------------------
Ran 1 test in 4.010s

FAILED (failures=1)
[...]
```

 At this point, if your FTs still can't talk to the server, something else must be in the way. Check your provider's firewall settings, and make sure ports 80 and 8000 are open to the world. On AWS, for example, you may need to configure the "security group" for your server.

Oops, spoke too soon! Another error. We didn't look closely enough at that `curl` output…

Hacking ALLOWED_HOSTS in settings.py

Don't be disheartened! We may have just fixed one problem only to run straight into another, but this problem is definitely a much easier one. At least we can talk to the server! And it's giving us a helpful pointer. Try opening the site manually (Figure 9-2):

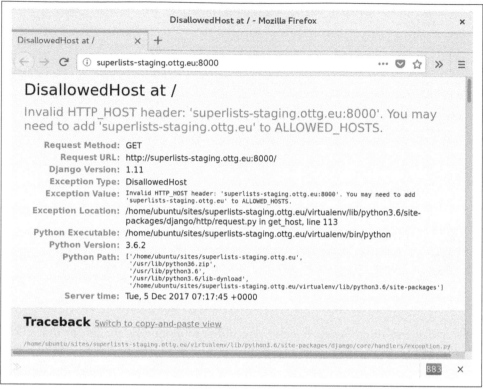

Figure 9-2. Another hitch along the way

ALLOWED_HOSTS is a security setting designed to reject requests that are likely to be forged, broken or malicious because they don't appear to be asking for your site (HTTP request contain the address they were intended for in a header called "Host").

By default, when DEBUG=True, ALLOWED_HOSTS effectively allows *localhost*, our own machine, so that's why it was working OK in dev, and from the server itself (where we ask for *localhost*), but not from our own machine (where we ask for *superlists-staging.ottg.eu*)

There's more information in the Django docs (*http://bit.ly/2u0R2d6*).

The upshot is that we need to adjust ALLOWED_HOSTS in *settings.py*. Since we're just hacking for now, let's set it to the totally insecure allow-everyone "*" setting:

superlists/settings.py

```
# SECURITY WARNING: don't run with debug turned on in production!
DEBUG = True

ALLOWED_HOSTS = ['*']
[...]
```

We commit that locally, then push it up to GitHub…

```
$ git commit -am "hack ALLOWED_HOSTS to be *"
$ git push
```

And pull it down on the server, and restart our runserver process:

```
elspeth@server:$ git pull
elspeth@server:$ ./virtualenv/bin/python manage.py runserver 0.0.0.0:8000
```

A quick visual inspection confirms—the site is up (Figure 9-3)!

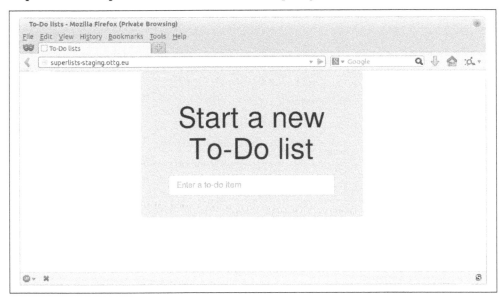

Figure 9-3. The staging site is up!

Let's see what our functional tests say:

```
$ STAGING_SERVER=superlists-staging.ottg.eu:8000 ./manage.py test functional_tests \
    --failfast
[...]
selenium.common.exceptions.NoSuchElementException: Message: Unable to locate
element: [id="id_list_table"]
```

The tests are failing as soon as they try to submit a new item, because we haven't set up the database. You'll probably have spotted the yellow Django debug page (Figure 9-4) telling us as much as the tests went through, or if you tried it manually.

The tests saved us from potential embarrassment there. The site *looked* fine when we loaded its front page. If we'd been a little hasty and only testing manually, we might have thought we were done, and it would have been the first users that discovered that nasty Django DEBUG page. Okay, slight exaggeration for effect, maybe we *would* have checked, but what happens as the site gets bigger and more complex? You can't check everything. The tests can.

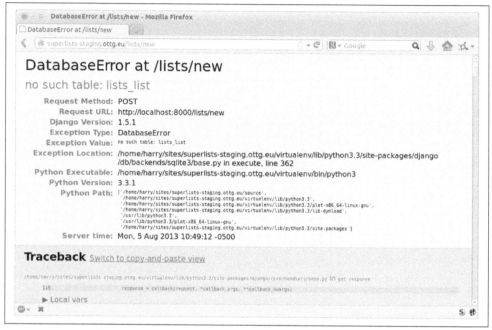

Figure 9-4. But the database isn't

Creating the Database with migrate

We run `migrate` using the `--noinput` argument to suppress the two little "are you sure" prompts:

```
elspeth@server:$ ./virtualenv/bin/python manage.py migrate --noinput
Operations to perform:
  Apply all migrations: auth, contenttypes, lists, sessions
Running migrations:
  Applying contenttypes.0001_initial... OK
  [...]
  Applying lists.0004_item_list... OK
  Applying sessions.0001_initial... OK
```

That looks good. We restart the server:

```
elspeth@server:$ ./virtualenv/bin/python manage.py runserver 0.0.0.0:8000
```

And try the FTs again:

```
$ STAGING_SERVER=superlists-staging.ottg.eu:8000 ./manage.py test functional_tests
[...]

...
----------------------------------------------------------------------
Ran 3 tests in 10.718s

OK
```

Hooray, that's a working deploy!

Time for a well-earned tea break I think, and perhaps a chocolate biscuit (*https://en.wikipedia.org/wiki/Digestive_biscuit*).

Success! Our Hack Deployment Works

Phew. Well, it took a bit of hacking about, but now we can be reassured that the basic piping works. Notice that the FT was able to guide us incrementally towards a working site.

But we really can't be using the Django dev server in production, or running on port 8000 forever. In the next chapter, we'll make our hacky deployment more production-ready.

Test-Driving Server Configuration and Deployment

Tests take some of the uncertainty out of deployment
> For developers, server administration is always "fun", by which I mean, a process full of uncertainty and surprises. My aim during this chapter was to show that a functional test suite can take some of the uncertainty out of the process.

Some typical pain points—networking, ports, static files, and the database
> The things that you need to keep an eye out for on any deployment include making sure your database configuration, static files, software dependencies, and custom settings that differ between development and production. You'll need to think through each of these for your own deployments.

Tests allow us to experiment and work incrementally
> Whenever we make a change to our server configuration, we can rerun the test suite, and be confident that everything works as well as it did before. It allows us to experiment with our setup with less fear (as we'll see in the next chapter).

Getting to a Production-Ready Deployment

Our deployment is working fine but it's not production-ready. Let's try to get it there, using the tests to guide us.

In a way we're applying the Red-Green-Refactor cycle to our server deployment. Our hacky deployment got us to Green, and now we're going to Refactor, working incrementally (just as we would while coding), trying to move from working state to working state, and using the FTs to detect any regressions.

What We Need to Do

What's wrong with our hacky deployment? A few things: first, we need to host our app on the "normal" port 80 so that people can access it using a regular URL.

Perhaps more importantly, we shouldn't use the Django dev server for production; it's not designed for real-life workloads. Instead, we'll use the popular combination of the Nginx web server and the Gunicorn Python/WSGI server.

Several settings in *settings.py* are currently unacceptable too. DEBUG=True, is strongly recommended against for production, and we'll want to fix ALLOWED_HOSTS, and set a unique SECRET_KEY too.

Finally, we don't want to have to SSH in to our server to actually start the site. Instead, we'll write a Systemd config file so that it starts up automatically whenever the server (re)boots.

Let's go through and see if we can fix each of these things one by one.

Switching to Nginx

Installation

We'll need a real web server, and all the cool kids are using Nginx these days, so we will too. Having fought with Apache for many years, I can tell you it's a blessed relief in terms of the readability of its config files, if nothing else!

Installing Nginx on my server was a matter of doing an `apt install`, and I could then see the default Nginx "Hello World" screen:

```
elspeth@server:$ sudo apt install nginx
elspeth@server:$ sudo systemctl start nginx
```

Now you should be able to go to the normal port-80 URL address of your server, and see the "Welcome to nginx" page at this point, as in Figure 10-1.

If you don't see it, it may be because your firewall does not open port 80 to the world. On AWS, for example, you may need to configure the "security group" for your server to open port 80.

Figure 10-1. Nginx—it works!

The FT Now Fails, But Show Nginx Is Running

We can also confirm that if we run the FT *without* specifying port 8000, we see them fail again—one of them in particular should now mention Nginx:

```
$ STAGING_SERVER=superlists-staging.ottg.eu python manage.py test functional_tests
[...]
selenium.common.exceptions.NoSuchElementException: Message: Unable to locate
element: [id="id_new_item"]
[...]
AssertionError: 'To-Do' not found in 'Welcome to nginx!'
```

Next we'll configure the Nginx web server to talk to Django

Simple Nginx Configuration

We create an Nginx config file to tell it to send requests for our staging site along to
Django. A minimal config looks like this:

server: /etc/nginx/sites-available/superlists-staging.ottg.eu

```
server {
    listen 80;
    server_name superlists-staging.ottg.eu;

    location / {
        proxy_pass http://localhost:8000;
    }
}
```

This config says it will only listen for our staging domain, and will "proxy" all
requests to the local port 8000 where it expects to find Django waiting to respond.

I saved this to a file called *superlists-staging.ottg.eu* inside the */etc/nginx/sites-available*
folder.

> Not sure how to edit a file on the server? There's always vi, which
> I'll keep encouraging you to learn a bit of, but perhaps today is
> already too full of new things. Try the relatively beginner-friendly
> nano (*http://www.howtogeek.com/howto/42980/the-beginners-guide-
> to-nano-the-linux-command-line-text-editor/*) instead. Note you'll
> also need to use sudo because the file is in a system folder.

We then add it to the enabled sites for the server by creating a symlink to it:

```
# reset our env var (if necessary)
elspeth@server:$ export SITENAME=superlists-staging.ottg.eu

elspeth@server:$ cd /etc/nginx/sites-enabled/
elspeth@server:$ sudo ln -s /etc/nginx/sites-available/$SITENAME $SITENAME

# check our symlink has worked:
elspeth@server:$ readlink -f $SITENAME
/etc/nginx/sites-available/superlists-staging.ottg.eu
```

That's the Debian/Ubuntu preferred way of saving Nginx configurations—the real config file in *sites-available*, and a symlink in *sites-enabled*; the idea is that it makes it easier to switch sites on or off.

We also may as well remove the default "Welcome to nginx" config, to avoid any confusion:

```
elspeth@server:$ sudo rm /etc/nginx/sites-enabled/default
```

And now to test it. First we reload nginx and restart our server:

```
elspeth@server:$ sudo systemctl reload nginx
elspeth@server:$ cd ~/sites/$SITENAME
elspeth@server:$ ./virtualenv/bin/python manage.py runserver 8000
```

 If you ever find that Nginx isn't behaving as expected, try the command sudo nginx -t, which does a config test and will warn you of any problems in your configuration files.

And now we can try our FTs without the port 8000:

```
$ STAGING_SERVER=superlists-staging.ottg.eu ./manage.py test functional_tests --failfast
[...]

...
-------------------------------------------------------------------
Ran 3 tests in 10.718s

OK
```

Hooray! Back to a working state.

 I also had to edit */etc/nginx/nginx.conf* and uncomment a line saying server_names_hash_bucket_size 64; to get my long domain name to work. You may not have this problem; Nginx will warn you when you do a reload if it has any trouble with its config files.

Tips on Debugging Nginx

Deployments are tricky! If ever things don't go exactly as expected, here are a few tips and things to look out for, particularly around Nginx.

- I'm sure you already have, but double-check that each file is exactly where it should be and has the right contents—a single stray character can make all the difference.

- Nginx error logs go into */var/log/nginx/error.log*.

- You can ask Nginx to "check" its config using the -t flag: `nginx -t`
- Make sure your browser isn't caching an out-of-date response. Use Ctrl-Refresh, or start a new private browser window.
- This may be clutching at straws, but I've sometimes seen inexplicable behaviour on the server that's only been resolved when I fully restarted it with a `sudo reboot`.

If you ever get completely stuck, there's always the option of blowing away your server and starting again from scratch! It should go faster the second time…

Switching to Gunicorn

Do you know why the Django mascot is a pony? The story is that Django comes with so many things you want: an ORM, all sorts of middleware, the admin site… "What else do you want, a pony?" Well, Gunicorn stands for "Green Unicorn", which I guess is what you'd want next if you already had a pony…

```
elspeth@server:$ ./virtualenv/bin/pip install gunicorn
```

Gunicorn will need to know a path to a WSGI server, which is usually a function called `application`. Django provides one in *superlists/wsgi.py*:

```
elspeth@server:$ ./virtualenv/bin/gunicorn superlists.wsgi:application
2013-05-27 16:22:01 [10592] [INFO] Starting gunicorn 0.19.7.1
2013-05-27 16:22:01 [10592] [INFO] Listening at: http://127.0.0.1:8000 (10592)
[...]
```

But if we run the functional tests, once again you'll see that they are warning us of a problem. The test for adding list items passes happily, but the test for layout + styling fails. Good job, tests!

```
$ STAGING_SERVER=superlists-staging.ottg.eu python manage.py test functional_tests
[...]
AssertionError: 106.5 != 512 within 10 delta
FAILED (failures=1)
```

And indeed, if you take a look at the site, you'll find the CSS is all broken, as in Figure 10-2.

The reason that the CSS is broken is that although the Django dev server will serve static files magically for you, Gunicorn doesn't. Now is the time to tell Nginx to do it instead.

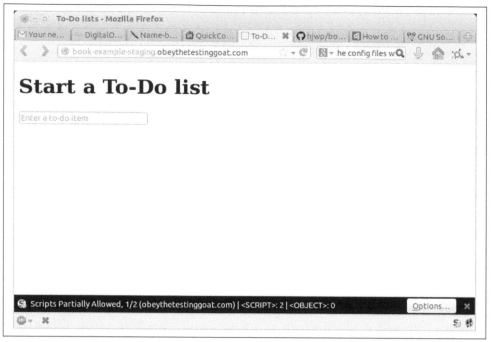

Figure 10-2. Broken CSS

One step forward, one step backward, but once again we've identified the problem nice and early. Moving on!

> At this point if you see a "502 - Bad Gateway", it's probably because you forgot to restart Gunicorn.

Getting Nginx to Serve Static Files

First we run `collectstatic` to copy all the static files to a folder where Nginx can find them:

```
elspeth@server:$ ./virtualenv/bin/python manage.py collectstatic --noinput
[...]
15 static files copied to '/home/elspeth/sites/superlists-staging.ottg.eu/static'
elspeth@server:$ ls static/
base.css  bootstrap
```

Now we tell Nginx to start serving those static files for us, by adding a second `location` directive to the config:

```
server {
    listen 80;
    server_name superlists-staging.ottg.eu;

    location /static {
        alias /home/elspeth/sites/superlists-staging.ottg.eu/static;
    }

    location / {
        proxy_pass http://localhost:8000;
    }
}
```

Reload Nginx and restart Gunicorn…

```
elspeth@server:$ sudo systemctl reload nginx
elspeth@server:$ ./virtualenv/bin/gunicorn superlists.wsgi:application
```

And if you take another manual look at your site, things should look much healthier. Let's rerun our FTs:

```
$ STAGING_SERVER=superlists-staging.ottg.eu python manage.py test functional_tests
[...]

...
.........   ---------------------------------------------
Ran 3 tests in 10.718s

OK
```

Phew.

Switching to Using Unix Sockets

When we want to serve both staging and live, we can't have both servers trying to use port 8000. We could decide to allocate different ports, but that's a bit arbitrary, and it would be dangerously easy to get it wrong and start the staging server on the live port, or vice versa.

A better solution is to use Unix domain sockets—they're like files on disk, but can be used by Nginx and Gunicorn to talk to each other. We'll put our sockets in */tmp*. Let's change the proxy settings in Nginx:

```
server {
    listen 80;
    server_name superlists-staging.ottg.eu;

    location /static {
        alias /home/elspeth/sites/superlists-staging.ottg.eu/static;
    }

    location / {
        proxy_pass http://unix:/tmp/superlists-staging.ottg.eu.socket;
    }
}
```

Now we restart Gunicorn, but this time telling it to listen on a socket instead of on the default port:

```
elspeth@server:$ sudo systemctl reload nginx
elspeth@server:$ ./virtualenv/bin/gunicorn --bind \
    unix:/tmp/superlists-staging.ottg.eu.socket superlists.wsgi:application
```

And again, we rerun the functional test again, to make sure things still pass:

```
$ STAGING_SERVER=superlists-staging.ottg.eu python manage.py test functional_tests
[...]
OK
```

Hooray, a change that went without a hitch for once! Moving on.

Using Environment Variables to Adjust Settings for Production

We know there are several things in *settings.py* that we want to change for production:

- ALLOWED_HOSTS is currently set to "*" which isn't secure. We want it to be set to only match the site we're supposed to be serving (*superlists-staging.ottg.eu*).

- DEBUG mode is all very well for hacking about on your own server, but leaving those pages full of tracebacks available to the world isn't secure (*https://docs.djan goproject.com/en/1.11/ref/settings/#debug*).

- SECRET_KEY is used by Django uses for some of its crypto—things like cookies and CSRF protection. It's good practice to make sure the secret key on the server is different from the one in your source code repo, because that code might be visible to strangers. We'll want to generate a new, random one but then keep it the same for the foreseeable future (find out more in the Django docs (*https://docs.djangoproject.com/en/1.11/topics/signing/*)).

Development, staging and live sites always have some differences in their configuration. Environment variables are a good place to store those different settings. See "the 12-factor app" (*http://www.clearlytech.com/2014/01/04/12-factor-apps-plain-english/*).[1]

Here's one way to make it work:

superlists/settings.py (ch08l004)

```
if 'DJANGO_DEBUG_FALSE' in os.environ:     ❶
    DEBUG = False
    SECRET_KEY = os.environ['DJANGO_SECRET_KEY']     ❷
    ALLOWED_HOSTS = [os.environ['SITENAME']]     ❷
else:
    DEBUG = True     ❸
    SECRET_KEY = 'insecure-key-for-dev'
    ALLOWED_HOSTS = []
```

❶ We say we'll use an environment variable called DJANGO_DEBUG_FALSE to switch debug mode off, and in effect require production settings (it doesn't matter what we set it to, just that it's there).

❷ And now we say that, if debug mode is off, we *require* the SECRET_KEY and ALLOWED_HOSTS to be set by two more environment variables (one of which can be the $SITENAME variable we've been using at the command-line so far).

❸ Otherwise we fall-back to the insecure, debug mode settings that are useful for Dev.

There are other ways you might set up the logic, making various variables optional, but I think this gives us a little bit of protection against accidentally forgetting to set one. The end result is that you don't need to set any of them for dev, but production needs all three, and it will error if any are missing.

 Better to fail hard than allow a typo in an environment variable name to leave you running with insecure settings.

Let's do our usual dance of committing locally, and pushing to GitHub:

---

1 Another common way of handling this is to have different versions of *settings.py* for dev and prod. That can work fine too, but it can get confusing to manage. Environment variables also have the advantage of working for non-Django stuff too…

```
$ git commit -am "use env vars for prod settings DEBUG, ALLOWED_HOSTS, SECRET_KEY"
$ git push
```

Then pull it down on the server, export a couple of environment variables, and restart
Gunicorn:

```
elspeth@server:$ git pull
elspeth@server:$ export DJANGO_DEBUG_FALSE=y DJANGO_SECRET_KEY=abc123
# we'll set the secret to something more secure later!
elspeth@server:$ ./virtualenv/bin/gunicorn --bind \
    unix:/tmp/superlists-staging.ottg.eu.socket superlists.wsgi:application
```

And use a test run to reassure ourselves that things still work…

```
$ STAGING_SERVER=superlists-staging.ottg.eu ./manage.py test functional_tests --failfast
[...]
AssertionError: 'To-Do' not found in ''
```

Oops. Let's take a look manually: Figure 10-3.

Figure 10-3. An ugly 400 error

Essential Googling the Error Message

Something's gone wrong. But once again, by running our FTs frequently, we're able to
identify the problem early, before we've changed too many things. In this case the
only thing we've changed is *settings.py*. We've changed three settings—which one
might be at fault?

Let's use the tried and tested "Googling the error message" technique (Figure 10-4).

The internet will make those bad words go away

Essential

Googling the
Error Message

O RLY?

The Practical Developer
@ThePracticalDev

Figure 10-4. An indispensable publication (source: https://news.ycombinator.com/item? id=11459601)

The very first link in my search results for Django 400 Bad Request (*https:// www.google.co.uk/?q=django+400+bad+request*) suggests that a 400 error is usually to do with ALLOWED_HOSTS. In the last chapter we had a nice Django Debug page saying "DisallowedHost error" (Figure 9-2), but now because we have DEBUG=False, we just get the minimal, unfriendly 400 page.

But what's wrong with ALLOWED_HOSTS? After double-checking it for typos, we might do a little more Googling with some relevant keywords: Django ALLOWED_HOSTS Nginx (*https://www.google.co.uk/search?q=django+allowed+hosts+nginx*). Once again, the first result (*https://www.digitalocean.com/community/questions/bad-request-400-django-nginx-gunicorn-on-debian-7*) gives us the clue we need.

Fixing ALLOWED_HOSTS with Nginx: passing on the Host header

The problem turns out to be that, by default, Nginx strips out the Host headers from requests it forwards, and it makes it "look like" they came from *localhost* after all. We can tell it to forward on the original host header by adding the proxy_set_header directive:

server: /etc/nginx/sites-available/superlists-staging.ottg.eu

```
server {
    listen 80;
    server_name superlists-staging.ottg.eu;

    location /static {
        alias /home/elspeth/sites/superlists-staging.ottg.eu/static;
    }

    location / {
        proxy_pass http://unix:/tmp/superlists-staging.ottg.eu.socket;
        proxy_set_header Host $host;
    }
}
```

Reload Nginx once more:

```
elspeth@server:$ sudo systemctl reload nginx
```

And then we try our FTs again:

```
$ STAGING_SERVER=superlists-staging.ottg.eu python manage.py test functional_tests
[...]
OK
```

Phew. Back to working again.

Using a .env File to Store Our Environment Variables

Another little refactor. Setting environment variables manually in various shells is a pain, and it'd be nice to have them all available in a single place. The Python world (and other people out there too) seems to be standardising around using the convention of a file called *.env* in the project root.

First we add it *.env* to our *.gitignore*—this file is going to be used for secrets, and we don't ever want them ending up on GitHub:

```
$ echo .env >> .gitignore
$ git commit -am"gitignore .env file"
$ git push
```

Next let's save our environment on the server:

```
elspeth@server:$ pwd
/home/elspeth/sites/superlists-staging.ottg.eu
elspeth@server:$ echo DJANGO_DEBUG_FALSE=y >> .env
elspeth@server:$ echo SITENAME=$SITENAME >>.env
```

 The way I've used the environment files in *settings.py* means that the *.env* file is not required on your own machine, only in staging/ production.

Generating a secure SECRET_KEY

While we're at it we'll also generate a more secure secret key using a little Python one-liner.

```
elspeth@server:$ echo DJANGO_SECRET_KEY=$(
python3.6 -c"import random; print(''.join(random.SystemRandom().
choices('abcdefghijklmnopqrstuvwxyz0123456789', k=50)))"
) >> .env
elspeth@server:$ cat .env
DJANGO_DEBUG_FALSE=y
SITENAME=superlists-staging.ottg.eu
DJANGO_SECRET_KEY=[...]
```

Now let's check our env file works, and restart gunicorn:

```
elspeth@server:$ unset DJANGO_SECRET_KEY DJANGO_DEBUG_FALSE SITENAME
elspeth@server:$ echo $DJANGO_DEBUG_FALSE-none
-none
elspeth@server:$ set -a; source .env; set +a
elspeth@server:$ echo $DJANGO_DEBUG_FALSE-none
y-none
elspeth@server:$ ./virtualenv/bin/gunicorn --bind \
    unix:/tmp/$SITENAME.socket superlists.wsgi:application
```

And we rerun our FTs to check that they agree, everything still works:

```
$ STAGING_SERVER=superlists-staging.ottg.eu python manage.py test functional_tests
[...]
OK
```

Excellent! That went without a hitch :)

I've shown the use of a *.env* file and manually extracting environment variables in *settings.py*, but there are some plugins that do this stuff for you that are definitely worth investigating. Look into django-environ (*https://django-environ.readthedocs.io/en/latest/*), django-dotenv (*https://github.com/jpadilla/django-dotenv*), and Pipenv (*https://docs.pipenv.org/*).

Using Systemd to Make Sure Gunicorn Starts on Boot

Our final step is to make sure that the server starts up Gunicorn automatically on boot, and reloads it automatically if it crashes. On Ubuntu, the way to do this is using Systemd.

Here's what a Systemd config file looks like

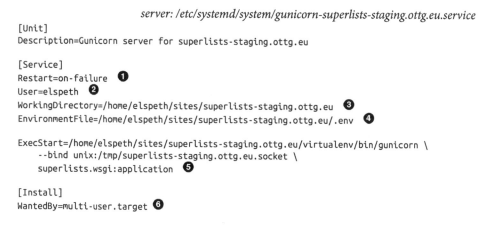

server: /etc/systemd/system/gunicorn-superlists-staging.ottg.eu.service

```
[Unit]
Description=Gunicorn server for superlists-staging.ottg.eu

[Service]
Restart=on-failure        ❶
User=elspeth               ❷
WorkingDirectory=/home/elspeth/sites/superlists-staging.ottg.eu        ❸
EnvironmentFile=/home/elspeth/sites/superlists-staging.ottg.eu/.env    ❹

ExecStart=/home/elspeth/sites/superlists-staging.ottg.eu/virtualenv/bin/gunicorn \
    --bind unix:/tmp/superlists-staging.ottg.eu.socket \
    superlists.wsgi:application        ❺

[Install]
WantedBy=multi-user.target        ❻
```

Systemd is joyously simple to configure (especially if you've ever had the dubious pleasure of writing an `init.d` script), and is fairly self-explanatory.

❶ `Restart=on-failure` will restart the process automatically if it crashes.

❷ `User=elspeth` makes the process run as the "elspeth" user.

❸ `WorkingDirectory` sets the current working directory.

❹ `EnvironmentFile` points Systemd towards our *.env* file and tells it to load environment variables from there.

❺ `ExecStart` is the actual process to execute. I'm using the \ line continuation characters to split the full command over multiple lines, for readability, but it could all go on one line.

❻ WantedBy in the [Install] section is what tells Systemd we want this service to start on boot.

Systemd scripts live in */etc/systemd/system*, and their names must end in *.service*.

Now we tell Systemd to start Gunicorn with the systemctl command:

```
# this command is necessary to tell Systemd to load our new config file
elspeth@server:$ sudo systemctl daemon-reload
# this command tells Systemd to always load our service on boot
elspeth@server:$ sudo systemctl enable gunicorn-superlists-staging.ottg.eu
# this command actually starts our service
elspeth@server:$ sudo systemctl start gunicorn-superlists-staging.ottg.eu
```

(You should find the systemctl command responds to tab completion, including of the service name, by the way.)

Now we can rerun the FTs to see that everything still works. You can even test that the site comes back up if you reboot the server!

```
$ STAGING_SERVER=superlists-staging.ottg.eu python manage.py test functional_tests
[...]
OK
```

More Debugging Tips and Commands

A few more places to look and things to try, now that we've introduced Gunicorn and Systemd into the mix, should things not go according to plan:

- You can check the Systemd logs using sudo journalctl -u gunicorn-superlists-staging.ottg.eu.

- You can ask Systemd to check the validity of your service configuration: systemd-analyze verify /path/to/my.service.

- Remember to restart both services whenever you make changes.

- If you make changes to the Systemd config file, you need to run daemon-reload before systemctl restart to see the effect of your changes.

Saving Our Changes: Adding Gunicorn to Our requirements.txt

Back in the *local* copy of your repo, we should add Gunicorn to the list of packages we need in our virtualenvs:

```
$ pip install gunicorn
$ pip freeze | grep gunicorn >> requirements.txt
$ git commit -am "Add gunicorn to virtualenv requirements"
$ git push
```

On Windows, at the time of writing, Gunicorn would `pip install` quite happily, but it wouldn't actually work if you tried to use it. Thankfully we only ever run it on the server, so that's not a problem. And, Windows support is being discussed (*http://stackover flow.com/questions/11087682/does-gunicorn-run-on-windows*)...

Thinking About Automating

Let's recap our provisioning and deployment procedures:

Provisioning

1. Assume we have a user account and home folder

2. `add-apt-repository ppa:deadsnakes/ppa && apt update`

3. `apt install nginx git python3.6 python3.6-venv`

4. Add Nginx config for virtual host

5. Add Systemd job for Gunicorn (including unique `SECRET_KEY`)

Deployment

1. Create directory in *~/sites*

2. Pull down source code

3. Start virtualenv in *virtualenv*

4. `pip install -r requirements.txt`

5. `manage.py migrate` for database

6. `collectstatic` for static files

7. Restart Gunicorn job

8. Run FTs to check everything works

Assuming we're not ready to entirely automate our provisioning process, how should we save the results of our investigation so far? I would say that the Nginx and Systemd config files should probably be saved somewhere, in a way that makes it easy to reuse them later. Let's save them in a new subfolder in our repo.

Saving Templates for Our Provisioning Config Files

First, we create the subfolder:

```
$ mkdir deploy_tools
```

Here's a generic template for our Nginx config:

deploy_tools/nginx.template.conf

```
server {
    listen 80;
    server_name DOMAIN;

    location /static {
        alias /home/elspeth/sites/DOMAIN/static;
    }

    location / {
        proxy_pass http://unix:/tmp/DOMAIN.socket;
        proxy_set_header Host $host;
    }
}
```

And here's one for the Gunicorn Sytemd service:

deploy_tools/gunicorn-systemd.template.service

```
[Unit]
Description=Gunicorn server for DOMAIN

[Service]
Restart=on-failure
User=elspeth
WorkingDirectory=/home/elspeth/sites/DOMAIN
EnvironmentFile=/home/elspeth/sites/DOMAIN/.env

ExecStart=/home/elspeth/sites/DOMAIN/virtualenv/bin/gunicorn \
    --bind unix:/tmp/DOMAIN.socket \
    superlists.wsgi:application

[Install]
WantedBy=multi-user.target
```

Now it's easy for us to use those two files to generate a new site, by doing a find and replace on DOMAIN.

For the rest, just keeping a few notes is OK. Why not keep them in a file in the repo too?

```
Provisioning a new site
=======================

## Required packages:

* nginx
* Python 3.6
* virtualenv + pip
* Git

eg, on Ubuntu:

    sudo add-apt-repository ppa:deadsnakes/ppa
    sudo apt update
    sudo apt install nginx git python36 python3.6-venv

## Nginx Virtual Host config

* see nginx.template.conf
* replace DOMAIN with, e.g., staging.my-domain.com

## Systemd service

* see gunicorn-systemd.template.service
* replace DOMAIN with, e.g., staging.my-domain.com

## Folder structure:

Assume we have a user account at /home/username

/home/username
└── sites
    ├── DOMAIN1
    │   ├── .env
    │   ├── db.sqlite3
    │   ├── manage.py etc
    │   ├── static
    │   └── virtualenv
    └── DOMAIN2
        ├── .env
        ├── db.sqlite3
        ├── etc
```

We can do a commit for those:

```
$ git add deploy_tools
$ git status # see three new files
$ git commit -m "Notes and template config files for provisioning"
```

Our source tree will now look something like this:

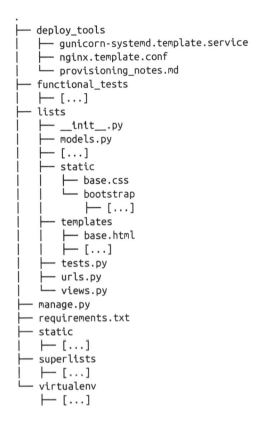

```
.
├── deploy_tools
│   ├── gunicorn-systemd.template.service
│   ├── nginx.template.conf
│   └── provisioning_notes.md
├── functional_tests
│   ├── [...]
├── lists
│   ├── __init__.py
│   ├── models.py
│   ├── [...]
│   ├── static
│   │   ├── base.css
│   │   └── bootstrap
│   │       ├── [...]
│   ├── templates
│   │   ├── base.html
│   │   │   ├── [...]
│   ├── tests.py
│   ├── urls.py
│   └── views.py
├── manage.py
├── requirements.txt
├── static
│   ├── [...]
├── superlists
│   ├── [...]
└── virtualenv
    ├── [...]
```

Saving Our Progress

Being able to run our FTs against a staging server can be very reassuring. But, in most cases, you don't want to run your FTs against your "real" server. In order to "save our work", and reassure ourselves that the production server will work just as well as the real server, we need to make our deployment process repeatable.

Automation is the answer, and it's the topic of the next chapter.

Production-Readiness for Server Deployments

A few things to think about when trying to build a production-ready server environment:

Don't use the Django dev server in production
Something like Gunicorn or uWSGI is a better tool for running Django; it will let you run multiple workers, for example.

Don't use Django to serve your static files
There's no point in using a Python process to do the simple job of serving static files. Nginx can do it, but so can other web servers like Apache or uWSGI.

Check your settings.py for dev-only settings
DEBUG=True, ALLOWED_HOSTS and SECRET_KEY are the ones we came across, but you will probably have others (we'll see more when we start to send emails from the server).

Security
A serious discussion of server security is beyond the scope of this book, and I'd warn against running your own servers without learning a good bit more about it. (One reason people choose to use a PaaS to host their code is that it means a slightly fewer security issues to worry about.) If you'd like a place to start, here's as good a place as any: My first 5 minutes on a server (*https://plusbryan.com/my-first-5-minutes-on-a-server-or-essential-security-for-linux-servers*). I can definitely recommend the eye-opening experience of installing fail2ban and watching its logfiles to see just how quickly it picks up on random drive-by attempts to brute force your SSH login. The internet is a wild place!

General Server Debugging Tips

The most important lesson to remember from this chapter is to work incrementally, make one change at a time, and run your tests frequently.

When things (inevitably) go wrong, resist the temptation to flail about and make other unrelated changes in the hope that things will start working again; instead, stop, go backward if necessary to get to a working state, and figure out what went wrong before moving forward again.

It's just as easy to fall into the Refactoring-Cat trap on the server!

Automating Deployment with Fabric

Automate, automate, automate.

—Cay Horstman

Automating deployment is critical for our staging tests to mean anything. By making sure the deployment procedure is repeatable, we give ourselves assurances that everything will go well when we deploy to production. (These days people sometimes use the words "Infrastructure as code" to describe automation of deployments, and provisioning.)

Fabric is a tool which lets you automate commands that you want to run on servers. "fabric3" is the Python 3 fork:

```
$ pip install fabric3
```

 It's safe to ignore any errors that say "failed building wheel" during the Fabric3 installation, as long as it says "Successfully installed..." at the end.

The usual setup is to have a file called *fabfile.py*, which will contain one or more functions that can later be invoked from a command-line tool called fab, like this:

```
fab function_name:host=SERVER_ADDRESS
```

That will call function_name, passing in a connection to the server at SERVER_ADDRESS. There are lots of other options for specifying usernames and passwords, which you can find out about using fab --help.

Breakdown of a Fabric Script for Our Deployment

The best way to see how it works is with an example. Here's one I made earlier (*http:// www.bbc.co.uk/cult/classic/bluepeter/valpetejohn/trivia.shtml*), automating all the deployment steps we've been going through. The main function is called deploy; that's the one we'll invoke from the command line. It then calls out to several helper functions, which we'll build together one by one, explaining as we go.

deploy_tools/fabfile.py (ch09l001)

```
import random
from fabric.contrib.files import append, exists
from fabric.api import cd, env, local, run

REPO_URL = 'https://github.com/hjwp/book-example.git'  ❶

def deploy():
    site_folder = f'/home/{env.user}/sites/{env.host}'  ❷
    run(f'mkdir -p {site_folder}')  ❸❹
    with cd(site_folder):  ❺
        _get_latest_source()
        _update_virtualenv()
        _create_or_update_dotenv()
        _update_static_files()
        _update_database()
```

❶ You'll want to update the REPO_URL variable with the URL of your own Git repo on its code-sharing site.

❷ env.user will contain the username you're using to log in to the server; env.host will be the address of the server we've specified at the command line (e.g., *super-lists.ottg.eu*).[1]

❸ run is the most common Fabric command. It says "run this shell command on the server". The run commands in this chapter will replicate many of the commands we did manually in the last two.

❹ mkdir -p is a useful flavour of mkdir, which is better in two ways: it can create directories several levels deep, and it only creates them if necessary. So, mkdir -p /tmp/foo/bar will create the directory *bar* but also its parent directory *foo* if it needs to. It also won't complain if *bar* already exists.

---

1 If you're wondering why we're building up paths manually with f-strings instead of the os.path.join command we saw earlier, it's because path.join will use backslashes if you run the script from Windows, but we definitely want forward slashes on the server. That's a common gotcha!

❺ cd is a fabric context manager that says "run all the following statements inside this working directory".[2]

Hopefully all of those helper functions have fairly self-descriptive names. Because any function in a fabfile can theoretically be invoked from the command line, I've used the convention of a leading underscore to indicate that they're not meant to be part of the "public API" of the fabfile. Let's take a look at each one, in chronological order.

Pulling Down Our Source Code with Git

Next we want to download the latest version of our source code to the server, like we did with git pull in the previous chapters:

deploy_tools/fabfile.py (ch09l003)

```python
def _get_latest_source():
    if exists('.git'):      ❶
        run('git fetch')    ❷
    else:
        run(f'git clone {REPO_URL} .')    ❸
    current_commit = local("git log -n 1 --format=%H", capture=True)    ❹
    run(f'git reset --hard {current_commit}')    ❺
```

❶ exists checks whether a directory or file already exists on the server. We look for the *.git* hidden folder to check whether the repo has already been cloned in our site folder.

❷ git fetch inside an existing repository pulls down all the latest commits from the web (it's like git pull, but without immediately updating the live source tree).

❸ Alternatively we use git clone with the repo URL to bring down a fresh source tree.

❹ Fabric's local command runs a command on your local machine—it's just a wrapper around subprocess.call really, but it's quite convenient. Here we capture the output from that git log invocation to get the ID of the current commit that's on your local PC. That means the server will end up with whatever code is currently checked out on your machine (as long as you've pushed it up to the server. Another common gotcha!).

---

2 You may be wondering why we didn't just use run to do the cd. It's because Fabric doesn't store any state from one command to the next—each run command runs in a separate shell session on the server.

❺ We reset --hard to that commit, which will blow away any current changes in the server's code directory.

The end result of this is that we either do a git clone if it's a fresh deploy, or we do a git fetch + git reset --hard if a previous version of the code is already there; the equivalent of the git pull we used when we did it manually, but with the reset --hard to force overwriting any local changes.

Updating the Virtualenv

Next we create or update the virtualenv:

deploy_tools/fabfile.py (ch09l004)

```
def _update_virtualenv():
    if not exists('virtualenv/bin/pip'):  ❶
        run(f'python3.6 -m venv virtualenv')
    run('./virtualenv/bin/pip install -r requirements.txt')  ❷
```

❶ We look inside the virtualenv folder for the pip executable as a way of checking whether it already exists.

❷ Then we use pip install -r like we did earlier.

Creating a New .env File if Necessary

Our deploy script can also save us some of the manual work creating a *.env* script:

deploy_tools/fabfile.py (ch09l005)

```
def _create_or_update_dotenv():
    append('.env', 'DJANGO_DEBUG_FALSE=y')  ❶
    append('.env', f'SITENAME={env.host}')
    current_contents = run('cat .env')  ❷
    if 'DJANGO_SECRET_KEY' not in current_contents:  ❷
        new_secret = ''.join(random.SystemRandom().choices(  ❸
            'abcdefghijklmnopqrstuvwxyz0123456789', k=50
        ))
        append('.env', f'DJANGO_SECRET_KEY={new_secret}')
```

❶ The append command conditionally adds a line to a file, if that line isn't already there.

❷ For the secret key we first manually check whether there's already an entry in the file…

❸ And if not, we use our little one-liner from earlier to generate a new one (we can't rely on the append's conditional logic here because our new key and any potential existing one won't be the same).

Updating Static Files

Updating static files is a single command:

deploy_tools/fabfile.py (ch09l006)

```
def _update_static_files():
    run('./virtualenv/bin/python manage.py collectstatic --noinput') ❶
```

❶ We use the virtualenv version of Python whenever we need to run a Django *manage.py* command, to make sure we get the virtualenv version of Django, not the system one.

Migrating the Database If Necessary

Finally, we update the database with `manage.py migrate`:

deploy_tools/fabfile.py (ch09l007)

```
def _update_database():
    run('./virtualenv/bin/python manage.py migrate --noinput') ❶
```

❶ The `--noinput` removes any interactive yes/no confirmations that Fabric would find hard to deal with.

And we're done! Lots of new things to take in, I imagine, but I hope you can see how this is all replicating the work we did manually earlier, with a bit of logic to make it work both for brand new deployments and for existing ones that just need updating. If you like words with Latin roots, you might describe it as *idempotent*, which means it has the same effect whether you run it once or multiple times.

Trying It Out

Before we try, we need to make sure our latest commits are up on GitHub, or we won't be able to sync the server with our local commits.

```
$ git push
```

Now let's try our Fabric script out on our existing staging site, and see it working to update a deployment that already exists:

```
$ cd deploy_tools
$ fab deploy:host=elspeth@superlists-staging.ottg.eu
[elspeth@superlists-staging.ottg.eu] Executing task 'deploy'
[elspeth@superlists-staging.ottg.eu] run: mkdir -p
/home/elspeth/sites/superlists-staging.ottg.eu
[elspeth@superlists-staging.ottg.eu] run: git fetch
[elspeth@superlists-staging.ottg.eu] out: remote: Counting objects: [...]
[elspeth@superlists-staging.ottg.eu] out: remote: Compressing objects: [...]
[localhost] local: git log -n 1 --format=%H
[elspeth@superlists-staging.ottg.eu] run: git reset --hard
[...]
[elspeth@superlists-staging.ottg.eu] out: HEAD is now at [...]
[elspeth@superlists-staging.ottg.eu] out:
[elspeth@superlists-staging.ottg.eu] run: ./virtualenv/bin/pip install -r
requirements.txt
[elspeth@superlists-staging.ottg.eu] out: Requirement already satisfied:
django==1.11 in ./virtualenv/lib/python3.6/site-packages (from -r
requirements.txt (line 1))
[elspeth@superlists-staging.ottg.eu] out: Requirement already satisfied:
gunicorn==19.7.1 in ./virtualenv/lib/python3.6/site-packages (from -r
requirements.txt (line 2))
[elspeth@superlists-staging.ottg.eu] out: Requirement already satisfied: pytz
in ./virtualenv/lib/python3.6/site-packages (from django==1.11->-r
requirements.txt (line 1))
[elspeth@superlists-staging.ottg.eu] out:
[elspeth@superlists-staging.ottg.eu] run: ./virtualenv/bin/python manage.py
collectstatic --noinput
[elspeth@superlists-staging.ottg.eu] out:
[elspeth@superlists-staging.ottg.eu] out: 0 static files copied to
'/home/elspeth/sites/superlists-staging.ottg.eu/static', 15 unmodified.
[elspeth@superlists-staging.ottg.eu] out:
[elspeth@superlists-staging.ottg.eu] run: ./virtualenv/bin/python manage.py
migrate --noinput
[elspeth@superlists-staging.ottg.eu] out: Operations to perform:
[elspeth@superlists-staging.ottg.eu] out:   Apply all migrations: auth,
contenttypes, lists, sessions
[elspeth@superlists-staging.ottg.eu] out: Running migrations:
[elspeth@superlists-staging.ottg.eu] out:   No migrations to apply.
[elspeth@superlists-staging.ottg.eu] out:
```

Awesome. I love making computers spew out pages and pages of output like that (in fact I find it hard to stop myself from making little '70s computer *<brrp, brrrp, brrrp>* noises like Mother in *Alien*). If we look through it we can see it is doing our bidding: the mkdir -p command goes through happily, even though the directory already exist. Next git pull pulls down the couple of commits we just made. Then pip install -r requirements.txt completes happily, noting that the existing virtualenv already has all the packages we need. collectstatic also notices that the static files are all already there, and finally the migrate completes without needing to apply anything.

For this script to work, you need to have done a `git push` of your current local commit, so that the server can pull it down and `reset` to it. If you see an error saying `Could not parse object`, try doing a `git push`.

Fabric Configuration

If you are using an SSH key to log in, are storing it in the default location, and are using the same username on the server as locally, then Fabric should "just work". If you aren't, there are several tweaks you may need to apply in order to get the `fab` command to do your bidding. They revolve around the username, the location of the SSH key to use, or the password.

You can pass these in to Fabric at the command line. Check out:

```
$ fab --help
```

Or see the Fabric documentation (*http://docs.fabfile.org*) for more info.

Deploying to Live

So, let's try using it for our live site!

```
$ fab deploy:host=elspeth@superlists.ottg.eu
[elspeth@superlists.ottg.eu] Executing task 'deploy'
[elspeth@superlists.ottg.eu] run: mkdir -p
/home/elspeth/sites/superlists.ottg.eu
[elspeth@superlists.ottg.eu] run: git clone
https://github.com/hjwp/book-example.git .
[elspeth@superlists.ottg.eu] out: Cloning into '.'...
[...]
[elspeth@superlists.ottg.eu] out: Receiving objects: 100% [...]
[...]
[elspeth@superlists.ottg.eu] out: Resolving deltas: 100% [...]
[elspeth@superlists.ottg.eu] out: Checking connectivity... done.
[elspeth@superlists.ottg.eu] out:
[localhost] local: git log -n 1 --format=%H
[elspeth@superlists.ottg.eu] run: git reset --hard [...]
[elspeth@superlists.ottg.eu] out: HEAD is now at [...]
[elspeth@superlists.ottg.eu] out:
```

```
[elspeth@superlists.ottg.eu] run: python3.6 -m venv virtualenv
[elspeth@superlists.ottg.eu] run: ./virtualenv/bin/pip install -r
requirements.txt
[elspeth@superlists.ottg.eu] out: Collecting django==1.11 [...]
[elspeth@superlists.ottg.eu] out:   Using cached [...]
[elspeth@superlists.ottg.eu] out: Collecting gunicorn==19.7.1 [...]
[elspeth@superlists.ottg.eu] out:   Using cached [...]
[elspeth@superlists.ottg.eu] out: Collecting pytz [...]
[elspeth@superlists.ottg.eu] out:   Using cached [...]
[elspeth@superlists.ottg.eu] out: Installing collected packages: pytz, django,
gunicorn
[elspeth@superlists.ottg.eu] out: Successfully installed django-1.11
gunicorn-19.7.1 pytz-2017.3

[elspeth@superlists.ottg.eu] run: echo 'DJANGO_DEBUG_FALSE=y' >> "$(echo .env)"
[elspeth@superlists.ottg.eu] run: echo 'SITENAME=superlists.ottg.eu' >> "$(echo
.env)"
[elspeth@superlists.ottg.eu] run: echo
'DJANGO_SECRET_KEY=[...]'
[elspeth@superlists.ottg.eu] run: ./virtualenv/bin/python manage.py
collectstatic --noinput
[elspeth@superlists.ottg.eu] out: Copying
'/home/elspeth/sites/superlists.ottg.eu/lists/static/base.css'
[...]
[elspeth@superlists.ottg.eu] out: 15 static files copied to
'/home/elspeth/sites/superlists.ottg.eu/static'.
[elspeth@superlists.ottg.eu] out:

[elspeth@superlists.ottg.eu] run: ./virtualenv/bin/python manage.py migrate
[...]
[elspeth@superlists.ottg.eu] out: Operations to perform:
[elspeth@superlists.ottg.eu] out:   Apply all migrations: auth, contenttypes,
lists, sessions
[elspeth@superlists.ottg.eu] out: Running migrations:
[elspeth@superlists.ottg.eu] out:   Applying contenttypes.0001_initial... OK
[elspeth@superlists.ottg.eu] out:   Applying
contenttypes.0002_remove_content_type_name... OK
[elspeth@superlists.ottg.eu] out:   Applying auth.0001_initial... OK
[elspeth@superlists.ottg.eu] out:   Applying
auth.0002_alter_permission_name_max_length... OK
[...]
[elspeth@superlists.ottg.eu] out:   Applying lists.0004_item_list... OK
[elspeth@superlists.ottg.eu] out:   Applying sessions.0001_initial... OK
[elspeth@superlists.ottg.eu] out:


Done.
Disconnecting from elspeth@superlists.ottg.eu... done.
```

Brrp brrp brpp. You can see the script follows a slightly different path, doing a git
clone to bring down a brand new repo instead of a git pull. It also needs to set up a
new virtualenv from scratch, including a fresh install of pip and Django. The collect
static actually creates new files this time, and the migrate seems to have worked
too.

Provisioning: Nginx and Gunicorn Config Using sed

What else do we need to do to get our live site into production? We refer to our provisioning notes, which tell us to use the template files to create our Nginx virtual host and the Systemd service.

Now let's use a little Unix command-line magic!

```
elspeth@server:$ cat ./deploy_tools/nginx.template.conf \
    | sed "s/DOMAIN/superlists.ottg.eu/g" \
    | sudo tee /etc/nginx/sites-available/superlists.ottg.eu
```

sed ("stream editor") takes a stream of text and performs edits on it. In this case we ask it to substitute the string *DOMAIN* for the address of our site, with the s/repla ceme/withthis/g syntax.[3] We pipe (|) that to another sed process to set our unique SECRET_KEY, and then we pipe the output once more output to a root-user process (sudo), which uses tee to write its input to a file, in this case the Nginx sites-available virtualhost config file.

 For bonus points, why not build an even bigger Bash "one-liner" that includes the python random.choices command to generate the secret key? Answers on a postcard!

Next we activate that file with a symlink:

```
elspeth@server:$ sudo ln -s /etc/nginx/sites-available/superlists.ottg.eu \
    /etc/nginx/sites-enabled/superlists.ottg.eu
```

And we write the Systemd service, with another, slightly simpler sed:

```
elspeth@server: cat ./deploy_tools/gunicorn-systemd.template.service \
    | sed "s/DOMAIN/superlists.ottg.eu/g" \
    | sudo tee /etc/systemd/system/gunicorn-superlists.ottg.eu.service
```

Finally we start both services:

```
elspeth@server:$ sudo systemctl daemon-reload
elspeth@server:$ sudo systemctl reload nginx
elspeth@server:$ sudo systemctl enable gunicorn-superlists.ottg.eu
elspeth@server:$ sudo systemctl start gunicorn-superlists.ottg.eu
```

And we take a look at our site: Figure 11-1. It works—hooray!

---

3 You might have seen nerdy people using this strange s/change-this/to-this/ notation on the internet. Now you know why!

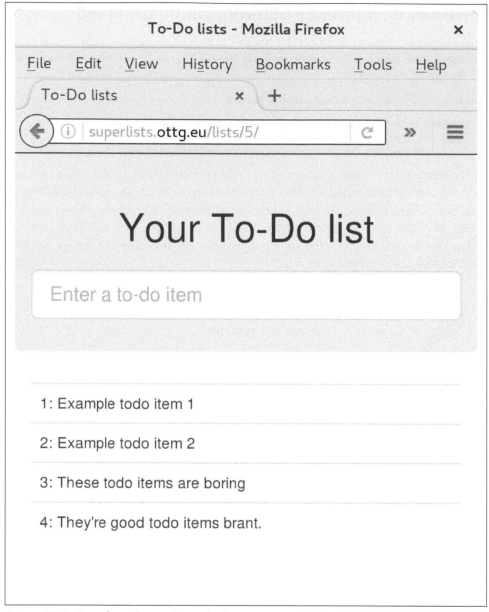

Figure 11-1. Brrp, brrp, brrp...it worked!

It's done a good job. Good fabfile, have a biscuit. You have earned the privilege of being added to the repo:

```
$ git add deploy_tools/fabfile.py
$ git commit -m "Add a fabfile for automated deploys"
```

Git Tag the Release

One final bit of admin. In order to preserve a historical marker, we'll use Git tags to mark the state of the codebase that reflects what's currently live on the server:

```
$ git tag LIVE
$ export TAG=$(date +DEPLOYED-%F/%H%M)  # this generates a timestamp
$ echo $TAG # should show "DEPLOYED-" and then the timestamp
$ git tag $TAG
$ git push origin LIVE $TAG # pushes the tags up
```

Now it's easy, at any time, to check what the difference is between our current codebase and what's live on the servers. This will come in useful in a few chapters, when we look at database migrations. Have a look at the tag in the history:

```
$ git log --graph --oneline --decorate
[...]
```

Anyway, you now have a live website! Tell all your friends! Tell your mum, if no one else is interested! And, in the next chapter, it's back to coding again.

Further Reading

There's no such thing as the One True Way in deployment, and I'm no grizzled expert in any case. I've tried to set you off on a reasonably sane path, but there's plenty of things you could do differently, and lots, lots more to learn besides. Here are some resources I used for inspiration:

- Solid Python Deployments for Everybody (*http://hynek.me/talks/python-deployments*) by Hynek Schlawack
- Git-based fabric deployments are awesome (*http://bit.ly/U6tUo5*) by Dan Bravender
- The deployment chapter of Two Scoops of Django by Dan Greenfeld and Audrey Roy
- The 12-factor App (*http://12factor.net/*) by the Heroku team

Automating Provisioning with Ansible

For some ideas on how you might go about automating the provisioning step, and an alternative to Fabric called Ansible, go check out Appendix C.

Automated Deployments

Fabric

Fabric lets you run commands on servers from inside Python scripts. This is a great tool for automating server admin tasks.

Idempotency

If your deployment script is deploying to existing servers, you need to design them so that they work against a fresh installation *and* against a server that's already configured.

Keep config files under source control

Make sure your only copy of a config file isn't on the server! They are critical to your application, and should be under version control like anything else.

Automating provisioning

Ultimately, *everything* should be automated, and that includes spinning up brand new servers and ensuring they have all the right software installed. This will involve interacting with the API of your hosting provider.

Configuration management tools

Fabric is very flexible, but its logic is still based on scripting. More advanced tools take a more "declarative" approach, and can make your life even easier. Ansible and Vagrant are two worth checking out (see Appendix C), but there are many more (Chef, Puppet, Salt, Juju…).

Splitting Our Tests into Multiple Files, and a Generic Wait Helper

The next feature we might like to implement is a little input validation. But as we start writing new tests, we'll notice that it's getting hard to find our way around a single *functional_tests.py*, and *tests.py*, so we'll reorganise them into multiple files—a little refactor of our tests, if you will.

We'll also build a generic explicit wait helper.

Start on a Validation FT: Preventing Blank Items

As our first few users start using the site, we've noticed they sometimes make mistakes that mess up their lists, like accidentally submitting blank list items, or accidentally inputting two identical items to a list. Computers are meant to help stop us from making silly mistakes, so let's see if we can get our site to help.

Here's the outline of an FT:

```
def test_cannot_add_empty_list_items(self):
    # Edith goes to the home page and accidentally tries to submit
    # an empty list item. She hits Enter on the empty input box

    # The home page refreshes, and there is an error message saying
    # that list items cannot be blank

    # She tries again with some text for the item, which now works

    # Perversely, she now decides to submit a second blank list item

    # She receives a similar warning on the list page

    # And she can correct it by filling some text in
    self.fail('write me!')
```

That's all very well, but before we go any further—our functional tests file is beginning to get a little crowded. Let's split it out into several files, in which each has a single test method.

Remember that functional tests are closely linked to "user stories". If you were using some sort of project management tool like an issue tracker, you might make it so that each file matched one issue or ticket, and its filename contained the ticket ID. Or, if you prefer to think about things in terms of "features", where one feature may have several user stories, then you might have one file and class for the feature, and several methods for each of its user stories.

We'll also have one base test class which they can all inherit from. Here's how to get there step by step.

Skipping a Test

It's always nice, when doing refactoring, to have a fully passing test suite. We've just written a test with a deliberate failure. Let's temporarily switch it off, using a decorator called "skip" from `unittest`:

```
from unittest import skip
[...]

    @skip
    def test_cannot_add_empty_list_items(self):
```

This tells the test runner to ignore this test. You can see it works—if we rerun the tests, it'll say it passes:

```
$ python manage.py test functional_tests
[...]
Ran 4 tests in 11.577s
OK
```

 Skips are dangerous—you need to remember to remove them before you commit your changes back to the repo. This is why line-by-line reviews of each of your diffs are a good idea!

Don't Forget the "Refactor" in "Red, Green, Refactor"

A criticism that's sometimes levelled at TDD is that it leads to badly architected code, as the developer just focuses on getting tests to pass rather than stopping to think about how the whole system should be designed. I think it's slightly unfair.

TDD is no silver bullet. You still have to spend time thinking about good design. But what often happens is that people forget the "Refactor" in "Red, Green, Refactor". The methodology allows you to throw together any old code to get your tests to pass, but it *also* asks you to then spend some time refactoring it to improve its design. Otherwise, it's too easy to allow "technical debt" (*https://martinfowler.com/bliki/Technical DebtQuadrant.html*) to build up.

Often, however, the best ideas for how to refactor code don't occur to you straight away. They may occur to you days, weeks, even months after you wrote a piece of code, when you're working on something totally unrelated and you happen to see some old code again with fresh eyes. But if you're halfway through something else, should you stop to refactor the old code?

The answer is that it depends. In the case at the beginning of the chapter, we haven't even started writing our new code. We know we are in a working state, so we can justify putting a skip on our new FT (to get back to fully passing tests) and do a bit of refactoring straight away.

Later in the chapter we'll spot other bits of code we want to alter. In those cases, rather than taking the risk of refactoring an application that's not in a working state, we'll make a note of the thing we want to change on our scratchpad and wait until we're back to a fully passing test suite before refactoring.

Splitting Functional Tests Out into Many Files

We start putting each test into its own class, still in the same file:

```python
class FunctionalTest(StaticLiveServerTestCase):

    def setUp(self):
        [...]
    def tearDown(self):
        [...]
    def wait_for_row_in_list_table(self, row_text):
        [...]


class NewVisitorTest(FunctionalTest):

    def test_can_start_a_list_for_one_user(self):
        [...]
    def test_multiple_users_can_start_lists_at_different_urls(self):
        [...]


class LayoutAndStylingTest(FunctionalTest):

    def test_layout_and_styling(self):
        [...]



class ItemValidationTest(FunctionalTest):

    @skip
    def test_cannot_add_empty_list_items(self):
        [...]
```

At this point we can rerun the FTs and see they all still work:

```
Ran 4 tests in 11.577s

OK
```

That's labouring it a little bit, and we could probably get away with doing this stuff in fewer steps, but, as I keep saying, practising the step-by-step method on the easy cases makes it that much easier when we have a complex case.

Now we switch from a single tests file to using one for each class, and one "base" file to contain the base class all the tests will inherit from. We'll make four copies of *tests.py*, naming them appropriately, and then delete the parts we don't need from each:

```
$ git mv functional_tests/tests.py functional_tests/base.py
$ cp functional_tests/base.py functional_tests/test_simple_list_creation.py
$ cp functional_tests/base.py functional_tests/test_layout_and_styling.py
$ cp functional_tests/base.py functional_tests/test_list_item_validation.py
```

---

base.py can be cut down to just the `FunctionalTest` class. We leave the helper method on the base class, because we suspect we're about to reuse it in our new FT:

functional_tests/base.py (ch11l003)

```python
import os
from django.contrib.staticfiles.testing import StaticLiveServerTestCase
from selenium import webdriver
from selenium.common.exceptions import WebDriverException
import time

MAX_WAIT = 10


class FunctionalTest(StaticLiveServerTestCase):

    def setUp(self):
        [...]
    def tearDown(self):
        [...]
    def wait_for_row_in_list_table(self, row_text):
        [...]
```

 Keeping helper methods in a base `FunctionalTest` class is one useful way of preventing duplication in FTs. Later in the book (in Chapter 25) we'll use the "Page pattern", which is related, but prefers composition over inheritance—always a good thing.

Our first FT is now in its own file, and should be just one class and one test method:

functional_tests/test_simple_list_creation.py (ch11l004)

```python
from .base import FunctionalTest
from selenium import webdriver
from selenium.webdriver.common.keys import Keys


class NewVisitorTest(FunctionalTest):

    def test_can_start_a_list_for_one_user(self):
        [...]
    def test_multiple_users_can_start_lists_at_different_urls(self):
        [...]
```

I used a relative import (`from .base`). Some people like to use them a lot in Django code (e.g., your views might import models using `from .models import List`, instead of `from list.models`). Ultimately this is a matter of personal preference. I prefer to use relative imports only when I'm super-super sure that the relative position of the thing I'm importing won't change. That applies in this case because I know for sure all the tests will sit next to *base.py*, which they inherit from.

The layout and styling FT should now be one file and one class:

functional_tests/test_layout_and_styling.py (ch11l005)

```python
from selenium.webdriver.common.keys import Keys
from .base import FunctionalTest


class LayoutAndStylingTest(FunctionalTest):
    [...]
```

Lastly our new validation test is in a file of its own too:

functional_tests/test_list_item_validation.py (ch11l006)

```python
from selenium.webdriver.common.keys import Keys
from unittest import skip
from .base import FunctionalTest


class ItemValidationTest(FunctionalTest):

    @skip
    def test_cannot_add_empty_list_items(self):
        [...]
```

And we can test that everything worked by rerunning `manage.py test func tional_tests`, and checking once again that all four tests are run:

```
Ran 4 tests in 11.577s

OK
```

Now we can remove our skip:

functional_tests/test_list_item_validation.py (ch11l007)

```python
class ItemValidationTest(FunctionalTest):

    def test_cannot_add_empty_list_items(self):
        [...]
```

Running a Single Test File

As a side bonus, we're now able to run an individual test file, like this:

```
$ python manage.py test functional_tests.test_list_item_validation
[...]
AssertionError: write me!
```

Brilliant—no need to sit around waiting for all the FTs when we're only interested in a single one. Although we need to remember to run all of them now and again, to check for regressions. Later in the book we'll see how to give that task over to an automated Continuous Integration loop. For now let's commit!

```
$ git status
$ git add functional_tests
$ git commit -m "Moved Fts into their own individual files"
```

Great. We've split our functional tests nicely out into different files. Next we'll start writing our FT, but before long, as you may be guessing, we'll do something similar to our unit test files.

A New Functional Test Tool: A Generic Explicit Wait Helper

First let's start implementing the test, or at least the beginning of it:

functional_tests/test_list_item_validation.py (ch11l008)

```
def test_cannot_add_empty_list_items(self):
    # Edith goes to the home page and accidentally tries to submit
    # an empty list item. She hits Enter on the empty input box
    self.browser.get(self.live_server_url)
    self.browser.find_element_by_id('id_new_item').send_keys(Keys.ENTER)

    # The home page refreshes, and there is an error message saying
    # that list items cannot be blank
    self.assertEqual(
        self.browser.find_element_by_css_selector('.has-error').text,   ❶
        "You can't have an empty list item"   ❷
    )

    # She tries again with some text for the item, which now works
    self.fail('finish this test!')
    [...]
```

This is how we might write the test naively:

❶ We specify we're going to use a CSS class called `.has-error` to mark our error text. We'll see that Bootstrap has some useful styling for those.

❷ And we can check that our error displays the message we want.

But can you guess what the potential problem is with the test as it's written now?

OK, I gave it away in the section header, but whenever we do something that causes a page refresh, we need an explicit wait; otherwise, Selenium might go looking for the `.has-error` element before the page has had a chance to load.

Whenever you submit a form with Keys.ENTER or click something that is going to cause a page to load, you probably want an explicit wait for your next assertion.

Our first explicit wait was built into a helper method. For this one, we might decide that building a specific helper method is overkill at this stage, but it might be nice to have some generic way of saying, in our tests, "wait until this assertion passes". Something like this:

functional_tests/test_list_item_validation.py (ch11l009)

```
[...]
    # The home page refreshes, and there is an error message saying
    # that list items cannot be blank
    self.wait_for(lambda: self.assertEqual(  ❶
        self.browser.find_element_by_css_selector('.has-error').text,
        "You can't have an empty list item"
    ))
```

❶ Rather than calling the assertion directly, we wrap it in a lambda function, and we pass it to a new helper method we imagine called wait_for.

If you've never seen lambda functions in Python before, see "Lambda Functions" on page 215.

So how would this magical wait_for method work? Let's head over to *base.py*, and make a copy of our existing wait_for_row_in_list_table method, and we'll adapt it slightly:

functional_tests/base.py (ch11l010)

```
def wait_for(self, fn):  ❶
    start_time = time.time()
    while True:
        try:
            table = self.browser.find_element_by_id('id_list_table')  ❷
            rows = table.find_elements_by_tag_name('tr')
            self.assertIn(row_text, [row.text for row in rows])
            return
        except (AssertionError, WebDriverException) as e:
            if time.time() - start_time > MAX_WAIT:
                raise e
            time.sleep(0.5)
```

❶ We make a copy of the method, but we name it `wait_for`, and we change its argument. It is expecting to be passed a function.

❷ For now we've still got the old code that's checking table rows. How to transform this into something that works for any generic `fn` that's been passed in?

Like this:

functional_tests/base.py (ch11l011)

```python
def wait_for(self, fn):
    start_time = time.time()
    while True:
        try:
            return fn()  ❶
        except (AssertionError, WebDriverException) as e:
            if time.time() - start_time > MAX_WAIT:
                raise e
            time.sleep(0.5)
```

❶ The body of our try/except, instead of being the specific code for examining table rows, just becomes a call to the function we passed in. We also `return` its return value to be able to exit the loop immediately if no exception is raised.

Lambda Functions

`lambda` in Python is the syntax for making a one-line, throwaway function—it saves you from having to use `def..():` and an indented block:

```python
>>> myfn = lambda x: x+1
>>> myfn(2)
3
>>> myfn(5)
6
>>> adder = lambda x, y: x + y
>>> adder(3, 2)
5
```

In our case, we're using it to transform a bit of code that would otherwise be executed immediately into a function that we can pass as an argument, and that can be executed later, and multiple times:

```
>>> def addthree(x):
...     return x + 3
...
>>> addthree(2)
5
>>> myfn = lambda: addthree(2)  # note addthree is not called immediately here
>>> myfn
<function <lambda> at 0x7f3b140339d8>
>>> myfn()
5
>>> myfn()
5
```

Let's see our funky wait_for helper in action:

```
$ python manage.py test functional_tests.test_list_item_validation
[...]
======================================================================
ERROR: test_cannot_add_empty_list_items
(functional_tests.test_list_item_validation.ItemValidationTest)
----------------------------------------------------------------------
Traceback (most recent call last):
  File "...python-tdd-book/functional_tests/test_list_item_validation.py", line
15, in test_cannot_add_empty_list_items
    self.wait_for(lambda: self.assertEqual(   ❶
  File "...python-tdd-book/functional_tests/base.py", line 37, in wait_for
    raise e  ❷
  File "...python-tdd-book/functional_tests/base.py", line 34, in wait_for
    return fn()  ❷
  File "...python-tdd-book/functional_tests/test_list_item_validation.py", line
16, in <lambda>  ❸
    self.browser.find_element_by_css_selector('.has-error').text,   ❸
[...]
selenium.common.exceptions.NoSuchElementException: Message: Unable to locate
element: .has-error
----------------------------------------------------------------------
Ran 1 test in 10.575s

FAILED (errors=1)
```

The order of the traceback is a little confusing, but we can more or less follow
through what happened:

❶ At line 15 in our FT, we go into our self.wait_for helper, passing it the lambda-
ified version of the assertEqual.

❷ We go into self.wait_for in *base.py*, where we can see that we've called the
lambda, enough times that we've dropped out to the raise e because our timeout
expired.

❸ To explain where the exception has actually come from, the traceback takes us back into *test_list_item_validation.py* and inside the body of the `lambda` function, and tells us that it was trying to find the `.has-error` element that failed.

We're into the realm of functional programming now, passing functions as arguments to other functions, and it can be a little mind-bending. I know it took me a little while to get used to! Have a couple of read-throughs of this code, and the code back in the FT, to let it sink in; and if you're still confused, don't worry about it too much, and let your confidence grow from working with it. We'll use it a few more times in this book and make it even more functionally fun, you'll see.

Finishing Off the FT

We'll finish off the FT like this:

```python
# The home page refreshes, and there is an error message saying
# that list items cannot be blank
self.wait_for(lambda: self.assertEqual(
    self.browser.find_element_by_css_selector('.has-error').text,
    "You can't have an empty list item"
))

# She tries again with some text for the item, which now works
self.browser.find_element_by_id('id_new_item').send_keys('Buy milk')
self.browser.find_element_by_id('id_new_item').send_keys(Keys.ENTER)
self.wait_for_row_in_list_table('1: Buy milk')

# Perversely, she now decides to submit a second blank list item
self.browser.find_element_by_id('id_new_item').send_keys(Keys.ENTER)

# She receives a similar warning on the list page
self.wait_for(lambda: self.assertEqual(
    self.browser.find_element_by_css_selector('.has-error').text,
    "You can't have an empty list item"
))

# And she can correct it by filling some text in
self.browser.find_element_by_id('id_new_item').send_keys('Make tea')
self.browser.find_element_by_id('id_new_item').send_keys(Keys.ENTER)
self.wait_for_row_in_list_table('1: Buy milk')
self.wait_for_row_in_list_table('2: Make tea')
```

Helper Methods in FTs

We've got two helper methods now, our generic `self.wait_for` helper, and `wait_for_row_in_list_table`. The former is a general utility—any of our FTs might need to do a wait.

The second also helps prevent duplication across your functional test code. The day we decide to change the implementation of how our list table works, we want to make sure we only have to change our FT code in one place, not in dozens of places across loads of FTs…

See also Chapter 25 and Appendix E for more on structuring your FT code.

I'll let you do your own "first-cut FT" commit.

Refactoring Unit Tests into Several Files

When we (finally!) start coding our solution, we're going to want to add another test for our *models.py*. Before we do so, it's time to tidy up our unit tests in a similar way to the functional tests.

A difference will be that, because the `lists` app contains real application code as well as tests, we'll separate out the tests into their own folder:

```
$ mkdir lists/tests
$ touch lists/tests/__init__.py
$ git mv lists/tests.py lists/tests/test_all.py
$ git status
$ git add lists/tests
$ python manage.py test lists
[...]
Ran 9 tests in 0.034s

OK
$ git commit -m "Move unit tests into a folder with single file"
```

If you get a message saying "Ran 0 tests", you probably forgot to add the dunderinit—it needs to be there or else the tests folder isn't a valid Python package...[1]

Now we turn *test_all.py* into two files, one called *test_views.py*, which will only contains view tests, and one called *test_models.py*. I'll start by making two copies:

```
$ git mv lists/tests/test_all.py lists/tests/test_views.py
$ cp lists/tests/test_views.py lists/tests/test_models.py
```

And strip *test_models.py* down to being just the one test—it means it needs far fewer imports:

lists/tests/test_models.py (ch11l016)

```
from django.test import TestCase
from lists.models import Item, List


class ListAndItemModelsTest(TestCase):
    [...]
```

Whereas *test_views.py* just loses one class:

---

1 "Dunder" is shorthand for double-underscore, so "dunderinit" means *__init__.py*.

```
--- a/lists/tests/test_views.py
+++ b/lists/tests/test_views.py
@@ -103,34 +104,3 @@ class ListViewTest(TestCase):
         self.assertNotContains(response, 'other list item 1')
         self.assertNotContains(response, 'other list item 2')
 
-
-
-class ListAndItemModelsTest(TestCase):
-
-    def test_saving_and_retrieving_items(self):
[...]
```

We rerun the tests to check that everything is still there:

```
$ python manage.py test lists
[...]
Ran 9 tests in 0.040s

OK
```

Great! That's another small, working step:

```
$ git add lists/tests
$ git commit -m "Split out unit tests into two files"
```

 Some people like to make their unit tests into a tests folder straight away, as soon as they start a project. That's a perfectly good idea; I just thought I'd wait until it became necessary, to avoid doing too much housekeeping all in the first chapter!

Well, that's our FTs and unit test nicely reorganised. In the next chapter we'll get down to some validation proper.

Tips on Organising Tests and Refactoring

Use a tests folder

Just as you use multiple files to hold your application code, you should split your tests out into multiple files.

- For functional tests, group them into tests for a particular feature or user story.

- For unit tests, use a folder called *tests*, with a *__init__.py*.

- You probably want a separate test file for each tested source code file. For Django, that's typically *test_models.py*, *test_views.py*, and *test_forms.py*.

- Have at least a placeholder test for *every* function and class.

Don't forget the "Refactor" in "Red, Green, Refactor"

The whole point of having tests is to allow you to refactor your code! Use them, and make your code (including your tests) as clean as you can.

Don't refactor against failing tests

- In general!

- But the FT you're currently working on doesn't count.

- You can occasionally put a skip on a test which is testing something you haven't written yet.

- More commonly, make a note of the refactor you want to do, finish what you're working on, and do the refactor a little later, when you're back to a working state.

- Don't forget to remove any skips before you commit your code! You should always review your diffs line by line to catch things like this.

Try a generic wait_for helper

Having specific helper methods that do explicit waits is great, and it helps to make your tests readable. But you'll also often need an ad-hoc one-line assertion or Selenium interaction that you'll want to add a wait to. `self.wait_for` does the job well for me, but you might find a slightly different pattern works for you.

Validation at the Database Layer

Over the next few chapters we'll talk about testing and implementing validation of user inputs.

In terms of content, there's going to be quite a lot of material here that's more about the specifics of Django, and less discussion of TDD philosophy. That doesn't mean you won't be learning anything about testing—there are plenty of little testing tidbits in here, but perhaps it's more about really getting into the swing of things, the rhythm of TDD, and how we get work done.

Once we get through these three short chapters, I've saved a bit of fun with JavaScript (!) for the end of Part II. Then it's on to Part III, where I promise we'll get right back into some of the real nitty-gritty discussions in TDD methodology—unit tests versus integrated tests, mocking, and more. Stay tuned!

But for now, a little validation. Let's just remind ourselves where our FT is pointing us:

```
$ python3 manage.py test functional_tests.test_list_item_validation
[...]
======================================================================
ERROR: test_cannot_add_empty_list_items
(functional_tests.test_list_item_validation.ItemValidationTest)
 ----------------------------------------------------------------------
Traceback (most recent call last):
  File "...python-tdd-book/functional_tests/test_list_item_validation.py", line
15, in test_cannot_add_empty_list_items
    self.wait_for(lambda: self.assertEqual(
[...]
  File "...python-tdd-book/functional_tests/test_list_item_validation.py", line
16, in <lambda>
    self.browser.find_element_by_css_selector('.has-error').text,
[...]
selenium.common.exceptions.NoSuchElementException: Message: Unable to locate
element: .has-error
```

It's expecting to see an error message if the user tries to input an empty item.

Model-Layer Validation

In a web app, there are two places you can do validation: on the client side (using JavaScript or HTML5 properties, as we'll see later), and on the server side. The server side is "safer" because someone can always bypass the client side, whether it's maliciously or due to some bug.

Similarly on the server side, in Django, there are two levels at which you can do validation. One is at the model level, and the other is higher up at the forms level. I like to use the lower level whenever possible, partially because I'm a bit too fond of databases and database integrity rules, and partially because, again, it's safer—you can sometimes forget which form you use to validate input, but you're always going to use the same database.

The self.assertRaises Context Manager

Let's go down and write a unit test at the models layer. Add a new test method to ListAndItemModelsTest, which tries to create a blank list item. This test is interesting because it's testing that the code under test should raise an exception:

```
from django.core.exceptions import ValidationError
[...]

class ListAndItemModelsTest(TestCase):
    [...]

    def test_cannot_save_empty_list_items(self):
        list_ = List.objects.create()
        item = Item(list=list_, text='')
        with self.assertRaises(ValidationError):
            item.save()
```

If you're new to Python, you may never have seen the with state-
ment. It's used with what are called "context managers", which wrap
a block of code, usually with some kind of setup, cleanup, or error-
handling code. There's a good write-up in the Python 2.5 release
notes (*http://docs.python.org/release/2.5/whatsnew/pep-343.html*).

This is a new unit testing technique: when we want to check that doing something
will raise an error, we can use the self.assertRaises context manager. We could
have used something like this instead:

```
try:
    item.save()
    self.fail('The save should have raised an exception')
except ValidationError:
    pass
```

But the with formulation is neater. Now, we can try running the test, and see its
expected failure:

```
    item.save()
AssertionError: ValidationError not raised
```

A Django Quirk: Model Save Doesn't Run Validation

And now we discover one of Django's little quirks. *This test should already pass.* If you
take a look at the docs for the Django model fields (*http://bit.ly/SuxPJO*), you'll see
that TextField actually defaults to blank=False, which means that it *should* disallow
empty values.

So why is the test still failing? Well, for slightly counterintuitive historical reasons
(*http://bit.ly/2v3SfRq*), Django models don't run full validation on save. As we'll see
later, any constraints that are actually implemented in the database will raise errors on
save, but SQLite doesn't support enforcing emptiness constraints on text columns,
and so our save method is letting this invalid value through silently.

There's a way of checking whether the constraint will happen at the database level or not: if it was at the database level, we would need a migration to apply the constraint. But Django knows that SQLite doesn't support this type of constraint, so if we try to run makemigrations, it will report there's nothing to do:

```
$ python manage.py makemigrations
No changes detected
```

Django does have a method to manually run full validation, however, called full_clean (more info in the docs (*http://bit.ly/2u5SIxA*)). Let's hack it in to see it work:

lists/tests/test_models.py

```
        with self.assertRaises(ValidationError):
            item.save()
            item.full_clean()
```

That gets the test to pass:

```
OK
```

Good. That taught us a little about Django validation, and the test is there to warn us if we ever forget our requirement and set blank=True on the text field (try it!).

Surfacing Model Validation Errors in the View

Let's try to enforce our model validation in the views layer and bring it up through into our templates, so the user can see them. Here's how we can optionally display an error in our HTML—we check whether the template has been passed an error variable, and if so, we display it next to the form:

lists/templates/base.html (ch11l020)

```
<form method="POST" action="{% block form_action %}{% endblock %}">
  <input name="item_text" id="id_new_item"
         class="form-control input-lg"
         placeholder="Enter a to-do item" />
  {% csrf_token %}
  {% if error %}
    <div class="form-group has-error">
      <span class="help-block">{{ error }}</span>
    </div>
  {% endif %}
</form>
```

Take a look at the Bootstrap docs (*http://getbootstrap.com/css/#forms*) for more info on form controls.

Passing this error to the template is the job of the view function. Let's take a look at the unit tests in the NewListTest class. I'm going to use two slightly different error-handling patterns here.

In the first case, our URL and view for new lists will optionally render the same template as the home page, but with the addition of an error message. Here's a unit test for that:

lists/tests/test_views.py (ch11l021)

```python
class NewListTest(TestCase):
    [...]

    def test_validation_errors_are_sent_back_to_home_page_template(self):
        response = self.client.post('/lists/new', data={'item_text': ''})
        self.assertEqual(response.status_code, 200)
        self.assertTemplateUsed(response, 'home.html')
        expected_error = "You can't have an empty list item"
        self.assertContains(response, expected_error)
```

As we're writing this test, we might get slightly offended by the */lists/new* URL, which we're manually entering as a string. We've got a lot of URLs hardcoded in our tests, in our views, and in our templates, which violates the DRY principle. I don't mind a bit of duplication in tests, but we should definitely be on the lookout for hardcoded URLs in our views and templates, and make a note to refactor them out. But we won't do them straight away, because right now our application is in a broken state. We want to get back to a working state first.

Back to our test, which is failing because the view is currently returning a 302 redirect, rather than a "normal" 200 response:

```
AssertionError: 302 != 200
```

Let's try calling full_clean() in the view:

lists/views.py

```python
def new_list(request):
    list_ = List.objects.create()
    item = Item.objects.create(text=request.POST['item_text'], list=list_)
    item.full_clean()
    return redirect(f'/lists/{list_.id}/')
```

As we're looking at the view code, we find a good candidate for a hardcoded URL to get rid of. Let's add that to our scratchpad:

Now the model validation raises an exception, which comes up through our view:

```
[...]
  File "...python-tdd-book/lists/views.py", line 11, in new_list
    item.full_clean()
[...]
django.core.exceptions.ValidationError: {'text': ['This field cannot be
blank.']}
```

So we try our first approach: using a try/except to detect errors. Obeying the Testing
Goat, we start with just the try/except and nothing else. The tests should tell us what
to code next…

lists/views.py (ch11l025)

```
from django.core.exceptions import ValidationError
[...]

def new_list(request):
    list_ = List.objects.create()
    item = Item.objects.create(text=request.POST['item_text'], list=list_)
    try:
        item.full_clean()
    except ValidationError:
        pass
    return redirect(f'/lists/{list_.id}/')
```

That gets us back to the 302 != 200:

```
AssertionError: 302 != 200
```

Let's return a rendered template then, which should take care of the template check as
well:

lists/views.py (ch11l026)

```
    except ValidationError:
        return render(request, 'home.html')
```

And the tests now tell us to put the error message into the template:

```
AssertionError: False is not true : Couldn't find 'You can't have an empty list
item' in response
```

We do that by passing a new template variable in:

```
    except ValidationError:
        error = "You can't have an empty list item"
        return render(request, 'home.html', {"error": error})
```

Hmm, it looks like that didn't quite work:

```
AssertionError: False is not true : Couldn't find 'You can't have an empty list
item' in response
```

A little print-based debug…

```
expected_error = "You can't have an empty list item"
print(response.content.decode())
self.assertContains(response, expected_error)
```

…will show us the cause—Django has HTML-escaped (*https://docs.djangopro ject.com/en/1.11/ref/templates/builtins/#autoescape*) the apostrophe:

```
[...]
<span class="help-block">You can&#39;t have an empty list
item</span>
```

We could hack something like this into our test:

```
    expected_error = "You can&#39;t have an empty list item"
```

But using Django's helper function is probably a better idea:

```
from django.utils.html import escape
[...]

        expected_error = escape("You can't have an empty list item")
        self.assertContains(response, expected_error)
```

That passes!

```
Ran 11 tests in 0.047s

OK
```

Checking That Invalid Input Isn't Saved to the Database

Before we go further though, did you notice a little logic error we've allowed to creep into our implementation? We're currently creating an object, even if validation fails:

```
item = Item.objects.create(text=request.POST['item_text'], list=list_)
try:
    item.full_clean()
except ValidationError:
    [...]
```

Let's add a new unit test to make sure that empty list items don't get saved:

```
class NewListTest(TestCase):
    [...]

    def test_validation_errors_are_sent_back_to_home_page_template(self):
        [...]

    def test_invalid_list_items_arent_saved(self):
        self.client.post('/lists/new', data={'item_text': ''})
        self.assertEqual(List.objects.count(), 0)
        self.assertEqual(Item.objects.count(), 0)
```

That gives:

```
[...]
Traceback (most recent call last):
  File "...python-tdd-book/lists/tests/test_views.py", line 40, in
test_invalid_list_items_arent_saved
    self.assertEqual(List.objects.count(), 0)
AssertionError: 1 != 0
```

We fix it like this:

```
def new_list(request):
    list_ = List.objects.create()
    item = Item(text=request.POST['item_text'], list=list_)
    try:
        item.full_clean()
        item.save()
    except ValidationError:
        list_.delete()
        error = "You can't have an empty list item"
        return render(request, 'home.html', {"error": error})
    return redirect(f'/lists/{list_.id}/')
```

Do the FTs pass?

```
$ python manage.py test functional_tests.test_list_item_validation
[...]
File "...python-tdd-book/functional_tests/test_list_item_validation.py", line
29, in test_cannot_add_empty_list_items
    self.wait_for(lambda: self.assertEqual(
[...]
selenium.common.exceptions.NoSuchElementException: Message: Unable to locate
element: .has-error
```

Not quite, but they did get a little further. Checking *line 29*, we can see that we've got past the first part of the test, and are now onto the second check—that submitting a second empty item also shows an error.

We've got some working code though, so let's have a commit:

```
$ git commit -am "Adjust new list view to do model validation"
```

Django Pattern: Processing POST Requests in the Same View as Renders the Form

This time we'll use a slightly different approach, one that's actually a very common pattern in Django, which is to use the same view to process POST requests as to render the form that they come from. Whilst this doesn't fit the REST-ful URL model quite as well, it has the important advantage that the same URL can display a form, and display any errors encountered in processing the user's input.

The current situation is that we have one view and URL for displaying a list, and one view and URL for processing additions to that list. We're going to combine them into one. So, in *list.html*, our form will have a different target:

lists/templates/list.html (ch11l030)

```
{% block form_action %}/lists/{{ list.id }}/{% endblock %}
```

Incidentally, that's another hardcoded URL. Let's add it to our to-do list, and while we're thinking about it, there's one in *home.html* too:

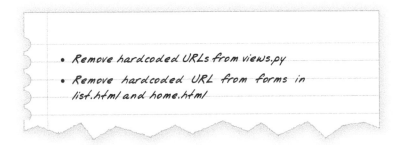

- *Remove hardcoded URLs from views.py*
- *Remove hardcoded URL from forms in list.html and home.html*

This will immediately break our original functional test, because the `view_list` page doesn't know how to process POST requests yet:

```
$ python manage.py test functional_tests
[...]
selenium.common.exceptions.NoSuchElementException: Message: Unable to locate
element: .has-error
[...]
AssertionError: '2: Use peacock feathers to make a fly' not found in ['1: Buy
peacock feathers']
```

 In this section we're performing a refactor at the application level. We execute our application-level refactor by changing or adding unit tests, and then adjusting our code. We use the functional tests to tell us when our refactor is complete and things are back to working as before. Have another look at the diagram from the end of Chapter 4 if you need to get your bearings.

Refactor: Transferring the new_item Functionality into view_list

Let's take all the old tests from `NewItemTest`, the ones that are about saving POST requests to existing lists, and move them into `ListViewTest`. As we do so, we also make them point at the base list URL, instead of .../*add_item*:

```
class ListViewTest(TestCase):

    def test_uses_list_template(self):
        [...]

    def test_passes_correct_list_to_template(self):
        [...]

    def test_displays_only_items_for_that_list(self):
        [...]

    def test_can_save_a_POST_request_to_an_existing_list(self):
        other_list = List.objects.create()
        correct_list = List.objects.create()

        self.client.post(
            f'/lists/{correct_list.id}/',
            data={'item_text': 'A new item for an existing list'}
        )

        self.assertEqual(Item.objects.count(), 1)
        new_item = Item.objects.first()
        self.assertEqual(new_item.text, 'A new item for an existing list')
        self.assertEqual(new_item.list, correct_list)


    def test_POST_redirects_to_list_view(self):
        other_list = List.objects.create()
        correct_list = List.objects.create()

        response = self.client.post(
            f'/lists/{correct_list.id}/',
            data={'item_text': 'A new item for an existing list'}
        )
        self.assertRedirects(response, f'/lists/{correct_list.id}/')
```

Note that the NewItemTest class disappears completely. I've also changed the name of
the redirect test to make it explicit that it only applies to POST requests.

That gives:

```
FAIL: test_POST_redirects_to_list_view (lists.tests.test_views.ListViewTest)
AssertionError: 200 != 302 : Response didn't redirect as expected: Response
code was 200 (expected 302)
[...]
FAIL: test_can_save_a_POST_request_to_an_existing_list
(lists.tests.test_views.ListViewTest)
AssertionError: 0 != 1
```

We change the view_list function to handle two types of request:

```
def view_list(request, list_id):
    list_ = List.objects.get(id=list_id)
    if request.method == 'POST':
        Item.objects.create(text=request.POST['item_text'], list=list_)
        return redirect(f'/lists/{list_.id}/')
    return render(request, 'list.html', {'list': list_})
```

That gets us passing tests:

```
Ran 12 tests in 0.047s

OK
```

Now we can delete the add_item view, since it's no longer needed...oops, an unexpected failure:

```
[...]
AttributeError: module 'lists.views' has no attribute 'add_item'
```

It's because we've deleted the view, but it's still being referred to in *urls.py*. We remove it from there:

```
urlpatterns = [
    url(r'^new$', views.new_list, name='new_list'),
    url(r'^(\d+)/$', views.view_list, name='view_list'),
]
```

And that gets us to the OK. Let's try a full FT run:

```
$ python manage.py test
[...]
ERROR: test_cannot_add_empty_list_items
[...]

Ran 16 tests in 15.276s
FAILED (errors=1)
```

We're back to the one failure in our new functional test. Our refactor of the add_item functionality is complete. We should commit there:

```
$ git commit -am "Refactor list view to handle new item POSTs"
```

So did I break the rule about never refactoring against failing tests? In this case, it's allowed, because the refactor is required to get our new functionality to work. You should definitely never refactor against failing *unit* tests. But in my book it's OK for the FT for the current story you're working on to be failing.[1]

Enforcing Model Validation in view_list

We still want the addition of items to existing lists to be subject to our model validation rules. Let's write a new unit test for that; it's very similar to the one for the home page, with just a couple of tweaks:

lists/tests/test_views.py (ch11l034)

```python
class ListViewTest(TestCase):
    [...]

    def test_validation_errors_end_up_on_lists_page(self):
        list_ = List.objects.create()
        response = self.client.post(
            f'/lists/{list_.id}/',
            data={'item_text': ''}
        )
        self.assertEqual(response.status_code, 200)
        self.assertTemplateUsed(response, 'list.html')
        expected_error = escape("You can't have an empty list item")
        self.assertContains(response, expected_error)
```

That should fail, because our view currently does not do any validation, and just redirects for all POSTs:

```
    self.assertEqual(response.status_code, 200)
AssertionError: 302 != 200
```

---

1 If you really want a "clean" test run, you could add a skip or an early return to the current FT, but you'd need to make sure you didn't accidentally forget it.

Here's an implementation:

lists/views.py (ch11l035)

```python
def view_list(request, list_id):
    list_ = List.objects.get(id=list_id)
    error = None

    if request.method == 'POST':
        try:
            item = Item(text=request.POST['item_text'], list=list_)
            item.full_clean()
            item.save()
            return redirect(f'/lists/{list_.id}/')
        except ValidationError:
            error = "You can't have an empty list item"

    return render(request, 'list.html', {'list': list_, 'error': error})
```

It's not deeply satisfying, is it? There's definitely some duplication of code here; that try/except occurs twice in *views.py*, and in general things are feeling clunky.

```
Ran 13 tests in 0.047s

OK
```

Let's wait a bit before we do more refactoring though, because we know we're about to do some slightly different validation coding for duplicate items. We'll just add it to our scratchpad for now:

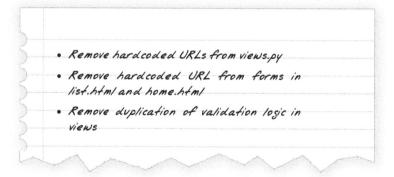

- *Remove hardcoded URLs from views.py*
- *Remove hardcoded URL from forms in list.html and home.html*
- *Remove duplication of validation logic in views*

One of the reasons that the "three strikes and refactor" rule exists is that, if you wait until you have three use cases, each might be slightly different, and it gives you a better view for what the common functionality is. If you refactor too early, you may find that the third use case doesn't quite fit with your refactored code...

At least our functional tests are back to passing:

```
$ python manage.py test functional_tests
[...]
OK
```

We're back to a working state, so we can take a look at some of the items on our scratchpad. This would be a good time for a commit. And possibly a tea break.

```
$ git commit -am "enforce model validation in list view"
```

Refactor: Removing Hardcoded URLs

Do you remember those `name=` parameters in *urls.py*? We just copied them across from the default example Django gave us, and I've been giving them some reasonably descriptive names. Now we find out what they're for:

lists/urls.py

```
url(r'^new$', views.new_list, name='new_list'),
url(r'^(\d+)/$', views.view_list, name='view_list'),
```

The {% url %} Template Tag

We can replace the hardcoded URL in *home.html* with a Django template tag which refers to the URL's "name":

lists/templates/home.html (ch11l036-1)

```
{% block form_action %}{% url 'new_list' %}{% endblock %}
```

We check that this doesn't break the unit tests:

```
$ python manage.py test lists
OK
```

Let's do the other template. This one is more interesting, because we pass it a parameter:

lists/templates/list.html (ch11l036-2)

```
{% block form_action %}{% url 'view_list' list.id %}{% endblock %}
```

See the Django docs on reverse URL resolution (*http://bit.ly/2uKaMzA*) for more info. We run the tests again, and check that they all pass:

```
$ python manage.py test lists
OK
$ python manage.py test functional_tests
OK
```

Excellent:

```
$ git commit -am "Refactor hard-coded URLs out of templates"
```

- *Remove hardcoded URLs from views.py*
- ~~*Remove hardcoded URL from forms in list.html and home.html*~~
- *Remove duplication of validation logic in views*

Using get_absolute_url for Redirects

Now let's tackle *views.py*. One way of doing it is just like in the template, passing in the name of the URL and a positional argument:

lists/views.py (ch11l036-3)

```python
def new_list(request):
    [...]
    return redirect('view_list', list_.id)
```

That would get the unit and functional tests passing, but the redirect function can do even better magic than that! In Django, because model objects are often associated with a particular URL, you can define a special function called get_absolute_url which says what page displays the item. It's useful in this case, but it's also useful in the Django admin (which I don't cover in the book, but you'll soon discover for yourself): it will let you jump from looking at an object in the admin view to looking at the object on the live site. I'd always recommend defining a get_absolute_url for a model whenever there is one that makes sense; it takes no time at all.

All it takes is a super-simple unit test in *test_models.py*:

lists/tests/test_models.py (ch11l036-4)

```python
def test_get_absolute_url(self):
    list_ = List.objects.create()
    self.assertEqual(list_.get_absolute_url(), f'/lists/{list_.id}/')
```

Which gives:

```
AttributeError: 'List' object has no attribute 'get_absolute_url'
```

The implementation is to use Django's `reverse` function, which essentially does the reverse of what Django normally does with *urls.py* (see the docs (*https://docs.django project.com/en/1.11/topics/http/urls/#reverse-resolution-of-urls*)):

lists/models.py (ch11l036-5)

```
from django.core.urlresolvers import reverse


class List(models.Model):

    def get_absolute_url(self):
        return reverse('view_list', args=[self.id])
```

And now we can use it in the view—the `redirect` function just takes the object we want to redirect to, and it uses `get_absolute_url` under the hood automagically!

lists/views.py (ch11l036-6)

```
def new_list(request):
    [...]
    return redirect(list_)
```

There's more info in the Django docs (*https://docs.djangoproject.com/en/1.11/topics/ http/shortcuts/#redirect*). Quick check that the unit tests still pass:

```
OK
```

Then we do the same to `view_list`:

lists/views.py (ch11l036-7)

```
def view_list(request, list_id):
    [...]

            item.save()
            return redirect(list_)
        except ValidationError:
            error = "You can't have an empty list item"
```

And a full unit test and functional test run to assure ourselves that everything still works:

```
$ python manage.py test lists
OK
$ python manage.py test functional_tests
OK
```

Cross off our to-dos...

- ~~Remove hardcoded URLs from views.py~~
- ~~Remove hardcoded URL from forms in list.html and home.html~~
- Remove duplication of validation logic in views

And a commit...

```
$ git commit -am "Use get_absolute_url on List model to DRY urls in views"
```

And we're done with that bit! We have working model-layer validation, and we've taken the opportunity to do a few refactors along the way.

That final scratchpad item will be the subject of the next chapter...

On Database-Layer Validation

I always like to push my validation logic down as low as possible.

Validation at the database layer is the ultimate guarantee of data integrity
It can ensure that, no matter how complex your code at the layers above gets, you have guarantees at the lowest level that your data is valid and consistent.

But it comes at the expense of flexibility
This benefit doesn't come for free! It's now impossible, even temporarily, to have inconsistent data. Sometimes you might have a good reason for temporarily storing data that breaks the rules rather than storing nothing at all. Perhaps you're importing data from an external source in several stages, for example.

And it's not designed for user-friendliness
Trying to store invalid data will cause a nasty IntegrityError to come back from your database, and possibly the user will see a confusing 500 error page. As we'll see in later chapters, forms-layer validation is designed with the user in mind, anticipating the kinds of helpful error messages we want to send them.

A Simple Form

At the end of the last chapter, we were left with the thought that there was too much duplication of code in the validation handling bits of our views. Django encourages you to use form classes to do the work of validating user input, and choosing what error messages to display. Let's see how that works.

As we go through the chapter, we'll also spend a bit of time tidying up our unit tests, and making sure each of them tests only one thing at a time.

Moving Validation Logic into a Form

 In Django, a complex view is a code smell. Could some of that logic be pushed out to a form? Or to some custom methods on the model class? Or maybe even to a non-Django module that represents your business logic?

Forms have several superpowers in Django:

- They can process user input and validate it for errors.
- They can be used in templates to render HTML input elements, and error messages too.
- And, as we'll see later, some of them can even save data to the database for you.

You don't have to use all three form superpowers in every form. You may prefer to roll your own HTML, or do your own saving. But they are an excellent place to keep validation logic.

Exploring the Forms API with a Unit Test

Let's do a little experimenting with forms by using a unit test. My plan is to iterate towards a complete solution, and hopefully introduce forms gradually enough that they'll make sense if you've never seen them before.

First we add a new file for our form unit tests, and we start with a test that just looks at the form HTML:

lists/tests/test_forms.py

```python
from django.test import TestCase

from lists.forms import ItemForm


class ItemFormTest(TestCase):

    def test_form_renders_item_text_input(self):
        form = ItemForm()
        self.fail(form.as_p())
```

`form.as_p()` renders the form as HTML. This unit test is using a `self.fail` for some exploratory coding. You could just as easily use a `manage.py shell` session, although you'd need to keep reloading your code for each change.

Let's make a minimal form. It inherits from the base `Form` class, and has a single field called `item_text`:

lists/forms.py

```python
from django import forms

class ItemForm(forms.Form):
    item_text = forms.CharField()
```

We now see a failure message which tells us what the autogenerated form HTML will look like:

```
    self.fail(form.as_p())
AssertionError: <p><label for="id_item_text">Item text:</label> <input
type="text" name="item_text" required id="id_item_text" /></p>
```

It's already pretty close to what we have in *base.html*. We're missing the placeholder attribute and the Bootstrap CSS classes. Let's make our unit test into a test for that:

```
class ItemFormTest(TestCase):

    def test_form_item_input_has_placeholder_and_css_classes(self):
        form = ItemForm()
        self.assertIn('placeholder="Enter a to-do item"', form.as_p())
        self.assertIn('class="form-control input-lg"', form.as_p())
```

That gives us a fail which justifies some real coding. How can we customise the input for a form field? Using a "widget". Here it is with just the placeholder:

```
class ItemForm(forms.Form):
    item_text = forms.CharField(
        widget=forms.fields.TextInput(attrs={
            'placeholder': 'Enter a to-do item',
        }),
    )
```

That gives:

```
AssertionError: 'class="form-control input-lg"' not found in '<p><label
for="id_item_text">Item text:</label> <input type="text" name="item_text"
placeholder="Enter a to-do item" required id="id_item_text" /></p>'
```

And then:

```
        widget=forms.fields.TextInput(attrs={
            'placeholder': 'Enter a to-do item',
            'class': 'form-control input-lg',
        }),
```

Doing this sort of widget customisation would get tedious if we had a much larger, more complex form. Check out django-crispy-forms (*https://django-crispy-forms.readthedocs.org/*) and django-floppyforms (*http://bit.ly/1rR5eyD*) for some help.

Switching to a Django ModelForm

What's next? We want our form to reuse the validation code that we've already defined on our model. Django provides a special class which can autogenerate a form for a model, called ModelForm. As you'll see, it's configured using a special attribute called Meta:

lists/forms.py

```python
from django import forms

from lists.models import Item

class ItemForm(forms.models.ModelForm):

    class Meta:
        model = Item
        fields = ('text',)
```

In Meta we specify which model the form is for, and which fields we want it to use.

ModelForms do all sorts of smart stuff, like assigning sensible HTML form input types to different types of field, and applying default validation. Check out the docs (*https://docs.djangoproject.com/en/1.11/topics/forms/modelforms/*) for more info.

We now have some different-looking form HTML:

```
AssertionError: 'placeholder="Enter a to-do item"' not found in '<p><label
for="id_text">Text:</label> <textarea name="text" cols="40" rows="10" required
id="id_text">\n</textarea></p>'
```

It's lost our placeholder and CSS class. But you can also see that it's using name="text" instead of name="item_text". We can probably live with that. But it's using a textarea instead of a normal input, and that's not the UI we want for our app. Thankfully, you can override widgets for ModelForm fields, similarly to the way we did it with the normal form:

```
class ItemForm(forms.models.ModelForm):

    class Meta:
        model = Item
        fields = ('text',)
        widgets = {
            'text': forms.fields.TextInput(attrs={
                'placeholder': 'Enter a to-do item',
                'class': 'form-control input-lg',
            }),
        }
```

That gets the test passing.

Testing and Customising Form Validation

Now let's see if the ModelForm has picked up the same validation rules which we defined on the model. We'll also learn how to pass data into the form, as if it came from the user:

```
def test_form_validation_for_blank_items(self):
    form = ItemForm(data={'text': ''})
    form.save()
```

That gives us:

```
ValueError: The Item could not be created because the data didn't validate.
```

Good: the form won't allow you to save if you give it an empty item text.

Now let's see if we can get it to use the specific error message that we want. The API for checking form validation *before* we try to save any data is a function called is_valid:

```
def test_form_validation_for_blank_items(self):
    form = ItemForm(data={'text': ''})
    self.assertFalse(form.is_valid())
    self.assertEqual(
        form.errors['text'],
        ["You can't have an empty list item"]
    )
```

Calling form.is_valid() returns True or False, but it also has the side effect of validating the input data, and populating the errors attribute. It's a dictionary mapping the names of fields to lists of errors for those fields (it's possible for a field to have more than one error).

That gives us:

```
AssertionError: ['This field is required.'] != ["You can't have an empty list
item"]
```

Django already has a default error message that we could present to the user—you might use it if you were in a hurry to build your web app, but we care enough to make our message special. Customising it means changing error_messages, another Meta variable:

lists/forms.py (ch11l010)

```python
class Meta:
    model = Item
    fields = ('text',)
    widgets = {
        'text': forms.fields.TextInput(attrs={
            'placeholder': 'Enter a to-do item',
            'class': 'form-control input-lg',
        }),
    }
    error_messages = {
        'text': {'required': "You can't have an empty list item"}
    }
```

OK

You know what would be even better than messing about with all these error strings? Having a constant:

lists/forms.py (ch11l011)

```python
EMPTY_ITEM_ERROR = "You can't have an empty list item"
[...]

    error_messages = {
        'text': {'required': EMPTY_ITEM_ERROR}
    }
```

Rerun the tests to see that they pass...OK. Now we change the test:

```
from lists.forms import EMPTY_ITEM_ERROR, ItemForm
[...]

    def test_form_validation_for_blank_items(self):
        form = ItemForm(data={'text': ''})
        self.assertFalse(form.is_valid())
        self.assertEqual(form.errors['text'], [EMPTY_ITEM_ERROR])
```

And the tests still pass:

```
OK
```

Great. Totes committable:

```
$ git status # should show lists/forms.py and tests/test_forms.py
$ git add lists
$ git commit -m "new form for list items"
```

Using the Form in Our Views

I had originally thought to extend this form to capture uniqueness validation as well as empty-item validation. But there's a sort of corollary to the "deploy as early as possible" lean methodology, which is "merge code as early as possible". In other words: while building this bit of forms code, it would be easy to go on for ages, adding more and more functionality to the form—I should know, because that's exactly what I did during the drafting of this chapter, and I ended up doing all sorts of work making an all-singing, all-dancing form class before I realised it wouldn't really work for our most basic use case.

So, instead, try to use your new bit of code as soon as possible. This makes sure you never have unused bits of code lying around, and that you start checking your code against "the real world" as soon as possible.

We have a form class which can render some HTML and do validation of at least one kind of error—let's start using it! We should be able to use it in our *base.html* template, and so in all of our views.

Using the Form in a View with a GET Request

Let's start in our unit tests for the home view. We'll add a new method that checks whether we're using the right kind of form:

```
from lists.forms import ItemForm

class HomePageTest(TestCase):

    def test_uses_home_template(self):
        [...]

    def test_home_page_uses_item_form(self):
        response = self.client.get('/')
        self.assertIsInstance(response.context['form'], ItemForm)   ❶
```

❶   `assertIsInstance` checks that our form is of the correct class.

That gives us:

```
KeyError: 'form'
```

So we use the form in our home page view:

```
[...]
from lists.forms import ItemForm
from lists.models import Item, List

def home_page(request):
    return render(request, 'home.html', {'form': ItemForm()})
```

OK, now let's try using it in the template—we replace the old `<input ..>` with `{{ form.text }}`:

```
<form method="POST" action="{% block form_action %}{% endblock %}">
    {{ form.text }}
    {% csrf_token %}
    {% if error %}
      <div class="form-group has-error">
```

`{{ form.text }}` renders just the HTML input for the `text` field of the form.

A Big Find and Replace

One thing we have done, though, is changed our form—it no longer uses the same `id` and `name` attributes. You'll see if we run our functional tests that they fail the first time they try to find the input box:

```
selenium.common.exceptions.NoSuchElementException: Message: Unable to locate
element: [id="id_new_item"]
```

We'll need to fix this, and it's going to involve a big find and replace. Before we do that, let's do a commit, to keep the rename separate from the logic change:

```
$ git diff # review changes in base.html, views.py and its tests
$ git commit -am "use new form in home_page, simplify tests. NB breaks stuff"
```

Let's fix the functional tests. A quick grep shows us there are several places where we're using id_new_item:

```
$ grep id_new_item functional_tests/test*
functional_tests/test_layout_and_styling.py:        inputbox =
self.browser.find_element_by_id('id_new_item')
functional_tests/test_layout_and_styling.py:        inputbox =
self.browser.find_element_by_id('id_new_item')
functional_tests/test_list_item_validation.py:
self.browser.find_element_by_id('id_new_item').send_keys(Keys.ENTER)
[...]
```

That's a good call for a refactor. Let's make a new helper method in *base.py*:

functional_tests/base.py (ch11l018)

```
class FunctionalTest(StaticLiveServerTestCase):
    [...]
    def get_item_input_box(self):
        return self.browser.find_element_by_id('id_text')
```

And then we use it throughout—I had to make four changes in *test_simple_list_cre-ation.py*, two in *test_layout_and_styling.py*, and six in *test_list_item_validation.py*, for example:

functional_tests/test_simple_list_creation.py

```
# She is invited to enter a to-do item straight away
inputbox = self.get_item_input_box()
```

Or:

functional_tests/test_list_item_validation.py

```
# an empty list item. She hits Enter on the empty input box
self.browser.get(self.live_server_url)
self.get_item_input_box().send_keys(Keys.ENTER)
```

I won't show you every single one; I'm sure you can manage this for yourself! You can redo the grep to check that you've caught them all.

We're past the first step, but now we have to bring the rest of the application code in line with the change. We need to find any occurrences of the old id (id_new_item) and name (item_text) and replace them too, with id_text and text, respectively:

```
$ grep -r id_new_item lists/
lists/static/base.css:#id_new_item {
```

That's one change, and similarly for the name:

```
$ grep -Ir item_text lists
[...]
lists/views.py:     item = Item(text=request.POST['item_text'], list=list_)
lists/views.py:            item = Item(text=request.POST['item_text'],
list=list_)
lists/tests/test_views.py:        self.client.post('/lists/new',
data={'item_text': 'A new list item'})
lists/tests/test_views.py:        response = self.client.post('/lists/new',
data={'item_text': 'A new list item'})
[...]
lists/tests/test_views.py:            data={'item_text': ''}
[...]
```

Once we're done, we rerun the unit tests to check that everything still works:

```
$ python manage.py test lists
[...]
.................
 -----------------------------------------------------------------
Ran 17 tests in 0.126s

OK
```

And the functional tests too:

```
$ python manage.py test functional_tests
[...]
  File "...python-tdd-book/functional_tests/test_simple_list_creation.py", line
37, in test_can_start_a_list_for_one_user
    return self.browser.find_element_by_id('id_text')
  File "...python-tdd-book/functional_tests/base.py", line 51, in
get_item_input_box
    return self.browser.find_element_by_id('id_text')
[...]
selenium.common.exceptions.NoSuchElementException: Message: Unable to locate
element: [id="id_text"]
[...]
FAILED (errors=3)
```

Not quite! Let's look at where this is happening—if you check the line number from one of the failures, you'll see that each time after we've submitted a first item, the input box has disappeared from the lists page.

Checking *views.py* and the new_list view we can see it's because if we detect a validation error, we're not actually passing the form to the *home.html* template:

```
except ValidationError:
    list_.delete()
    error = "You can't have an empty list item"
    return render(request, 'home.html', {"error": error})
```

We'll want to use the form in this view too. Before we make any more changes though, let's do a commit:

```
$ git status
$ git commit -am "rename all item input ids and names. still broken"
```

Using the Form in a View That Takes POST Requests

Now we want to adjust the unit tests for the new_list view, especially the one that deals with validation. Let's take a look at it now:

```
class NewListTest(TestCase):
    [...]

    def test_validation_errors_are_sent_back_to_home_page_template(self):
        response = self.client.post('/lists/new', data={'text': ''})
        self.assertEqual(response.status_code, 200)
        self.assertTemplateUsed(response, 'home.html')
        expected_error = escape("You can't have an empty list item")
        self.assertContains(response, expected_error)
```

Adapting the Unit Tests for the new_list View

For a start this test is testing too many things at once, so we've got an opportunity to clarify things here. We should split out two different assertions:

- If there's a validation error, we should render the home template, with a 200.
- If there's a validation error, the response should contain our error text.

And we can add a new one too:

- If there's a validation error, we should pass our form object to the template.

And while we're at it, we'll use our constant instead of the hardcoded string for that error message:

```
from lists.forms import ItemForm, EMPTY_ITEM_ERROR
[...]

class NewListTest(TestCase):
    [...]

    def test_for_invalid_input_renders_home_template(self):
        response = self.client.post('/lists/new', data={'text': ''})
        self.assertEqual(response.status_code, 200)
        self.assertTemplateUsed(response, 'home.html')


    def test_validation_errors_are_shown_on_home_page(self):
        response = self.client.post('/lists/new', data={'text': ''})
        self.assertContains(response, escape(EMPTY_ITEM_ERROR))


    def test_for_invalid_input_passes_form_to_template(self):
        response = self.client.post('/lists/new', data={'text': ''})
        self.assertIsInstance(response.context['form'], ItemForm)
```

Much better. Each test is now clearly testing one thing, and, with a bit of luck, just one will fail and tell us what to do:

```
$ python manage.py test lists
[...]
======================================================================
ERROR: test_for_invalid_input_passes_form_to_template
(lists.tests.test_views.NewListTest)
----------------------------------------------------------------------
Traceback (most recent call last):
  File "...python-tdd-book/lists/tests/test_views.py", line 49, in
test_for_invalid_input_passes_form_to_template
    self.assertIsInstance(response.context['form'], ItemForm)
[...]
KeyError: 'form'


----------------------------------------------------------------------
Ran 19 tests in 0.041s

FAILED (errors=1)
```

Using the Form in the View

And here's how we use the form in the view:

```
def new_list(request):
    form = ItemForm(data=request.POST)   ❶
    if form.is_valid():   ❷
        list_ = List.objects.create()
        Item.objects.create(text=request.POST['text'], list=list_)
        return redirect(list_)
    else:
        return render(request, 'home.html', {"form": form})   ❸
```

❶ We pass the `request.POST` data into the form's constructor.

❷ We use `form.is_valid()` to determine whether this is a good or a bad submission.

❸ In the invalid case, we pass the form down to the template, instead of our hardcoded error string.

That view is now looking much nicer! And all our tests pass, except one:

```
    self.assertContains(response, escape(EMPTY_ITEM_ERROR))
[...]
AssertionError: False is not true : Couldn't find 'You can&#39;t have an empty
list item' in response
```

Using the Form to Display Errors in the Template

We're failing because we're not yet using the form to display errors in the template:

```
<form method="POST" action="{% block form_action %}{% endblock %}">
    {{ form.text }}
    {% csrf_token %}
    {% if form.errors %}   ❶
        <div class="form-group has-error">
            <div class="help-block">{{ form.text.errors }}</div>   ❷
        </div>
    {% endif %}
</form>
```

❶ `form.errors` contains a list of all the errors for the form.

❷ `form.text.errors` is a list of just the errors for the `text` field.

What does that do to our tests?

```
FAIL: test_validation_errors_end_up_on_lists_page
(lists.tests.test_views.ListViewTest)
[...]
AssertionError: False is not true : Couldn't find 'You can&#39;t have an empty
list item' in response
```

An unexpected failure—it's actually in the tests for our final view, view_list. Because we've changed the way errors are displayed in *all* templates, we're no longer showing the error that we manually pass into the template.

That means we're going to need to rework view_list as well, before we can get back to a working state.

Using the Form in the Other View

This view handles both GET and POST requests. Let's start with checking that the form is used in GET requests. We can have a new test for that:

lists/tests/test_views.py

```python
class ListViewTest(TestCase):
    [...]

    def test_displays_item_form(self):
        list_ = List.objects.create()
        response = self.client.get(f'/lists/{list_.id}/')
        self.assertIsInstance(response.context['form'], ItemForm)
        self.assertContains(response, 'name="text"')
```

That gives:

```
KeyError: 'form'
```

Here's a minimal implementation:

lists/views.py (ch11l028)

```python
def view_list(request, list_id):
    [...]
    form = ItemForm()
    return render(request, 'list.html', {
        'list': list_, "form": form, "error": error
    })
```

A Helper Method for Several Short Tests

Next we want to use the form errors in the second view. We'll split our current single test for the invalid case (test_validation_errors_end_up_on_lists_page) into several separate ones:

```python
class ListViewTest(TestCase):
    [...]

    def post_invalid_input(self):
        list_ = List.objects.create()
        return self.client.post(
            f'/lists/{list_.id}/',
            data={'text': ''}
        )

    def test_for_invalid_input_nothing_saved_to_db(self):
        self.post_invalid_input()
        self.assertEqual(Item.objects.count(), 0)

    def test_for_invalid_input_renders_list_template(self):
        response = self.post_invalid_input()
        self.assertEqual(response.status_code, 200)
        self.assertTemplateUsed(response, 'list.html')

    def test_for_invalid_input_passes_form_to_template(self):
        response = self.post_invalid_input()
        self.assertIsInstance(response.context['form'], ItemForm)

    def test_for_invalid_input_shows_error_on_page(self):
        response = self.post_invalid_input()
        self.assertContains(response, escape(EMPTY_ITEM_ERROR))
```

By making a little helper function, `post_invalid_input`, we can make four separate tests without duplicating lots of lines of code.

We've seen this several times now. It often feels more natural to write view tests as a single, monolithic block of assertions—the view should do this and this and this, then return that with this. But breaking things out into multiple tests is definitely worthwhile; as we saw in previous chapters, it helps you isolate the exact problem you may have, when you later come and change your code and accidentally introduce a bug. Helper methods are one of the tools that lower the psychological barrier.

For example, now we can see there's just one failure, and it's a clear one:

```
FAIL: test_for_invalid_input_shows_error_on_page
(lists.tests.test_views.ListViewTest)
AssertionError: False is not true : Couldn't find 'You can&#39;t have an empty
list item' in response
```

Now let's see if we can properly rewrite the view to use our form. Here's a first cut:

```
def view_list(request, list_id):
    list_ = List.objects.get(id=list_id)
    form = ItemForm()
    if request.method == 'POST':
        form = ItemForm(data=request.POST)
        if form.is_valid():
            Item.objects.create(text=request.POST['text'], list=list_)
            return redirect(list_)
    return render(request, 'list.html', {'list': list_, "form": form})
```

That gets the unit tests passing:

```
Ran 23 tests in 0.086s

OK
```

How about the FTs?

```
ERROR: test_cannot_add_empty_list_items
(functional_tests.test_list_item_validation.ItemValidationTest)
 -------------------------------------------------------------------
Traceback (most recent call last):
File "...python-tdd-book/functional_tests/test_list_item_validation.py", line
15, in test_cannot_add_empty_list_items
[...]
selenium.common.exceptions.NoSuchElementException: Message: Unable to locate
element: .has-error
```

Nope.

An Unexpected Benefit: Free Client-Side Validation from HTML5

What's going on here? Let's add our usual `time.sleep` before the error, and take a look at what's happening (or spin up the site manually with `manage.py runserver` if you prefer (see Figure 14-1).

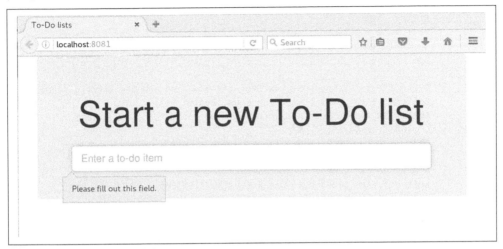

Figure 14-1. HTML5 validation says no

It seems like the browser is preventing the user from even submitting the input when it's empty.

It's because Django has added the `required` attribute to the HTML input[1] (take another look at our `as_p()` printouts from earlier if you don't believe me). This is a new feature of HTML5 (*https://developer.mozilla.org/en-US/docs/Web/HTML/Element/Input#attr-required*), and browsers nowadays will do some validation at the client side if they see it, preventing users from even submitting invalid input.

Let's change our FT to reflect that:

---

1 This is a new feature in Django 1.11.

```
def test_cannot_add_empty_list_items(self):
    # Edith goes to the home page and accidentally tries to submit
    # an empty list item. She hits Enter on the empty input box
    self.browser.get(self.live_server_url)
    self.get_item_input_box().send_keys(Keys.ENTER)

    # The browser intercepts the request, and does not load the
    # list page
    self.wait_for(lambda: self.browser.find_elements_by_css_selector(
        '#id_text:invalid'  ❶
    ))

    # She starts typing some text for the new item and the error disappears
    self.get_item_input_box().send_keys('Buy milk')
    self.wait_for(lambda: self.browser.find_elements_by_css_selector(
        '#id_text:valid'  ❷
    ))

    # And she can submit it successfully
    self.get_item_input_box().send_keys(Keys.ENTER)
    self.wait_for_row_in_list_table('1: Buy milk')

    # Perversely, she now decides to submit a second blank list item
    self.get_item_input_box().send_keys(Keys.ENTER)

    # Again, the browser will not comply
    self.wait_for_row_in_list_table('1: Buy milk')
    self.wait_for(lambda: self.browser.find_elements_by_css_selector(
        '#id_text:invalid'
    ))

    # And she can correct it by filling some text in
    self.get_item_input_box().send_keys('Make tea')
    self.wait_for(lambda: self.browser.find_elements_by_css_selector(
        '#id_text:valid'
    ))
    self.get_item_input_box().send_keys(Keys.ENTER)
    self.wait_for_row_in_list_table('1: Buy milk')
    self.wait_for_row_in_list_table('2: Make tea')
```

❶ Instead of checking for our custom error message, we check using the CSS pseudoselector :invalid, which the browser applies to any HTML5 input that has invalid input.

❷ And its converse in the case of valid inputs.

See how useful and flexible our self.wait_for function is turning out to be?

Our FT does look quite different from how it started though, doesn't it? I'm sure that's raising a lot of questions in your mind right now. Put a pin in them for a moment; I promise we'll talk. Let's first see if we're back to passing tests:

```
$ python manage.py test functional_tests
[...]
....
----------------------------------------------------------------
Ran 4 tests in 12.154s

OK
```

A Pat on the Back

First let's give ourselves a massive pat on the back: we've just made a major change to our small app—that input field, with its name and ID, is absolutely critical to making everything work. We've touched seven or eight different files, doing a refactor that's quite involved…this is the kind of thing that, without tests, would seriously worry me. In fact, I might well have decided that it wasn't worth messing with code that works. But, because we have a full tests suite, we can delve around, tidying things up, safe in the knowledge that the tests are there to spot any mistakes we make. It just makes it that much likelier that you're going to keep refactoring, keep tidying up, keep gardening, keep tending your code, keep everything neat and tidy and clean and smooth and precise and concise and functional and good.

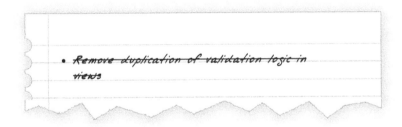

And it's definitely time for a commit:

```
$ git diff
$ git commit -am "use form in all views, back to working state"
```

But Have We Wasted a Lot of Time?

But what about our custom error message? What about all that effort rendering the form in our HTML template? We're not even passing those errors from Django to the user if the browser is intercepting the requests before the user even makes them? And our FT isn't even testing that stuff any more!

Well, you're quite right. But there are two or three reasons all our time hasn't been wasted. Firstly, client-side validation isn't enough to guarantee you're protected from bad inputs, so you always need the server side as well if you really care about data integrity; using a form is a nice way of encapsulating that logic.

Also, not all browsers (*cough—Safari—cough*) fully implement HTML5, so some users are still going to see our custom error message. And if or when we come to letting users access our data via an API (see Appendix F), then our validation messages will come back into use.

On top of that, we'll be able to reuse all our validation and forms code and the front-end `.has-error` classes in the next chapter, when we do some more advanced validation that can't be done by HTML5 magic.

But you know, even if all that wasn't true, you still can't beat yourself up for occasionally going down a blind alley while you're coding. None of us can see the future, and we should concentrate on finding the right solution rather than the time "wasted" on the wrong solution.

Using the Form's Own Save Method

There are a couple more things we can do to make our views even simpler. I've mentioned that forms are supposed to be able to save data to the database for us. Our case won't quite work out of the box, because the item needs to know what list to save to, but it's not hard to fix that.

We start, as always, with a test. Just to illustrate what the problem is, let's see what happens if we just try to call `form.save()`:

lists/tests/test_forms.py (ch11l033)

```python
def test_form_save_handles_saving_to_a_list(self):
    form = ItemForm(data={'text': 'do me'})
    new_item = form.save()
```

Django isn't happy, because an item needs to belong to a list:

```
django.db.utils.IntegrityError: NOT NULL constraint failed: lists_item.list_id
```

Our solution is to tell the form's save method what list it should save to:

lists/tests/test_forms.py

```python
from lists.models import Item, List
[...]

    def test_form_save_handles_saving_to_a_list(self):
        list_ = List.objects.create()
        form = ItemForm(data={'text': 'do me'})
        new_item = form.save(for_list=list_)
        self.assertEqual(new_item, Item.objects.first())
        self.assertEqual(new_item.text, 'do me')
        self.assertEqual(new_item.list, list_)
```

We then make sure that the item is correctly saved to the database, with the right attributes:

```
TypeError: save() got an unexpected keyword argument 'for_list'
```

And here's how we can implement our custom save method:

lists/forms.py (ch11l035)

```python
    def save(self, for_list):
        self.instance.list = for_list
        return super().save()
```

The .instance attribute on a form represents the database object that is being modified or created. And I only learned that as I was writing this chapter! There are other ways of getting this to work, including manually creating the object yourself, or using the commit=False argument to save, but this is the neatest I think. We'll explore a different way of making a form "know" what list it's for in the next chapter:

```
Ran 24 tests in 0.086s
OK
```

Finally we can refactor our views. new_list first:

lists/views.py

```python
def new_list(request):
    form = ItemForm(data=request.POST)
    if form.is_valid():
        list_ = List.objects.create()
        form.save(for_list=list_)
        return redirect(list_)
    else:
        return render(request, 'home.html', {"form": form})
```

Rerun the test to check that everything still passes:

```
Ran 24 tests in 0.086s
OK
```

And now `view_list`:

lists/views.py

```python
def view_list(request, list_id):
    list_ = List.objects.get(id=list_id)
    form = ItemForm()
    if request.method == 'POST':
        form = ItemForm(data=request.POST)
        if form.is_valid():
            form.save(for_list=list_)
            return redirect(list_)
    return render(request, 'list.html', {'list': list_, "form": form})
```

And we still have full passes:

```
Ran 24 tests in 0.111s
OK
```

and:

```
Ran 4 tests in 14.367s
OK
```

Great! Our two views are now looking very much like "normal" Django views: they take information from a user's request, combine it with some custom logic or information from the URL (`list_id`), pass it to a form for validation and possible saving, and then redirect or render a template.

Forms and validation are really important in Django, and in web programming in general, so let's try to make a slightly more complicated one in the next chapter.

Tips

Thin views

If you find yourself looking at complex views, and having to write a lot of tests for them, it's time to start thinking about whether that logic could be moved elsewhere: possibly to a form, like we've done here.

Another possible place would be a custom method on the model class. And—once the complexity of the app demands it—out of Django-specific files and into your own classes and functions, that capture your core business logic.

Each test should test one thing

The heuristic is to be suspicious if there's more than one assertion in a test. Sometimes two assertions are closely related, so they belong together. But often your first draft of a test ends up testing multiple behaviours, and it's worth rewriting it as several tests. Helper functions can keep them from getting too bloated.

More Advanced Forms

Now let's look at some more advanced forms usage. We've helped our users to avoid blank list items, so now let's help them avoid duplicate items.

This chapter goes into more intricate details of Django's form validation, and you have my official permission to skip it if you already know all about customising Django forms, or if you're reading this book for the TDD rather than for the Django.

If you're still learning Django, there's good stuff in here. If you want to skip ahead, that's OK too. Make sure you take a quick look at the aside on developer stupidity, and the recap on testing views at the end.

Another FT for Duplicate Items

We add a second test method to `ItemValidationTest`:

```
def test_cannot_add_duplicate_items(self):
    # Edith goes to the home page and starts a new list
    self.browser.get(self.live_server_url)
    self.get_item_input_box().send_keys('Buy wellies')
    self.get_item_input_box().send_keys(Keys.ENTER)
    self.wait_for_row_in_list_table('1: Buy wellies')

    # She accidentally tries to enter a duplicate item
    self.get_item_input_box().send_keys('Buy wellies')
    self.get_item_input_box().send_keys(Keys.ENTER)

    # She sees a helpful error message
    self.wait_for(lambda: self.assertEqual(
        self.browser.find_element_by_css_selector('.has-error').text,
        "You've already got this in your list"
    ))
```

Why have two test methods rather than extending one, or having a new file and class?
It's a judgement call. These two feel closely related; they're both about validation on
the same input field, so it feels right to keep them in the same file. On the other hand,
they're logically separate enough that it's practical to keep them in different methods:

```
$ python manage.py test functional_tests.test_list_item_validation
[...]
selenium.common.exceptions.NoSuchElementException: Message: Unable to locate
element: .has-error

Ran 2 tests in 9.613s
```

OK, so we know the first of the two tests passes now. Is there a way to run just the
failing one, I hear you ask? Why, yes indeed:

```
$ python manage.py test functional_tests.\
test_list_item_validation.ItemValidationTest.test_cannot_add_duplicate_items
[...]
selenium.common.exceptions.NoSuchElementException: Message: Unable to locate
element: .has-error
```

Preventing Duplicates at the Model Layer

Here's what we really wanted to do. It's a new test that checks that duplicate items in
the same list raise an error:

```
def test_duplicate_items_are_invalid(self):
    list_ = List.objects.create()
    Item.objects.create(list=list_, text='bla')
    with self.assertRaises(ValidationError):
        item = Item(list=list_, text='bla')
        item.full_clean()
```

And, while it occurs to us, we add another test to make sure we don't overdo it on our integrity constraints:

```
def test_CAN_save_same_item_to_different_lists(self):
    list1 = List.objects.create()
    list2 = List.objects.create()
    Item.objects.create(list=list1, text='bla')
    item = Item(list=list2, text='bla')
    item.full_clean()  # should not raise
```

I always like to put a little comment for tests which are checking that a particular use case should *not* raise an error; otherwise, it can be hard to see what's being tested:

```
AssertionError: ValidationError not raised
```

If we want to get it deliberately wrong, we can do this:

```
class Item(models.Model):
    text = models.TextField(default='', unique=True)
    list = models.ForeignKey(List, default=None)
```

That lets us check that our second test really does pick up on this problem:

```
Traceback (most recent call last):
  File "...python-tdd-book/lists/tests/test_models.py", line 62, in
test_CAN_save_same_item_to_different_lists
    item.full_clean()  # should not raise
    [...]
django.core.exceptions.ValidationError: {'text': ['Item with this Text already
exists.']}
```

An Aside on When to Test for Developer Stupidity

One of the judgement calls in testing is when you should write tests that sound like "check that we haven't done something stupid". In general, you should be wary of these.

In this case, we've written a test to check that you can't save duplicate items to the same list. Now, the simplest way to get that test to pass, the way in which you'd write the fewest lines of code, would be to make it impossible to save *any* duplicate items. That justifies writing another test, despite the fact that it would be a "stupid" or "wrong" thing for us to code.

But you can't be writing tests for every possible way we could have coded something wrong. If you have a function that adds two numbers, you can write a couple of tests:

```
assert adder(1, 1) == 2
assert adder(2, 1) == 3
```

But you have the right to assume that the implementation isn't deliberately screwy or perverse:

```
def adder(a, b):
    # unlikely code!
    if a == 3:
        return 666
    else:
        return a + b
```

One way of putting it is that you should trust yourself not to do something *deliberately* stupid, but not something *accidentally* stupid.

Just like ModelForms, models have a class Meta, and that's where we can implement a constraint which says that an item must be unique for a particular list, or in other words, that text and list must be unique together:

lists/models.py (ch09l031)

```
class Item(models.Model):
    text = models.TextField(default='')
    list = models.ForeignKey(List, default=None)

    class Meta:
        unique_together = ('list', 'text')
```

You might want to take a quick peek at the Django docs on model Meta attributes (*https://docs.djangoproject.com/en/1.11/ref/models/options/*) at this point.

A Little Digression on Queryset Ordering and String Representations

When we run the tests they reveal an unexpected failure:

```
======================================================================
FAIL: test_saving_and_retrieving_items
(lists.tests.test_models.ListAndItemModelsTest)
----------------------------------------------------------------------
Traceback (most recent call last):
  File "...python-tdd-book/lists/tests/test_models.py", line 31, in
test_saving_and_retrieving_items
    self.assertEqual(first_saved_item.text, 'The first (ever) list item')
AssertionError: 'Item the second' != 'The first (ever) list item'
- Item the second
[...]
```

 Depending on your platform and its SQLite installation, you may not see this error. You can follow along anyway; the code and tests are interesting in their own right.

That's a bit of a puzzler. A bit of print-based debugging:

lists/tests/test_models.py

```python
first_saved_item = saved_items[0]
print(first_saved_item.text)
second_saved_item = saved_items[1]
print(second_saved_item.text)
self.assertEqual(first_saved_item.text, 'The first (ever) list item')
```

will show us...

```
.....Item the second
The first (ever) list item
F.....
```

It looks like our uniqueness constraint has messed with the default ordering of queries like `Item.objects.all()`. Although we already have a failing test, it's best to add a new test that explicitly tests for ordering:

```
def test_list_ordering(self):
    list1 = List.objects.create()
    item1 = Item.objects.create(list=list1, text='i1')
    item2 = Item.objects.create(list=list1, text='item 2')
    item3 = Item.objects.create(list=list1, text='3')
    self.assertEqual(
        Item.objects.all(),
        [item1, item2, item3]
    )
```

That gives us a new failure, but it's not a very readable one:

```
AssertionError: <QuerySet [<Item: Item object>, <Item: Item object>, <Item:
Item object>]> != [<Item: Item object>, <Item: Item object>, <Item: Item
object>]
```

We need a better string representation for our objects. Let's add another unit test:

Ordinarily you would be wary of adding more failing tests when you already have some—it makes reading test output that much more complicated, and just generally makes you nervous. Will we ever get back to a working state? In this case, they're all quite simple tests, so I'm not worried.

lists/tests/test_models.py (ch13l008)

```
def test_string_representation(self):
    item = Item(text='some text')
    self.assertEqual(str(item), 'some text')
```

That gives us:

```
AssertionError: 'Item object' != 'some text'
```

As well as the other two failures. Let's start fixing them all now:

lists/models.py (ch09l034)

```
class Item(models.Model):
    [...]

    def __str__(self):
        return self.text
```

In Python 2.x versions of Django, the string representation method used to be __unicode__. Like much string handling, this is simplified in Python 3. See the Django docs (*https://docs.djangoproject.com/en/1.11/topics/python3/#str-and-unicode-methods*).

Now we're down to two failures, and the ordering test has a more readable failure message:

```
AssertionError: <QuerySet [<Item: i1>, <Item: item 2>, <Item: 3>]> != [<Item:
i1>, <Item: item 2>, <Item: 3>]
```

We can fix that in the class Meta:

lists/models.py (ch09l035)

```
class Meta:
    ordering = ('id',)
    unique_together = ('list', 'text')
```

Does that work?

```
AssertionError: <QuerySet [<Item: i1>, <Item: item 2>, <Item: 3>]> != [<Item:
i1>, <Item: item 2>, <Item: 3>]
```

Urp? It has worked; you can see the items *are* in the same order, but the tests are confused. I keep running into this problem actually—Django querysets don't compare well with lists. We can fix it by converting the queryset to a list[1] in our test:

lists/tests/test_models.py (ch09l036)

```
self.assertEqual(
    list(Item.objects.all()),
    [item1, item2, item3]
)
```

That works; we get a fully passing test suite:

```
OK
```

Rewriting the Old Model Test

That long-winded model test did serendipitously help us find an unexpected bug, but now it's time to rewrite it. I wrote it in a very verbose style to introduce the Django ORM, but in fact, now that we have the explicit test for ordering, we can get the same coverage from a couple of much shorter tests. Delete test_saving_and_retriev ing_items and replace with this:

---

1 You could also check out assertSequenceEqual from unittest, and assertQuerysetEqual from Django's test tools, although I confess when I last looked at assertQuerysetEqual I was quite baffled...

```python
class ListAndItemModelsTest(TestCase):

    def test_default_text(self):
        item = Item()
        self.assertEqual(item.text, '')


    def test_item_is_related_to_list(self):
        list_ = List.objects.create()
        item = Item()
        item.list = list_
        item.save()
        self.assertIn(item, list_.item_set.all())

    [...]
```

That's more than enough really—a check of the default values of attributes on a freshly initialized model object is enough to sanity-check that we've probably set some fields up in *models.py*. The "item is related to list" test is a real "belt and braces" test to make sure that our foreign key relationship works.

While we're at it, we can split this file out into tests for Item and tests for List (there's only one of the latter, test_get_absolute_url):

```python
class ItemModelTest(TestCase):

    def test_default_text(self):
        [...]


class ListModelTest(TestCase):

    def test_get_absolute_url(self):
        [...]
```

That's neater and tidier:

```
$ python manage.py test lists
[...]
Ran 29 tests in 0.092s

OK
```

Some Integrity Errors Do Show Up on Save

A final aside before we move on. Do you remember I mentioned in Chapter 13 that some data integrity errors *are* picked up on save? It all depends on whether the integrity constraint is actually being enforced by the database.

Try running `makemigrations` and you'll see that Django wants to add the `unique_together` constraint to the database itself, rather than just having it as an application-layer constraint:

```
$ python manage.py makemigrations
Migrations for 'lists':
  lists/migrations/0005_auto_20140414_2038.py
    - Change Meta options on item
    - Alter unique_together for item (1 constraint(s))
```

Now if we change our duplicates test to do a `.save` instead of a `.full_clean`...

lists/tests/test_models.py

```python
def test_duplicate_items_are_invalid(self):
    list_ = List.objects.create()
    Item.objects.create(list=list_, text='bla')
    with self.assertRaises(ValidationError):
        item = Item(list=list_, text='bla')
        # item.full_clean()
        item.save()
```

It gives:

```
ERROR: test_duplicate_items_are_invalid (lists.tests.test_models.ItemModelTest)
[...]
    return Database.Cursor.execute(self, query, params)
sqlite3.IntegrityError: UNIQUE constraint failed: lists_item.list_id,
lists_item.text
[...]
django.db.utils.IntegrityError: UNIQUE constraint failed: lists_item.list_id,
lists_item.text
```

You can see that the error bubbles up from SQLite, and it's a different error from the one we want, an `IntegrityError` instead of a `ValidationError`.

Let's revert our changes to the test, and see them all passing again:

```
$ python manage.py test lists
[...]
Ran 29 tests in 0.092s
OK
```

And now it's time to commit our model-layer changes:

```
$ git status # should show changes to tests + models and new migration
# let's give our new migration a better name
$ mv lists/migrations/0005_auto* lists/migrations/0005_list_item_unique_together.py
$ git add lists
$ git diff --staged
$ git commit -am "Implement duplicate item validation at model layer"
```

Experimenting with Duplicate Item Validation at the Views Layer

Let's try running our FT, just to see where we are:

```
selenium.common.exceptions.NoSuchElementException: Message: Unable to locate
element: .has-error
```

In case you didn't see it as it flew past, the site is 500ing.[2] A quick unit test at the view level ought to clear this up:

lists/tests/test_views.py (ch13l014)

```
class ListViewTest(TestCase):
    [...]

    def test_for_invalid_input_shows_error_on_page(self):
        [...]


    def test_duplicate_item_validation_errors_end_up_on_lists_page(self):
        list1 = List.objects.create()
        item1 = Item.objects.create(list=list1, text='textey')
        response = self.client.post(
            f'/lists/{list1.id}/',
            data={'text': 'textey'}
        )

        expected_error = escape("You've already got this in your list")
        self.assertContains(response, expected_error)
        self.assertTemplateUsed(response, 'list.html')
        self.assertEqual(Item.objects.all().count(), 1)
```

Gives:

```
django.db.utils.IntegrityError: UNIQUE constraint failed: lists_item.list_id,
lists_item.text
```

We want to avoid integrity errors! Ideally, we want the call to is_valid to somehow notice the duplication error before we even try to save, but to do that, our form will need to know in advance what list it's being used for.

---

2 It's showing a server error, code 500. Gotta get with the jargon!

Let's put a skip on that test for now:

lists/tests/test_views.py (ch13l015)

```
from unittest import skip
[...]

    @skip
    def test_duplicate_item_validation_errors_end_up_on_lists_page(self):
```

A More Complex Form to Handle Uniqueness Validation

The form to create a new list only needs to know one thing, the new item text. A form which validates that list items are unique needs to know the list too. Just as we overrode the save method on our `ItemForm`, this time we'll override the constructor on our new form class so that it knows what list it applies to.

We duplicate our tests for the previous form, tweaking them slightly:

lists/tests/test_forms.py (ch13l016)

```
from lists.forms import (
    DUPLICATE_ITEM_ERROR, EMPTY_ITEM_ERROR,
    ExistingListItemForm, ItemForm
)
[...]

class ExistingListItemFormTest(TestCase):

    def test_form_renders_item_text_input(self):
        list_ = List.objects.create()
        form = ExistingListItemForm(for_list=list_)
        self.assertIn('placeholder="Enter a to-do item"', form.as_p())


    def test_form_validation_for_blank_items(self):
        list_ = List.objects.create()
        form = ExistingListItemForm(for_list=list_, data={'text': ''})
        self.assertFalse(form.is_valid())
        self.assertEqual(form.errors['text'], [EMPTY_ITEM_ERROR])


    def test_form_validation_for_duplicate_items(self):
        list_ = List.objects.create()
        Item.objects.create(list=list_, text='no twins!')
        form = ExistingListItemForm(for_list=list_, data={'text': 'no twins!'})
        self.assertFalse(form.is_valid())
        self.assertEqual(form.errors['text'], [DUPLICATE_ITEM_ERROR])
```

Next we iterate through a few TDD cycles until we get a form with a custom constructor, which just ignores its `for_list` argument. (I won't show them all, but I'm sure you'll do them, right? Remember, the Goat sees all.)

lists/forms.py (ch09l071)

```
DUPLICATE_ITEM_ERROR = "You've already got this in your list"
[...]
class ExistingListItemForm(forms.models.ModelForm):
    def __init__(self, for_list, *args, **kwargs):
        super().__init__(*args, **kwargs)
```

At this point our error should be:

```
ValueError: ModelForm has no model class specified.
```

Then let's see if making it inherit from our existing form helps:

lists/forms.py (ch09l072)

```
class ExistingListItemForm(ItemForm):
    def __init__(self, for_list, *args, **kwargs):
        super().__init__(*args, **kwargs)
```

Yes, that takes us down to just one failure:

```
FAIL: test_form_validation_for_duplicate_items
(lists.tests.test_forms.ExistingListItemFormTest)
    self.assertFalse(form.is_valid())
AssertionError: True is not false
```

The next step requires a little knowledge of Django's internals, but you can read up on it in the Django docs on model validation (*https://docs.djangoproject.com/en/1.11/ref/ models/instances/#validating-objects*) and form validation (*https://docs.djangopro ject.com/en/1.11/ref/forms/validation/*).

Django uses a method called `validate_unique`, both on forms and models, and we can use both, in conjunction with the `instance` attribute:

```python
from django.core.exceptions import ValidationError
[...]

class ExistingListItemForm(ItemForm):

    def __init__(self, for_list, *args, **kwargs):
        super().__init__(*args, **kwargs)
        self.instance.list = for_list


    def validate_unique(self):
        try:
            self.instance.validate_unique()
        except ValidationError as e:
            e.error_dict = {'text': [DUPLICATE_ITEM_ERROR]}
            self._update_errors(e)
```

That's a bit of Django voodoo right there, but we basically take the validation error, adjust its error message, and then pass it back into the form.

And we're there! A quick commit:

```
$ git diff
$ git commit -a
```

Using the Existing List Item Form in the List View

Now let's see if we can put this form to work in our view.

We remove the skip, and while we're at it, we can use our new constant. Tidy.

lists/tests/test_views.py (ch13l049)

```python
from lists.forms import (
    DUPLICATE_ITEM_ERROR, EMPTY_ITEM_ERROR,
    ExistingListItemForm, ItemForm,
)
[...]

    def test_duplicate_item_validation_errors_end_up_on_lists_page(self):
        [...]
        expected_error = escape(DUPLICATE_ITEM_ERROR)
```

That brings back our integrity error:

```
django.db.utils.IntegrityError: UNIQUE constraint failed: lists_item.list_id,
lists_item.text
```

Our fix for this is to switch to using the new form class. Before we implement it, let's find the tests where we check the form class, and adjust them:

```
class ListViewTest(TestCase):
    [...]

    def test_displays_item_form(self):
        list_ = List.objects.create()
        response = self.client.get(f'/lists/{list_.id}/')
        self.assertIsInstance(response.context['form'], ExistingListItemForm)
        self.assertContains(response, 'name="text"')

    [...]

    def test_for_invalid_input_passes_form_to_template(self):
        response = self.post_invalid_input()
        self.assertIsInstance(response.context['form'], ExistingListItemForm)
```

That gives us:

```
AssertionError: <ItemForm bound=False, valid=False, fields=(text)> is not an
instance of <class 'lists.forms.ExistingListItemForm'>
```

So we can adjust the view:

```
from lists.forms import ExistingListItemForm, ItemForm
[...]
def view_list(request, list_id):
    list_ = List.objects.get(id=list_id)
    form = ExistingListItemForm(for_list=list_)
    if request.method == 'POST':
        form = ExistingListItemForm(for_list=list_, data=request.POST)
        if form.is_valid():
            form.save()
            [...]
```

And that *almost* fixes everything, except for an unexpected fail:

```
TypeError: save() missing 1 required positional argument: 'for_list'
```

Our custom save method from the parent ItemForm is no longer needed. Let's make a quick unit test for that:

```
def test_form_save(self):
    list_ = List.objects.create()
    form = ExistingListItemForm(for_list=list_, data={'text': 'hi'})
    new_item = form.save()
    self.assertEqual(new_item, Item.objects.all()[0])
```

We can make our form call the grandparent save method:

```
def save(self):
    return forms.models.ModelForm.save(self)
```

 Personal opinion here: I could have used super, but I prefer not to use super when it requires arguments, say, to get a grandparent method. I find Python 3's super() with no args awesome to get the immediate parent. Anything else is too error-prone, and I find it ugly besides. YMMV.

And we're there! All the unit tests pass:

```
$ python manage.py test lists
[...]
Ran 34 tests in 0.082s

OK
```

And so does our FT for validation:

```
$ python manage.py test functional_tests.test_list_item_validation
[...]
..
 ----------------------------------------------------------------
Ran 2 tests in 12.040s

OK
```

As a final check, we rerun *all* the FTs:

```
$ python manage.py test functional_tests
[...]
.....
 ----------------------------------------------------------------
Ran 5 tests in 19.048s

OK
```

Hooray! Time for a final commit, and a wrap-up of what we've learned about testing views over the last few chapters.

Wrapping Up: What We've Learned About Testing Django

We're now at a point where our app looks a lot more like a "standard" Django app, and it implements the three common Django layers: models, forms, and views. We no longer have any "training wheels"-style tests, and our code looks pretty much like code we'd be happy to see in a real app.

We have one unit test file for each of our key source code files. Here's a recap of the biggest (and highest-level) one, *test_views* (the listing shows just the key tests and assertions):

What to Test in Views

lists/tests/test_views.py

```python
class ListViewTest(TestCase):
    def test_uses_list_template(self):
        response = self.client.get(f'/lists/{list_.id}/')  ❶
        self.assertTemplateUsed(response, 'list.html')  ❷
    def test_passes_correct_list_to_template(self):
        self.assertEqual(response.context['list'], correct_list)  ❸
    def test_displays_item_form(self):
        self.assertIsInstance(response.context['form'], ExistingListItemForm)  ❹
        self.assertContains(response, 'name="text"')
    def test_displays_only_items_for_that_list(self):
        self.assertContains(response, 'itemey 1')  ❺
        self.assertContains(response, 'itemey 2')  ❺
        self.assertNotContains(response, 'other list item 1')  ❺
    def test_can_save_a_POST_request_to_an_existing_list(self):
        self.assertEqual(Item.objects.count(), 1)  ❻
        self.assertEqual(new_item.text, 'A new item for an existing list')  ❻
    def test_POST_redirects_to_list_view(self):
        self.assertRedirects(response, f'/lists/{correct_list.id}/')  ❻
    def test_for_invalid_input_nothing_saved_to_db(self):
        self.assertEqual(Item.objects.count(), 0)  ❻
    def test_for_invalid_input_renders_list_template(self):
        self.assertEqual(response.status_code, 200)
        self.assertTemplateUsed(response, 'list.html')  ❻
    def test_for_invalid_input_passes_form_to_template(self):
        self.assertIsInstance(response.context['form'], ExistingListItemForm)  ❼
    def test_for_invalid_input_shows_error_on_page(self):
        self.assertContains(response, escape(EMPTY_ITEM_ERROR))  ❼
    def test_duplicate_item_validation_errors_end_up_on_lists_page(self):
        self.assertContains(response, expected_error)
        self.assertTemplateUsed(response, 'list.html')
        self.assertEqual(Item.objects.all().count(), 1)
```

❶ Use the Django Test Client.

❷ Check the template used. Then, check each item in the template context.

❸ Check that any objects are the right ones, or querysets have the correct items.

❹ Check that any forms are of the correct class.

❺ Think about testing template logic: any for or if might deserve a minimal test.

---

❻ For POST requests, make sure you test both the valid case and the invalid case.

❼ Optionally, sanity-check that your form is rendered, and its errors are displayed.

Why these points? Skip ahead to Appendix B, and I'll show how they are sufficient to ensure that our views are still correct if we refactor them to start using class-based views.

Next we'll try to make our data validation more friendly by using a bit of client-side code. Uh-oh, you know what that means…

Dipping Our Toes, Very Tentatively, into JavaScript

If the Good Lord had wanted us to enjoy ourselves, he wouldn't have granted us his precious gift of relentless misery.

—John Calvin (as portrayed in Calvin and the Chipmunks (*http://onemillion points.blogspot.co.uk/2008/08/calvin-and-chipmunks.html*))

Our new validation logic is good, but wouldn't it be nice if the duplicate item error messages disappeared once the user started fixing the problem? Just like our nice HTML5 validation errors do? For that we'd need a teeny-tiny bit of JavaScript.

We are utterly spoiled by programming every day in such a joyful language as Python. JavaScript is our punishment. For a web developer though, there's no way around it. So let's dip our toes in, very gingerly.

 I'm going to assume you know the basics of JavaScript syntax. If you haven't read *JavaScript: The Good Parts*, go and get yourself a copy right away! It's not a very long book.

Starting with an FT

Let's add a new functional test to the `ItemValidationTest` class:

functional_tests/test_list_item_validation.py (ch14l001)

```python
def test_error_messages_are_cleared_on_input(self):
    # Edith starts a list and causes a validation error:
    self.browser.get(self.live_server_url)
    self.get_item_input_box().send_keys('Banter too thick')
    self.get_item_input_box().send_keys(Keys.ENTER)
    self.wait_for_row_in_list_table('1: Banter too thick')
    self.get_item_input_box().send_keys('Banter too thick')
    self.get_item_input_box().send_keys(Keys.ENTER)

    self.wait_for(lambda: self.assertTrue(              ❶
        self.browser.find_element_by_css_selector('.has-error').is_displayed()   ❷
    ))

    # She starts typing in the input box to clear the error
    self.get_item_input_box().send_keys('a')

    # She is pleased to see that the error message disappears
    self.wait_for(lambda: self.assertFalse(
        self.browser.find_element_by_css_selector('.has-error').is_displayed()   ❷
    ))
```

❶   We use another of our `wait_for` invocations, this time with `assertTrue`.

❷   `is_displayed()` tells you whether an element is visible or not. We can't just rely on checking whether the element is present in the DOM, because now we're starting to hide elements.

That fails appropriately, but before we move on: three strikes and refactor! We've got several places where we find the error element using CSS. Let's move it to a helper function:

functional_tests/test_list_item_validation.py (ch14l002)

```python
class ItemValidationTest(FunctionalTest):

    def get_error_element(self):
        return self.browser.find_element_by_css_selector('.has-error')

    [...]
```

 I like to keep helper functions in the FT class that's using them, and only promote them to the base class when they're actually needed elsewhere. It stops the base class from getting too cluttered. YAGNI.

And we then make three replacements in *test_list_item_validation*, like this:

```
    self.wait_for(lambda: self.assertEqual(
        self.get_error_element().text,
        "You've already got this in your list"
    ))
[...]
    self.wait_for(lambda: self.assertTrue(
        self.get_error_element().is_displayed()
    ))
[...]
    self.wait_for(lambda: self.assertFalse(
        self.get_error_element().is_displayed()
    ))
```

We have an expected failure:

```
$ python manage.py test functional_tests.test_list_item_validation
[...]
    self.get_error_element().is_displayed()
AssertionError: True is not false
```

And we can commit this as the first cut of our FT.

Setting Up a Basic JavaScript Test Runner

Choosing your testing tools in the Python and Django world is fairly straightforward. The standard library unittest package is perfectly adequate, and the Django test runner also makes a good default choice. There are some alternatives out there—nose (*http://nose.readthedocs.org/*) is popular, Green (*https://github.com/CleanCut/green*) is the new kid on the block, and I've personally found pytest (*http://pytest.org/*) to be very impressive. But there is a clear default option, and it's just fine.[1]

Not so in the JavaScript world! We use YUI and Jest at work, but I thought I'd go out and see whether there were any new tools out there. I was overwhelmed with options —jsUnit, Qunit, Mocha, Chutzpah, Karma, Jasmine, and many more. And it doesn't end there either: as I had almost settled on one of them, Mocha,[2] I find out that I now need to choose an *assertion framework* and a *reporter*, and maybe a *mocking library*, and it never ends!

In the end I decided we should use QUnit (*http://qunitjs.com/*) because it's simple, has a similar look and feel to Python unit tests, and it works well with jQuery.

Make a directory called *tests* inside *lists/static*, and download the QUnit JavaScript and CSS files into it. We'll also put a file called *tests.html* in there:

---

1 Admittedly once you start looking for Python BDD tools, things are a little more confusing.

2 Purely because it features the NyanCat (*https://mochajs.org/#nyan*) test runner.

```
$ tree lists/static/tests/
lists/static/tests/
├── qunit-2.0.1.css
├── qunit-2.0.1.js
└── tests.html
```

The boilerplate for a QUnit HTML file looks like this, including a smoke test:

```html
<!DOCTYPE html>
<html>
<head>
  <meta charset="utf-8">
  <meta name="viewport" content="width=device-width">
  <title>Javascript tests</title>
  <link rel="stylesheet" href="qunit-2.0.1.css">
</head>
<body>
  <div id="qunit"></div>
  <div id="qunit-fixture"></div>
  <script src="qunit-2.0.1.js"></script>

  <script>

QUnit.test("smoke test", function (assert) {
  assert.equal(1, 1, "Maths works!");
});

  </script>
</body>
</html>
```

Dissecting that, the important things to pick up are the fact that we pull in *qunit-2.0.1.js* using the first <script> tag, and then use the second one to write the main body of tests.

If you open up the file using your web browser (no need to run the dev server, just find the file on disk), you should see something like Figure 16-1.

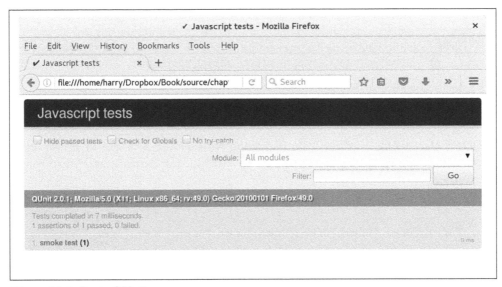

Figure 16-1. Basic QUnit screen

Looking at the test itself, we'll find many similarities with the Python tests we've been writing so far:

```
QUnit.test("smoke test", function (assert) { ❶
    assert.equal(1, 1, "Maths works!"); ❷
});
```

❶ The `QUnit.test` function defines a test case, a bit like `def test_some thing(self)` did in Python. Its first argument is a name for the test, and the second is a function for the body of the test.

❷ The `assert.equal` function is an assertion; very much like `assertEqual`, it compares two arguments. Unlike in Python, though, the message is displayed both for failures and for passes, so it should be phrased as a positive rather than a negative.

Why not try changing those arguments to see a deliberate failure?

Using jQuery and the Fixtures Div

Let's get a bit more comfortable with what our testing framework can do, and start using a bit of jQuery—an almost indispensable library that gives you a cross-browser-compatible API for manipulating the DOM.

If you've never seen jQuery before, I'm going to try to explain it as we go, just enough so that you won't be totally lost; but this isn't a jQuery tutorial. You may find it helpful to spend an hour or two investigating jQuery at some point during this chapter.

Download the latest jQuery from jquery.com (*https://jquery.com/download/*) and save it into the *lists/static* folder.

Then let's start using it in our tests file, along with adding a couple of HTML elements. We'll start by seeing if we can show and hide an element, and write some assertions about its visibility:

lists/static/tests/tests.html

```
<div id="qunit-fixture"></div>

<form>  ❶
  <input name="text" />
  <div class="has-error">Error text</div>
</form>

<script src="../jquery-3.1.1.min.js"></script>  ❷
<script src="qunit-2.0.1.js"></script>

<script>

QUnit.test("smoke test", function (assert) {
  assert.equal($('.has-error').is(':visible'), true);  ❸❹
  $('.has-error').hide();  ❺
  assert.equal($('.has-error').is(':visible'), false);  ❻
});

</script>
```

❶ The `<form>` and its contents are there to represent what will be on the real list page.

❷ Here's where we load jQuery.

❸ jQuery magic starts here! $ is the jQuery Swiss Army knife. It's used to find bits of the DOM. Its first argument is a CSS selector; here, we're telling it to find all elements that have the class "has-error". It returns an object that represents one or more DOM elements. That, in turn, has various useful methods that allow us to manipulate or find out about those elements.

④ One of which is `.is`, which can tell us whether an element matches a particular CSS property. Here we use `:visible` to check whether the element is displayed or hidden.

⑤ We then use jQuery's `.hide()` method to hide the div. Behind the scenes, it dynamically sets a `style="display: none"` on the element.

⑥ And finally we check that it's worked, with a second `assert.equal`.

If you refresh the browser, you should see that all passes:

Expected results from QUnit in the browser

```
2 assertions of 2 passed, 0 failed.
1. smoke test (2)
```

Time to see how fixtures work. Let's just dupe up this test:

lists/static/tests/tests.html

```
<script>

QUnit.test("smoke test", function (assert) {
  assert.equal($('.has-error').is(':visible'), true);
  $('.has-error').hide();
  assert.equal($('.has-error').is(':visible'), false);
});
QUnit.test("smoke test 2", function (assert) {
  assert.equal($('.has-error').is(':visible'), true);
  $('.has-error').hide();
  assert.equal($('.has-error').is(':visible'), false);
});

</script>
```

Slightly unexpectedly, we find one of them fails—see Figure 16-2.

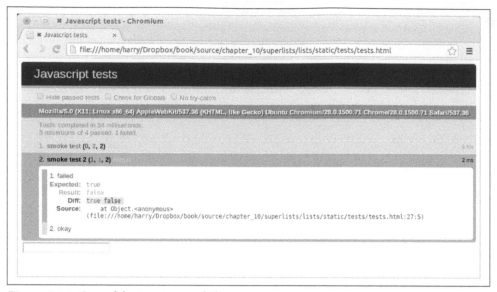

Figure 16-2. One of the two tests is failing

What's happening here is that the first test hides the error div, so when the second test runs, it starts out invisible.

> QUnit tests do not run in a predictable order, so you can't rely on the first test running before the second one. Try hitting refresh a few times, and you'll find that the test which fails changes...

We need some way of tidying up between tests, a bit like `setUp` and `tearDown`, or like the Django test runner would reset the database between each test. The `qunit-fixture` div is what we're looking for. Move the form in there:

lists/static/tests/tests.html

```html
<div id="qunit"></div>
<div id="qunit-fixture">
    <form>
        <input name="text" />
        <div class="has-error">Error text</div>
    </form>
</div>

<script src="../jquery-3.1.1.min.js"></script>
```

As you've probably guessed, jQuery resets the content of the fixtures div before each test, so that gets us back to two neatly passing tests:

```
4 assertions of 4 passed, 0 failed.
1. smoke test (2)
2. smoke test 2 (2)
```

Building a JavaScript Unit Test for Our Desired Functionality

Now that we're acquainted with our JavaScript testing tools, we can switch back to just one test and start to write the real thing:

lists/static/tests/tests.html

```
<script>

QUnit.test("errors should be hidden on keypress", function (assert) {
    $('input[name="text"]').trigger('keypress'); ❶
    assert.equal($('.has-error').is(':visible'), false);
});

</script>
```

❶ The jQuery `.trigger` method is mainly used for testing. It says "fire off a JavaScript DOM event on the element(s)". Here we use the *keypress* event, which is fired off by the browser behind the scenes whenever a user types something into a particular input element.

 jQuery is hiding a lot of complexity behind the scenes here. Check out Quirksmode.org (*http://www.quirksmode.org/dom/events/index.html*) for a view on the hideous nest of differences between the different browsers' interpretation of events. The reason that jQuery is so popular is that it just makes all this stuff go away.

And that gives us:

```
0 assertions of 1 passed, 1 failed.
1. errors should be hidden on keypress (1, 0, 1)
    1. failed
        Expected: false
        Result: true
```

Let's say we want to keep our code in a standalone JavaScript file called *list.js*.

```
<script src="../jquery-3.1.1.min.js"></script>
<script src="../list.js"></script>
<script src="qunit-2.0.1.js"></script>

<script>
  [...]
```

Here's the minimal code to get that test to pass:

```
$('.has-error').hide();
```

And it works...

```
1 assertions of 1 passed, 0 failed.
1. errors should be hidden on keypress (1)
```

But it has an obvious problem. We'd better add another test:

```
QUnit.test("errors should be hidden on keypress", function (assert) {
  $('input[name="text"]').trigger('keypress');
  assert.equal($('.has-error').is(':visible'), false);
});

QUnit.test("errors aren't hidden if there is no keypress", function (assert) {
  assert.equal($('.has-error').is(':visible'), true);
});
```

Now we get an expected failure:

```
1 assertions of 2 passed, 1 failed.
1. errors should be hidden on keypress (1)
2. errors aren't hidden if there is no keypress (1, 0, 1)
    1. failed
        Expected: true
        Result: false
[...]
```

And we can make a more realistic implementation:

```
$('input[name="text"]').on('keypress', function () {  ❶
  $('.has-error').hide();
});
```

❶ This line says: find any input elements whose name attribute is "text", and add an event listener which reacts *on* keypress events. The event listener is the inline function, which hides all elements that have the class `.has-error`.

Does it work? No.

```
1 assertions of 2 passed, 1 failed.
1. errors should be hidden on keypress (1, 0, 1)
    1. failed
        Expected: false
        Result: true
[...]
2. errors aren't hidden if there is no keypress (1)
```

Curses! Why is that?

Fixtures, Execution Order, and Global State: Key Challenges of JS Testing

One of the difficulties with JavaScript in general, and testing in particular, is in understanding the order of execution of our code (i.e., what happens when). When does our code in *list.js* run, and when does each of our tests run? And how does that interact with global state, that is, the DOM of our web page, and the fixtures that we've already seen are supposed to be cleaned up after each test?

console.log for Debug Printing

Let's add a couple of debug prints, or "console.logs":

lists/static/tests/tests.html

```
<script>

console.log('qunit tests start');

QUnit.test("errors should be hidden on keypress", function (assert) {
  console.log('in test 1');
  $('input[name="text"]').trigger('keypress');
  assert.equal($('.has-error').is(':visible'), false);
});

QUnit.test("errors aren't hidden if there is no keypress", function (assert) {
  console.log('in test 2');
  assert.equal($('.has-error').is(':visible'), true);
});
  </script>
```

And the same in our actual JS code:

```
$('input[name="text"]').on('keypress', function () {
  console.log('in keypress handler');
  $('.has-error').hide();
});
console.log('list.js loaded');
```

Rerun the tests, opening up the browser debug console (Ctrl-Shift-I usually) and you should see something like Figure 16-3.

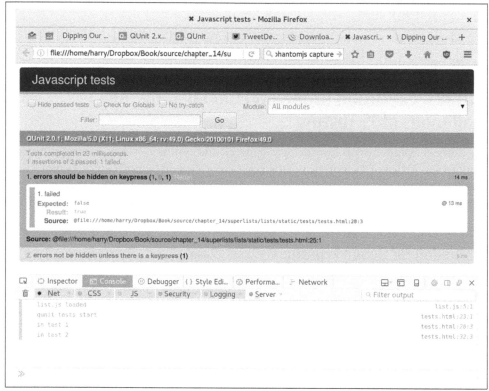

Figure 16-3. QUnit tests with console.log debug outputs

What do we see?

- *list.js* loads first. So our event listener should be attached to the input element.
- Then our QUnit tests file loads.
- Then each test runs.

But, thinking it through, each test is going to "reset" the fixtures div, which means destroying and re-creating the input element. So the input element that *list.js* sees and attaches the event listener to will be replaced with a new one by the time each test runs.

Using an Initialize Function for More Control Over Execution Time

We need more control over the order of execution of our JavaScript. Rather than just relying on the code in *list.js* running whenever it is loaded by a <script> tag, we can use a common pattern, which is to define an "initialize" function, and call that when we want to in our tests (and later in real life):

lists/static/list.js

```
var initialize = function () {
  console.log('initialize called');
  $('input[name="text"]').on('keypress', function () {
    console.log('in keypress handler');
    $('.has-error').hide();
  });
};
console.log('list.js loaded');
```

And in our tests file, we call `initialize` with each test:

lists/static/tests/tests.html (ch14l017)

```
QUnit.test("errors should be hidden on keypress", function (assert) {
  console.log('in test 1');
  initialize();
  $('input[name="text"]').trigger('keypress');
  assert.equal($('.has-error').is(':visible'), false);
});

QUnit.test("errors aren't hidden if there is no keypress", function (assert) {
  console.log('in test 2');
  initialize();
  assert.equal($('.has-error').is(':visible'), true);
});
```

Now we should see our tests pass, and our debug output should make more sense:

```
2 assertions of 2 passed, 0 failed.
1. errors should be hidden on keypress (1)
2. errors aren't hidden if there is no keypress (1)

list.js loaded
qunit tests start
in test 1
initialize called
in keypress handler
in test 2
initialize called
```

Hooray! Let's strip out those console.logs:

lists/static/list.js

```
var initialize = function () {
  $('input[name="text"]').on('keypress', function () {
    $('.has-error').hide();
  });
};
```

And from the tests too…

lists/static/tests/tests.html

```
QUnit.test("errors should be hidden on keypress", function (assert) {
  initialize();
  $('input[name="text"]').trigger('keypress');
  assert.equal($('.has-error').is(':visible'), false);
});

QUnit.test("errors aren't hidden if there is no keypress", function (assert) {
  initialize();
  assert.equal($('.has-error').is(':visible'), true);
});
```

And for the moment of truth, we'll pull in jQuery, our script, and invoke our initialize function on our real pages:

lists/templates/base.html (ch14l020)

```
    </div>
    <script src="/static/jquery-3.1.1.min.js"></script>
    <script src="/static/list.js"></script>

    <script>
      initialize();
    </script>

  </body>
</html>
```

 It's good practice to put your script loads at the end of your body HTML, as it means the user doesn't have to wait for all your JavaScript to load before they can see something on the page. It also helps to make sure most of the DOM has loaded before any scripts run.

Aaaand we run our FT:

```
$ python manage.py test functional_tests.test_list_item_validation.\
ItemValidationTest.test_error_messages_are_cleared_on_input
[...]

Ran 1 test in 3.023s

OK
```

Hooray! That's a commit!

```
$ git add lists/static
$ git commit -m"add jquery, qunit tests, list.js with keypress listeners"
```

Columbo Says: Onload Boilerplate and Namespacing

Oh, and one more thing. Our `initialize` function name is too generic—what if we include some third-party JavaScript tool later that also defines a function called `initialize`? Let's give ourselves a "namespace" that's unlikely to be used by anyone else:

lists/static/list.js

```
window.Superlists = {}; ❶
window.Superlists.initialize = function () { ❷
  $('input[name="text"]').on('keypress', function () {
    $('.has-error').hide();
  });
};
```

❶ We explicitly declare an object as a property of the "window" global, giving it a name that we think no one else is likely to use.

❷ Then we make our `initialize` function an attribute of that namespace object.

 There are lots of other, much cleverer ways of dealing with namespaces in JavaScript, but they are all more complicated, and I'm not enough of an expert to be able to steer you around them. If you do want to learn more, search for *require.js*, which seemed to be the done thing, or at least it was in the last JavaScript femtosecond.

```
    <script>
QUnit.test("errors should be hidden on keypress", function (assert) {
    window.Superlists.initialize();
    $('input[name="text"]').trigger('keypress');
    assert.equal($('.has-error').is(':visible'), false);
});

QUnit.test("errors aren't hidden if there is no keypress", function (assert) {
    window.Superlists.initialize();
    assert.equal($('.has-error').is(':visible'), true);
});
    </script>
```

Finally, whenever you have some JavaScript that interacts with the DOM, it's always good to wrap it in some "onload" boilerplate code to make sure that the page has fully loaded before it tries to do anything. Currently it works anyway, because we've placed the <script> tag right at the bottom of the page, but we shouldn't rely on that.

The jQuery onload boilerplate is quite minimal:

```
    <script>

$(document).ready(function () {
    window.Superlists.initialize();
});

    </script>
```

Read more in the jQuery .ready() docs (*http://api.jquery.com/ready/*).

JavaScript Testing in the TDD Cycle

You may be wondering how these JavaScript tests fit in with our "double loop" TDD cycle. The answer is that they play exactly the same role as our Python unit tests.

1. Write an FT and see it fail.

2. Figure out what kind of code you need next: Python or JavaScript?

3. Write a unit test in either language, and see it fail.

4. Write some code in either language, and make the test pass.

5. Rinse and repeat.

Want a little more practice with JavaScript? See if you can get our error messages to be hidden when the user clicks inside the input element, as well as just when they type in it. You should be able to FT it too.

We're almost ready to move on to Part III. The last step is to deploy our new code to our servers. Don't forget to do a final commit including *base.html* first!

A Few Things That Didn't Make It

In this chapter I wanted to cover the very basics of JavaScript testing and how it fits into our TDD workflow in this chapter. Here are a few pointers for further research:

- At the moment, our test only checks that the JavaScript works on one page. It works because we're including it in *base.html*, but if we'd only added it to *home.html* the tests would still pass. It's a judgement call, but you could choose to write an extra test here.

- When writing JavaScript, get as much help from your editor as you can to avoid common "gotchas". Check out syntax/error-checking tools like "jslint" and "jshint", also known as "linters".

- QUnit mainly expects you to "run" your tests using an actual web browser. This has the advantage that it's easy to create some HTML fixtures that match the kind of HTML your site actually contains, for tests to run against. But it's also possible to run JS tests from the command line. We'll see an example in Chapter 24.

- The new shiny thing in the world of frontend development are MVC frameworks like *angular.js* and React. Most tutorials for these use an RSpec-like assertion library called Jasmine (*https://jasmine.github.io/*). If you're going to use one of them, you'll probably find life easier if you use Jasmine rather than QUnit.

There is more JavaScript fun in this book too! Have a look at the Rest API appendix when you're ready for it.

JavaScript Testing Notes

- One of the great advantages of Selenium is that it allows you to test that your JavaScript really works, just as it tests your Python code.

- There are many JavaScript test running libraries out there. QUnit is closely tied to jQuery, which is the main reason I chose it.

- No matter which testing library you use, you'll always need to find solutions to the main challenge of JavaScript testing, which is about *managing global state*. That includes:

  — the DOM / HTML fixtures

  — namespacing

  — understanding and controlling execution order.

- I don't really mean it when I say that JavaScript is awful. It can actually be quite fun. But I'll say it again: make sure you've read *JavaScript: The Good Parts*.

Deploying Our New Code

It's time to deploy our brilliant new validation code to our live servers. This will be a chance to see our automated deploy scripts in action for the second time.

 At this point I want to say a huge thanks to Andrew Godwin and the whole Django team. Up until Django 1.7, I used to have a whole long section, entirely devoted to migrations. Migrations now "just work", so I was able to drop it altogether. Thanks for all the great work, gang!

Staging Deploy

We start with the staging server:

```
$ git push
$ cd deploy_tools
$ fab deploy:host=elspeth@superlists-staging.ottg.eu
[...]
Disconnecting from superlists-staging.ottg.eu... done.
```

Restart Gunicorn:

```
elspeth@server:$ sudo systemctl restart gunicorn-superlists-staging.ottg.eu
```

And run the tests against staging:

```
$ STAGING_SERVER=superlists-staging.ottg.eu python manage.py test functional_tests
OK
```

Live Deploy

Assuming all is well, we then run our deploy against live:

```
$ fab deploy:host=elspeth@superlists.ottg.eu

elspeth@server:$ sudo service gunicorn-superlists.ottg.eu restart
```

What to Do If You See a Database Error

Because our migrations introduce a new integrity constraint, you may find that it fails to apply because some existing data violates that constraint.

At this point you have two choices:

- Delete the database on the server and try again. After all, it's only a toy project!
- Learn about data migrations. See Appendix D.

Wrap-Up: git tag the New Release

The last thing to do is to tag the release in our VCS—it's important that we're always able to keep track of what's live:

```
$ git tag -f LIVE   # needs the -f because we are replacing the old tag
$ export TAG=`date +DEPLOYED-%F/%H%M`
$ git tag $TAG
$ git push -f origin LIVE $TAG
```

Some people don't like to use push -f and update an existing tag, and will instead use some kind of version number to tag their releases. Use whatever works for you.

And on that note, we can wrap up Part II, and move on to the more exciting topics that comprise Part III. Can't wait!

Deployment Procedure Review

We've done a couple of deploys now, so this is a good time for a little recap:

- `git push` latest code
- Deploy to staging and run functional tests against staging
- Deploy to live
- Tag the release

Deployment procedures evolve and get more complex as projects grow, and it's an area that can grow hard to maintain, full of manual checks and procedures, if you're not careful to keep things automated. There's lots more to say about this, but it's out of scope for this book. Do be sure to check out Appendix C, and have a read around on the topic of "continuous deployment."

More Advanced Topics in Testing

"Oh my gosh, what? Another section? Harry, I'm exhausted, it's already been three hundred pages, I don't think I can handle a whole 'nother section of the book. Particularly not if it's called 'Advanced'…maybe I can get away with just skipping it?"

Oh no, you can't! This may be called the advanced section, but it's full of really important topics for TDD and web development. No way can you skip it. If anything, it's *even more important* than the first two sections.

We'll be talking about how to integrate third-party systems, and how to test them. Modern web development is all about reusing existing components. We'll cover mocking and test isolation, which is really a core part of TDD, and a technique you're going to need for all but the simplest of codebases. We'll talk about server-side debugging, and test fixtures, and how to set up a Continuous Integration environment. None of these things are take-it-or-leave-it optional luxury extras for your project—they're all vital!

Inevitably, the learning curve does get a little steeper in this section. You may find yourself having to read things a couple of times before they sink in, or you may find that things don't work on the first go, and that you need to do a bit of debugging on your own. But persist with it! The harder it is, the more rewarding it is. And I'm always happy to help if you're stuck; just drop me an email at *obeythetesting-goat@gmail.com*.

Come on; I promise the best is yet to come!

User Authentication, Spiking, and De-Spiking

Our beautiful lists site has been live for a few days, and our users are starting to come back to us with feedback. "We love the site", they say, "but we keep losing our lists. Manually remembering URLs is hard. It'd be great if it could remember what lists we'd started".

Remember Henry Ford and faster horses. Whenever you hear a user requirement, it's important to dig a little deeper and think—what is the real requirement here? And how can I make it involve a cool new technology I've been wanting to try out?

Clearly the requirement here is that people want to have some kind of user account on the site. So, without further ado, let's dive into authentication.

Naturally we're not going to mess about with remembering passwords ourselves—besides being *so* '90s, secure storage of user passwords is a security nightmare we'd rather leave to someone else. We'll use something fun called passwordless auth instead.

(If you *insist* on storing your own passwords, Django's default auth module is ready and waiting for you. It's nice and straightforward, and I'll leave it to you to discover on your own.)

Passwordless Auth

What authentication system could we use to avoid storing passwords ourselves? Oauth? Openid? "Login with Facebook"? Ugh. For me those all have unacceptable creepy overtones; why should Google or Facebook know what sites you're logging into and when?

In the first edition I used an experimental project called "Persona", cooked up by a some of the wonderful techno-hippy-idealists at Mozilla, but sadly that project was abandoned.

Instead I've found a fun approach to authentication that goes by the name of "Passwordless", but you might call it "just use email".

The system was invented by someone annoyed at having to create new passwords for so many websites, who found himself just using random, throwaway passwords, not even trying to remember them, and using the "forgot my password" feature whenever he needed to log in again. You can read all about it on Medium (*https://medium.com/@ninjudd/passwords-are-obsolete-9ed56d483eb#.cx8iber30*).

The concept is: just use email to verify someone's identity. If you're going to have a "forgot my password" feature, then you're trusting email anyway, so why not just go the whole hog? Whenever someone wants to log in, we generate a unique URL for them to use, email it to them, and they then click through that to get into the site.

It's by no means a perfect system, and in fact there are lots of subtleties to be thought through before it would really make a good login solution for a production website, but this is just a fun toy project so let's give it a go.

Exploratory Coding, aka "Spiking"

Before I wrote this chapter all I knew about passwordless auth was the outline I'd read in the article linked above. I'd never seen any code for it, and didn't really know where to start in building it.

In Chapters 13 and 14 we saw that you can use a unit test as a way of exploring a new API or tool, but sometimes you just want to hack something together without any tests at all, just to see if it works, to learn it or get a feel for it. That's absolutely fine. When learning a new tool or exploring a new possible solution, it's often appropriate to leave the rigorous TDD process to one side, and build a little prototype without tests, or perhaps with very few tests. The goat doesn't mind looking the other way for a bit.

This kind of prototyping activity is often called a "spike", for reasons best known (*http://stackoverflow.com/questions/249969/why-are-tdd-spikes-called-spikes*).

The first thing I did was take a look at existing Python and Django authentication packages, like django-allauth (*http://www.intenct.nl/projects/django-allauth/*) and python-social-auth (*https://github.com/omab/python-social-auth*), but both of them looked overcomplicated for this stage (and besides, it'll be more fun to code our own!).

So instead I dived in and hacked about, and after a few dead ends and wrong turns, I had something which just about works. I'll take you on a tour, and then we'll go through and "de-spike" the implementation—that is, replace the prototype with tested, production-ready code.

You should go ahead and add this code to your own site too, and then you can have a play with it, try logging in with your own email address, and convince yourself that it really does work.

Starting a Branch for the Spike

Before embarking on a spike, it's a good idea to start a new branch, so you can still use your VCS without worrying about your spike commits getting mixed up with your production code:

```
$ git checkout -b passwordless-spike
```

Let's keep track of some of the things we're hoping to learn from the spike:

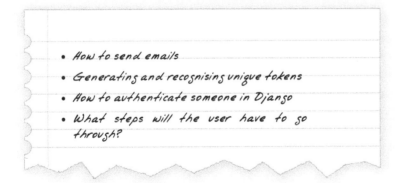

- How to send emails
- Generating and recognising unique tokens
- How to authenticate someone in Django
- What steps will the user have to go through?

Frontend Log in UI

Let's start with the frontend, hacking in an actual form to be able to enter your email address into the navbar, and a logout link for users who are already authenticated:

```html
<body>
  <div class="container">

    <div class="navbar">
      {% if user.is_authenticated %}
        <p>Logged in as {{ user.email }}</p>
        <p><a id="id_logout" href="{% url 'logout' %}">Log out</a></p>
      {% else %}
        <form method="POST" action ="{% url 'send_login_email' %}">
          Enter email to log in: <input name="email" type="text" />
          {% csrf_token %}
        </form>
      {% endif %}
    </div>

    <div class="row">
    [...]
```

Sending Emails from Django

The login theory will be something like this:

- When someone wants to log in, we generate a unique secret token for them, store it in the database linked to their email, and send it to them.

- They then check their email, which will have a link to a URL that includes that token.

- When they click that link, we check whether the token exists in database, and if so, they are logged in as the associated user.

First we prep an app for our accounts stuff:

```
$ python manage.py startapp accounts
```

And we'll wire up *urls.py* with at least one URL. In the top-level *superlists/urls.py*...

```python
from django.conf.urls import include, url
from lists import views as list_views
from lists import urls as list_urls
from accounts import urls as accounts_urls

urlpatterns = [
    url(r'^$', list_views.home_page, name='home'),
    url(r'^lists/', include(list_urls)),
    url(r'^accounts/', include(accounts_urls)),
]
```

And in the accounts module's *urls.py*:

accounts/urls.py (ch16l004)

```python
from django.conf.urls import url
from accounts import views

urlpatterns = [
    url(r'^send_email$', views.send_login_email, name='send_login_email'),
]
```

Here's the view that's in charge of creating a token associated with the email address the user puts in our login form:

accounts/views.py (ch16l005)

```python
import uuid
import sys
from django.shortcuts import render
from django.core.mail import send_mail

from accounts.models import Token


def send_login_email(request):
    email = request.POST['email']
    uid = str(uuid.uuid4())
    Token.objects.create(email=email, uid=uid)
    print('saving uid', uid, 'for email', email, file=sys.stderr)
    url = request.build_absolute_uri(f'/accounts/login?uid={uid}')
    send_mail(
        'Your login link for Superlists',
        f'Use this link to log in:\n\n{url}',
        'noreply@superlists',
        [email],
    )
    return render(request, 'login_email_sent.html')
```

For that to work we'll need a placeholder message confirming the email was sent:

accounts/templates/login_email_sent.html (ch16l006)

```html
<html>
<h1>Email sent</h1>

<p>Check your email, you'll find a message with a link that will log you into
the site.</p>

</html>
```

(You can see how hacky this code is—we'd want to integrate this template with our *base.html* in the real version.)

More importantly, for the Django send_mail function to work, we need to tell Django our email server address. I'm just using my Gmail[1] account for now. You can use any email provider you like, as long as they support SMTP:

superlists/settings.py (ch16l007)

```python
EMAIL_HOST = 'smtp.gmail.com'
EMAIL_HOST_USER = 'obeythetestinggoat@gmail.com'
EMAIL_HOST_PASSWORD = os.environ.get('EMAIL_PASSWORD')
EMAIL_PORT = 587
EMAIL_USE_TLS = True
```

 If you want to use Gmail as well, you'll probably have to visit your Google account security settings page. If you're using two-factor auth, you'll want to set up an app-specific password (*https://myac count.google.com/apppasswords*). If you're not, you will probably still need to allow access for less secure apps (*https://www.google.com/settings/security/lesssecureapps*). You might want to consider creating a new Google account for this purpose, rather than using one containing sensitive data.

Another Secret, Another Environment Variable

Once again, we have a "secret" that we want to avoid keeping directly in our source code or on GitHub, so another environment variable gets used in the os.envi ron.get.

To get this to work, we need to set it in the shell that's running my dev server:

```
$ export EMAIL_PASSWORD="sekrit"
```

Later we'll see about adding that to the *.env* on the staging server as well.

Storing Tokens in the Database

How are we doing?

---

1 Didn't I just spend a whole intro banging on about the privacy implications of using Google for login, only to go on and use Gmail? Yes, it's a contradiction (honest, I will move off Gmail one day!). But in this case I'm just using it for testing, and the important thing is that I'm not forcing Google on my users.

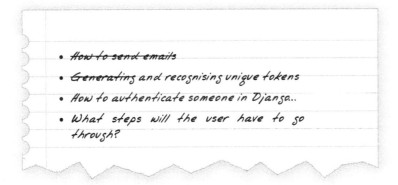

- How to send emails
- Generating and recognising unique tokens
- How to authenticate someone in Django
- What steps will the user have to go through?

We'll need a model to store our tokens in the database—they link an email address with a unique ID. Pretty simple:

accounts/models.py (ch16l008)

```
from django.db import models

class Token(models.Model):
    email = models.EmailField()
    uid = models.CharField(max_length=255)
```

Custom Authentication Models

While we're messing about with models, let's start experimenting with authentication in Django.

- How to send emails
- Generating and recognising unique tokens
- How to authenticate someone in Django...
- What steps will the user have to go through?

The first thing we'll need is a user model. When I first wrote this, custom user models were a new thing in Django, so I dived into the Django auth documentation (*https:// docs.djangoproject.com/en/1.11/topics/auth/customizing/*) and tried to hack in the simplest possible one:

```
[...]
from django.contrib.auth.models import (
    AbstractBaseUser, BaseUserManager, PermissionsMixin
)


class ListUser(AbstractBaseUser, PermissionsMixin):
    email = models.EmailField(primary_key=True)
    USERNAME_FIELD = 'email'
    #REQUIRED_FIELDS = ['email', 'height']

    objects = ListUserManager()

    @property
    def is_staff(self):
        return self.email == 'harry.percival@example.com'

    @property
    def is_active(self):
        return True
```

That's what I call a minimal user model! One field, none of this firstname/lastname/username nonsense, and, pointedly, no password! Somebody else's problem!

But, again, you can see that this code isn't ready for production, from the commented-out lines to the hardcoded harry email address. We'll neaten this up quite a lot when we de-spike.

To get it to work, you need a model manager for the user:

```
[...]
class ListUserManager(BaseUserManager):

    def create_user(self, email):
        ListUser.objects.create(email=email)

    def create_superuser(self, email, password):
        self.create_user(email)
```

No need to worry about what a model manager is at this stage; for now we just need it because we need it, and it just works. When we de-spike, we'll examine each bit of code that actually ends up in production and make sure we understand it fully.

Finishing the Custom Django Auth

Almost there—our last step combines recognising the token and then actually logging the user in. Once we've done this, we'll be able to pretty much strike off all the items on our scratchpad:

So here's the view that actually handles the click through from the link in the email:

accounts/views.py (ch16l011)

```
import uuid
import sys
from django.contrib.auth import authenticate
from django.contrib.auth import login as auth_login
from django.core.mail import send_mail
from django.shortcuts import redirect, render
[...]

def login(request):
    print('login view', file=sys.stderr)
    uid = request.GET.get('uid')
    user = authenticate(uid=uid)
    if user is not None:
        auth_login(request, user)
    return redirect('/')
```

The "authenticate" function invokes Django's authentication framework, which we configure using a "custom authentication backend", whose job it is to validate the UID and return a user with the right email.

We could have done this stuff directly in the view, but we may as well structure things the way Django expects. It makes for a reasonably neat separation of concerns:

```
import sys
from accounts.models import ListUser, Token

class PasswordlessAuthenticationBackend(object):

    def authenticate(self, uid):
        print('uid', uid, file=sys.stderr)
        if not Token.objects.filter(uid=uid).exists():
            print('no token found', file=sys.stderr)
            return None
        token = Token.objects.get(uid=uid)
        print('got token', file=sys.stderr)
        try:
            user = ListUser.objects.get(email=token.email)
            print('got user', file=sys.stderr)
            return user
        except ListUser.DoesNotExist:
            print('new user', file=sys.stderr)
            return ListUser.objects.create(email=token.email)


    def get_user(self, email):
        return ListUser.objects.get(email=email)
```

Again, lots of debug prints in there, and some duplicated code, not something we'd want in production, but it works…

Finally, a logout view:

```
from django.contrib.auth import login as auth_login, logout as auth_logout
[...]

def logout(request):
    auth_logout(request)
    return redirect('/')
```

Add login and logout to our *urls.py*…

```
from django.conf.urls import url
from accounts import views

urlpatterns = [
    url(r'^send_email$', views.send_login_email, name='send_login_email'),
    url(r'^login$', views.login, name='login'),
    url(r'^logout$', views.logout, name='logout'),
]
```

Almost there! We switch on the auth backend and our new accounts app in *settings.py*:

superlists/settings.py (ch16l015)

```
INSTALLED_APPS = [
    #'django.contrib.admin',
    'django.contrib.auth',
    'django.contrib.contenttypes',
    'django.contrib.sessions',
    'django.contrib.messages',
    'django.contrib.staticfiles',
    'lists',
    'accounts',
]

AUTH_USER_MODEL = 'accounts.ListUser'
AUTHENTICATION_BACKENDS = [
    'accounts.authentication.PasswordlessAuthenticationBackend',
]

MIDDLEWARE = [
[...]
```

A quick `makemigrations` to make the token and user models real:

```
$ python manage.py makemigrations
Migrations for 'accounts':
  accounts/migrations/0001_initial.py
    - Create model ListUser
    - Create model Token
```

And a `migrate` to build the database:

```
$ python manage.py migrate
[...]
Running migrations:
  Applying accounts.0001_initial... OK
```

And we should be all done! Why not spin up a dev server with `runserver` and see how it all looks (Figure 18-1)?

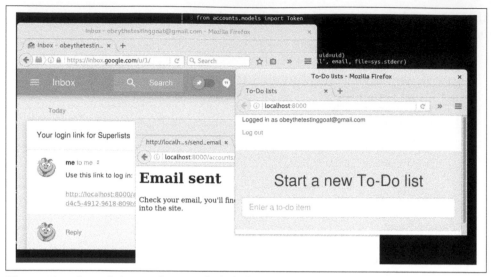

Figure 18-1. It works! It works! Mwahahahaha.

 If you get an `SMTPSenderRefused` error message, don't forget to set the `EMAIL_PASSWORD` environment variable in the shell that's running `runserver`.

That's pretty much it! Along the way, I had to fight pretty hard, including clicking around the Gmail account security UI for a while, stumbling over several missing attributes on my custom user model (because I didn't read the docs properly), and even at one point switching to the dev version of Django to overcome a bug, which thankfully turned out to be irrelevant.

Aside: Logging to stderr

While spiking, it's pretty critical to be able to see exceptions that are being generated by your code. Annoyingly, Django doesn't send all exceptions to the terminal by default, but you can make it do so with a variable called LOGGING in *settings.py*:

superlists/settings.py (ch16l017)

```python
LOGGING = {
    'version': 1,
    'disable_existing_loggers': False,
    'handlers': {
        'console': {
            'level': 'DEBUG',
            'class': 'logging.StreamHandler',
        },
    },
    'loggers': {
        'django': {
            'handlers': ['console'],
        },
    },
    'root': {'level': 'INFO'},
}
```

Django uses the rather "enterprisey" logging package from the Python standard library, which, although very fully featured, does suffer from a fairly steep learning curve. It's covered a little more in Chapter 21, and in the Django docs (*https://docs.djangoproject.com/en/1.11/topics/logging/*).

But we now have a working solution! Let's commit it on our spike branch:

```
$ git status
$ git add accounts
$ git commit -am "spiked in custom passwordless auth backend"
```

Time to de-spike!

De-spiking

De-spiking means rewriting your prototype code using TDD. We now have enough information to "do it properly". So what's the first step? An FT, of course!

We'll stay on the spike branch for now, to see our FT pass against our spiked code. Then we'll go back to master and commit just the FT.

Here's a first, simple version of the FT:

```python
from django.core import mail
from selenium.webdriver.common.keys import Keys
import re

from .base import FunctionalTest

TEST_EMAIL = 'edith@example.com'
SUBJECT = 'Your login link for Superlists'


class LoginTest(FunctionalTest):

    def test_can_get_email_link_to_log_in(self):
        # Edith goes to the awesome superlists site
        # and notices a "Log in" section in the navbar for the first time
        # It's telling her to enter her email address, so she does
        self.browser.get(self.live_server_url)
        self.browser.find_element_by_name('email').send_keys(TEST_EMAIL)
        self.browser.find_element_by_name('email').send_keys(Keys.ENTER)

        # A message appears telling her an email has been sent
        self.wait_for(lambda: self.assertIn(
            'Check your email',
            self.browser.find_element_by_tag_name('body').text
        ))

        # She checks her email and finds a message
        email = mail.outbox[0]  ❶
        self.assertIn(TEST_EMAIL, email.to)
        self.assertEqual(email.subject, SUBJECT)

        # It has a url link in it
        self.assertIn('Use this link to log in', email.body)
        url_search = re.search(r'http://.+/.+$', email.body)
        if not url_search:
            self.fail(f'Could not find url in email body:\n{email.body}')
        url = url_search.group(0)
        self.assertIn(self.live_server_url, url)

        # she clicks it
        self.browser.get(url)

        # she is logged in!
        self.wait_for(
            lambda: self.browser.find_element_by_link_text('Log out')
        )
        navbar = self.browser.find_element_by_css_selector('.navbar')
        self.assertIn(TEST_EMAIL, navbar.text)
```

❶ Were you worried about how we were going to handle retrieving emails in our tests? Thankfully we can cheat for now! When running tests, Django gives us access to any emails the server tries to send via the `mail.outbox` attribute. We'll save checking "real" emails for later (but we will do it!).

And if we run the FT, it works!

```
$ python manage.py test functional_tests.test_login
[...]
Not Found: /favicon.ico
saving uid [...]
login view
uid [...]
got token
new user


.
-----------------------------------------------------------------
Ran 1 test in 3.729s

OK
```

You can even see some of the debug output I left in my spiked view implementations. Now it's time to revert all of our temporary changes, and reintroduce them one by one in a test-driven way.

Reverting Our Spiked Code

```
$ git checkout master # switch back to master branch
$ rm -rf accounts # remove any trace of spiked code
$ git add functional_tests/test_login.py
$ git commit -m "FT for login via email"
```

Now we rerun the FT and let it drive our development:

```
$ python manage.py test functional_tests.test_login
selenium.common.exceptions.NoSuchElementException: Message: Unable to locate
element: [name="email"]
[...]
```

The first thing it wants us to do is add an email input element. Bootstrap has some built-in classes for navigation bars, so we'll use them, and include a form for the login email:

```
<div class="container">

  <nav class="navbar navbar-default" role="navigation">
    <div class="container-fluid">
      <a class="navbar-brand" href="/">Superlists</a>
      <form class="navbar-form navbar-right" method="POST" action="#">
        <span>Enter email to log in:</span>
        <input class="form-control" name="email" type="text" />
        {% csrf_token %}
      </form>
    </div>
  </nav>

  <div class="row">
  [...]
```

Now our FT fails because the login form doesn't actually do anything:

```
$ python manage.py test functional_tests.test_login
[...]
AssertionError: 'Check your email' not found in 'Superlists\nEnter email to log
in:\nStart a new To-Do list'
```

 I recommend reintroducing the LOGGING setting from earlier at this point. There's no need for an explicit test for it; our current test suite will let us know in the unlikely event that it breaks anything. As we'll find out in Chapter 21, it'll be useful for debugging later.

Time to start writing some Django code. We begin by creating an app called `accounts` to hold all the files related to login:

```
$ python manage.py startapp accounts
```

You could even do a commit just for that, to be able to distinguish the placeholder app files from our modifications.

Next let's rebuild our minimal user model, with tests this time, and see if it turns out neater than it did in the spike.

A Minimal Custom User Model

Django's built-in user model makes all sorts of assumptions about what information you want to track about users, from explicitly recording first name and last name[2] to

---

2 A decision which you'll find prominent Django maintainers saying they now regret. Not everyone has a first name and a last name.

---

forcing you to use a username. I'm a great believer in not storing information about users unless you absolutely must, so a user model that records an email address and nothing else sounds good to me!

By now I'm sure you can manage to create the tests folder and its *__init__.py*, remove *tests.py*, and then add a *test_models.py* to say:

accounts/tests/test_models.py (ch16l024)

```python
from django.test import TestCase
from django.contrib.auth import get_user_model

User = get_user_model()


class UserModelTest(TestCase):

    def test_user_is_valid_with_email_only(self):
        user = User(email='a@b.com')
        user.full_clean()  # should not raise
```

That gives us an expected failure:

```
django.core.exceptions.ValidationError: {'password': ['This field cannot be
blank.'], 'username': ['This field cannot be blank.']}
```

Password? Username? Bah! How about this?

accounts/models.py

```python
from django.db import models

class User(models.Model):
    email = models.EmailField()
```

And we wire it up inside *settings.py*, adding `accounts` to INSTALLED_APPS and a variable called AUTH_USER_MODEL:

superlists/settings.py (ch16l026)

```python
INSTALLED_APPS = [
    #'django.contrib.admin',
    'django.contrib.auth',
    'django.contrib.contenttypes',
    'django.contrib.sessions',
    'django.contrib.messages',
    'django.contrib.staticfiles',
    'lists',
    'accounts',
]

AUTH_USER_MODEL = 'accounts.User'
```

The next error is a database error:

```
django.db.utils.OperationalError: no such table: accounts_user
```

That prompts us, as usual, to do a migration… When we try, Django complains that our custom user model is missing a couple of bits of metadata:

```
$ python manage.py makemigrations
Traceback (most recent call last):
[...]
    if not isinstance(cls.REQUIRED_FIELDS, (list, tuple)):
AttributeError: type object 'User' has no attribute 'REQUIRED_FIELDS'
```

Sigh. Come on, Django, it's only got one field, so you should be able to figure out the answers to these questions for yourself. Here you go:

accounts/models.py

```python
class User(models.Model):
    email = models.EmailField()
    REQUIRED_FIELDS = []
```

Next silly question?[3]

```
$ python manage.py makemigrations
[...]
AttributeError: type object 'User' has no attribute 'USERNAME_FIELD'
```

And we go through a few more of these, until we get to:

accounts/models.py

```python
class User(models.Model):
    email = models.EmailField()

    REQUIRED_FIELDS = []
    USERNAME_FIELD = 'email'
    is_anonymous = False
    is_authenticated = True
```

And now we get a slightly different error:

```
$ python manage.py makemigrations
SystemCheckError: System check identified some issues:

ERRORS:
accounts.User: (auth.E003) 'User.email' must be unique because it is named as
the 'USERNAME_FIELD'.
```

---

3 You might ask, if I think Django is so silly, why don't I submit a pull request to fix it? Should be quite a simple fix. Well, I promise I will, as soon as I've finished writing the book. For now, snarky comments will have to suffice.

Well, the simple way to fix that would be like this:

accounts/models.py (ch16l028-1)

```
email = models.EmailField(unique=True)
```

Now the migration is successful:

```
$ python manage.py makemigrations
Migrations for 'accounts':
  accounts/migrations/0001_initial.py
    - Create model User
```

And the test passes:

```
$ python manage.py test accounts
[...]
Ran 1 tests in 0.001s
OK
```

But our model isn't quite as simple as it could be. It has the email field, and also an autogenerated "ID" field as its primary key. We could make it even simpler!

Tests as Documentation

Let's go all the way and make the email field into the primary key,[4] and thus implicitly remove the autogenerated id column.

Although we could just do it and our test would still pass, and conceivably claim it was "just a refactor", it would be better to have a specific test:

accounts/tests/test_models.py (ch16l028-3)

```
def test_email_is_primary_key(self):
    user = User(email='a@b.com')
    self.assertEqual(user.pk, 'a@b.com')
```

It'll help us remember if we ever come back and look at the code again in future:

```
    self.assertEqual(user.pk, 'a@b.com')
AssertionError: None != 'a@b.com'
```

---

4 Emails may not be the perfect primary key IRL. One reader, clearly deeply emotionally scarred, wrote me a tearful email about how much they've suffered for over a decade from trying to deal with the effects of email primary keys, due to their making multiuser account management impossible. So, as ever, YMMV.

Your tests can be a form of documentation for your code—they express what your requirements are of a particular class or function. Sometimes, if you forget why you've done something a particular way, going back and looking at the tests will give you the answer. That's why it's important to give your tests explicit, verbose method names.

And here's the implementation (feel free to check what happens with unique=True first):

accounts/models.py (ch16l028-4)

```python
email = models.EmailField(primary_key=True)
```

And we mustn't forget to adjust our migrations:

```
$ rm accounts/migrations/0001_initial.py
$ python manage.py makemigrations
Migrations for 'accounts':
  accounts/migrations/0001_initial.py
    - Create model User
```

And both our tests pass:

```
$ python manage.py test accounts
[...]
Ran 2 tests in 0.001s
OK
```

A Token Model to Link Emails with a Unique ID

Next let's build a token model. Here's a short unit test that captures the essence—you should be able to link an email to a unique ID, and that ID shouldn't be the same two times in a row:

accounts/tests/test_models.py (ch16l030)

```python
from accounts.models import Token
[...]


class TokenModelTest(TestCase):

    def test_links_user_with_auto_generated_uid(self):
        token1 = Token.objects.create(email='a@b.com')
        token2 = Token.objects.create(email='a@b.com')
        self.assertNotEqual(token1.uid, token2.uid)
```

I won't show every single listing for creating the Token class in *models.py*; I'll let you do that yourself instead. Driving Django models with basic TDD involves jumping

through a few hoops because of the migration, so you'll see a few iterations like this—
minimal code change, make migrations, get new error, delete migrations, re-create
new migrations, another code change, and so on…

```
$ python manage.py makemigrations
Migrations for 'accounts':
  accounts/migrations/0002_token.py
    - Create model Token
$ python manage.py test accounts
[...]
TypeError: 'email' is an invalid keyword argument for this function
```

I'll trust you to go through these conscientiously—remember, I may not be able to see
you, but the Testing Goat can!

```
$ rm accounts/migrations/0002_token.py
$ python manage.py makemigrations
Migrations for 'accounts':
  accounts/migrations/0002_token.py
    - Create model Token
$ python manage.py test accounts
AttributeError: 'Token' object has no attribute 'uid'
```

Eventually you should get to this code…

accounts/models.py (ch16l033)

```python
class Token(models.Model):
    email = models.EmailField()
    uid = models.CharField(max_length=40)
```

And this error:

```
$ python manage.py test accounts
[...]

    self.assertNotEqual(token1.uid, token2.uid)
AssertionError: '' == ''
```

And here we have to decide how to generate our random unique ID field. We could
use the random module, but Python actually comes with another module specifically
designed for generating unique IDs called "uuid" (for "universally unique id").

We can use that like this:

accounts/models.py (ch16l035)

```python
import uuid
[...]

class Token(models.Model):
    email = models.EmailField()
    uid = models.CharField(default=uuid.uuid4, max_length=40)
```

And, with a bit more wrangling of migrations, that should get us to passing tests:

```
$ python manage.py test accounts
[...]
Ran 3 tests in 0.015s

OK
```

Well, that gets us on our way! The models layer is done, at least. In the next chapter, we'll get into mocking, a key technique for testing external dependencies like email.

Exploratory Coding, Spiking, and De-spiking

Spiking

Exploratory coding to find out about a new API, or to explore the feasibility of a new solution. Spiking can be done without tests. It's a good idea to do your spike on a new branch, and go back to master when de-spiking.

De-spiking

Taking the work from a spike and making it part of the production codebase. The idea is to throw away the old spike code altogether, and start again from scratch, using TDD once again. De-spiked code can often come out looking quite different from the original spike, and usually much nicer.

Writing your FT against spiked code

Whether or not this is a good idea depends on your circumstances. The reason it can be useful is because it can help you write the FT correctly—figuring out how to test your spike can be just as challenging as the spike itself. On the other hand, it might constrain you towards reimplementing a very similar solution to your spiked one—something to watch out for.

Using Mocks to Test External Dependencies or Reduce Duplication

In this chapter we'll start testing the parts of our code that send emails. In the FT, you saw that Django gives us a way of retrieving any emails it sends by using the `mail.out` box attribute. But in this chapter, I want to demonstrate a very important testing technique called *mocking*, so for the purpose of these unit tests, we'll pretend that this nice Django shortcut doesn't exist.

Am I telling you not to use Django's `mail.outbox`? No; use it, it's a neat shortcut. But I want to teach mocks because they're a useful general-purpose tool for unit testing external dependencies. You may not always be using Django! And even if you are, you may not be sending email—any interaction with a third-party API is a good candidate for testing with mocks.

Before We Start: Getting the Basic Plumbing In

Let's just get a basic view and URL set up first. We can do so with a simple test that our new URL for sending the login email should eventually redirect back to the home page:

```python
from django.test import TestCase


class SendLoginEmailViewTest(TestCase):

    def test_redirects_to_home_page(self):
        response = self.client.post('/accounts/send_login_email', data={
            'email': 'edith@example.com'
        })
        self.assertRedirects(response, '/')
```

Wire up the `include` in *superlists/urls.py*, plus the `url` in *accounts/urls.py*, and get the test passing with something a bit like this:

```python
from django.core.mail import send_mail
from django.shortcuts import redirect


def send_login_email(request):
    return redirect('/')
```

I've added the import of the `send_mail` function as a placeholder for now:

```
$ python manage.py test accounts
[...]
Ran 4 tests in 0.015s

OK
```

OK, now we have a starting point, so let's get mocking!

Mocking Manually, aka Monkeypatching

When we call `send_mail` in real life we expect Django to be making a connection to our email provider, and sending an actual email across the public internet. That's not something we want to happen in our tests. It's a similar problem whenever you have code that has external side effects—calling an API, sending out a tweet or an SMS or whatever it may be. In our unit tests, we don't want to be sending out real tweets or API calls across the internet. But we would still like a way of testing that our code is correct. Mocks[1] are the answer.

---

[1] I'm using the generic term "mock", but testing enthusiasts like to distinguish other types of a general class of test tools called "Test Doubles", including spies, fakes, and stubs. The differences don't really matter for this book, but if you want to get into the nitty-gritty, check out this amazing wiki by Justin Searls (*https://github.com/testdouble/contributing-tests/wiki/Test-Double*). Warning: absolutely chock full of great testing content.

Actually, one of the great things about Python is that its dynamic nature makes it very easy to do things like mocking, or what's sometimes called monkeypatching (*https://en.wikipedia.org/wiki/Monkey_patch*). Let's suppose that, as a first step, we want to get to some code that invokes send_mail with the right subject line, from address, and to address. That would look something like this:

accounts/views.py

```python
def send_login_email(request):
    email = request.POST['email']
    # send_mail(
    #     'Your login link for Superlists',
    #     'body text tbc',
    #     'noreply@superlists',
    #     [email],
    # )
    return redirect('/')
```

How can we test this, without calling the *real* send_mail function? The answer is that our test can ask Python to replace the send_mail function with a fake version, at runtime, before we invoke the send_login_email view. Check this out:

accounts/tests/test_views.py (ch17l005)

```python
from django.test import TestCase
import accounts.views   ❷

class SendLoginEmailViewTest(TestCase):
    [...]

    def test_sends_mail_to_address_from_post(self):
        self.send_mail_called = False

        def fake_send_mail(subject, body, from_email, to_list):   ❶
            self.send_mail_called = True
            self.subject = subject
            self.body = body
            self.from_email = from_email
            self.to_list = to_list

        accounts.views.send_mail = fake_send_mail   ❷

        self.client.post('/accounts/send_login_email', data={
            'email': 'edith@example.com'
        })

        self.assertTrue(self.send_mail_called)
        self.assertEqual(self.subject, 'Your login link for Superlists')
        self.assertEqual(self.from_email, 'noreply@superlists')
        self.assertEqual(self.to_list, ['edith@example.com'])
```

❶ We define a `fake_send_mail` function, which looks like the real `send_mail` function, but all it does is save some information about how it was called, using some variables on `self`.

❷ Then, before we execute the code under test by doing the `self.client.post`, we swap out the real `accounts.views.send_mail` with our fake version—it's as simple as just assigning it.

It's important to realise that there isn't really anything magical going on here; we're just taking advantage of Python's dynamic nature and scoping rules.

Up until we actually invoke a function, we can modify the variables it has access to, as long as we get into the right namespace (that's why we import the top-level accounts module, to be able to get down to the `accounts.views` module, which is the scope that the `accounts.views.send_login_email` function will run in).

This isn't even something that only works inside unit tests. You can do this kind of "monkeypatching" in any kind of Python code!

That may take a little time to sink in. See if you can convince yourself that it's not all totally crazy, before reading a couple of bits of further detail.

- Why do we use `self` as a way of passing information around? It's just a convenient variable that's available both inside the scope of the `fake_send_mail` function and outside of it. We could use any mutable object, like a list or a dictionary, as long as we are making in-place changes to an existing variable that exists outside our fake function. (Feel free to have a play around with different ways of doing this, if you're curious, and see what works and doesn't work.)

- The "before" is critical! I can't tell you how many times I've sat there, wondering why a mock isn't working, only to realise that I didn't mock *before* I called the code under test.

Let's see if our hand-rolled mock object will let us test-drive some code:

```
$ python manage.py test accounts
[...]
    self.assertTrue(self.send_mail_called)
AssertionError: False is not true
```

So let's call `send_mail`, naively:

accounts/views.py

```
def send_login_email(request):
    send_mail()
    return redirect('/')
```

That gives:

```
TypeError: fake_send_mail() missing 4 required positional arguments: 'subject',
'body', 'from_email', and 'to_list'
```

Looks like our monkeypatch is working! We've called send_mail, and it's gone into our fake_send_mail function, which wants more arguments. Let's try this:

accounts/views.py

```
def send_login_email(request):
    send_mail('subject', 'body', 'from_email', ['to email'])
    return redirect('/')
```

That gives:

```
    self.assertEqual(self.subject, 'Your login link for Superlists')
AssertionError: 'subject' != 'Your login link for Superlists'
```

That's working pretty well. And now we can work all the way through to something like this:

accounts/views.py

```
def send_login_email(request):
    email = request.POST['email']
    send_mail(
        'Your login link for Superlists',
        'body text tbc',
        'noreply@superlists',
        [email]
    )
    return redirect('/')
```

and passing tests!

```
$ python manage.py test accounts

Ran 5 tests in 0.016s

OK
```

Brilliant! We've managed to write tests for some code, that ordinarily[2] would go out and try to send real emails across the internet, and by "mocking out" the send_email function, we're able to write the tests and code all the same.

---

2 Yes, I know Django already mocks out emails using mail.outbox for us, but, again, let's pretend it doesn't. What if you were using Flask? Or what if this was an API call, not an email?

The Python Mock Library

The popular *mock* package was added to the standard library as part of Python 3.3.[3] It provides a magical object called a Mock; try this out in a Python shell:

```
>>> from unittest.mock import Mock
>>> m = Mock()
>>> m.any_attribute
<Mock name='mock.any_attribute' id='140716305179152'>
>>> type(m.any_attribute)
<class 'unittest.mock.Mock'>
>>> m.any_method()
<Mock name='mock.any_method()' id='140716331211856'>
>>> m.foo()
<Mock name='mock.foo()' id='140716331251600'>
>>> m.called
False
>>> m.foo.called
True
>>> m.bar.return_value = 1
>>> m.bar(42, var='thing')
1
>>> m.bar.call_args
call(42, var='thing')
```

A magical object that responds to any request for an attribute or method call with other mocks, that you can configure to return specific values for its calls, and that allows you to inspect what it was called with? Sounds like a useful thing to be able to use in our unit tests!

Using unittest.patch

And as if that weren't enough, the mock module also provides a helper function called patch, which we can use to do the monkeypatching we did by hand earlier.

I'll explain how it all works shortly, but let's see it in action first:

---

3 In Python 2, you can install it with pip install mock.

```
from django.test import TestCase
from unittest.mock import patch
[...]

    @patch('accounts.views.send_mail')
    def test_sends_mail_to_address_from_post(self, mock_send_mail):
        self.client.post('/accounts/send_login_email', data={
            'email': 'edith@example.com'
        })

        self.assertEqual(mock_send_mail.called, True)
        (subject, body, from_email, to_list), kwargs = mock_send_mail.call_args
        self.assertEqual(subject, 'Your login link for Superlists')
        self.assertEqual(from_email, 'noreply@superlists')
        self.assertEqual(to_list, ['edith@example.com'])
```

If you rerun the tests, you'll see they still pass. And since we're always suspicious of any test that still passes after a big change, let's deliberately break it just to see:

```
        self.assertEqual(to_list, ['schmedith@example.com'])
```

And let's add a little debug print to our view:

```
def send_login_email(request):
    email = request.POST['email']
    print(type(send_mail))
    send_mail(
        [...]
```

And run the tests again:

```
$ python manage.py test accounts
[...]
<class 'function'>
<class 'unittest.mock.MagicMock'>
[...]
AssertionError: Lists differ: ['edith@example.com'] !=
['schmedith@example.com']
[...]

Ran 5 tests in 0.024s

FAILED (failures=1)
```

Sure enough, the tests fail. And we can see just before the failure message that when we print the `type` of the `send_mail` function, in the first unit test it's a normal function, but in the second unit test we're seeing a mock object.

Let's remove the deliberate mistake and dive into exactly what's going on:

accounts/tests/test_views.py (ch17l011)

```
@patch('accounts.views.send_mail')  ❶
def test_sends_mail_to_address_from_post(self, mock_send_mail):  ❷
    self.client.post('/accounts/send_login_email', data={
        'email': 'edith@example.com'  ❸
    })

    self.assertEqual(mock_send_mail.called, True)  ❹
    (subject, body, from_email, to_list), kwargs = mock_send_mail.call_args  ❺
    self.assertEqual(subject, 'Your login link for Superlists')
    self.assertEqual(from_email, 'noreply@superlists')
    self.assertEqual(to_list, ['edith@example.com'])
```

❶ The `patch` decorator takes a dot-notation name of an object to monkeypatch. That's the equivalent of manually replacing the `send_mail` in `accounts.views`. The advantage of the decorator is that, firstly, it automatically replaces the target with a mock. And secondly, it automatically puts the original object back at the end! (Otherwise, the object stays monkeypatched for the rest of the test run, which might cause problems in other tests.)

❷ `patch` then injects the mocked object into the test as an argument to the test method. We can choose whatever name we want for it, but I usually use a convention of `mock_` plus the original name of the object.

❸ We call our function under test as usual, but everything inside this test method has our mock applied to it, so the view won't call the real `send_mail` object; it'll be seeing `mock_send_mail` instead.

❹ And we can now make assertions about what happened to that mock object during the test. We can see it was called...

❺ ...and we can also unpack its various positional and keyword call arguments, and examine what it was called with. (We'll discuss `call_args` in a bit more detail later.)

All crystal-clear? No? Don't worry, we'll do a couple more tests with mocks, to see if they start to make more sense as we use them more.

Getting the FT a Little Further Along

First let's get back to our FT and see where it's failing:

```
$ python manage.py test functional_tests.test_login
[...]
AssertionError: 'Check your email' not found in 'Superlists\nEnter email to log
in:\nStart a new To-Do list'
```

Submitting the email address currently has no effect, because the form isn't sending the data anywhere. Let's wire it up in *base.html*:[4]

lists/templates/base.html (ch17l012)

```
<form class="navbar-form navbar-right"
      method="POST"
      action="{% url 'send_login_email' %}">
```

Does that help? Nope, same error. Why? Because we're not actually displaying a success message after we send the user an email. Let's add a test for that.

Testing the Django Messages Framework

We'll use Django's "messages framework", which is often used to display ephemeral "success" or "warning" messages to show the results of an action. Have a look at the django messages docs (*https://docs.djangoproject.com/en/1.11/ref/contrib/messages/*) if you haven't come across it already.

Testing Django messages is a bit contorted—we have to pass `follow=True` to the test client to tell it to get the page after the 302-redirect, and examine its context for a list of messages (which we have to listify before it'll play nicely). Here's what it looks like:

accounts/tests/test_views.py (ch17l013)

```
def test_adds_success_message(self):
    response = self.client.post('/accounts/send_login_email', data={
        'email': 'edith@example.com'
    }, follow=True)

    message = list(response.context['messages'])[0]
    self.assertEqual(
        message.message,
        "Check your email, we've sent you a link you can use to log in."
    )
    self.assertEqual(message.tags, "success")
```

---

4 I've split the form tag across three lines so it fits nicely in the book. If you've not seen it before, it may look a little weird to you, but it is valid HTML. You don't have to use it if you don't like it though. :)

That gives:

```
$ python manage.py test accounts
[...]
    message = list(response.context['messages'])[0]
IndexError: list index out of range
```

And we can get it passing with:

accounts/views.py (ch17l014)

```
from django.contrib import messages
[...]

def send_login_email(request):
    [...]
    messages.success(
        request,
        "Check your email, we've sent you a link you can use to log in."
    )
    return redirect('/')
```

Mocks Can Leave You Tightly Coupled to the Implementation

 This sidebar is an intermediate-level testing tip. If it goes over your head the first time around, come back and take another look when you've finished this chapter and Chapter 23.

I said testing messages is a bit contorted; it took me several goes to get it right. In fact, at work, we gave up on testing them like this and decided to just use mocks. Let's see what that would look like in this case:

accounts/tests/test_views.py (ch17l014-2)

```
from unittest.mock import patch, call
[...]

    @patch('accounts.views.messages')
    def test_adds_success_message_with_mocks(self, mock_messages):
        response = self.client.post('/accounts/send_login_email', data={
            'email': 'edith@example.com'
        })

        expected = "Check your email, we've sent you a link you can use to log in."
        self.assertEqual(
            mock_messages.success.call_args,
            call(response.wsgi_request, expected),
        )
```

We mock out the `messages` module, and check that `messages.success` was called with the right args: the original request, and the message we want.

And you could get it passing by using the exact same code as earlier. Here's the problem though: the `messages` framework gives you more than one way to achieve the same result. I could write the code like this:

accounts/views.py (ch17l014-3)

```
messages.add_message(
    request,
    messages.SUCCESS,
    "Check your email, we've sent you a link you can use to log in."
)
```

And the original, nonmocky test would still pass. But our mocky test will fail, because we're no longer calling `messages.success`, we're calling `messages.add_message`. Even though the end result is the same and our code is "correct," the test is broken.

This is what people mean when they say that using mocks can leave you "tightly coupled with the implementation". We usually say it's better to test behaviour, not implementation details; test what happens, not how you do it. Mocks often end up erring too much on the side of the "how" rather than the "what".

There's more detailed discussion of the pros and cons of mocks in later chapters.

Adding Messages to Our HTML

What happens next in the functional test? Ah. Still nothing. We need to actually add the messages to the page. Something like this:

lists/templates/base.html (ch17l015)

```
[...]
</nav>

{% if messages %}
  <div class="row">
    <div class="col-md-8">
      {% for message in messages %}
        {% if message.level_tag == 'success' %}
          <div class="alert alert-success">{{ message }}</div>
        {% else %}
          <div class="alert alert-warning">{{ message }}</div>
        {% endif %}
      {% endfor %}
    </div>
  </div>
{% endif %}
```

Now do we get a little further? Yes!

```
$ python manage.py test accounts
[...]
Ran 6 tests in 0.023s

OK


$ python manage.py test functional_tests.test_login
[...]
AssertionError: 'Use this link to log in' not found in 'body text tbc'
```

We need to fill out the body text of the email, with a link that the user can use to log in.

Let's just cheat for now though, by changing the value in the view:

accounts/views.py

```python
send_mail(
    'Your login link for Superlists',
    'Use this link to log in',
    'noreply@superlists',
    [email]
)
```

That gets the FT a little further:

```
$ python manage.py test functional_tests.test_login
[...]
AssertionError: Could not find url in email body:
Use this link to log in
```

Starting on the Login URL

We're going to have to build some kind of URL! Let's build one that, again, just cheats:

accounts/tests/test_views.py (ch17l017)

```python
class LoginViewTest(TestCase):

    def test_redirects_to_home_page(self):
        response = self.client.get('/accounts/login?token=abcd123')
        self.assertRedirects(response, '/')
```

We're imagining we'll pass the token in as a GET parameter, after the ?. It doesn't need to do anything for now.

I'm sure you can find your way through to getting the boilerplate for a basic URL and view in, via errors like these:

- No URL:

  ```
  AssertionError: 404 != 302 : Response didn't redirect as expected: Response
  code was 404 (expected 302)
  ```

- No view:

  ```
  AttributeError: module 'accounts.views' has no attribute 'login'
  ```

- Broken view:

  ```
  ValueError: The view accounts.views.login didn't return an HttpResponse object.
  It returned None instead.
  ```

- OK!

  ```
  $ python manage.py test accounts
  [...]

  Ran 7 tests in 0.029s
  OK
  ```

And now we can give them a link to use. It still won't do much though, because we still don't have a token to give to the user.

Checking That We Send the User a Link with a Token

Back in our send_login_email view, we've tested the email subject, from, and to fields. The body is the part that will have to include a token or URL they can use to log in. Let's spec out two tests for that:

accounts/tests/test_views.py (ch17l021)

```python
from accounts.models import Token
[...]

    def test_creates_token_associated_with_email(self):
        self.client.post('/accounts/send_login_email', data={
            'email': 'edith@example.com'
        })
        token = Token.objects.first()
        self.assertEqual(token.email, 'edith@example.com')


    @patch('accounts.views.send_mail')
    def test_sends_link_to_login_using_token_uid(self, mock_send_mail):
        self.client.post('/accounts/send_login_email', data={
            'email': 'edith@example.com'
        })

        token = Token.objects.first()
        expected_url = f'http://testserver/accounts/login?token={token.uid}'
        (subject, body, from_email, to_list), kwargs = mock_send_mail.call_args
        self.assertIn(expected_url, body)
```

The first test is fairly straightforward; it checks that the token we create in the database is associated with the email address from the post request.

The second one is our second test using mocks. We mock out the `send_mail` function again using the `patch` decorator, but this time we're interested in the body argument from the call arguments.

Running them now will fail because we're not creating any kind of token:

```
$ python manage.py test accounts
[...]
AttributeError: 'NoneType' object has no attribute 'email'
[...]
AttributeError: 'NoneType' object has no attribute 'uid'
```

We can get the first one to pass by creating a token:

accounts/views.py (ch17l022)

```
from accounts.models import Token
[...]

def send_login_email(request):
    email = request.POST['email']
    token = Token.objects.create(email=email)
    send_mail(
        [...]
```

And now the second test prompts us to actually use the token in the body of our email:

```
[...]
AssertionError:
'http://testserver/accounts/login?token=[...]'
not found in 'Use this link to log in'

FAILED (failures=1)
```

So we can insert the token into our email like this:

```
from django.core.urlresolvers import reverse
[...]

def send_login_email(request):
    email = request.POST['email']
    token = Token.objects.create(email=email)
    url = request.build_absolute_uri(  ❶
        reverse('login') + '?token=' + str(token.uid)
    )
    message_body = f'Use this link to log in:\n\n{url}'
    send_mail(
        'Your login link for Superlists',
        message_body,
        'noreply@superlists',
        [email]
    )
    [...]
```

❶ `request.build_absolute_uri` deserves a mention—it's one way to build a "full" URL, including the domain name and the http(s) part, in Django. There are other ways, but they usually involve getting into the "sites" framework, and that gets overcomplicated pretty quickly. You can find lots more discussion on this if you're curious by doing a bit of googling.

Two more pieces in the puzzle. We need an authentication backend, whose job it will be to examine tokens for validity and then return the corresponding users; then we need to get our login view to actually log users in, if they can authenticate.

De-spiking Our Custom Authentication Backend

Our custom authentication backend is next. Here's how it looked in the spike:

```
class PasswordlessAuthenticationBackend(object):

    def authenticate(self, uid):
        print('uid', uid, file=sys.stderr)
        if not Token.objects.filter(uid=uid).exists():
            print('no token found', file=sys.stderr)
            return None
        token = Token.objects.get(uid=uid)
        print('got token', file=sys.stderr)
        try:
            user = ListUser.objects.get(email=token.email)
            print('got user', file=sys.stderr)
            return user
        except ListUser.DoesNotExist:
            print('new user', file=sys.stderr)
            return ListUser.objects.create(email=token.email)


    def get_user(self, email):
        return ListUser.objects.get(email=email)
```

Decoding this:

- We take a UID and check if it exists in the database.

- We return None if it doesn't.

- If it does exist, we extract an email address, and either find an existing user with that address, or create a new one.

1 if = 1 More Test

A rule of thumb for these sorts of tests: any if means an extra test, and any try/ except means an extra test, so this should be about three tests. How about something like this?

```python
from django.test import TestCase
from django.contrib.auth import get_user_model
from accounts.authentication import PasswordlessAuthenticationBackend
from accounts.models import Token
User = get_user_model()


class AuthenticateTest(TestCase):

    def test_returns_None_if_no_such_token(self):
        result = PasswordlessAuthenticationBackend().authenticate(
            'no-such-token'
        )
        self.assertIsNone(result)


    def test_returns_new_user_with_correct_email_if_token_exists(self):
        email = 'edith@example.com'
        token = Token.objects.create(email=email)
        user = PasswordlessAuthenticationBackend().authenticate(token.uid)
        new_user = User.objects.get(email=email)
        self.assertEqual(user, new_user)


    def test_returns_existing_user_with_correct_email_if_token_exists(self):
        email = 'edith@example.com'
        existing_user = User.objects.create(email=email)
        token = Token.objects.create(email=email)
        user = PasswordlessAuthenticationBackend().authenticate(token.uid)
        self.assertEqual(user, existing_user)
```

In *authenticate.py* we'll just have a little placeholder:

```python
class PasswordlessAuthenticationBackend(object):

    def authenticate(self, uid):
        pass
```

How do we get on?

```
$ python manage.py test accounts

.FE........
======================================================================
ERROR: test_returns_new_user_with_correct_email_if_token_exists
(accounts.tests.test_authentication.AuthenticateTest)
 ----------------------------------------------------------------------
Traceback (most recent call last):
  File "...python-tdd-book/accounts/tests/test_authentication.py", line 21, in
test_returns_new_user_with_correct_email_if_token_exists
    new_user = User.objects.get(email=email)
[...]
accounts.models.DoesNotExist: User matching query does not exist.


======================================================================
FAIL: test_returns_existing_user_with_correct_email_if_token_exists
(accounts.tests.test_authentication.AuthenticateTest)
 ----------------------------------------------------------------------
Traceback (most recent call last):
  File "...python-tdd-book/accounts/tests/test_authentication.py", line 30, in
test_returns_existing_user_with_correct_email_if_token_exists
    self.assertEqual(user, existing_user)
AssertionError: None != <User: User object>


 ----------------------------------------------------------------------
Ran 12 tests in 0.038s

FAILED (failures=1, errors=1)
```

Here's a first cut:

accounts/authentication.py (ch17l026)

```python
from accounts.models import User, Token

class PasswordlessAuthenticationBackend(object):

    def authenticate(self, uid):
        token = Token.objects.get(uid=uid)
        return User.objects.get(email=token.email)
```

That gets one test passing but breaks another one:

```
$ python manage.py test accounts
ERROR: test_returns_None_if_no_such_token
(accounts.tests.test_authentication.AuthenticateTest)

accounts.models.DoesNotExist: Token matching query does not exist.

ERROR: test_returns_new_user_with_correct_email_if_token_exists
(accounts.tests.test_authentication.AuthenticateTest)
[...]
accounts.models.DoesNotExist: User matching query does not exist.
```

Let's fix each of those in turn:

accounts/authentication.py (ch17l027)

```python
def authenticate(self, uid):
    try:
        token = Token.objects.get(uid=uid)
        return User.objects.get(email=token.email)
    except Token.DoesNotExist:
        return None
```

That gets us down to one failure:

```
ERROR: test_returns_new_user_with_correct_email_if_token_exists
(accounts.tests.test_authentication.AuthenticateTest)
[...]
accounts.models.DoesNotExist: User matching query does not exist.

FAILED (errors=1)
```

And we can handle the final case like this:

accounts/authentication.py (ch17l028)

```python
def authenticate(self, uid):
    try:
        token = Token.objects.get(uid=uid)
        return User.objects.get(email=token.email)
    except User.DoesNotExist:
        return User.objects.create(email=token.email)
    except Token.DoesNotExist:
        return None
```

That's turned out neater than our spike!

The get_user Method

We've handled the authenticate function which Django will use to log new users in. The second part of the protocol we have to implement is the get_user method, whose job is to retrieve a user based on their unique identifier (the email address), or to return None if it can't find one (have another look at the spiked code if you need a reminder).

Here are a couple of tests for those two requirements:

```
class GetUserTest(TestCase):

    def test_gets_user_by_email(self):
        User.objects.create(email='another@example.com')
        desired_user = User.objects.create(email='edith@example.com')
        found_user = PasswordlessAuthenticationBackend().get_user(
            'edith@example.com'
        )
        self.assertEqual(found_user, desired_user)


    def test_returns_None_if_no_user_with_that_email(self):
        self.assertIsNone(
            PasswordlessAuthenticationBackend().get_user('edith@example.com')
        )
```

And our first failure:

```
AttributeError: 'PasswordlessAuthenticationBackend' object has no attribute
'get_user'
```

Let's create a placeholder one then:

accounts/authentication.py (ch17l031)

```
class PasswordlessAuthenticationBackend(object):

    def authenticate(self, uid):
        [...]

    def get_user(self, email):
        pass
```

Now we get:

```
    self.assertEqual(found_user, desired_user)
AssertionError: None != <User: User object>
```

And (step by step, just to see if our test fails the way we think it will):

accounts/authentication.py (ch17l033)

```
    def get_user(self, email):
        return User.objects.first()
```

That gets us past the first assertion, and onto:

```
    self.assertEqual(found_user, desired_user)
AssertionError: <User: User object> != <User: User object>
```

And so we call get with the email as an argument:

```
def get_user(self, email):
    return User.objects.get(email=email)
```

Now our test for the None case fails:

```
ERROR: test_returns_None_if_no_user_with_that_email
[...]
accounts.models.DoesNotExist: User matching query does not exist.
```

Which prompts us to finish the method like this:

```
def get_user(self, email):
    try:
        return User.objects.get(email=email)
    except User.DoesNotExist:
        return None     ❶
```

❶ You could just use `pass` here, and the function would return `None` by default. However, because we specifically need the function to return `None`, the "explicit is better than implicit" rule applies here.

That gets us to passing tests:

```
OK
```

And we have a working authentication backend!

Using Our Auth Backend in the Login View

The final step is to use the backend in our login view. First we add it to *settings.py*:

```
AUTH_USER_MODEL = 'accounts.User'
AUTHENTICATION_BACKENDS = [
    'accounts.authentication.PasswordlessAuthenticationBackend',
]

[...]
```

Next let's write some tests for what should happen in our view. Looking back at the spike again:

```
def login(request):
    print('login view', file=sys.stderr)
    uid = request.GET.get('uid')
    user = auth.authenticate(uid=uid)
    if user is not None:
        auth.login(request, user)
    return redirect('/')
```

We need the view to call `django.contrib.auth.authenticate`, and then, if it returns a user, we call `django.contrib.auth.login`.

This is a good time to check out the Django docs on authentication (*https://docs.djangoproject.com/en/1.11/topics/auth/default/#how-to-log-a-user-in*) for a little more context.

An Alternative Reason to Use Mocks: Reducing Duplication

So far we've used mocks to test external dependencies, like Django's mail-sending function. The main reason to use a mock was to isolate ourselves from external side effects, in this case, to avoid sending out actual emails during our tests.

In this section we'll look at a different kind of use of mocks. Here we don't have any side effects we're worried about, but there are still some reasons you might want to use a mock here.

The nonmocky way of testing this login view would be to see whether it does actually log the user in, by checking whether the user gets assigned an authenticated session cookie in the right circumstances.

But our authentication backend does have a few different code paths: it returns None for invalid tokens, existing users if they already exist, and creates new users for valid tokens if they don't exist yet. So, to fully test this view, I'd have to write tests for all three of those cases.

One good justification for using mocks is when they will reduce duplication between tests. It's one way of avoiding *combinatorial explosion*.

On top of that, the fact that we're using the Django `auth.authenticate` function rather than calling our own code directly is relevant: it allows us the option to add further backends in future.

So in this case (in contrast to the example in "Mocks Can Leave You Tightly Coupled to the Implementation" on page 338) the implementation does matter, and using a mock will save us from having duplication in our tests. Let's see how it looks:

accounts/tests/test_views.py (ch17l037)

```python
from unittest.mock import patch, call
[...]

    @patch('accounts.views.auth')  ❶
    def test_calls_authenticate_with_uid_from_get_request(self, mock_auth):  ❷
        self.client.get('/accounts/login?token=abcd123')
        self.assertEqual(
            mock_auth.authenticate.call_args,  ❸
            call(uid='abcd123')  ❹
        )
```

❶ We expect to be using the `django.contrib.auth` module in *views.py*, and we mock it out here. Note that this time, we're not mocking out a function, we're mocking out a whole module, and thus implicitly mocking out all the functions (and any other objects) that module contains.

❷ As usual, the mocked object is injected into our test method.

❸ This time, we've mocked out a module rather than a function. So we examine the `call_args` not of the `mock_auth` module, but of the `mock_auth.authenticate` function. Because all the attributes of a mock are more mocks, that's a mock too. You can start to see why `Mock` objects are so convenient, compared to trying to build your own.

❹ Now, instead of "unpacking" the call args, we use the `call` function for a neater way of saying what it should have been called with-- that is, the token from the GET request. (See the following sidebar.)

On Mock call_args

The `call_args` property on a mock represents the positional and keyword arguments that the mock was called with. It's a special "call" object type, which is essentially a tuple of (`positional_args`, `keyword_args`). `positional_args` is itself a tuple, consisting of the set of positional arguments. `keyword_args` is a dictionary.

```
>>> from unittest.mock import Mock, call
>>> m = Mock()
>>> m(42, 43, 'positional arg 3', key='val', thing=666)
<Mock name='mock()' id='139909729163528'>

>>> m.call_args
call(42, 43, 'positional arg 3', key='val', thing=666)

>>> m.call_args == ((42, 43, 'positional arg 3'), {'key': 'val', 'thing': 666})
True
>>> m.call_args == call(42, 43, 'positional arg 3', key='val', thing=666)
True
```

So in our test, we could have done this instead:

accounts/tests/test_views.py

```
self.assertEqual(
    mock_auth.authenticate.call_args,
    ((,), {'uid': 'abcd123'})
)
# or this
args, kwargs = mock_auth.authenticate.call_args
self.assertEqual(args, (,))
self.assertEqual(kwargs, {'uid': 'abcd123'})
```

But you can see how using the `call` helper is nicer.

What happens when we run the test? The first error is this:

```
$ python manage.py test accounts
[...]
AttributeError: <module 'accounts.views' from
'...python-tdd-book/accounts/views.py'> does not have the attribute 'auth'
```

`module foo does not have the attribute bar` is a common first failure in a test that uses mocks. It's telling you that you're trying to mock out something that doesn't yet exist (or isn't yet imported) in the target module.

Once we import `django.contrib.auth`, the error changes:

```
from django.contrib import auth, messages
[...]
```

Now we get:

```
AssertionError: None != call(uid='abcd123')
```

Now it's telling us that the view doesn't call the `auth.authenticate` function at all. Let's fix that, but get it deliberately wrong, just to see:

```
def login(request):
    auth.authenticate('bang!')
    return redirect('/')
```

Bang indeed!

```
$ python manage.py test accounts
[...]
AssertionError: call('bang!') != call(uid='abcd123')
[...]
FAILED (failures=1)
```

Let's give authenticate the arguments it expects then:

```
def login(request):
    auth.authenticate(uid=request.GET.get('token'))
    return redirect('/')
```

That gets us to passing tests:

```
$ python manage.py test accounts
[...]
Ran 15 tests in 0.041s

OK
```

Using mock.return_value

Next we want to check that if the authenticate function returns a user, we pass that into `auth.login`. Let's see how that test looks:

```
@patch('accounts.views.auth')  ❶
def test_calls_auth_login_with_user_if_there_is_one(self, mock_auth):
    response = self.client.get('/accounts/login?token=abcd123')
    self.assertEqual(
        mock_auth.login.call_args,  ❷
        call(response.wsgi_request, mock_auth.authenticate.return_value)  ❸
    )
```

❶ We mock the `contrib.auth` module again.

❷ This time we examine the call args for the `auth.login` function.

❸ We check that it's called with the request object that the view sees, and the "user"
   object that the `authenticate` function returns. Because `authenticate` is also
   mocked out, we can use its special "return_value" attribute.

When you call a mock, you get another mock. But you can also get a copy of that
returned mock from the original mock that you called. Boy, it sure is hard to explain
this stuff without saying "mock" a lot! Another little console illustration might help
here:

```
>>> m = Mock()
>>> thing = m()
>>> thing
<Mock name='mock()' id='140652722034952'>
>>> m.return_value
<Mock name='mock()' id='140652722034952'>
>>> thing == m.return_value
True
```

In any case, what do we get from running the test?

```
$ python manage.py test accounts
[...]
    call(response.wsgi_request, mock_auth.authenticate.return_value)
AssertionError: None != call(<WSGIRequest: GET '/accounts/login?t[...]
```

Sure enough, it's telling us that we're not calling `auth.login` at all yet. Let's try doing
that. Deliberately wrong as usual first!

```
def login(request):
    auth.authenticate(uid=request.GET.get('token'))
    auth.login('ack!')
    return redirect('/')
```

Ack indeed!

```
TypeError: login() missing 1 required positional argument: 'user'
[...]
AssertionError: call('ack!') != call(<WSGIRequest: GET
'/accounts/login?token=[...]
```

Let's fix that:

accounts/views.py (ch17l043)

```
def login(request):
    user = auth.authenticate(uid=request.GET.get('token'))
    auth.login(request, user)
    return redirect('/')
```

Now we get this unexpected complaint:

```
ERROR: test_redirects_to_home_page (accounts.tests.test_views.LoginViewTest)
[...]
AttributeError: 'AnonymousUser' object has no attribute '_meta'
```

It's because we're still calling auth.login indiscriminately on any kind of user, and that's causing problems back in our original test for the redirect, which *isn't* currently mocking out auth.login. We need to add an if (and therefore another test), and while we're at it we'll learn about patching at the class level.

Patching at the Class Level

We want to add another test, with another @patch('accounts.views.auth'), and that's starting to get repetitive. We use the "three strikes" rule, and we can move the patch decorator to the class level. This will have the effect of mocking out accounts.views.auth in every single test method in that class. That also means our original redirect test will now also have the mock_auth variable injected:

```
@patch('accounts.views.auth')  ❶
class LoginViewTest(TestCase):

    def test_redirects_to_home_page(self, mock_auth):  ❷
        [...]

    def test_calls_authenticate_with_uid_from_get_request(self, mock_auth):  ❸
        [...]

    def test_calls_auth_login_with_user_if_there_is_one(self, mock_auth):  ❸
        [...]


    def test_does_not_login_if_user_is_not_authenticated(self, mock_auth):
        mock_auth.authenticate.return_value = None  ❹
        self.client.get('/accounts/login?token=abcd123')
        self.assertEqual(mock_auth.login.called, False)  ❺
```

❶ We move the patch to the class level…

❷ which means we get an extra argument injected into our first test method…

❸ And we can remove the decorators from all the other tests.

❹ In our new test, we explicitly set the `return_value` on the `auth.authenticate` mock, *before* we call the `self.client.get`.

❺ We assert that, if `authenticate` returns `None`, we should not call `auth.login` at all.

That cleans up the spurious failure, and gives us a specific, expected failure to work on:

```
    self.assertEqual(mock_auth.login.called, False)
AssertionError: True != False
```

And we get it passing like this:

```
def login(request):
    user = auth.authenticate(uid=request.GET.get('token'))
    if user:
        auth.login(request, user)
    return redirect('/')
```

So are we there yet?

The Moment of Truth: Will the FT Pass?

I think we're just about ready to try our functional test!

Let's just make sure our base template shows a different nav bar for logged-in and non–logged-in users (which our FT relies on):

lists/templates/base.html (ch17l046)

```
<nav class="navbar navbar-default" role="navigation">
  <div class="container-fluid">
    <a class="navbar-brand" href="/">Superlists</a>
    {% if user.email %}
      <ul class="nav navbar-nav navbar-right">
        <li class="navbar-text">Logged in as {{ user.email }}</li>
        <li><a href="#">Log out</a></li>
      </ul>
    {% else %}
      <form class="navbar-form navbar-right"
            method="POST"
            action="{% url 'send_login_email' %}">
        <span>Enter email to log in:</span>
        <input class="form-control" name="email" type="text" />
        {% csrf_token %}
      </form>
    {% endif %}
  </div>
</nav>
```

And see if that…

```
$ python manage.py test functional_tests.test_login
Internal Server Error: /accounts/login
[...]
  File "...python-tdd-book/accounts/views.py", line 31, in login
    auth.login(request, user)
[...]
ValueError: The following fields do not exist in this model or are m2m fields:
last_login
[...]
selenium.common.exceptions.NoSuchElementException: Message: Unable to locate
element: Log out
```

Oh no! Something's not right. But assuming you've kept the LOGGING config in *settings.py*, you should see the explanatory traceback, as just shown. It's saying something about a last_login field.

In my opinion (*https://code.djangoproject.com/ticket/26823*) this is a bug in Django, but essentially the auth framework expects the user model to have a last_login field. We don't have one. But never fear! There's a way of handling this failure.

Let's write a unit test that reproduces the bug first. Since it's to do with our custom user model, as good a place to have it as any might be *test_models.py*:

accounts/tests/test_models.py (ch17l047)

```
from django.test import TestCase
from django.contrib import auth
from accounts.models import Token
User = auth.get_user_model()


class UserModelTest(TestCase):

    def test_user_is_valid_with_email_only(self):
        [...]
    def test_email_is_primary_key(self):
        [...]


    def test_no_problem_with_auth_login(self):
        user = User.objects.create(email='edith@example.com')
        user.backend = ''
        request = self.client.request().wsgi_request
        auth.login(request, user)  # should not raise
```

We create a request object and a user, and then we pass them into the auth.login function.

That will raise our error:

```
          auth.login(request, user)  # should not raise
    [...]
    ValueError: The following fields do not exist in this model or are m2m fields:
    last_login
```

The specific reason for this bug isn't really important for the purposes of this book, but if you're curious about what exactly is going on here, take a look through the Django source lines listed in the traceback, and have a read up of Django's docs on signals (*https://docs.djangoproject.com/en/1.11/topics/signals/*).

The upshot is that we can fix it like this:

accounts/models.py (ch17l048)

```
import uuid
from django.contrib import auth
from django.db import models


auth.signals.user_logged_in.disconnect(auth.models.update_last_login)


class User(models.Model):
    [...]
```

How does our FT look now?

```
$ python manage.py test functional_tests.test_login
[...]
.
 ---------------------------------------------------------------
Ran 1 test in 3.282s

OK
```

It Works in Theory! Does It Work in Practice?

Wow! Can you believe it? I scarcely can! Time for a manual look around with run server:

```
$ python manage.py runserver
[...]
Internal Server Error: /accounts/send_login_email
Traceback (most recent call last):
  File "...python-tdd-book/accounts/views.py", line 20, in send_login_email

ConnectionRefusedError: [Errno 111] Connection refused
```

Using Our New Environment Variable, and Saving It to .env

You'll probably get an error, like I did, when you try to run things manually. It's because of two things:

- Firstly, we need to re-add the email configuration to *settings.py*.

superlists/settings.py (ch17l049)

```
EMAIL_HOST = 'smtp.gmail.com'
EMAIL_HOST_USER = 'obeythetestinggoat@gmail.com'
EMAIL_HOST_PASSWORD = os.environ.get('EMAIL_PASSWORD')
EMAIL_PORT = 587
EMAIL_USE_TLS = True
```

- Secondly, we (probably) need to re-set the EMAIL_PASSWORD in our shell.

```
$ export EMAIL_PASSWORD="yoursekritpasswordhere"
```

Using a Local .env File for Development

Until now we've only used the *.env* file on the server, because all the other settings have sensible defaults for dev, but there's just no way to get a working login system without this one.

Just as we do on the server, you can also use a *.env* file to save project-specific environment variables:

```
$ echo EMAIL_PASSWORD="yoursekritpasswordhere" >> .env
$ set -a; source .env; set +a;
```

It does mean you have to remember to do that weird set -a; source... dance, every time you start working on the project, as well as remembering to activate your virtualenv.

If you search or ask around, you'll find there are some tools and shell plugins that load virtualenvs and *.env* files automatically, and/or django plugins that do this stuff too.

- Django-specific: django-environ (*https://django-environ.readthedocs.io/en/latest/*) or django-dotenv (*https://github.com/jpadilla/django-dotenv*)
- More general Python project management Pipenv (*https://docs.pipenv.org/*)
- Or even roll your own (*https://stackoverflow.com/questions/19331497/set-environment-variables-from-file/34093548#34093548*)

And now...

```
$ python manage.py runserver
```

...you should see something like Figure 19-1.

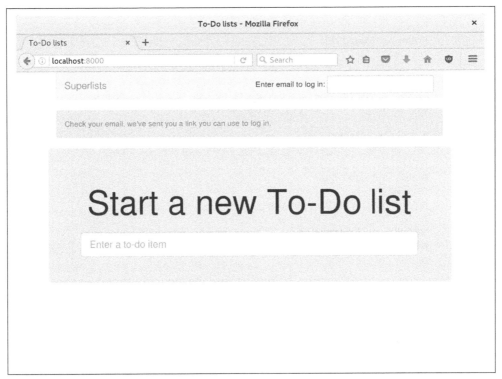

Figure 19-1. Check your email....

Woohoo!

I've been waiting to do a commit up until this moment, just to make sure everything works. At this point, you could make a series of separate commits—one for the login view, one for the auth backend, one for the user model, one for wiring up the template. Or you could decide that, since they're all interrelated, and none will work without the others, you may as well just have one big commit:

```
$ git status
$ git add .
$ git diff --staged
$ git commit -m "Custom passwordless auth backend + custom user model"
```

Finishing Off Our FT, Testing Logout

The last thing we need to do before we call it a day is to test the logout link. We extend the FT with a couple more steps:

```
[...]
# she is logged in!
self.wait_for(
    lambda: self.browser.find_element_by_link_text('Log out')
)
navbar = self.browser.find_element_by_css_selector('.navbar')
self.assertIn(TEST_EMAIL, navbar.text)

# Now she logs out
self.browser.find_element_by_link_text('Log out').click()

# She is logged out
self.wait_for(
    lambda: self.browser.find_element_by_name('email')
)
navbar = self.browser.find_element_by_css_selector('.navbar')
self.assertNotIn(TEST_EMAIL, navbar.text)
```

With that, we can see that the test is failing because the logout button doesn't work:

```
$ python manage.py test functional_tests.test_login
[...]
selenium.common.exceptions.NoSuchElementException: Message: Unable to locate
element: [name="email"]
```

Implementing a logout button is actually very simple: we can use Django's built-in logout view (*http://bit.ly/SuI0hA*), which clears down the user's session and redirects them to a page of our choice:

```
from django.contrib.auth.views import logout
[...]

urlpatterns = [
    url(r'^send_login_email$', views.send_login_email, name='send_login_email'),
    url(r'^login$', views.login, name='login'),
    url(r'^logout$', logout, {'next_page': '/'}, name='logout'),
]
```

And in *base.html*, we just make the logout into a real URL link:

```
<li><a href="{% url 'logout' %}">Log out</a></li>
```

And that gets us a fully passing FT—indeed, a fully passing test suite:

```
$ python manage.py test functional_tests.test_login
[...]
OK
$ python manage.py test
[...]
Ran 59 tests in 78.124s

OK
```

 We're nowhere near a truly secure or acceptable login system here. Since this is just an example app for a book, we'll leave it at that, but in "real life" you'd want to explore a lot more security and usability issues before calling the job done. We're dangerously close to "rolling our own crypto" here, and relying on a more established login system would be much safer.

In the next chapter, we'll start trying to put our login system to good use. In the meantime, do a commit and enjoy this recap:

On Mocking in Python

Mocking and external dependencies

We use mocking in unit tests when we have an external dependency that we don't want to actually use in our tests. A mock is used to simulate the third-party API. Whilst it is possible to "roll your own" mocks in Python, a mocking framework like the mock module provides a lot of helpful shortcuts which will make it easier to write (and more importantly, read) your tests.

Monkeypatching

Replacing an object in a namespace at runtime. We use it in our unit tests to replace a real function which has undesirable side effects with a mock object, using the patch decorator.

The Mock library

Michael Foord (who used to work for the company that spawned PythonAnywhere, just before I joined) wrote the excellent "Mock" library that's now been integrated into the standard library of Python 3. It contains most everything you might need for mocking in Python.

The patch decorator

unittest.mock provides a function called patch, which can be used to "mock out" any object from the module you're testing. It's commonly used as a decorator on a test method, or even at the class level, where it's applied to all the test methods of that class.

Mocks can leave you tightly coupled to the implementation
>As we saw in "Mocks Can Leave You Tightly Coupled to the Implementation" on page 338, mocks can leave you tightly coupled to your implementation. For that reason, you shouldn't use them unless you have a good reason.

Mocks can save you from duplication in your tests
>On the other hand, there's no point in duplicating all of your tests for a function inside a higher-level piece of code that uses that function. Using a mock in this case reduces duplication.

There's lots more discussion of the pros and cons of mocks coming up soon. Read on!

Test Fixtures and a Decorator for Explicit Waits

Now that we have a functional authentication system, we want to use it to identify users, and be able to show them all the lists they have created.

To do that, we're going to have to write FTs that have a logged-in user. Rather than making each test go through the (time-consuming) login email dance, we want to be able to skip that part.

This is about separation of concerns. Functional tests aren't like unit tests, in that they don't usually have a single assertion. But, conceptually, they should be testing a single thing. There's no need for every single FT to test the login/logout mechanisms. If we can figure out a way to "cheat" and skip that part, we'll spend less time waiting for duplicated test paths.

Don't overdo de-duplication in FTs. One of the benefits of an FT is that it can catch strange and unpredictable interactions between different parts of your application.

This chapter has only just been rewritten for the new edition, so let me know via *obeythetestinggoat@gmail.com* if you spot any problems or have any suggestions for improvement!

Skipping the Login Process by Pre-creating a Session

It's quite common for a user to return to a site and still have a cookie, which means they are "pre-authenticated", so this isn't an unrealistic cheat at all. Here's how you can set it up:

functional_tests/test_my_lists.py

```python
from django.conf import settings
from django.contrib.auth import BACKEND_SESSION_KEY, SESSION_KEY, get_user_model
from django.contrib.sessions.backends.db import SessionStore
from .base import FunctionalTest
User = get_user_model()


class MyListsTest(FunctionalTest):

    def create_pre_authenticated_session(self, email):
        user = User.objects.create(email=email)
        session = SessionStore()
        session[SESSION_KEY] = user.pk  ❶
        session[BACKEND_SESSION_KEY] = settings.AUTHENTICATION_BACKENDS[0]
        session.save()
        ## to set a cookie we need to first visit the domain.
        ## 404 pages load the quickest!
        self.browser.get(self.live_server_url + "/404_no_such_url/")
        self.browser.add_cookie(dict(
            name=settings.SESSION_COOKIE_NAME,
            value=session.session_key,  ❷
            path='/',
        ))
```

❶ We create a session object in the database. The session key is the primary key of the user object (which is actually the user's email address).

❷ We then add a cookie to the browser that matches the session on the server—on our next visit to the site, the server should recognise us as a logged-in user.

Note that, as it is, this will only work because we're using `LiveServerTestCase`, so the `User` and `Session` objects we create will end up in the same database as the test server. Later we'll need to modify it so that it works against the database on the staging server too.

Django Sessions: How a User's Cookies Tell the Server She Is Authenticated

Being an attempt to explain sessions, cookies, and authentication in Django.

Because HTTP is stateless, servers need a way of recognising different clients with *every single request*. IP addresses can be shared, so the usual solution is to give each client a unique session ID, which it will store in a cookie, and submit with every request. The server will store that ID somewhere (by default, in the database), and then it can recognise each request that comes in as being from a particular client.

If you log in to the site using the dev server, you can actually take a look at your session ID by hand if you like. It's stored under the key `sessionid` by default. See Figure 20-1.

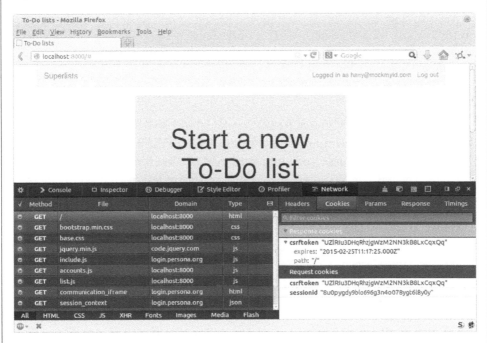

Figure 20-1. Examining the session cookie in the Debug toolbar

These session cookies are set for all visitors to a Django site, whether they're logged in or not.

When we want to recognise a client as being a logged-in and authenticated user, again, rather than asking the client to send their username and password with every single request, the server can actually just mark that client's session as being an authenticated session, and associate it with a user ID in its database.

A session is a dictionary-like data structure, and the user ID is stored under the key given by django.contrib.auth.SESSION_KEY. You can check this out in a ./manage.py shell if you like:

```
$ python manage.py shell
[...]
In [1]: from django.contrib.sessions.models import Session

# substitute your session id from your browser cookie here
In [2]: session = Session.objects.get(
    session_key="8u0pygdy9blo696g3n4o078ygt6l8y0y"
)

In [3]: print(session.get_decoded())
{'_auth_user_id': 'obeythetestinggoat@gmail.com', '_auth_user_backend':
'accounts.authentication.PasswordlessAuthenticationBackend'}
```

You can also store any other information you like on a user's session, as a way of temporarily keeping track of some state. This works for non–logged-in users too. Just use request.session inside any view, and it works as a dict. There's more information in the Django docs on sessions (*http://bit.ly/2tGVbQE*).

Checking That It Works

To check that it works, it would be good to use some of the code from our previous test. Let's make a couple of functions called wait_to_be_logged_in and wait_to_be_logged_out. To access them from a different test, we'll need to pull them up into FunctionalTest. We'll also tweak them slightly so that they can take an arbitrary email address as a parameter:

functional_tests/base.py (ch18l002)

```python
class FunctionalTest(StaticLiveServerTestCase):
    [...]

    def wait_to_be_logged_in(self, email):
        self.wait_for(
            lambda: self.browser.find_element_by_link_text('Log out')
        )
        navbar = self.browser.find_element_by_css_selector('.navbar')
        self.assertIn(email, navbar.text)


    def wait_to_be_logged_out(self, email):
        self.wait_for(
            lambda: self.browser.find_element_by_name('email')
        )
        navbar = self.browser.find_element_by_css_selector('.navbar')
        self.assertNotIn(email, navbar.text)
```

Hm, that's not bad, but I'm not quite happy with the amount of duplication of `wait_for` stuff in here. Let's make a note to come back to it, and get these helpers working.

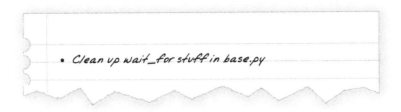

• *Clean up wait_for stuff in base.py*

First we use them in *test_login.py*:

functional_tests/test_login.py (ch18l003)

```python
def test_can_get_email_link_to_log_in(self):
    [...]
    # she is logged in!
    self.wait_to_be_logged_in(email=TEST_EMAIL)

    # Now she logs out
    self.browser.find_element_by_link_text('Log out').click()

    # She is logged out
    self.wait_to_be_logged_out(email=TEST_EMAIL)
```

Just to make sure we haven't broken anything, we rerun the login test:

```
$ python manage.py test functional_tests.test_login
[...]
OK
```

And now we can write a placeholder for the "My Lists" test, to see if our pre-authenticated session creator really does work:

functional_tests/test_my_lists.py (ch18l004)

```python
def test_logged_in_users_lists_are_saved_as_my_lists(self):
    email = 'edith@example.com'
    self.browser.get(self.live_server_url)
    self.wait_to_be_logged_out(email)

    # Edith is a logged-in user
    self.create_pre_authenticated_session(email)
    self.browser.get(self.live_server_url)
    self.wait_to_be_logged_in(email)
```

That gets us:

```
$ python manage.py test functional_tests.test_my_lists
[...]
OK
```

That's a good place for a commit:

```
$ git add functional_tests
$ git commit -m "test_my_lists: precreate sessions, move login checks into base"
```

JSON Test Fixtures Considered Harmful

When we pre-populate the database with test data, as we've done here with the User object and its associated Session object, what we're doing is setting up a "test fixture".

Django comes with built-in support for saving database objects as JSON (using the manage.py dumpdata), and automatically loading them in your test runs using the fixtures class attribute on TestCase.

More and more people are starting to say: don't use JSON fixtures (*http://bit.ly/ 1kSTyrb*). They're a nightmare to maintain when your model changes. Plus it's difficult for the reader to tell which of the many attribute values specified in the JSON are critical for the behaviour under test, and which are just filler. Finally, even if tests start out sharing fixtures, sooner or later one test will want slightly different versions of the data, and you end up copying the whole thing around to keep them isolated, and again it's hard to tell what's relevant to the test and what is just happenstance.

It's usually much more straightforward to just load the data directly using the Django ORM.

Once you have more than a handful of fields on a model, and/or several related models, even using the ORM can be cumbersome. In this case, there's a tool that lots of people swear by called factory_boy (*https://factoryboy.readthe docs.org/*).

Our Final Explicit Wait Helper: A Wait Decorator

We've used decorators a few times in our code so far, but it's time to learn how they actually work by making one of our own.

First, let's imagine how we might want our decorator to work. It would be nice to be able to replace all the custom wait/retry/timeout logic in wait_for_row_ in_list_table and the inline self.wait_fors in the wait_to_be_logged_in/out. Something like this would look lovely:

```
    @wait
    def wait_for_row_in_list_table(self, row_text):
        table = self.browser.find_element_by_id('id_list_table')
        rows = table.find_elements_by_tag_name('tr')
        self.assertIn(row_text, [row.text for row in rows])


    @wait
    def wait_to_be_logged_in(self, email):
        self.browser.find_element_by_link_text('Log out')
        navbar = self.browser.find_element_by_css_selector('.navbar')
        self.assertIn(email, navbar.text)


    @wait
    def wait_to_be_logged_out(self, email):
        self.browser.find_element_by_name('email')
        navbar = self.browser.find_element_by_css_selector('.navbar')
        self.assertNotIn(email, navbar.text)
```

Are you ready to dive in? Although decorators are quite difficult to wrap your head around (I know it took me a long time before I was comfortable with them, and I still have to think about them quite carefully whenever I make one), the nice thing is that we've already dipped our toes into functional programming in our self.wait_for helper function. That's a function that takes another function as an argument, and a decorator is the same. The difference is that the decorator doesn't actually execute any code itself—it returns a modified version of the function that it was given.

Our decorator wants to return a new function which will keep calling the function it was given, catching our usual exceptions, until a timeout occurs. Here's a first cut:

```
def wait(fn):  ❶
    def modified_fn():  ❸
        start_time = time.time()
        while True:  ❹
            try:
                return fn()  ❺
            except (AssertionError, WebDriverException) as e:  ❹
                if time.time() - start_time > MAX_WAIT:
                    raise e
                time.sleep(0.5)
    return modified_fn  ❷
```

❶ A decorator is a way of modifying a function; it takes a function as an argument...

❷ and returns another function as the modified (or "decorated") version.

❸ Here's where we create our modified function.

❹ And here's our familiar loop, which will keep going, catching the usual exceptions, until our timeout expires.

❺ And as always, we call our function and return immediately if there are no exceptions.

That's *almost* right, but not quite; try running it?

```
$ python manage.py test functional_tests.test_my_lists
[...]
    self.wait_to_be_logged_out(email)
TypeError: modified_fn() takes 0 positional arguments but 2 were given
```

Unlike in `self.wait_for`, the decorator is being applied to functions that have arguments:

functional_tests/base.py

```
@wait
def wait_to_be_logged_in(self, email):
    self.browser.find_element_by_link_text('Log out')
```

`wait_to_be_logged_in` takes `self` and `email` as positional arguments. But when it's decorated, it's replaced with `modified_fn`, which takes no arguments. How do we magically make it so our `modified_fn` can handle the same arguments as whatever `fn` the decorator gets given has?

The answer is a bit of Python magic, `*args` and `**kwargs`, more formally known as "variadic arguments" (*https://docs.python.org/3/tutorial/controlflow.html#keyword-arguments*), apparently (I only just learned that):

functional_tests/base.py (ch18l007)

```
def wait(fn):
    def modified_fn(*args, **kwargs):    ❶
        start_time = time.time()
        while True:
            try:
                return fn(*args, **kwargs)    ❷
            except (AssertionError, WebDriverException) as e:
                if time.time() - start_time > MAX_WAIT:
                    raise e
                time.sleep(0.5)
    return modified_fn
```

❶ Using *args and **kwargs, we specify that modified_fn may take any arbitrary positional and keyword arguments.

❷ As we've captured them in the function definition, we make sure to pass those same arguments to fn when we actually call it.

One of the fun things this can be used for is to make a decorator that changes the arguments of a function. But we won't get into that now. The main thing is that our decorator now works:

```
$ python manage.py test functional_tests.test_my_lists
[...]
OK
```

And do you know what's truly satisfying? We can use our wait decorator for our self.wait_for helper as well! Like this:

functional_tests/base.py (ch18l008)

```
@wait
def wait_for(self, fn):
    return fn()
```

Lovely! Now all our wait/retry logic is encapsulated in a single place, and we have a nice easy way of applying those waits, either inline in our FTs using self.wait_for, or on any helper function using the @wait decorator.

In the next chapter we'll try to deploy our code to staging, and use the pre-authenticated session fixtures on the server. As we'll see it'll help us catch a little bug or two!

Lessons Learned

Decorators are nice
> Decorators can be a great way of abstracting out different levels of concerns. They let us write our test assertions without having to think about waits at the same time.

De-duplicate your FTs, with caution

Every single FT doesn't need to test every single part of your application. In our case, we wanted to avoid going through the full login process for every FT that needs an authenticated user, so we used a test fixture to "cheat" and skip that part. You might find other things you want to skip in your FTs. A word of caution, however: functional tests are there to catch unpredictable interactions between different parts of your application, so be wary of pushing de-duplication to the extreme.

Test fixtures

Test fixtures refers to test data that needs to be set up as a precondition before a test is run—often this means populating the database with some information, but as we've seen (with browser cookies), it can involve other types of preconditions.

Avoid JSON fixtures

Django makes it easy to save and restore data from the database in JSON format (and others) using the `dumpdata` and `loaddata` management commands. Most people recommend against using these for test fixtures, as they are painful to manage when your database schema changes. Use the ORM, or a tool like `factory_boy` (*https://factoryboy.readthedocs.org/*).

Server-Side Debugging

Popping a few layers off the stack of things we're working on: we have nice wait-for helpers; what were we using them for? Oh yes, waiting to be logged in. And why was that? Ah yes, we had just built a way of pre-authenticating a user.

The Proof Is in the Pudding: Using Staging to Catch Final Bugs

They're all very well for running the FTs locally, but how would they work against the staging server? Let's try to deploy our site. Along the way we'll catch an unexpected bug (that's what staging is for!), and then we'll have to figure out a way of managing the database on the test server:

```
$ git push  # if you haven't already
$ cd deploy_tools
$ fab deploy --host=elspeth@superlists-staging.ottg.eu
[...]
```

And restart Gunicorn…

```
elspeth@server:$ sudo systemctl daemon-reload
elspeth@server:$ sudo systemctl restart gunicorn-superlists-staging.ottg.eu
```

Here's what happens when we run the functional tests:

```
$ STAGING_SERVER=superlists-staging.ottg.eu python manage.py test functional_tests
======================================================================
ERROR: test_logged_in_users_lists_are_saved_as_my_lists
(functional_tests.test_my_lists.MyListsTest)
----------------------------------------------------------------------
Traceback (most recent call last):
  File "...python-tdd-book/functional_tests/test_my_lists.py", line 34, in
test_logged_in_users_lists_are_saved_as_my_lists
    self.wait_to_be_logged_in(email)
[...]
selenium.common.exceptions.NoSuchElementException: Message: Unable to locate
element: Log out


======================================================================
FAIL: test_can_get_email_link_to_log_in (functional_tests.test_login.LoginTest)
----------------------------------------------------------------------
Traceback (most recent call last):
  File "...python-tdd-book/functional_tests/test_login.py", line 22, in
test_can_get_email_link_to_log_in
    self.wait_for(lambda: self.assertIn(
[...]
AssertionError: 'Check your email' not found in 'Server Error (500)'

----------------------------------------------------------------------
Ran 8 tests in 68.602s

FAILED (failures=1, errors=1)
```

We can't log in—either with the real email system or with our pre-authenticated session. Looks like our nice new authentication system is crashing the server.

Let's practice a bit of server-side debugging!

Inspecting Logs on the Server

In order to track this problem down, we need to get some logging information out of Django.

First, make sure your *settings.py* still contains the LOGGING settings which will actually send stuff to the console:

```
LOGGING = {
    'version': 1,
    'disable_existing_loggers': False,
    'handlers': {
        'console': {
            'level': 'DEBUG',
            'class': 'logging.StreamHandler',
        },
    },
    'loggers': {
        'django': {
            'handlers': ['console'],
        },
    },
    'root': {'level': 'INFO'},
}
```

Restart Gunicorn again if necessary, and then either rerun the FT, or just try to log in manually. While that happens, we watch the logs on the server with `journalctl -f`:

```
elspeth@server:$ sudo journalctl -f -u gunicorn-superlists-staging.ottg.eu
```

You should see an error like this:

```
Internal Server Error: /accounts/send_login_email
Traceback (most recent call last):
  File "/home/elspeth/sites/superlists-staging.ottg.eu/virtualenv/lib/python3.6/[...]
    response = wrapped_callback(request, *callback_args, **callback_kwargs)
  File
"/home/elspeth/sites/superlists-staging.ottg.eu/accounts/views.py", line
20, in send_login_email
    [email]
[...]
    self.connection.sendmail(from_email, recipients, message.as_bytes(linesep=|r|n))
  File "/usr/lib/python3.6/smtplib.py", line 862, in sendmail
    raise SMTPSenderRefused(code, resp, from_addr)
smtplib.SMTPSenderRefused: (530, b'5.5.1 Authentication Required. Learn more
at\n5.5.1  https://support.google.com/mail/?p=WantAuthError [...]
- gsmtp', noreply@superlists)
```

Hm, Gmail is refusing to send our emails, is it? Now why might that be? Ah yes, we haven't told the server what our password is!

Another Environment Variable

Just as in Chapter 10, the place we set environment variables on the server is in the *.env* file:

```
elspeth@server:$ cd ~/sites/superlists-staging.ottg.eu/
elspeth@server:$ echo EMAIL_PASSWORD=yoursekritpasswordhere >> .env
elspeth@server:$ sudo systemctl daemon-reload
elspeth@server:$ sudo systemctl restart gunicorn-superlists-staging.ottg.eu
elspeth@server:$ sudo journalctl -f -u gunicorn-superlists-staging.ottg.eu
```

Now if we rerun our FTs, we see a change:

```
$ STAGING_SERVER=superlists-staging.ottg.eu python manage.py test functional_tests

[...]
Traceback (most recent call last):
  File "...python-tdd-book/functional_tests/test_login.py", line 28, in
test_can_get_email_link_to_log_in
    email = mail.outbox[0]
IndexError: list index out of range

[...]

selenium.common.exceptions.NoSuchElementException: Message: Unable to locate
element: Log out
```

The my_lists failure is still the same, but we have more information in our login test: the FT gets further, and the site now looks like it's sending emails correctly (and the server log no longer shows any errors), but we can't check the email in the mail.out box...

Adapting Our FT to Be Able to Test Real Emails via POP3

Ah. That explains it. Now that we're running against a real server rather than the Live ServerTestCase, we can no longer inspect the local django.mail.outbox to see sent emails.

First, we'll need to know, in our FTs, whether we're running against the staging server or not. Let's save the staging_server variable on self in *base.py*:

functional_tests/base.py (ch18l009)

```python
def setUp(self):
    self.browser = webdriver.Firefox()
    self.staging_server = os.environ.get('STAGING_SERVER')
    if self.staging_server:
        self.live_server_url = 'http://' + self.staging_server
```

Then we build a helper function that can retrieve a real email from a real POP3 email server, using the horrifically tortuous Python standard library POP3 client:

```python
import os
import poplib
import re
import time
[...]

    def wait_for_email(self, test_email, subject):
        if not self.staging_server:
            email = mail.outbox[0]
            self.assertIn(test_email, email.to)
            self.assertEqual(email.subject, subject)
            return email.body

        email_id = None
        start = time.time()
        inbox = poplib.POP3_SSL('pop.mail.yahoo.com')
        try:
            inbox.user(test_email)
            inbox.pass_(os.environ['YAHOO_PASSWORD'])
            while time.time() - start < 60:
                # get 10 newest messages
                count, _ = inbox.stat()
                for i in reversed(range(max(1, count - 10), count + 1)):
                    print('getting msg', i)
                    _, lines, __ = inbox.retr(i)
                    lines = [l.decode('utf8') for l in lines]
                    print(lines)
                    if f'Subject: {subject}' in lines:
                        email_id = i
                        body = '\n'.join(lines)
                        return body
                time.sleep(5)
        finally:
            if email_id:
                inbox.dele(email_id)
            inbox.quit()
```

I'm using a Yahoo account for testing, but you can use any email service you like, as long as it offers POP3 access. You will need to set the YAHOO_PASSWORD environment variable in the console that's running the FT.

```
$ echo YAHOO_PASSWORD=otheremailpasswordhere >> .env
$ source .env
```

And then we feed through the rest of the changes to the FT that are required as a result. Firstly, populating a test_email variable, differently for local and staging tests:

```
@@ -7,7 +7,7 @@ from selenium.webdriver.common.keys import Keys

 from .base import FunctionalTest

-TEST_EMAIL = 'edith@example.com'
+
 SUBJECT = 'Your login link for Superlists'


@@ -33,7 +33,6 @@ class LoginTest(FunctionalTest):
                     print('getting msg', i)
                     _, lines, __ = inbox.retr(i)
                     lines = [l.decode('utf8') for l in lines]
-                    print(lines)
                     if f'Subject: {subject}' in lines:
                         email_id = i
                         body = '\n'.join(lines)
@@ -49,6 +48,11 @@ class LoginTest(FunctionalTest):
         # Edith goes to the awesome superlists site
         # and notices a "Log in" section in the navbar for the first time
         # It's telling her to enter her email address, so she does
+        if self.staging_server:
+            test_email = 'edith.testuser@yahoo.com'
+        else:
+            test_email = 'edith@example.com'
+
         self.browser.get(self.live_server_url)
```

And then modifications involving using that variable and calling our new helper function:

```
@@ -54,7 +54,7 @@ class LoginTest(FunctionalTest):
            test_email = 'edith@example.com'

            self.browser.get(self.live_server_url)
-           self.browser.find_element_by_name('email').send_keys(TEST_EMAIL)
+           self.browser.find_element_by_name('email').send_keys(test_email)
            self.browser.find_element_by_name('email').send_keys(Keys.ENTER)

            # A message appears telling her an email has been sent
@@ -64,15 +64,13 @@ class LoginTest(FunctionalTest):
            ))

            # She checks her email and finds a message
-           email = mail.outbox[0]
-           self.assertIn(TEST_EMAIL, email.to)
-           self.assertEqual(email.subject, SUBJECT)
+           body = self.wait_for_email(test_email, SUBJECT)

            # It has a url link in it
-           self.assertIn('Use this link to log in', email.body)
-           url_search = re.search(r'http://.+/.+$', email.body)
+           self.assertIn('Use this link to log in', body)
+           url_search = re.search(r'http://.+/.+$', body)
            if not url_search:
-               self.fail(f'Could not find url in email body:\n{email.body}')
+               self.fail(f'Could not find url in email body:\n{body}')
            url = url_search.group(0)
            self.assertIn(self.live_server_url, url)

@@ -80,11 +78,11 @@ class LoginTest(FunctionalTest):
            self.browser.get(url)

            # she is logged in!
-           self.wait_to_be_logged_in(email=TEST_EMAIL)
+           self.wait_to_be_logged_in(email=test_email)

            # Now she logs out
            self.browser.find_element_by_link_text('Log out').click()

            # She is logged out
-           self.wait_to_be_logged_out(email=TEST_EMAIL)
+           self.wait_to_be_logged_out(email=test_email)
```

And, believe it or not, that'll actually work, and give us an FT that can actually check for logins that work, involving real emails!

```
$ STAGING_SERVER=superlists-staging.ottg.eu python manage.py test functional_tests.test_login
[...]
OK
```

I've just hacked this email-checking code together, and it's currently pretty ugly and brittle (one common problem is picking up the wrong email from a previous test run). With some cleanup and a few more retry loops it could grow into something more reliable. Alternatively, services like *mailinator.com* will give you throwaway email addresses and an API to check them, for a small fee.

Managing the Test Database on Staging

Now we can rerun our full FT suite and get to the next failure: our attempt to create pre-authenticated sessions doesn't work, so the "My Lists" test fails:

```
$ STAGING_SERVER=superlists-staging.ottg.eu python manage.py test functional_tests

ERROR: test_logged_in_users_lists_are_saved_as_my_lists
(functional_tests.test_my_lists.MyListsTest)
[...]
selenium.common.exceptions.TimeoutException: Message: Could not find element
with id id_logout. Page text was:
Superlists
Sign in
Start a new To-Do list

Ran 8 tests in 72.742s

FAILED (errors=1)
```

It's because our test utility function `create_pre_authenticated_session` only acts on the local database. Let's find out how our tests can manage the database on the server.

A Django Management Command to Create Sessions

To do things on the server, we'll need to build a self-contained script that can be run from the command line on the server, most probably via Fabric.

When trying to build a standalone script that works with Django (i.e., can talk to the database and so on), there are some fiddly issues you need to get right, like setting the `DJANGO_SETTINGS_MODULE` environment variable, and getting `sys.path` correctly.

Instead of messing about with all that, Django lets you create your own "management commands" (commands you can run with `python manage.py`), which will do all that path mangling for you. They live in a folder called *management/commands* inside your apps:

```
$ mkdir -p functional_tests/management/commands
$ touch functional_tests/management/__init__.py
$ touch functional_tests/management/commands/__init__.py
```

The boilerplate in a management command is a class that inherits from `django.core.management.BaseCommand`, and that defines a method called `handle`:

---

functional_tests/management/commands/create_session.py

```python
from django.conf import settings
from django.contrib.auth import BACKEND_SESSION_KEY, SESSION_KEY, get_user_model
User = get_user_model()
from django.contrib.sessions.backends.db import SessionStore
from django.core.management.base import BaseCommand


class Command(BaseCommand):

    def add_arguments(self, parser):
        parser.add_argument('email')

    def handle(self, *args, **options):
        session_key = create_pre_authenticated_session(options['email'])
        self.stdout.write(session_key)


def create_pre_authenticated_session(email):
    user = User.objects.create(email=email)
    session = SessionStore()
    session[SESSION_KEY] = user.pk
    session[BACKEND_SESSION_KEY] = settings.AUTHENTICATION_BACKENDS[0]
    session.save()
    return session.session_key
```

We've taken the code for create_pre_authenticated_session from *test_my_lists.py*.
handle will pick up an email address from the parser, and then return the session key
that we'll want to add to our browser cookies, and the management command prints
it out at the command line. Try it out:

```
$ python manage.py create_session a@b.com
Unknown command: 'create_session'
```

One more step: we need to add functional_tests to our *settings.py* for it to recognise it as a real app that might have management commands as well as tests:

superlists/settings.py

```
+++ b/superlists/settings.py
@@ -42,6 +42,7 @@ INSTALLED_APPS = [
     'lists',
     'accounts',
+    'functional_tests',
 ]
```

Now it works:

```
$ python manage.py create_session a@b.com
qnslckvp2aga7tm6xuivyb0ob1akzzwl
```

If you see an error saying the auth_user table is missing, you may need to run manage.py migrate. In case that doesn't work, delete the *db.sqlite3* file and run migrate again, to get a clean slate.

Getting the FT to Run the Management Command on the Server

Next we need to adjust test_my_lists so that it runs the local function when we're on the local server, and make it run the management command on the staging server if we're on that:

functional_tests/test_my_lists.py (ch18l016)

```python
from django.conf import settings
from .base import FunctionalTest
from .server_tools import create_session_on_server
from .management.commands.create_session import create_pre_authenticated_session

class MyListsTest(FunctionalTest):

    def create_pre_authenticated_session(self, email):
        if self.staging_server:
            session_key = create_session_on_server(self.staging_server, email)
        else:
            session_key = create_pre_authenticated_session(email)
        ## to set a cookie we need to first visit the domain.
        ## 404 pages load the quickest!
        self.browser.get(self.live_server_url + "/404_no_such_url/")
        self.browser.add_cookie(dict(
            name=settings.SESSION_COOKIE_NAME,
            value=session_key,
            path='/',
        ))

    [...]
```

Let's also tweak *base.py*, to gather a bit more information when we populate self.against_staging:

```
from .server_tools import reset_database  ❶
[...]

class FunctionalTest(StaticLiveServerTestCase):

    def setUp(self):
        self.browser = webdriver.Firefox()
        self.staging_server = os.environ.get('STAGING_SERVER')
        if self.staging_server:
            self.live_server_url = 'http://' + self.staging_server
            reset_database(self.staging_server)  ❶
```

❶ This will be our function to reset the server database in between each test. We'll write that next, using Fabric.

Using Fabric Directly from Python

Rather than using the fab command, Fabric provides an API that lets you run Fabric server commands directly inline in your Python code. You just need to let it know the "host string" you're connecting to:

```
from fabric.api import run
from fabric.context_managers import settings, shell_env


def _get_manage_dot_py(host):
    return f'~/sites/{host}/virtualenv/bin/python ~/sites/{host}/manage.py'


def reset_database(host):
    manage_dot_py = _get_manage_dot_py(host)
    with settings(host_string=f'elspeth@{host}'):  ❶
        run(f'{manage_dot_py} flush --noinput')  ❷
```

❶ Here's the context manager that sets the host string, in the form *user@server-address* (I've hardcoded my server username, elspeth, so adjust as necessary).

❷ Then, once we're inside the context manager, we can just call Fabric commands as if we're in a fabfile.

For creating the session, we have a slightly more complex procedure, because we need to extract the SECRET_KEY and other env vars from the current running server, to be able to generate a session key that's cryptographically valid for the server:

```
def _get_server_env_vars(host):
    env_lines = run(f'cat ~/sites/{host}/.env').splitlines()  ❶
    return dict(l.split('=') for l in env_lines if l)


def create_session_on_server(host, email):
    manage_dot_py = _get_manage_dot_py(host)
    with settings(host_string=f'elspeth@{host}'):
        env_vars = _get_server_env_vars(host)
        with shell_env(**env_vars):  ❷
            session_key = run(f'{manage_dot_py} create_session {email}')  ❸
            return session_key.strip()
```

❶ We extract and parse the server's current environment variables from the *.env* file…

❷ In order to use them in another fabric context manager, shell_env, which sets the environment for the next command…

❸ Which is to run our create_session management command, which calls the same create_pre_authenticated_session function, but on the server.

Recap: Creating Sessions Locally Versus Staging

Does that all make sense? Perhaps a little ascii-art diagram will help:

Locally:

```
+------------------------------------+        +------------------------------------+
| MyListsTest                        |  -->   | .management.commands.create_session |
| .create_pre_authenticated_session  |        |  .create_pre_authenticated_session  |
|          (locally)                 |        |             (locally)              |
+------------------------------------+        +------------------------------------+
```

Against staging:

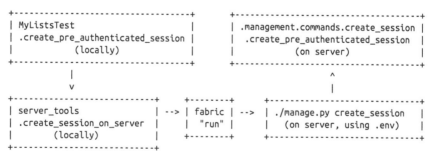

```
+------------------------------------+        +------------------------------------+
| MyListsTest                        |        | .management.commands.create_session |
| .create_pre_authenticated_session  |        |  .create_pre_authenticated_session  |
|          (locally)                 |        |            (on server)             |
+------------------------------------+        +------------------------------------+
                 |                                             ^
                 v                                             |
+---------------------------+   +--------+   +------------------------------+
| server_tools              | --> | fabric | --> | ./manage.py create_session |
| .create_session_on_server |   |  "run" |   |   (on server, using .env)   |
|          (locally)        |   +--------+   +------------------------------+
+---------------------------+
```

In any case, let's see if it works. First, locally, to check that we didn't break anything:

```
$ python manage.py test functional_tests.test_my_lists
[...]
OK
```

Next, against the server. We push our code up first:

```
$ git push  # you'll need to commit changes first.
$ cd deploy_tools
$ fab deploy --host=elspeth@superlists-staging.ottg.eu
```

And now we run the test:

```
$ STAGING_SERVER=superlists-staging.ottg.eu python manage.py test \
  functional_tests.test_my_lists
[...]
[elspeth@superlists-staging.ottg.eu] run:
~/sites/superlists-staging.ottg.eu/virtualenv/bin/python
~/sites/superlists-staging.ottg.eu/manage.py flush --noinput
[...]
[elspeth@superlists-staging.ottg.eu] run:
~/sites/superlists-staging.ottg.eu/virtualenv/bin/python
~/sites/superlists-staging.ottg.eu/manage.py create_session edith@example.com
[...]
.
-----------------------------------------------------------------
Ran 1 test in 5.701s

OK
```

Looking good! We can rerun all the tests to make sure…

```
$ STAGING_SERVER=superlists-staging.ottg.eu python manage.py test functional_tests
[...]
[elspeth@superlists-staging.ottg.eu] run:
~/sites/superlists-staging.ottg.eu/virtualenv/bin/python
[...]
Ran 8 tests in 89.494s

OK
```

Hooray!

 I've shown one way of managing the test database, but you could experiment with others—for example, if you were using MySQL or Postgres, you could open up an SSH tunnel to the server, and use port forwarding to talk to the database directly. You could then amend settings.DATABASES during FTs to talk to the tunnelled port. You'd still need some way of pulling in the staging server environment variables though.

Updating our Deploy Script

Before we finish, let's update our deployment fabfile so that it can automatically add the EMAIL_PASSWORD to the *.env* file on the server:

deploy_tools/fabfile.py (ch18l021)

```
import os
[...]


def _create_or_update_dotenv():
    append('.env', 'DJANGO_DEBUG_FALSE=y')
    append('.env', f'SITENAME={env.host}')
    current_contents = run('cat .env')
    if 'DJANGO_SECRET_KEY' not in current_contents:
        new_secret = ''.join(random.SystemRandom().choices(
            'abcdefghijklmnopqrstuvwxyz0123456789', k=50
        ))
        append('.env', f'DJANGO_SECRET_KEY={new_secret}')
    email_password = os.environ['EMAIL_PASSWORD']    ❶
    append('.env', f'EMAIL_PASSWORD={email_password}')    ❶
```

❶ We just add two lines at the end of the script which will essentially copy the local EMAIL_PASSWORD environment variable up to the server's *.env* file.

Wrap-Up

Actually getting your new code up and running on a server always tends to flush out some last-minute bugs and unexpected issues. We had to do a bit of work to get through them, but we've ended up with several useful things as a result.

We now have a lovely generic `wait` decorator which will be a nice Pythonic helper for our FTs from now on. We have test fixtures that work both locally and on the server, including the ability to test "real" email integration. And we've got some more robust logging configuration.

But before we can deploy our actual live site, we'd better actually give the users what they wanted—the next chapter describes how to give them the ability to save their lists on a "My Lists" page.

Lessons Learned Catching Bugs in Staging

Fixtures also have to work remotely

LiveServerTestCase makes it easy to interact with the test database using the Django ORM for tests running locally. Interacting with the database on the staging server is not so straightforward. One solution is Fabric and Django management commands, as I've shown, but you should explore what works for you— SSH tunnels, for example.

Be very careful when resetting data on your servers

A command that can remotely wipe the entire database on one of your servers is a dangerous weapon, and you want to be really, really sure it's never accidentally going to hit your production data.

Logging is critical to debugging issues on the server

At the very least, you'll want to be able to see any error messages that are being generated by the server. For thornier bugs, you'll also want to be able to do the occasional "debug print", and see it end up in a file somewhere.

Finishing "My Lists": Outside-In TDD

In this chapter I'd like to talk about a technique called Outside-In TDD. It's pretty much what we've been doing all along. Our "double-loop" TDD process, in which we write the functional test first and then the unit tests, is already a manifestation of outside-in—we design the system from the outside, and build up our code in layers. Now I'll make it explicit, and talk about some of the common issues involved.

The Alternative: "Inside-Out"

The alternative to "outside-in" is to work "inside-out", which is the way most people intuitively work before they encounter TDD. After coming up with a design, the natural inclination is sometimes to implement it starting with the innermost, lowest-level components first.

For example, when faced with our current problem, providing users with a "My Lists" page of saved lists, the temptation is to start by adding an "owner" attribute to the List model object, reasoning that an attribute like this is "obviously" going to be required. Once that's in place, we would modify the more peripheral layers of code, such as views and templates, taking advantage of the new attribute, and then finally add URL routing to point to the new view.

It feels comfortable because it means you're never working on a bit of code that is dependent on something that hasn't yet been implemented. Each bit of work on the inside is a solid foundation on which to build the next layer out.

But working inside-out like this also has some weaknesses.

Why Prefer "Outside-In"?

The most obvious problem with inside-out is that it requires us to stray from a TDD workflow. Our functional test's first failure might be due to missing URL routing, but we decide to ignore that and go off adding attributes to our database model objects instead.

We might have ideas in our head about the new desired behaviour of our inner layers like database models, and often these ideas will be pretty good, but they are actually just speculation about what's really required, because we haven't yet built the outer layers that will use them.

One problem that can result is to build inner components that are more general or more capable than we actually need, which is a waste of time, and an added source of complexity for your project. Another common problem is that you create inner components with an API which is convenient for their own internal design, but which later turns out to be inappropriate for the calls your outer layers would like to make… worse still, you might end up with inner components which, you later realise, don't actually solve the problem that your outer layers need solved.

In contrast, working outside-in allows you to use each layer to imagine the most convenient API you could want from the layer beneath it. Let's see it in action.

The FT for "My Lists"

As we work through the following functional test, we start with the most outward-facing (presentation layer), through to the view functions (or "controllers"), and lastly the innermost layers, which in this case will be model code.

We know our `create_pre_authenticated_session` code works now, so we can just write our FT to look for a "My Lists" page:

```python
def test_logged_in_users_lists_are_saved_as_my_lists(self):
    # Edith is a logged-in user
    self.create_pre_authenticated_session('edith@example.com')

    # She goes to the home page and starts a list
    self.browser.get(self.live_server_url)
    self.add_list_item('Reticulate splines')
    self.add_list_item('Immanentize eschaton')
    first_list_url = self.browser.current_url

    # She notices a "My lists" link, for the first time.
    self.browser.find_element_by_link_text('My lists').click()

    # She sees that her list is in there, named according to its
    # first list item
    self.wait_for(
        lambda: self.browser.find_element_by_link_text('Reticulate splines')
    )
    self.browser.find_element_by_link_text('Reticulate splines').click()
    self.wait_for(
        lambda: self.assertEqual(self.browser.current_url, first_list_url)
    )
```

We create a list with a couple of items, and then we check that this list appears on a new "My Lists" page, and that it's "named" after the first item in the list.

Let's validate that it really works by creating a second list, and seeing that appear on the My Lists page as well. The FT continues, and while we're at it, we check that only logged-in users can see the "My Lists" page:

```
[...]
self.wait_for(
    lambda: self.assertEqual(self.browser.current_url, first_list_url)
)

# She decides to start another list, just to see
self.browser.get(self.live_server_url)
self.add_list_item('Click cows')
second_list_url = self.browser.current_url

# Under "my lists", her new list appears
self.browser.find_element_by_link_text('My lists').click()
self.wait_for(
    lambda: self.browser.find_element_by_link_text('Click cows')
)
self.browser.find_element_by_link_text('Click cows').click()
self.wait_for(
    lambda: self.assertEqual(self.browser.current_url, second_list_url)
)

# She logs out.  The "My lists" option disappears
self.browser.find_element_by_link_text('Log out').click()
self.wait_for(lambda: self.assertEqual(
    self.browser.find_elements_by_link_text('My lists'),
    []
))
```

Our FT uses a new helper method, `add_list_item`, which abstracts away entering text into the right input box. We define it in *base.py*:

```
from selenium.webdriver.common.keys import Keys
[...]

    def add_list_item(self, item_text):
        num_rows = len(self.browser.find_elements_by_css_selector('#id_list_table tr'))
        self.get_item_input_box().send_keys(item_text)
        self.get_item_input_box().send_keys(Keys.ENTER)
        item_number = num_rows + 1
        self.wait_for_row_in_list_table(f'{item_number}: {item_text}')
```

And while we're at it we can use it in a few of the other FTs, like this:

```
        self.add_list_item('Buy wellies')
```

I think it makes the FTs a lot more readable. I made a total of six changes—see if you agree with me.

A quick run of all FTs, a commit, and then back to the FT we're working on. The first error should look like this:

```
$ python3 manage.py test functional_tests.test_my_lists
[...]
selenium.common.exceptions.NoSuchElementException: Message: Unable to locate
element: My lists
```

The Outside Layer: Presentation and Templates

The test is currently failing saying that it can't find a link saying "My Lists". We can address that at the presentation layer, in *base.html*, in our navigation bar. Here's the minimal code change:

lists/templates/base.html (ch19l002-1)

```
{% if user.email %}
  <ul class="nav navbar-nav navbar-left">
    <li><a href="#">My lists</a></li>
  </ul>
  <ul class="nav navbar-nav navbar-right">
    <li class="navbar-text">Logged in as {{ user.email }}</li>
    <li><a href="{% url 'logout' %}">Log out</a></li>
  </ul>
```

Of course, that link doesn't actually go anywhere, but it does get us along to the next failure:

```
$ python3 manage.py test functional_tests.test_my_lists
[...]
    lambda: self.browser.find_element_by_link_text('Reticulate splines')
[...]
selenium.common.exceptions.NoSuchElementException: Message: Unable to locate
element: Reticulate splines
```

Which is telling us we're going to have to build a page that lists all of a user's lists by title. Let's start with the basics—a URL and a placeholder template for it.

Again, we can go outside-in, starting at the presentation layer with just the URL and nothing else:

lists/templates/base.html (ch19l002-2)

```
<ul class="nav navbar-nav navbar-left">
  <li><a href="{% url 'my_lists' user.email %}">My lists</a></li>
</ul>
```

Moving Down One Layer to View Functions (the Controller)

That will cause a template error, so we'll start to move down from the presentation layer and URLs down to the controller layer, Django's view functions.

As always, we start with a test:

lists/tests/test_views.py (ch19l003)

```python
class MyListsTest(TestCase):

    def test_my_lists_url_renders_my_lists_template(self):
        response = self.client.get('/lists/users/a@b.com/')
        self.assertTemplateUsed(response, 'my_lists.html')
```

That gives:

```
AssertionError: No templates used to render the response
```

And we fix it, still at the presentation level, in *urls.py*:

lists/urls.py

```python
urlpatterns = [
    url(r'^new$', views.new_list, name='new_list'),
    url(r'^(\d+)/$', views.view_list, name='view_list'),
    url(r'^users/(.+)/$', views.my_lists, name='my_lists'),
]
```

That gives us a test failure, which informs us of what we should do as we move down to the next level:

```
AttributeError: module 'lists.views' has no attribute 'my_lists'
```

We move in from the presentation layer to the views layer, and create a minimal placeholder:

lists/views.py (ch19l005)

```python
def my_lists(request, email):
    return render(request, 'my_lists.html')
```

And a minimal template:

lists/templates/my_lists.html

```
{% extends 'base.html' %}

{% block header_text %}My Lists{% endblock %}
```

That gets our unit tests passing, but our FT is still at the same point, saying that the "My Lists" page doesn't yet show any lists. It wants them to be clickable links named after the first item:

```
$ python3 manage.py test functional_tests.test_my_lists
[...]
selenium.common.exceptions.NoSuchElementException: Message: Unable to locate
element: Reticulate splines
```

Another Pass, Outside-In

At each stage, we still let the FT drive what development we do.

Starting again at the outside layer, in the template, we begin to write the template code we'd like to use to get the "My Lists" page to work the way we want it to. As we do so, we start to specify the API we want from the code at the layers below.

A Quick Restructure of the Template Inheritance Hierarchy

Currently there's no place in our base template for us to put any new content. Also, the "My Lists" page doesn't need the new item form, so we'll put that into a block too, making it optional:

lists/templates/base.html (ch19l007-1)

```html
<div class="row">
  <div class="col-md-6 col-md-offset-3 jumbotron">
    <div class="text-center">
      <h1>{% block header_text %}{% endblock %}</h1>
      {% block list_form %}
        <form method="POST" action="{% block form_action %}{% endblock %}">
          {{ form.text }}
          {% csrf_token %}
          {% if form.errors %}
            <div class="form-group has-error">
              <div class="help-block">{{ form.text.errors }}</div>
            </div>
          {% endif %}
        </form>
      {% endblock %}
    </div>
  </div>
</div>
```

```
  <div class="row">
    <div class="col-md-6 col-md-offset-3">
      {% block table %}
      {% endblock %}
    </div>
  </div>

  <div class="row">
    <div class="col-md-6 col-md-offset-3">
      {% block extra_content %}
      {% endblock %}
    </div>
  </div>

</div>
<script src="/static/jquery-3.1.1.min.js"></script>
[...]
```

Designing Our API Using the Template

Meanwhile, in *my_lists.html* we override the list_form and say it should be empty…

```
{% extends 'base.html' %}

{% block header_text %}My Lists{% endblock %}

{% block list_form %}{% endblock %}
```

And then we can just work inside the extra_content block:

```
[...]

{% block list_form %}{% endblock %}

{% block extra_content %}
  <h2>{{ owner.email }}'s lists</h2>       ❶
  <ul>
    {% for list in owner.list_set.all %}     ❷
      <li><a href="{{ list.get_absolute_url }}">{{ list.name }}</a></li>     ❸
    {% endfor %}
  </ul>
{% endblock %}
```

We've made several design decisions in this template which are going to filter their way down through the code:

---

❶ We want a variable called `owner` to represent the user in our template.

❷ We want to be able to iterate through the lists created by the user using `owner.list_set.all` (I happen to know we get this for free from the Django ORM).

❸ We want to use `list.name` to print out the "name" of the list, which is currently specified as the text of its first element.

 Outside-In TDD is sometimes called "programming by wishful thinking", and you can see why. We start writing code at the higher levels based on what we wish we had at the lower levels, even though it doesn't exist yet!

We can rerun our FTs, to check that we didn't break anything, and to see whether we've got any further:

```
$ python manage.py test functional_tests
[...]
selenium.common.exceptions.NoSuchElementException: Message: Unable to locate
element: Reticulate splines


 ------------------------------------------------------------------
Ran 8 tests in 77.613s

FAILED (errors=1)
```

Well, no further, but at least we didn't break anything. Time for a commit:

```
$ git add lists
$ git diff --staged
$ git commit -m "url, placeholder view, and first-cut templates for my_lists"
```

Moving Down to the Next Layer: What the View Passes to the Template

Now our views layer needs to respond to the requirements we've laid out in the template layer, by giving it the objects it needs. In this case, the list owner:

```
from django.contrib.auth import get_user_model
User = get_user_model()
[...]
class MyListsTest(TestCase):

    def test_my_lists_url_renders_my_lists_template(self):
        [...]

    def test_passes_correct_owner_to_template(self):
        User.objects.create(email='wrong@owner.com')
        correct_user = User.objects.create(email='a@b.com')
        response = self.client.get('/lists/users/a@b.com/')
        self.assertEqual(response.context['owner'], correct_user)
```

Gives:

```
KeyError: 'owner'
```

So:

```
from django.contrib.auth import get_user_model
User = get_user_model()
[...]

def my_lists(request, email):
    owner = User.objects.get(email=email)
    return render(request, 'my_lists.html', {'owner': owner})
```

That gets our new test passing, but we'll also see an error from the previous test. We just need to add a user for it as well:

```
    def test_my_lists_url_renders_my_lists_template(self):
        User.objects.create(email='a@b.com')
        [...]
```

And we get to an OK:

```
OK
```

The Next "Requirement" from the Views Layer: New Lists Should Record Owner

Before we move down to the model layer, there's another part of the code at the views layer that will need to use our model: we need some way for newly created lists to be assigned to an owner, if the current user is logged in to the site.

Here's a first crack at writing the test:

lists/tests/test_views.py (ch19l014)

```python
class NewListTest(TestCase):
    [...]

    def test_list_owner_is_saved_if_user_is_authenticated(self):
        user = User.objects.create(email='a@b.com')
        self.client.force_login(user)  ❶
        self.client.post('/lists/new', data={'text': 'new item'})
        list_ = List.objects.first()
        self.assertEqual(list_.owner, user)
```

❶ force_login() is the way you get the test client to make requests with a logged-in user.

The test fails as follows:

```
AttributeError: 'List' object has no attribute 'owner'
```

To fix this, we can try writing code like this:

lists/views.py (ch19l015)

```python
def new_list(request):
    form = ItemForm(data=request.POST)
    if form.is_valid():
        list_ = List()
        list_.owner = request.user
        list_.save()
        form.save(for_list=list_)
        return redirect(list_)
    else:
        return render(request, 'home.html', {"form": form})
```

But it won't actually work, because we don't know how to save a list owner yet:

```
        self.assertEqual(list_.owner, user)
AttributeError: 'List' object has no attribute 'owner'
```

A Decision Point: Whether to Proceed to the Next Layer with a Failing Test

In order to get this test passing, as it's written now, we have to move down to the model layer. However, it means doing more work with a failing test, which is not ideal.

The alternative is to rewrite the test to make it more *isolated* from the level below, using mocks.

On the one hand, it's a lot more effort to use mocks, and it can lead to tests that are harder to read. On the other hand, imagine if our app was more complex, and there were several more layers between the outside and the inside. Imagine leaving three or four or five layers of tests, all failing while we wait to get to the bottom layer to implement our critical feature. While tests are failing, we're not sure that layer really works, on its own terms, or not. We have to wait until we get to the bottom layer.

This is a decision point you're likely to run into in your own projects. Let's investigate both approaches. We'll start by taking the shortcut, and leaving the test failing. In the next chapter, we'll come back to this exact point, and investigate how things would have gone if we'd used more isolation.

Let's do a commit, and then *tag* the commit as a way of remembering our position for the next chapter:

```
$ git commit -am "new_list view tries to assign owner but cant"
$ git tag revisit_this_point_with_isolated_tests
```

Moving Down to the Model Layer

Our outside-in design has driven out two requirements for the model layer: we want to be able to assign an owner to a list using the attribute .owner, and we want to be able to access the list's owner with the API owner.list_set.all.

Let's write a test for that:

lists/tests/test_models.py (ch19l018)

```
from django.contrib.auth import get_user_model
User = get_user_model()
[...]

class ListModelTest(TestCase):

    def test_get_absolute_url(self):
        [...]

    def test_lists_can_have_owners(self):
        user = User.objects.create(email='a@b.com')
        list_ = List.objects.create(owner=user)
        self.assertIn(list_, user.list_set.all())
```

And that gives us a new unit test failure:

```
    list_ = List.objects.create(owner=user)
    [...]
TypeError: 'owner' is an invalid keyword argument for this function
```

The naive implementation would be this:

```
from django.conf import settings
[...]

class List(models.Model):
    owner = models.ForeignKey(settings.AUTH_USER_MODEL)
```

But we want to make sure the list owner is optional. Explicit is better than implicit, and tests are documentation, so let's have a test for that too:

lists/tests/test_models.py (ch19l020)

```
def test_list_owner_is_optional(self):
    List.objects.create()  # should not raise
```

The correct implementation is this:

lists/models.py

```
from django.conf import settings
[...]

class List(models.Model):
    owner = models.ForeignKey(settings.AUTH_USER_MODEL, blank=True, null=True)

    def get_absolute_url(self):
        return reverse('view_list', args=[self.id])
```

Now running the tests gives the usual database error:

```
    return Database.Cursor.execute(self, query, params)
django.db.utils.OperationalError: no such column: lists_list.owner_id
```

Because we need to make some migrations:

```
$ python manage.py makemigrations
Migrations for 'lists':
  lists/migrations/0006_list_owner.py
    - Add field owner to list
```

We're almost there; a couple more failures:

```
ERROR: test_redirects_after_POST (lists.tests.test_views.NewListTest)
[...]
ValueError: Cannot assign "<SimpleLazyObject:
<django.contrib.auth.models.AnonymousUser object at 0x7f364795ef90>>":
"List.owner" must be a "User" instance.
ERROR: test_can_save_a_POST_request (lists.tests.test_views.NewListTest)

[...]
ValueError: Cannot assign "<SimpleLazyObject:
<django.contrib.auth.models.AnonymousUser object at 0x7f364795ef90>>":
"List.owner" must be a "User" instance.
```

We're moving back up to the views layer now, just doing a little tidying up. Notice that these are in the old test for the `new_list` view, when we haven't got a logged-in user. We should only save the list owner when the user is actually logged in. The `.is_authenticated` attribute we defined in Chapter 19 comes in useful now (when they're not logged in, Django represents users using a class called AnonymousUser, whose `.is_authenticated` is always `False`):

lists/views.py (ch19l023)

```python
if form.is_valid():
    list_ = List()
    if request.user.is_authenticated:
        list_.owner = request.user
    list_.save()
    form.save(for_list=list_)
    [...]
```

And that gets us passing!

```
$ python manage.py test lists
[...]
.......................................
---------------------------------------------------------------------
Ran 39 tests in 0.237s

OK
```

This is a good time for a commit:

```
$ git add lists
$ git commit -m "lists can have owners, which are saved on creation."
```

Final Step: Feeding Through the .name API from the Template

The last thing our outside-in design wanted came from the templates, which wanted to be able to access a list "name" based on the text of its first item:

lists/tests/test_models.py (ch19l024)

```python
def test_list_name_is_first_item_text(self):
    list_ = List.objects.create()
    Item.objects.create(list=list_, text='first item')
    Item.objects.create(list=list_, text='second item')
    self.assertEqual(list_.name, 'first item')
```

lists/models.py (ch19l025)

```python
@property
def name(self):
    return self.item_set.first().text
```

And that, believe it or not, actually gets us a passing test, and a working "My Lists" page (Figure 22-1)!

```
$ python manage.py test functional_tests
[...]
Ran 8 tests in 93.819s

OK
```

The @property Decorator in Python

If you haven't seen it before, the @property decorator transforms a method on a class to make it appear to the outside world like an attribute.

This is a powerful feature of the language, because it makes it easy to implement "duck typing", to change the implementation of a property without changing the interface of the class. In other words, if we decide to change .name into being a "real" attribute on the model, which is stored as text in the database, then we will be able to do so entirely transparently—as far as the rest of our code is concerned, they will still be able to just access .name and get the list name, without needing to know about the implementation. Raymond Hettinger gave a great, beginner-friendly talk on this topic at Pycon a few years ago (*https://www.youtube.com/watch?v=HTLu2DFOdTg*), which I enthusiastically recommend (it covers about a million good practices for Pythonic class design besides).

Of course, in the Django template language, .name would still call the method even if it didn't have @property, but that's a particularity of Django, and doesn't apply to Python in general...

But we know we cheated to get there. The Testing Goat is eyeing us suspiciously. We left a test failing at one layer while we implemented its dependencies at the lower layer. Let's see how things would play out if we were to use better test isolation...

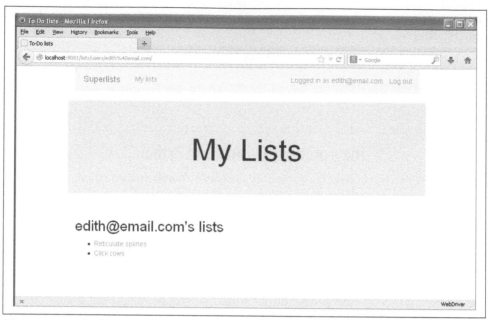

Figure 22-1. The "My Lists" page, in all its glory (and proof I did test on Windows)

Outside-In TDD

Outside-In TDD

> A methodology for building code, driven by tests, which proceeds by starting from the "outside" layers (presentation, GUI), and moving "inwards" step by step, via view/controller layers, down towards the model layer. The idea is to drive the design of your code from the use to which it is going to be put, rather than trying to anticipate requirements from the ground up.

Programming by wishful thinking

> The outside-in process is sometimes called "programming by wishful thinking". Actually, any kind of TDD involves some wishful thinking. We're always writing tests for things that don't exist yet.

The pitfalls of outside-in

> Outside-in isn't a silver bullet. It encourages us to focus on things that are immediately visible to the user, but it won't automatically remind us to write other critical tests that are less user-visible—things like security, for example. You'll need to remember them yourself.

Test Isolation, and "Listening to Your Tests"

In the preceding chapter, we made the decision to leave a unit test failing in the views layer while we proceeded to write more tests and more code at the models layer to get it to pass.

We got away with it because our app was simple, but I should stress that, in a more complex application, this would be a dangerous decision. Proceeding to work on lower levels while you're not sure that the higher levels are *really* finished or not is a risky strategy.

 I'm grateful to Gary Bernhardt, who took a look at an early draft of the previous chapter, and encouraged me to get into a longer discussion of test isolation.

Ensuring isolation between layers does involve more effort (and more of the dreaded mocks!), but it can also help to drive out improved design, as we'll see in this chapter.

Revisiting Our Decision Point: The Views Layer Depends on Unwritten Models Code

Let's revisit the point we were at halfway through the last chapter, when we couldn't get the new_list view to work because lists didn't have the .owner attribute yet.

We'll actually go back in time and check out the old codebase using the tag we saved earlier, so that we can see how things would have worked if we'd used more isolated tests:

```
$ git checkout -b more-isolation  # a branch for this experiment
$ git reset --hard revisit_this_point_with_isolated_tests
```

Here's what our failing test looks like:

lists/tests/test_views.py

```python
class NewListTest(TestCase):
    [...]

    def test_list_owner_is_saved_if_user_is_authenticated(self):
        user = User.objects.create(email='a@b.com')
        self.client.force_login(user)
        self.client.post('/lists/new', data={'text': 'new item'})
        list_ = List.objects.first()
        self.assertEqual(list_.owner, user)
```

And here's what our attempted solution looked like:

lists/views.py

```python
def new_list(request):
    form = ItemForm(data=request.POST)
    if form.is_valid():
        list_ = List()
        list_.owner = request.user
        list_.save()
        form.save(for_list=list_)
        return redirect(list_)
    else:
        return render(request, 'home.html', {"form": form})
```

And at this point, the view test is failing because we don't have the model layer yet:

```
    self.assertEqual(list_.owner, user)
AttributeError: 'List' object has no attribute 'owner'
```

 You won't see this error unless you actually check out the old code and revert *lists/models.py*. You should definitely do this; part of the objective of this chapter is to see whether we really can write tests for a models layer that doesn't exist yet.

A First Attempt at Using Mocks for Isolation

Lists don't have owners yet, but we can let the views layer tests pretend they do by using a bit of mocking:

```
from unittest.mock import patch
[...]

    @patch('lists.views.List')        ❶
    @patch('lists.views.ItemForm')    ❷
    def test_list_owner_is_saved_if_user_is_authenticated(
        self, mockItemFormClass, mockListClass    ❸
    ):
        user = User.objects.create(email='a@b.com')
        self.client.force_login(user)

        self.client.post('/lists/new', data={'text': 'new item'})

        mock_list = mockListClass.return_value    ❹
        self.assertEqual(mock_list.owner, user)   ❺
```

❶ We mock out the List class to be able to get access to any lists that might be created by the view.

❷ We also mock out the ItemForm. Otherwise, our form will raise an error when we call form.save(), because it can't use a mock object as the foreign key for the Item it wants to create. Once you start mocking, it can be hard to stop!

❸ The mock objects are injected into the test's arguments in the opposite order to which they're declared. Tests with lots of mocks often have this strange signature, with the dangling):. You get used to it!

❹ The list instance that the view will have access to will be the return value of the mocked List class.

❺ And we can make assertions about whether the .owner attribute is set on it.

If we try to run this test now, it should pass:

```
$ python manage.py test lists
[...]
Ran 37 tests in 0.145s
OK
```

If you don't see a pass, make sure that your views code in *views.py* is exactly as I've shown it, using List(), not List.objects.create.

Using mocks does tie you to specific ways of using an API. This is one of the many trade-offs involved in the use of mock objects.

Using Mock side_effects to Check the Sequence of Events

The trouble with this test is that it can still let us get away with writing the wrong code by mistake. Imagine if we accidentally call save before we we assign the owner:

lists/views.py

```
if form.is_valid():
    list_ = List()
    list_.save()
    list_.owner = request.user
    form.save(for_list=list_)
    return redirect(list_)
```

The test, as it's written now, still passes:

```
OK
```

So strictly speaking, we need to check not just that the owner is assigned, but that it's assigned *before* we call save on our list object.

Here's how we could test the sequence of events using mocks—you can mock out a function, and use it as a spy to check on the state of the world at the moment it's called:

lists/tests/test_views.py (ch20l005)

```
@patch('lists.views.List')
@patch('lists.views.ItemForm')
def test_list_owner_is_saved_if_user_is_authenticated(
    self, mockItemFormClass, mockListClass
):
    user = User.objects.create(email='a@b.com')
    self.client.force_login(user)
    mock_list = mockListClass.return_value

    def check_owner_assigned():          ❶
        self.assertEqual(mock_list.owner, user)
    mock_list.save.side_effect = check_owner_assigned    ❷

    self.client.post('/lists/new', data={'text': 'new item'})

    mock_list.save.assert_called_once_with()    ❸
```

❶ We define a function that makes the assertion about the thing we want to happen first: checking that the list's owner has been set.

❷ We assign that check function as a side_effect to the thing we want to check happened second. When the view calls our mocked save function, it will go through this assertion. We make sure to set this up before we actually call the function we're testing.

❸ Finally, we make sure that the function with the `side_effect` was actually triggered—that is, that we did `.save()`. Otherwise, our assertion may actually never have been run.

 Two common mistakes when you're using mock side effects are assigning the side effect too late (i.e., *after* you call the function under test), and forgetting to check that the side-effect function was actually called. And by common, I mean, "I made both these mistakes several times *while writing this chapter*."

At this point, if you've still got the "broken" code from earlier, where we assign the owner but call `save` in the wrong order, you should now see a fail:

```
FAIL: test_list_owner_is_saved_if_user_is_authenticated
(lists.tests.test_views.NewListTest)
[...]
  File "...python-tdd-book/lists/views.py", line 17, in new_list
    list_.save()
[...]
  File "...python-tdd-book/lists/tests/test_views.py", line 74, in
check_owner_assigned
    self.assertEqual(mock_list.owner, user)
AssertionError: <MagicMock name='List().owner' id='140691452447208'> != <User:
User object>
```

Notice how the failure happens when we try to save, and then go inside our `side_effect` function.

We can get it passing again like this:

lists/views.py

```python
if form.is_valid():
    list_ = List()
    list_.owner = request.user
    list_.save()
    form.save(for_list=list_)
    return redirect(list_)
```

```
...

OK
```

But, boy, that's getting to be an ugly test!

Listen to Your Tests: Ugly Tests Signal a Need to Refactor

Whenever you find yourself having to write a test like this, and you're finding it hard work, it's likely that your tests are trying to tell you something. Eight lines of setup (two lines for mocks, three to set up a user, and three more for our side-effect function) is way too many.

What this test is trying to tell us is that our view is doing too much work, dealing with creating a form, creating a new list object, *and* deciding whether or not to save an owner for the list.

We've already seen that we can make our views simpler and easier to understand by pushing some of the work down to a form class. Why does the view need to create the list object? Perhaps our `ItemForm.save` could do that? And why does the view need to make decisions about whether or not to save the `request.user`? Again, the form could do that.

While we're giving this form more responsibilities, it feels like it should probably get a new name too. We could call it `NewListForm` instead, since that's a better representation of what it does…something like this?

lists/views.py

```python
# don't enter this code yet, we're only imagining it.

def new_list(request):
    form = NewListForm(data=request.POST)
    if form.is_valid():
        list_ = form.save(owner=request.user)  # creates both List and Item
        return redirect(list_)
    else:
        return render(request, 'home.html', {"form": form})
```

That would be neater! Let's see how we'd get to that state by using fully isolated tests.

Rewriting Our Tests for the View to Be Fully Isolated

Our first attempt at a test suite for this view was highly *integrated*. It needed the database layer and the forms layer to be fully functional in order for it to pass. We've started trying to make it more isolated, so let's now go all the way.

Keep the Old Integrated Test Suite Around as a Sanity Check

Let's rename our old `NewListTest` class to `NewListViewIntegratedTest`, and throw away our attempt at a mocky test for saving the owner, putting back the integrated version, with a skip on it for now:

```
import unittest
[...]

class NewListViewIntegratedTest(TestCase):

    def test_can_save_a_POST_request(self):
        [...]

    @unittest.skip
    def test_list_owner_is_saved_if_user_is_authenticated(self):
        user = User.objects.create(email='a@b.com')
        self.client.force_login(user)
        self.client.post('/lists/new', data={'text': 'new item'})
        list_ = List.objects.first()
        self.assertEqual(list_.owner, user)
```

 Have you heard the term "integration test" and are wondering what the difference is from an "integrated test"? Go and take a peek at the definitions box in Chapter 26.

```
$ python manage.py test lists
[...]
Ran 37 tests in 0.139s
OK
```

A New Test Suite with Full Isolation

Let's start with a blank slate, and see if we can use isolated tests to drive a replacement of our new_list view. We'll call it new_list2, build it alongside the old view, and when we're ready, swap it in and see if the old integrated tests all still pass:

```
def new_list(request):
    [...]

def new_list2(request):
    pass
```

Thinking in Terms of Collaborators

In order to rewrite our tests to be fully isolated, we need to throw out our old way of thinking about the tests in terms of the "real" effects of the view on things like the database, and instead think of it in terms of the objects it collaborates with, and how it interacts with them.

In the new world, the view's main collaborator will be a form object, so we mock that out in order to be able to fully control it, and in order to be able to define, by wishful thinking, the way we want our form to work:

lists/tests/test_views.py (ch20l010)

```python
from unittest.mock import patch
from django.http import HttpRequest
from lists.views import new_list2
[...]

@patch('lists.views.NewListForm')  ❷
class NewListViewUnitTest(unittest.TestCase):  ❶

    def setUp(self):
        self.request = HttpRequest()
        self.request.POST['text'] = 'new list item'  ❸

    def test_passes_POST_data_to_NewListForm(self, mockNewListForm):
        new_list2(self.request)
        mockNewListForm.assert_called_once_with(data=self.request.POST)  ❹
```

❶   The Django `TestCase` class makes it too easy to write integrated tests. As a way of making sure we're writing "pure", isolated unit tests, we'll only use `unittest.TestCase`.

❷   We mock out the `NewListForm` class (which doesn't even exist yet). It's going to be used in all the tests, so we mock it out at the class level.

❸   We set up a basic POST request in `setUp`, building up the request by hand rather than using the (overly integrated) Django Test Client.

❹   And we check the first thing about our new view: it initialises its collaborator, the `NewListForm`, with the correct constructor—the data from the request.

That will start with a failure, saying we don't have a `NewListForm` in our view yet:

```
AttributeError: <module 'lists.views' from '...python-tdd-book/lists/views.py'>
does not have the attribute 'NewListForm'
```

Let's create a placeholder for it:

lists/views.py (ch20l011)

```python
from lists.forms import ExistingListItemForm, ItemForm, NewListForm
[...]
```

and:

```
class ItemForm(forms.models.ModelForm):
    [...]

class NewListForm(object):
    pass

class ExistingListItemForm(ItemForm):
    [...]
```

Next we get a real failure:

```
AssertionError: Expected 'NewListForm' to be called once. Called 0 times.
```

And we implement like this:

```
def new_list2(request):
    NewListForm(data=request.POST)
```

```
$ python manage.py test lists
[...]
Ran 38 tests in 0.143s
OK
```

Let's continue. If the form is valid, we want to call **save** on it:

```
from unittest.mock import patch, Mock
[...]

@patch('lists.views.NewListForm')
class NewListViewUnitTest(unittest.TestCase):

    def setUp(self):
        self.request = HttpRequest()
        self.request.POST['text'] = 'new list item'
        self.request.user = Mock()


    def test_passes_POST_data_to_NewListForm(self, mockNewListForm):
        new_list2(self.request)
        mockNewListForm.assert_called_once_with(data=self.request.POST)


    def test_saves_form_with_owner_if_form_valid(self, mockNewListForm):
        mock_form = mockNewListForm.return_value
        mock_form.is_valid.return_value = True
        new_list2(self.request)
        mock_form.save.assert_called_once_with(owner=self.request.user)
```

That takes us to this:

lists/views.py (ch20l014)

```python
def new_list2(request):
    form = NewListForm(data=request.POST)
    form.save(owner=request.user)
```

In the case where the form is valid, we want the view to return a redirect, to send us to see the object that the form has just created. So we mock out another of the view's collaborators, the redirect function:

lists/tests/test_views.py (ch20l015)

```python
@patch('lists.views.redirect')    ❶
def test_redirects_to_form_returned_object_if_form_valid(
    self, mock_redirect, mockNewListForm    ❷
):
    mock_form = mockNewListForm.return_value
    mock_form.is_valid.return_value = True    ❸

    response = new_list2(self.request)

    self.assertEqual(response, mock_redirect.return_value)    ❹
    mock_redirect.assert_called_once_with(mock_form.save.return_value)    ❺
```

❶ We mock out the redirect function, this time at the method level.

❷ patch decorators are applied innermost first, so the new mock is injected to our method as before the mockNewListForm.

❸ We specify that we're testing the case where the form is valid.

❹ We check that the response from the view is the result of the redirect function.

❺ And we check that the redirect function was called with the object that the form returns on save.

That takes us to here:

lists/views.py (ch20l016)

```python
def new_list2(request):
    form = NewListForm(data=request.POST)
    list_ = form.save(owner=request.user)
    return redirect(list_)
```

```
$ python manage.py test lists
[...]
Ran 40 tests in 0.163s
OK
```

And now the failure case—if the form is invalid, we want to render the home page template:

lists/tests/test_views.py (ch20l017)

```python
@patch('lists.views.render')
def test_renders_home_template_with_form_if_form_invalid(
    self, mock_render, mockNewListForm
):
    mock_form = mockNewListForm.return_value
    mock_form.is_valid.return_value = False

    response = new_list2(self.request)

    self.assertEqual(response, mock_render.return_value)
    mock_render.assert_called_once_with(
        self.request, 'home.html', {'form': mock_form}
    )
```

That gives us:

```
AssertionError: <HttpResponseRedirect status_code=302, "te[114 chars]%3E"> !=
<MagicMock name='render()' id='140244627467408'>
```

 When using assert methods on mocks, like assert_called_once_with, it's doubly important to make sure you run the test and see it fail. It's all too easy to make a typo in your assert function name and end up calling a mock method that does nothing (mine was to write asssert_called_once_with with three esssses; try it!).

We make a deliberate mistake, just to make sure our tests are comprehensive:

lists/views.py (ch20l018)

```python
def new_list2(request):
    form = NewListForm(data=request.POST)
    list_ = form.save(owner=request.user)
    if form.is_valid():
        return redirect(list_)
    return render(request, 'home.html', {'form': form})
```

That passes, but it shouldn't! One more test then:

```
def test_does_not_save_if_form_invalid(self, mockNewListForm):
    mock_form = mockNewListForm.return_value
    mock_form.is_valid.return_value = False
    new_list2(self.request)
    self.assertFalse(mock_form.save.called)
```

Which fails:

```
    self.assertFalse(mock_form.save.called)
AssertionError: True is not false
```

And we get to to our neat, small finished view:

```
def new_list2(request):
    form = NewListForm(data=request.POST)
    if form.is_valid():
        list_ = form.save(owner=request.user)
        return redirect(list_)
    return render(request, 'home.html', {'form': form})
```

...

```
$ python manage.py test lists
[...]
Ran 42 tests in 0.163s
OK
```

Moving Down to the Forms Layer

So we've built up our view function based on a "wishful thinking" version of a form called NewListForm, which doesn't even exist yet.

We'll need the form's save method to create a new list, and a new item based on the text from the form's validated POST data. If we were to just dive in and use the ORM, the code might look something a bit like this:

```
class NewListForm(models.Form):

    def save(self, owner):
        list_ = List()
        if owner:
            list_.owner = owner
        list_.save()
        item = Item()
        item.list = list_
        item.text = self.cleaned_data['text']
        item.save()
```

This implementation depends on two classes from the model layer, `Item` and `List`. So, what would a well-isolated test look like?

```python
class NewListFormTest(unittest.TestCase):

    @patch('lists.forms.List')  ❶
    @patch('lists.forms.Item')  ❶
    def test_save_creates_new_list_and_item_from_post_data(
        self, mockItem, mockList  ❶
    ):
        mock_item = mockItem.return_value
        mock_list = mockList.return_value
        user = Mock()
        form = NewListForm(data={'text': 'new item text'})
        form.is_valid()  ❷

        def check_item_text_and_list():
            self.assertEqual(mock_item.text, 'new item text')
            self.assertEqual(mock_item.list, mock_list)
            self.assertTrue(mock_list.save.called)
        mock_item.save.side_effect = check_item_text_and_list  ❸

        form.save(owner=user)

        self.assertTrue(mock_item.save.called)  ❹
```

❶ We mock out the two collaborators for our form from the models layer below.

❷ We need to call `is_valid()` so that the form populates the `.cleaned_data` dictionary where it stores validated data.

❸ We use the `side_effect` method to make sure that, when we save the new item object, we're doing so with a saved `List` and with the correct item text.

❹ As always, we double-check that our side-effect function was actually called.

Yuck! What an ugly test! Let's not even bother saving that to disk, we can do better.

Keep Listening to Your Tests: Removing ORM Code from Our Application

Again, these tests are trying to tell us something: the Django ORM is hard to mock out, and our form class needs to know too much about how it works. Programming by wishful thinking again, what would be a simpler API that our form could use? How about something like this:

```python
def save(self):
    List.create_new(first_item_text=self.cleaned_data['text'])
```

Our wishful thinking says: how about a helper method that would live on the `List` class[1] and encapsulate all the logic of saving a new list object and its associated first item?

So let's write a test for that instead:

lists/tests/test_forms.py (ch20l021)

```python
import unittest
from unittest.mock import patch, Mock
from django.test import TestCase

from lists.forms import (
    DUPLICATE_ITEM_ERROR, EMPTY_ITEM_ERROR,
    ExistingListItemForm, ItemForm, NewListForm
)
from lists.models import Item, List
[...]


class NewListFormTest(unittest.TestCase):

    @patch('lists.forms.List.create_new')
    def test_save_creates_new_list_from_post_data_if_user_not_authenticated(
        self, mock_List_create_new
    ):
        user = Mock(is_authenticated=False)
        form = NewListForm(data={'text': 'new item text'})
        form.is_valid()
        form.save(owner=user)
        mock_List_create_new.assert_called_once_with(
            first_item_text='new item text'
        )
```

---

[1] It could easily just be a standalone function, but hanging it on the model class is a nice way to keep track of where it lives, and gives a bit more of a hint as to what it will do.

And while we're at it, we can test the case where the user is an authenticated user too:

lists/tests/test_forms.py (ch20l022)

```python
@patch('lists.forms.List.create_new')
def test_save_creates_new_list_with_owner_if_user_authenticated(
    self, mock_List_create_new
):
    user = Mock(is_authenticated=True)
    form = NewListForm(data={'text': 'new item text'})
    form.is_valid()
    form.save(owner=user)
    mock_List_create_new.assert_called_once_with(
        first_item_text='new item text', owner=user
    )
```

You can see this is a much more readable test. Let's start implementing our new form. We start with the import:

lists/forms.py (ch20l023)

```python
from lists.models import Item, List
```

Now mock tells us to create a placeholder for our `create_new` method:

```
AttributeError: <class 'lists.models.List'> does not have the attribute
'create_new'
```

lists/models.py

```python
class List(models.Model):

    def get_absolute_url(self):
        return reverse('view_list', args=[self.id])

    def create_new():
        pass
```

And after a few steps, we should end up with a form save method like this:

lists/forms.py (ch20l025)

```python
class NewListForm(ItemForm):

    def save(self, owner):
        if owner.is_authenticated:
            List.create_new(first_item_text=self.cleaned_data['text'], owner=owner)
        else:
            List.create_new(first_item_text=self.cleaned_data['text'])
```

And passing tests:

```
$ python manage.py test lists
Ran 44 tests in 0.192s
OK
```

Hiding ORM Code Behind Helper Methods

One of the techniques that emerged from our use of isolated tests was the "ORM helper method".

Django's ORM lets you get things done quickly with a reasonably readable syntax (it's certainly much nicer than raw SQL!). But some people like to try to minimise the amount of ORM code in the application—particularly removing it from the views and forms layers.

One reason is that it makes it much easier to test those layers. But another is that it forces us to build helper functions that express our domain logic more clearly. Compare:

```
list_ = List()
list_.save()
item = Item()
item.list = list_
item.text = self.cleaned_data['text']
item.save()
```

With:

```
List.create_new(first_item_text=self.cleaned_data['text'])
```

This applies to read queries as well as write. Imagine something like this:

```
Book.objects.filter(in_print=True, pub_date__lte=datetime.today())
```

Versus a helper method, like:

```
Book.all_available_books()
```

When we build helper functions, we can give them names that express what we are doing in terms of the business domain, which can actually make our code more legible, as well as giving us the benefit of keeping all ORM calls at the model layer, and thus making our whole application more loosely coupled.

Finally, Moving Down to the Models Layer

At the models layer, we no longer need to write isolated tests—the whole point of the models layer is to integrate with the database, so it's appropriate to write integrated tests:

```
class ListModelTest(TestCase):

    def test_get_absolute_url(self):
        list_ = List.objects.create()
        self.assertEqual(list_.get_absolute_url(), f'/lists/{list_.id}/')


    def test_create_new_creates_list_and_first_item(self):
        List.create_new(first_item_text='new item text')
        new_item = Item.objects.first()
        self.assertEqual(new_item.text, 'new item text')
        new_list = List.objects.first()
        self.assertEqual(new_item.list, new_list)
```

Which gives:

```
TypeError: create_new() got an unexpected keyword argument 'first_item_text'
```

And that will take us to a first cut implementation that looks like this:

lists/models.py (ch20l027)

```
class List(models.Model):

    def get_absolute_url(self):
        return reverse('view_list', args=[self.id])

    @staticmethod
    def create_new(first_item_text):
        list_ = List.objects.create()
        Item.objects.create(text=first_item_text, list=list_)
```

Notice we've been able to get all the way down to the models layer, driving a nice design for the views and forms layers, and the List model still doesn't support having an owner!

Now let's test the case where the list should have an owner, and add:

lists/tests/test_models.py (ch20l028)

```
from django.contrib.auth import get_user_model
User = get_user_model()
[...]

    def test_create_new_optionally_saves_owner(self):
        user = User.objects.create()
        List.create_new(first_item_text='new item text', owner=user)
        new_list = List.objects.first()
        self.assertEqual(new_list.owner, user)
```

And while we're at it, we can write the tests for the new owner attribute:

lists/tests/test_models.py (ch20l029)

```python
class ListModelTest(TestCase):
    [...]

    def test_lists_can_have_owners(self):
        List(owner=User())  # should not raise

    def test_list_owner_is_optional(self):
        List().full_clean()  # should not raise
```

These two are almost exactly the same tests we used in the last chapter, but I've rewritten them slightly so they don't actually save objects—just having them as in-memory objects is enough for this test.

 Use in-memory (unsaved) model objects in your tests whenever you can; it makes your tests faster.

That gives:

```
$ python manage.py test lists
[...]
ERROR: test_create_new_optionally_saves_owner
TypeError: create_new() got an unexpected keyword argument 'owner'
[...]
ERROR: test_lists_can_have_owners (lists.tests.test_models.ListModelTest)
TypeError: 'owner' is an invalid keyword argument for this function
[...]
Ran 48 tests in 0.204s
FAILED (errors=2)
```

We implement, just like we did in the last chapter:

lists/models.py (ch20l030-1)

```python
from django.conf import settings
[...]


class List(models.Model):
    owner = models.ForeignKey(settings.AUTH_USER_MODEL, blank=True, null=True)
    [...]
```

That will give us the usual integrity failures, until we do a migration:

```
django.db.utils.OperationalError: no such column: lists_list.owner_id
```

Building the migration will get us down to three failures:

```
ERROR: test_create_new_optionally_saves_owner
TypeError: create_new() got an unexpected keyword argument 'owner'
[...]
ValueError: Cannot assign "<SimpleLazyObject:
<django.contrib.auth.models.AnonymousUser object at 0x7f5b2380b4e0>>":
"List.owner" must be a "User" instance.
ValueError: Cannot assign "<SimpleLazyObject:
<django.contrib.auth.models.AnonymousUser object at 0x7f5b237a12e8>>":
"List.owner" must be a "User" instance.
```

Let's deal with the first one, which is for our `create_new` method:

lists/models.py (ch20l030-3)

```python
@staticmethod
def create_new(first_item_text, owner=None):
    list_ = List.objects.create(owner=owner)
    Item.objects.create(text=first_item_text, list=list_)
```

Back to Views

Two of our old integrated tests for the views layer are failing. What's happening?

```
ValueError: Cannot assign "<SimpleLazyObject:
<django.contrib.auth.models.AnonymousUser object at 0x7fbad1cb6c10>>":
"List.owner" must be a "User" instance.
```

Ah, the old view isn't discerning enough about what it does with list owners yet:

lists/views.py

```python
if form.is_valid():
    list_ = List()
    list_.owner = request.user
    list_.save()
```

This is the point at which we realise that our old code wasn't fit for purpose. Let's fix it to get all our tests passing:

```
def new_list(request):
    form = ItemForm(data=request.POST)
    if form.is_valid():
        list_ = List()
        if request.user.is_authenticated:
            list_.owner = request.user
        list_.save()
        form.save(for_list=list_)
        return redirect(list_)
    else:
        return render(request, 'home.html', {"form": form})


def new_list2(request):
    [...]
```

 One of the benefits of integrated tests is that they help you to catch less predictable interactions like this. We'd forgotten to write a test for the case where the user is not authenticated, but because the integrated tests use the stack all the way down, errors from the model layer came up to let us know we'd forgotten something:

```
$ python manage.py test lists
[...]
Ran 48 tests in 0.175s
OK
```

The Moment of Truth (and the Risks of Mocking)

So let's try switching out our old view, and activating our new view. We can make the swap in *urls.py*:

```
    [...]
    url(r'^new$', views.new_list2, name='new_list'),
```

We should also remove the unittest.skip from our integrated test class, to see if our new code for list owners really works:

```
class NewListViewIntegratedTest(TestCase):

    def test_can_save_a_POST_request(self):
        [...]

    def test_list_owner_is_saved_if_user_is_authenticated(self):
        [...]
        self.assertEqual(list_.owner, user)
```

So what happens when we run our tests? Oh no!

```
ERROR: test_list_owner_is_saved_if_user_is_authenticated
[...]
ERROR: test_can_save_a_POST_request
[...]
ERROR: test_redirects_after_POST
(lists.tests.test_views.NewListViewIntegratedTest)
  File "...python-tdd-book/lists/views.py", line 30, in new_list2
    return redirect(list_)
[...]
TypeError: argument of type 'NoneType' is not iterable

FAILED (errors=3)
```

Here's an important lesson to learn about test isolation: it might help you to drive out good design for individual layers, but it won't automatically verify the integration *between* your layers.

What's happened here is that the view was expecting the form to return a list item:

```
list_ = form.save(owner=request.user)
return redirect(list_)
```

But we forgot to make it return anything:

```
def save(self, owner):
    if owner.is_authenticated:
        List.create_new(first_item_text=self.cleaned_data['text'], owner=owner)
    else:
        List.create_new(first_item_text=self.cleaned_data['text'])
```

Thinking of Interactions Between Layers as "Contracts"

Ultimately, even if we had been writing nothing but isolated unit tests, our functional tests would have picked up this particular slip-up. But ideally we'd want our feedback cycle to be quicker—functional tests may take a couple of minutes to run, or even a few hours once your app starts to grow. Is there any way to avoid this sort of problem before it happens?

Methodologically, the way to do it is to think about the interaction between your layers in terms of contracts. Whenever we mock out the behaviour of one layer, we have to make a mental note that there is now an implicit contract between the layers, and that a mock on one layer should probably translate into a test at the layer below.

Here's the part of the contract that we missed:

lists/tests/test_views.py

```python
@patch('lists.views.redirect')
def test_redirects_to_form_returned_object_if_form_valid(
    self, mock_redirect, mockNewListForm
):
    mock_form = mockNewListForm.return_value
    mock_form.is_valid.return_value = True

    response = new_list2(self.request)

    self.assertEqual(response, mock_redirect.return_value)
    mock_redirect.assert_called_once_with(mock_form.save.return_value)  ❶
```

❶ The mocked `form.save` function is returning an object, which we expect our view to be able to use.

Identifying Implicit Contracts

It's worth reviewing each of the tests in `NewListViewUnitTest` and seeing what each mock is saying about the implicit contract:

```python
def test_passes_POST_data_to_NewListForm(self, mockNewListForm):
    [...]
    mockNewListForm.assert_called_once_with(data=self.request.POST)   ❶


def test_saves_form_with_owner_if_form_valid(self, mockNewListForm):
    mock_form = mockNewListForm.return_value
    mock_form.is_valid.return_value = True   ❷
    new_list2(self.request)
    mock_form.save.assert_called_once_with(owner=self.request.user)   ❸


def test_does_not_save_if_form_invalid(self, mockNewListForm):
    [...]
    mock_form.is_valid.return_value = False   ❷
    [...]


@patch('lists.views.redirect')
def test_redirects_to_form_returned_object_if_form_valid(
    self, mock_redirect, mockNewListForm
):
    [...]
    mock_redirect.assert_called_once_with(mock_form.save.return_value)   ❹


@patch('lists.views.render')
def test_renders_home_template_with_form_if_form_invalid(
    [...]
```

❶ We need to be able to initialise our form by passing it a POST request as data.

❷ It should have an `is_valid()` function which returns `True` or `False` appropriately, based on the input data.

❸ The form should have a `.save` method which will accept a `request.user`, which may or may not be a logged-in user, and deal with it appropriately.

❹ The form's `.save` method should return a new list object, for our view to redirect the user to.

If we have a look through our form tests, we'll see that, actually, only item (3) is tested explicitly. On items (1) and (2) we were lucky—they're default features of a Django `ModelForm`, and they are actually covered by our tests for the parent `ItemForm` class.

But contract clause number (4) managed to slip through the net.

When doing Outside-In TDD with isolated tests, you need to keep track of each test's implicit assumptions about the contract which the next layer should implement, and remember to test each of those in turn later. You could use our scratchpad for this, or create a placeholder test with a self.fail.

Fixing the Oversight

Let's add a new test that our form should return the new saved list:

lists/tests/test_forms.py (ch20l038-1)

```python
@patch('lists.forms.List.create_new')
def test_save_returns_new_list_object(self, mock_List_create_new):
    user = Mock(is_authenticated=True)
    form = NewListForm(data={'text': 'new item text'})
    form.is_valid()
    response = form.save(owner=user)
    self.assertEqual(response, mock_List_create_new.return_value)
```

And, actually, this is a good example—we have an implicit contract with the List.cre ate_new; we want it to return the new list object. Let's add a placeholder test for that:

lists/tests/test_models.py (ch20l038-2)

```python
class ListModelTest(TestCase):
    [...]

    def test_create_returns_new_list_object(self):
        self.fail()
```

So, we have one test failure that's telling us to fix the form save:

```
AssertionError: None != <MagicMock name='create_new()' id='139802647565536'>
FAILED (failures=2, errors=3)
```

Like this:

lists/forms.py (ch20l039-1)

```python
class NewListForm(ItemForm):

    def save(self, owner):
        if owner.is_authenticated:
            return List.create_new(first_item_text=self.cleaned_data['text'], owner=owner)
        else:
            return List.create_new(first_item_text=self.cleaned_data['text'])
```

That's a start; now we should look at our placeholder test:

```
[...]
FAIL: test_create_returns_new_list_object
    self.fail()
AssertionError: None

FAILED (failures=1, errors=3)
```

We flesh it out:

lists/tests/test_models.py (ch20l039-2)

```
    def test_create_returns_new_list_object(self):
        returned = List.create_new(first_item_text='new item text')
        new_list = List.objects.first()
        self.assertEqual(returned, new_list)
```

...

```
    AssertionError: None != <List: List object>
```

And we add our return value:

lists/models.py (ch20l039-3)

```
    @staticmethod
    def create_new(first_item_text, owner=None):
        list_ = List.objects.create(owner=owner)
        Item.objects.create(text=first_item_text, list=list_)
        return list_
```

And that gets us to a fully passing test suite:

```
$ python manage.py test lists
[...]
Ran 50 tests in 0.169s

OK
```

One More Test

That's our code for saving list owners, test-driven all the way down and working. But our functional test isn't passing quite yet:

```
$ python manage.py test functional_tests.test_my_lists
selenium.common.exceptions.NoSuchElementException: Message: Unable to locate
element: Reticulate splines
```

It's because we have one last feature to implement, the .name attribute on list objects. Again, we can grab the test and code from the last chapter:

```
def test_list_name_is_first_item_text(self):
    list_ = List.objects.create()
    Item.objects.create(list=list_, text='first item')
    Item.objects.create(list=list_, text='second item')
    self.assertEqual(list_.name, 'first item')
```

(Again, since this is a model-layer test, it's OK to use the ORM. You could conceivably write this test using mocks, but there wouldn't be much point.)

lists/models.py (ch20l041)

```
@property
def name(self):
    return self.item_set.first().text
```

And that gets us to a passing FT!

```
$ python manage.py test functional_tests.test_my_lists

Ran 1 test in 21.428s

OK
```

Tidy Up: What to Keep from Our Integrated Test Suite

Now everything is working, we can remove some redundant tests, and decide whether we want to keep any of our old integrated tests.

Removing Redundant Code at the Forms Layer

We can get rid of the test for the old save method on the `ItemForm`:

lists/tests/test_forms.py

```
--- a/lists/tests/test_forms.py
+++ b/lists/tests/test_forms.py
@@ -23,14 +23,6 @@ class ItemFormTest(TestCase):

        self.assertEqual(form.errors['text'], [EMPTY_ITEM_ERROR])


-    def test_form_save_handles_saving_to_a_list(self):
-        list_ = List.objects.create()
-        form = ItemForm(data={'text': 'do me'})
-        new_item = form.save(for_list=list_)
-        self.assertEqual(new_item, Item.objects.first())
-        self.assertEqual(new_item.text, 'do me')
-        self.assertEqual(new_item.list, list_)
-
```

And in our actual code, we can get rid of two redundant save methods in *forms.py*:

lists/forms.py

```
--- a/lists/forms.py
+++ b/lists/forms.py
@@ -22,11 +22,6 @@ class ItemForm(forms.models.ModelForm):

        self.fields['text'].error_messages['required'] = EMPTY_ITEM_ERROR


-    def save(self, for_list):
-        self.instance.list = for_list
-        return super().save()
-
-

 class NewListForm(ItemForm):

@@ -52,8 +47,3 @@ class ExistingListItemForm(ItemForm):

            e.error_dict = {'text': [DUPLICATE_ITEM_ERROR]}
            self._update_errors(e)

-
-    def save(self):
-        return forms.models.ModelForm.save(self)
-
```

Removing the Old Implementation of the View

We can now completely remove the old `new_list` view, and rename `new_list2` to `new_list`:

```
-from lists.views import new_list, new_list2
+from lists.views import new_list


 class HomePageTest(TestCase):
@@ -75,7 +75,7 @@ class NewListViewIntegratedTest(TestCase):
        request = HttpRequest()
        request.user = User.objects.create(email='a@b.com')
        request.POST['text'] = 'new list item'
-       new_list2(request)
+       new_list(request)
        list_ = List.objects.first()
        self.assertEqual(list_.owner, request.user)


@@ -91,21 +91,21 @@ class NewListViewUnitTest(unittest.TestCase):

    def test_passes_POST_data_to_NewListForm(self, mockNewListForm):
-       new_list2(self.request)
+       new_list(self.request)

[.. several more]
```

```
--- a/lists/urls.py
+++ b/lists/urls.py
@@ -3,7 +3,7 @@ from django.conf.urls import url
 from lists import views

 urlpatterns = [
-    url(r'^new$', views.new_list2, name='new_list'),
+    url(r'^new$', views.new_list, name='new_list'),
     url(r'^(\d+)/$', views.view_list, name='view_list'),
     url(r'^users/(.+)/$', views.my_lists, name='my_lists'),
 ]
```

```
def new_list(request):
    form = NewListForm(data=request.POST)
    if form.is_valid():
        list_ = form.save(owner=request.user)
        [...]
```

And a quick check that all the tests still pass:

```
OK
```

Removing Redundant Code at the Forms Layer

Finally, we have to decide what (if anything) to keep from our integrated test suite.

One option is to throw them all away, and decide that the FTs will pick up any integration problems. That's perfectly valid.

On the other hand, we saw how integrated tests can warn you when you've made small mistakes in integrating your layers. We could keep just a couple of tests around as "sanity checks", to give us a quicker feedback cycle.

How about these three:

lists/tests/test_views.py (ch20l048)

```python
class NewListViewIntegratedTest(TestCase):

    def test_can_save_a_POST_request(self):
        self.client.post('/lists/new', data={'text': 'A new list item'})
        self.assertEqual(Item.objects.count(), 1)
        new_item = Item.objects.first()
        self.assertEqual(new_item.text, 'A new list item')


    def test_for_invalid_input_doesnt_save_but_shows_errors(self):
        response = self.client.post('/lists/new', data={'text': ''})
        self.assertEqual(List.objects.count(), 0)
        self.assertContains(response, escape(EMPTY_ITEM_ERROR))


    def test_list_owner_is_saved_if_user_is_authenticated(self):
        user = User.objects.create(email='a@b.com')
        self.client.force_login(user)
        self.client.post('/lists/new', data={'text': 'new item'})
        list_ = List.objects.first()
        self.assertEqual(list_.owner, user)
```

If you're going to keep any intermediate-level tests at all, I like these three because they feel like they're doing the most "integration" jobs: they test the full stack, from the request down to the actual database, and they cover the three most important use cases of our view.

Conclusions: When to Write Isolated Versus Integrated Tests

Django's testing tools make it very easy to quickly put together integrated tests. The test runner helpfully creates a fast, in-memory version of your database and resets it for you in between each test. The TestCase class and the test client make it easy to test your views, from checking whether database objects are modified, confirming that your URL mappings work, and inspecting the rendering of the templates. This lets you get started with testing very easily and get good coverage across your whole stack.

On the other hand, these kinds of integrated tests won't necessarily deliver the full benefit that rigorous unit testing and Outside-In TDD are meant to confer in terms of design.

If we look at the example in this chapter, compare the code we had before and after:

```python
def new_list(request):
    form = ItemForm(data=request.POST)
    if form.is_valid():
        list_ = List()
        if not isinstance(request.user, AnonymousUser):
            list_.owner = request.user
        list_.save()
        form.save(for_list=list_)
        return redirect(list_)
    else:
        return render(request, 'home.html', {"form": form})


def new_list(request):
    form = NewListForm(data=request.POST)
    if form.is_valid():
        list_ = form.save(owner=request.user)
        return redirect(list_)
    return render(request, 'home.html', {'form': form})
```

If we hadn't bothered to go down the isolation route, would we have bothered to refactor the view function? I know I didn't in the first draft of this book. I'd like to think I would have "in real life", but it's hard to be sure. But writing isolated tests does make you very aware of where the complexities in your code lie.

Let Complexity Be Your Guide

I'd say the point at which isolated tests start to become worth it is to do with complexity. The example in this book is extremely simple, so it's not usually been worth it so far. Even in the example in this chapter, I can convince myself I didn't really *need* to write those isolated tests.

But once an application gains a little more complexity—if it starts growing any more layers between views and models, if you find yourself writing helper methods, or if you're writing your own classes, then you will probably gain from writing more isolated tests.

Should You Do Both?

We already have our suite of functional tests, which will serve the purpose of telling us if we ever make any mistakes in integrating the different parts of our code together. Writing isolated tests can help us to drive out better design for our code, and to verify correctness in finer detail. Would a middle layer of integration tests serve any additional purpose?

I think the answer is potentially yes, if they can provide a faster feedback cycle, and help you identify more clearly what integration problems you suffer from—their tracebacks may provide you with better debug information than you would get from a functional test, for example.

There may even be a case for building them as a separate test suite—you could have one suite of fast, isolated unit tests that don't even use `manage.py`, because they don't need any of the database cleanup and teardown that the Django test runner gives you, and then the intermediate layer that uses Django, and finally the functional tests layer that, say, talks to a staging server. It may be worth it if each layer delivers incremental benefits.

It's a judgement call. I hope that, by going through this chapter, I've given you a feel for what the trade-offs are. There's more discussion on this in Chapter 26.

Onwards!

We're happy with our new version, so let's bring it across to master:

```
$ git add .
$ git commit -m "add list owners via forms. more isolated tests"
$ git checkout master
$ git checkout -b master-noforms-noisolation-bak # optional backup
$ git checkout master
$ git reset --hard more-isolation  # reset master to our branch.
```

In the meantime—those FTs are taking an annoyingly long time to run. I wonder if there's something we can do about that?

On the Pros and Cons of Different Types of Tests, and Decoupling ORM Code

Functional tests

- Provide the best guarantee that your application really works correctly, from the point of view of the user

- But: it's a slower feedback cycle

- And they don't necessarily help you write clean code

Integrated tests (reliant on, for example, the ORM or the Django Test Client)

- Are quick to write

- Are easy to understand

- Will warn you of any integration issues

- But: may not always drive good design (that's up to you!)

- And are usually slower than isolated tests

Isolated ("mocky") tests

- Involve the most hard work

- Can be harder to read and understand

- But: are the best ones for guiding you towards better design

- And run the fastest

Decoupling our application from ORM code

One of the consequences of striving to write isolated tests is that we find ourselves forced to remove ORM code from places like views and forms, by hiding it behind helper functions or methods. This can be beneficial in terms of decoupling your application from the ORM, but also just because it makes your code more readable. As with all things, it's a judgement call as to whether the additional effort is worth it in particular circumstances.

Continuous Integration (CI)

As our site grows, it takes longer and longer to run all of our functional tests. If this continues, the danger is that we're going to stop bothering.

Rather than let that happen, we can automate the running of functional tests by setting up a "Continuous Integration" or CI server. That way, in day-to-day development, we can just run the FT that we're working on at that time, and rely on the CI server to run all the tests automatically and let us know if we've broken anything accidentally. The unit tests should stay fast enough that we can keep running them every few seconds.

The CI server of choice these days is called Jenkins. It's a bit Java, a bit crashy, a bit ugly, but it's what everyone uses, and it has a great plugin ecosystem, so let's get it up and running.

Installing Jenkins

There are several hosted-CI services out there that essentially provide you with a Jenkins server, ready to go. I've come across Sauce Labs, Travis, Circle-CI, ShiningPanda, and there are probably lots more. But I'm going to assume we're installing everything on a server we control.

 It's not a good idea to install Jenkins on the same server as our staging or production servers. Apart from anything else, we may want Jenkins to be able to reboot the staging server!

We'll install the latest version from the official Jenkins apt repo, because the Ubuntu default still has a few annoying bugs with locale/unicode support, and it also doesn't set itself up to listen on the public internet by default:

```
root@server:$ wget -q -O - https://pkg.jenkins.io/debian/jenkins-ci.org.key |\
    apt-key add -
root@server:$ echo deb http://pkg.jenkins.io/debian-stable binary/ | tee \
    /etc/apt/sources.list.d/jenkins.list
root@server:$ apt update
root@server:$ apt install jenkins
```

(Instructions lifted from the Jenkins site (*https://wiki.jenkins-ci.org/display/JENKINS/ Installing+Jenkins+on+Ubuntu*).)

While we're at it, we'll install a few other dependencies:

```
root@server:$ add-apt-repository ppa:deadsnakes/ppa
root@server:$ apt update
root@server:$ apt install firefox python3.6-venv python3.6-dev xvfb
# and, to build fabric3:
root@server:$ apt install build-essential libssl-dev libffi-dev
```

And we'll download, unzip, and install geckodriver too (it was v0.17 at the time of writing, but substitute the latest version as you read this):

```
root@server:$ wget https://github.com/mozilla/geckodriver/releases\
/download/v0.17.0/geckodriver-v0.17.0-linux64.tar.gz
root@server:$ tar -xvzf geckodriver-v0.17.0-linux64.tar.gz
root@server:$ mv geckodriver /usr/local/bin
root@server:$ geckodriver --version
geckodriver 0.17.0
```

Adding Some Swap

Jenkins is quite memory-hungry, and if you're running this on a small VM with less than a couple of gigs for RAM, you'll probably find it gets OOM-killed unless you add some swap:

```
$ fallocate -l 4G /swapfile
$ mkswap /swapfile
$ chmod 600 /swapfile
$ swapon /swapfile
```

That should be plenty.

Configuring Jenkins

You should now be able to visit Jenkins at the URL/IP for your server on port 8080, and see something like Figure 24-1.

Figure 24-1. Jenkins unlock screen

Initial Unlock

The unlock screen is telling us to read a file from disk to unlock the server for first-time use. I jumped over to a terminal and printed it like this:

```
root@server$ cat /var/lib/jenkins/secrets/initialAdminPassword
```

Suggested Plugins for Now

Next we're offered the choice to choose "suggested" plugins. Suggested ones are fine for now. (As a self-respecting nerd, our instinct is to hit "customize" immediately, and that's what I did first time round, but it turns out that screen won't give us what we want. Don't worry, we'll add some more plugins later.)

Configuring the Admin User

Next we set up a username and password to log in to Jenkins with; see Figure 24-2.

Figure 24-2. Jenkins admin user config

And once we log in, we should see a welcome screen (Figure 24-3).

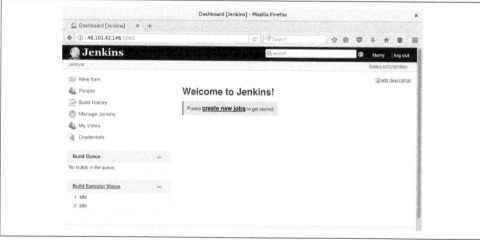

Figure 24-3. A butler—how quaint

Adding Plugins

Follow the links for *Manage Jenkins → Manage Plugins → Available.*

We'll want the plugins for:

- *ShiningPanda*
- *Xvfb*

And hit install (Figure 24-4).

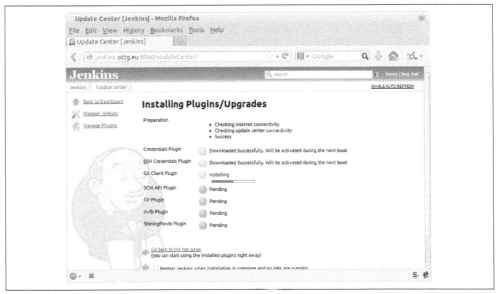

Figure 24-4. Installing plugins…

Telling Jenkins Where to Find Python 3 and Xvfb

We need to tell the ShiningPanda plugin where Python 3 is installed (usually */usr/bin/python3*, but you can check with a which python3):

- *Manage Jenkins → Global Tool Configuration*
- *Python → Python installations → Add Python* (see Figure 24-5; it's safe to ignore the warning message)
- *Xvfb installation → Add Xvfb installation*; enter **/usr/bin** as the installation directory

Figure 24-5. Where did I leave that Python?

Finishing Off with HTTPS

To finish off securing your Jenkins instance, you'll want to set up HTTPS, by getting nginx HTTPS to use a self-signed cert, and proxy requests from port 443 to port 8080. Then you can even block port 8080 on the firewall. I won't go into detail on that now, but here are a few links to instructions which I found useful:

- Official Jenkins Ubuntu installation guide (*https://wiki.jenkins-ci.org/display/JENKINS/Installing+Jenkins+on+Ubuntu*)

- How to create a self-signed SSL certificate (*https://www.digitalocean.com/community/tutorials/how-to-create-an-ssl-certificate-on-nginx-for-ubuntu-14-04*)

- How to redirect HTTP to HTTPS (*http://serverfault.com/questions/250476/how-to-force-or-redirect-to-ssl-in-nginx#424016*)

Setting Up Our Project

Now we've got the basic Jenkins configured, let's set up our project:

- Hit the New Item button.

- Enter *Superlists* as the name, and then choose "Freestyle project", and hit OK.

- Add the Git repo, as in Figure 24-6.

Figure 24-6. Get it from Git

- Set it to poll every hour (Figure 24-7; check out the help text here—there are many other options for ways of triggering builds).

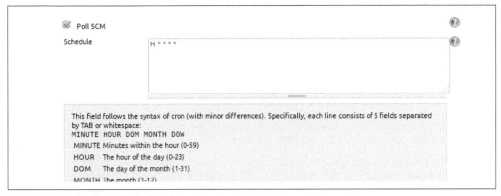

Figure 24-7. Poll GitHub for changes

- Run the tests inside a Python 3 virtualenv.
- Run the unit tests and functional tests separately. See Figure 24-8.

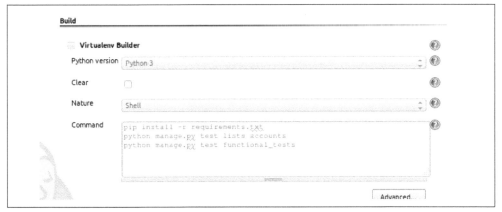

Figure 24-8. Virtualenv build steps

First Build!

Hit "Build Now", then go and take a look at the "Console Output". You should see something like this:

```
Started by user harry
Building in workspace /var/lib/jenkins/jobs/Superlists/workspace
Fetching changes from the remote Git repository
Fetching upstream changes from https://github.com/hjwp/book-example.git
Checking out Revision d515acebf7e173f165ce713b30295a4a6ee17c07 (origin/master)
[workspace] $ /bin/sh -xe /tmp/shiningpanda7260707941304155464.sh
+ pip install -r requirements.txt
Requirement already satisfied (use --upgrade to upgrade): Django==1.11 in
/var/lib/jenkins/shiningpanda/jobs/ddc1aed1/virtualenvs/d41d8cd9/lib/python3.6/site-packages
(from -r requirements.txt (line 1))

Requirement already satisfied (use --upgrade to upgrade): gunicorn==17.5 in
/var/lib/jenkins/shiningpanda/jobs/ddc1aed1/virtualenvs/d41d8cd9/lib/python3.6/site-packages
(from -r requirements.txt (line 3))
Downloading/unpacking requests==2.0.0 (from -r requirements.txt (line 4))
  Running setup.py egg_info for package requests

Installing collected packages: requests
  Running setup.py install for requests

Successfully installed requests
Cleaning up...
+ python manage.py test lists accounts
........................................................................
 -------------------------------------------------------------------
Ran 67 tests in 0.429s

OK
Creating test database for alias 'default'...
Destroying test database for alias 'default'...
+ python manage.py test functional_tests
EEEEEE
======================================================================
ERROR: functional_tests.test_layout_and_styling (unittest.loader._FailedTest)
 ----------------------------------------------------------------------
ImportError: Failed to import test module: functional_tests.test_layout_and_styling
[...]
ImportError: No module named 'selenium'

Ran 6 tests in 0.001s

FAILED (errors=6)

Build step 'Virtualenv Builder' marked build as failure
```

Ah. We need Selenium in our virtualenv.

Let's add a manual installation of Selenium to our build steps:

```
pip install -r requirements.txt
python manage.py test accounts lists
pip install selenium fabric3
python manage.py test functional_tests
```

Some people like to use a file called *test-requirements.txt* to specify packages that are needed for the tests, but not the main app.

And hit "Build Now" again.

Next one of two things will happen. Either you'll see some error messages like this in your console output:

```
    self.browser = webdriver.Firefox()
[...]
selenium.common.exceptions.WebDriverException: Message: 'The browser appears to
have exited before we could connect. The output was: b"\\n(process:19757):
GLib-CRITICAL **: g_slice_set_config: assertion \'sys_page_size == 0\'
failed\\nError: no display specified\\n"'
[...]
selenium.common.exceptions.WebDriverException: Message: connection refused
```

Or possibly your build will just hang altogether (that happened to me at least once). The reason is that Firefox can't start, because it doesn't have a display to run on.

Setting Up a Virtual Display So the FTs Can Run Headless

As you can see from the traceback, Firefox is unable to start because the server doesn't have a display.

There are two ways to deal with this problem. The first is to switch to using a headless browser, like PhantomJS or SlimerJS. Those tools definitely have their place—they're faster, for one thing—but they also have disadvantages. The first is that they're not "real" web browsers, so you can't be sure you're going to catch all the strange quirks and behaviours of the actual browsers your users use. The second is that they can behave quite differently inside Selenium, and often require some rewriting of FT code.

I would look into using headless browsers as a "dev-only" tool, to speed up the running of FTs on the developer's machine, while the tests on the CI server use actual browsers.

The alternative is to set up a virtual display: we get the server to pretend it has a screen attached to it, so Firefox runs happily. There are a few tools out there to do this; we'll use one called "Xvfb" (X Virtual Framebuffer)[1] because it's easy to install and use, and because it has a convenient Jenkins plugin (now you know why we installed it earlier).

We go back to our project and hit "Configure" again, then find the section called "Build Environment". Using the virtual display is as simple as ticking the box marked "Start Xvfb before the build, and shut it down after", as in Figure 24-9.

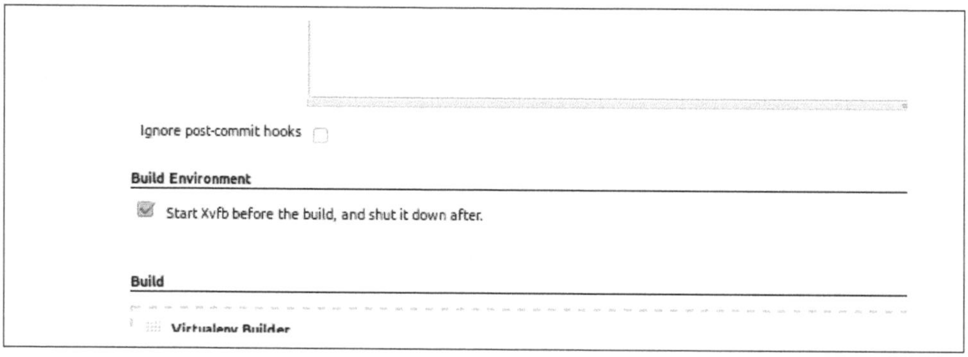

Figure 24-9. Sometimes config is easy

The build does much better now:

```
[...]
Xvfb starting$ /usr/bin/Xvfb :2 -screen 0 1024x768x24 -fbdir
/var/lib/jenkins/2013-11-04_03-27-221510012427739470928xvfb
[...]
+ python manage.py test lists accounts
...........................................................
 ------------------------------------------------------------
Ran 63 tests in 0.410s

OK
Creating test database for alias 'default'...
Destroying test database for alias 'default'...

+ pip install selenium
Requirement already satisfied (use --upgrade to upgrade): selenium in
/var/lib/jenkins/shiningpanda/jobs/ddc1aed1/virtualenvs/d41d8cd9/lib/python3.6/site-packages
Cleaning up...
```

---

1 Check out pyvirtualdisplay (*https://pypi.python.org/pypi/PyVirtualDisplay*) as a way of controlling virtual displays from Python.

```
+ python manage.py test functional_tests
......F.
======================================================================
FAIL: test_can_start_a_list_for_one_user
(functional_tests.test_simple_list_creation.NewVisitorTest)
----------------------------------------------------------------------
Traceback (most recent call last):
  File "...python-tdd-book/functional_tests/test_simple_list_creation.py", line
43, in test_can_start_a_list_for_one_user
    self.wait_for_row_in_list_table('2: Use peacock feathers to make a fly')
  File "...python-tdd-book/functional_tests/base.py", line 51, in
wait_for_row_in_list_table
    raise e
  File "...python-tdd-book/functional_tests/base.py", line 47, in
wait_for_row_in_list_table
    self.assertIn(row_text, [row.text for row in rows])
AssertionError: '2: Use peacock feathers to make a fly' not found in ['1: Buy
peacock feathers']
----------------------------------------------------------------------
Ran 8 tests in 89.275s

FAILED (errors=1)
Creating test database for alias 'default'...
[{'secure': False, 'domain': 'localhost', 'name': 'sessionid', 'expiry':
1920011311, 'path': '/', 'value': 'a8d8bbde33nreq6gihw8a7r1cc8bf02k'}]
Destroying test database for alias 'default'...
Build step 'Virtualenv Builder' marked build as failure
Xvfb stopping
Finished: FAILURE
```

Pretty close! To debug that failure, we'll need screenshots though.

 This error was due to the performance of my Jenkins instance—you may see a different error, or none at all. In any case, the following tools for taking screenshots and dealing with race conditions will come in useful. Read on!

Taking Screenshots

To be able to debug unexpected failures that happen on a remote PC, it would be good to see a picture of the screen at the moment of the failure, and maybe also a dump of the HTML of the page. We can do that using some custom logic in our FT class tearDown. We have to do a bit of introspection of unittest internals, a private attribute called _outcomeForDoCleanups, but this will work:

```
import os
from datetime import datetime
[...]

SCREEN_DUMP_LOCATION = os.path.join(
    os.path.dirname(os.path.abspath(__file__)), 'screendumps'
)
[...]

    def tearDown(self):
        if self._test_has_failed():
            if not os.path.exists(SCREEN_DUMP_LOCATION):
                os.makedirs(SCREEN_DUMP_LOCATION)
            for ix, handle in enumerate(self.browser.window_handles):
                self._windowid = ix
                self.browser.switch_to_window(handle)
                self.take_screenshot()
                self.dump_html()
        self.browser.quit()
        super().tearDown()


    def _test_has_failed(self):
        # slightly obscure but couldn't find a better way!
        return any(error for (method, error) in self._outcome.errors)
```

We first create a directory for our screenshots if necessary. Then we iterate through all the open browser tabs and pages, and use some Selenium methods, get_screen shot_as_file and browser.page_source, for our image and HTML dumps:

```
    def take_screenshot(self):
        filename = self._get_filename() + '.png'
        print('screenshotting to', filename)
        self.browser.get_screenshot_as_file(filename)


    def dump_html(self):
        filename = self._get_filename() + '.html'
        print('dumping page HTML to', filename)
        with open(filename, 'w') as f:
            f.write(self.browser.page_source)
```

And finally here's a way of generating a unique filename identifier, which includes the name of the test and its class, as well as a timestamp:

functional_tests/base.py (ch21l008)

```python
def _get_filename(self):
    timestamp = datetime.now().isoformat().replace(':', '.')[:19]
    return '{folder}/{classname}.{method}-window{windowid}-{timestamp}'.format(
        folder=SCREEN_DUMP_LOCATION,
        classname=self.__class__.__name__,
        method=self._testMethodName,
        windowid=self._windowid,
        timestamp=timestamp
    )
```

You can test this first locally by deliberately breaking one of the tests, with a self.fail() for example, and you'll see something like this:

```
[...]
screenshotting to ...python-tdd-book/functional_tests/screendumps/MyListsTest.t
est_logged_in_users_lists_are_saved_as_my_lists-window0-2014-03-09T11.19.12.png
dumping page HTML to ...python-tdd-book/functional_tests/screendumps/MyListsTes
t.test_logged_in_users_lists_are_saved_as_my_lists-window0-[...]
```

Revert the self.fail(), then commit and push:

```
$ git diff  # changes in base.py
$ echo "functional_tests/screendumps" >> .gitignore
$ git commit -am "add screenshot on failure to FT runner"
$ git push
```

And when we rerun the build on Jenkins, we see something like this:

```
screenshotting to /var/lib/jenkins/jobs/Superlists/.../functional_tests/
screendumps/LoginTest.test_login_with_persona-window0-2014-01-22T17.45.12.png
dumping page HTML to /var/lib/jenkins/jobs/Superlists/.../functional_tests/
screendumps/LoginTest.test_login_with_persona-window0-2014-01-22T17.45.12.html
```

We can go and visit these in the "workspace", which is the folder Jenkins uses to store our source code and run the tests in, as in Figure 24-10.

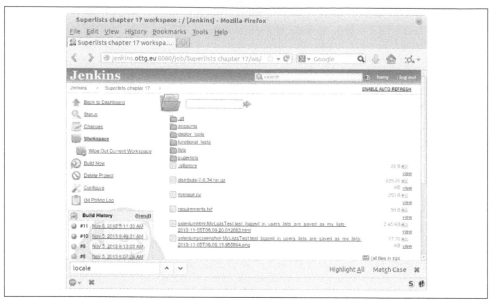

Figure 24-10. Visiting the project workspace

And then we look at the screenshot, as shown in Figure 24-11.

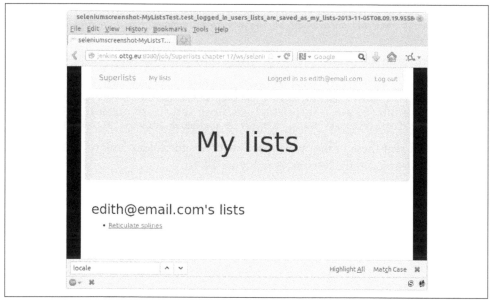

Figure 24-11. Screenshot looking normal

If in Doubt, Try Bumping the Timeout!

Hm. No obvious clues there. Well, when in doubt, bump the timeout, as the old adage goes:

functional_tests/base.py

```
MAX_WAIT = 20
```

Then we can rerun the build on Jenkins using "Build Now", and confirm it now works, as in Figure 24-12.

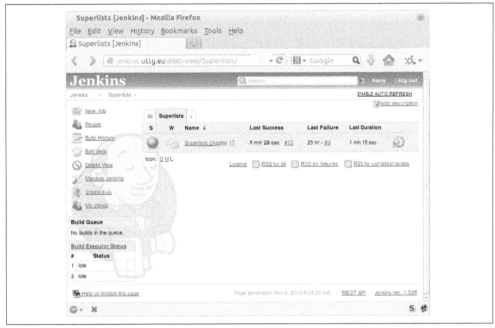

Figure 24-12. The outlook is brighter

Jenkins uses blue to indicate passing builds rather than green, which is a bit disappointing, but look at the sun peeking through the clouds: that's cheery! It's an indicator of a moving average ratio of passing builds to failing builds. Things are looking up!

Running Our QUnit JavaScript Tests in Jenkins with PhantomJS

There's a set of tests we almost forgot—the JavaScript tests. Currently our "test runner" is an actual web browser. To get Jenkins to run them, we need a command-line test runner. Here's a chance to use PhantomJS.

Installing node

It's time to stop pretending we're not in the JavaScript game. We're doing web development. That means we do JavaScript. That means we're going to end up with node.js on our computers. It's just the way it has to be.

Follow the instructions on the node.js homepage (*http://nodejs.org/*). There are installers for Windows and Mac, and repositories for popular Linux distros.[2]

Once we have node, we can install phantom:

```
$ npm install -g phantomjs-prebuilt  # the -g means "system-wide".
```

Next we pull down a QUnit/PhantomJS test runner. There are several out there (I even wrote a basic one to be able to test the QUnit listings in this book), but the best one to get is probably the one that's linked from the QUnit plugins page (*http://qunitjs.com/plugins/*). At the time of writing, its repo was at *https://github.com/jonkemp/qunit-phantomjs-runner*. The only file you need is *runner.js*.

You should end up with this:

```
$ tree lists/static/tests/
lists/static/tests/
├── qunit-2.0.1.css
├── qunit-2.0.1.js
├── runner.js
└── tests.html

0 directories, 4 files
```

Let's try it out:

```
$ phantomjs lists/static/tests/runner.js lists/static/tests/tests.html
Took 24ms to run 2 tests. 2 passed, 0 failed.
```

Just to be sure, let's deliberately break something:

---

2 Make sure you get the latest version. On Ubuntu, use the PPA rather than the default package.

```
$('input[name="text"]').on('keypress', function () {
  // $('.has-error').hide();
});
```

Sure enough:

```
$ phantomjs lists/static/tests/runner.js lists/static/tests/tests.html
```

```
Test failed: errors should be hidden on keypress
    Failed assertion: expected: false, but was: true
file://...python-tdd-book/lists/static/tests/tests.html:27:15
```

```
Took 27ms to run 2 tests. 1 passed, 1 failed.
```

All right! Let's unbreak that, commit and push the runner, and then add it to our Jenkins build:

```
$ git checkout lists/static/list.js
$ git add lists/static/tests/runner.js
$ git commit -m "Add phantomjs test runner for javascript tests"
$ git push
```

Adding the Build Steps to Jenkins

Edit the project configuration again, and add a step for each set of JavaScript tests, as per Figure 24-13.

Figure 24-13. Add a build step for our JavaScript unit tests

You'll also need to install PhantomJS on the server:

```
root@server:$ add-apt-repository -y ppa:chris-lea/node.js
root@server:$ apt update
root@server:$ apt install nodejs
root@server:$ npm install -g phantomjs-prebuilt
```

And there we are! A complete CI build featuring all of our tests!

```
Started by user harry
Building in workspace /var/lib/jenkins/jobs/Superlists/workspace
Fetching changes from the remote Git repository
Fetching upstream changes from https://github.com/hjwp/book-example.git
Checking out Revision 936a484038194b289312ff62f10d24e6a054fb29 (origin/chapter_1
Xvfb starting$ /usr/bin/Xvfb :1 -screen 0 1024x768x24 -fbdir /var/lib/jenkins/20
[workspace] $ /bin/sh -xe /tmp/shiningpanda7092102504259037999.sh

+ pip install -r requirements.txt
[...]

+ python manage.py test lists
...............................
----------------------------------------------------------------------
Ran 43 tests in 0.229s

OK
Creating test database for alias 'default'...
Destroying test database for alias 'default'...

+ python manage.py test accounts
..................
----------------------------------------------------------------------
Ran 18 tests in 0.078s

OK
Creating test database for alias 'default'...
Destroying test database for alias 'default'...

[workspace] $ /bin/sh -xe /tmp/hudson2967478575201471277.sh
+ phantomjs lists/static/tests/runner.js lists/static/tests/tests.html
Took 32ms to run 2 tests. 2 passed, 0 failed.
+ phantomjs lists/static/tests/runner.js accounts/static/tests/tests.html
Took 47ms to run 11 tests. 11 passed, 0 failed.

[workspace] $ /bin/sh -xe /tmp/shiningpanda7526089957247195819.sh
+ pip install selenium
Requirement already satisfied (use --upgrade to upgrade): selenium in /var/lib/

Cleaning up...
[workspace] $ /bin/sh -xe /tmp/shiningpanda2420240268202055029.sh
+ python manage.py test functional_tests
........
----------------------------------------------------------------------
Ran 8 tests in 76.804s

OK
```

Nice to know that, no matter how lazy I get about running the full test suite on my
own machine, the CI server will catch me. Another one of the Testing Goat's agents in
cyberspace, watching over us…

More Things to Do with a CI Server

I've only scratched the surface of what you can do with Jenkins and CI servers. For example, you can make it much smarter about how it monitors your repo for new commits.

Perhaps more interestingly, you can use your CI server to automate your staging tests as well as your normal functional tests. If all the FTs pass, you can add a build step that deploys the code to staging, and then reruns the FTs against that—automating one more step of the process, and ensuring that your staging server is automatically kept up to date with the latest code.

Some people even use a CI server as the way of deploying their production releases!

Tips on CI and Selenium Best Practices

Set up CI as soon as possible for your project
> As soon as your functional tests take more than a few seconds to run, you'll find yourself avoiding running them all. Give this job to a CI server, to make sure that all your tests are getting run somewhere.

Set up screenshots and HTML dumps for failures
> Debugging test failures is easier if you can see what the page looked like when the failure occurred. This is particularly useful for debugging CI failures, but it's also very useful for tests that you run locally.

Be prepared to bump your timeouts
> A CI server may not be as speedy as your laptop, especially if it's under load, running multiple tests at the same time. Be prepared to be even more generous with your timeouts, in order to minimise the chance of random failures.

Look into hooking up CI and staging
> Tests that use `LiveServerTestCase` are all very well for dev boxes, but the true reassurance comes from running your tests against a real server. Look into getting your CI server to deploy to your staging server, and run the functional tests against that instead. It has the side benefit of testing your automated deploy scripts.

The Token Social Bit, the Page Pattern, and an Exercise for the Reader

Are jokes about how "everything has to be social now" slightly old hat? Everything has to be all A/B tested big data get-more-clicks lists of 10 Things This Inspiring Teacher Said That Will Make You Change Your Mind About Blah Blah now…anyway. Lists, be they inspirational or otherwise, are often better shared. Let's allow our users to collaborate on their lists with other users.

Along the way we'll improve our FTs by starting to implement something called the Page object pattern.

Then, rather than showing you explicitly what to do, I'm going to let you write your unit tests and application code by yourself. Don't worry, you won't be totally on your own! I'll give an outline of the steps to take, as well as some hints and tips.

An FT with Multiple Users, and addCleanup

Let's get started—we'll need two users for this FT:

```
from selenium import webdriver
from .base import FunctionalTest


def quit_if_possible(browser):
    try: browser.quit()
    except: pass


class SharingTest(FunctionalTest):

    def test_can_share_a_list_with_another_user(self):
        # Edith is a logged-in user
        self.create_pre_authenticated_session('edith@example.com')
        edith_browser = self.browser
        self.addCleanup(lambda: quit_if_possible(edith_browser))

        # Her friend Oniciferous is also hanging out on the lists site
        oni_browser = webdriver.Firefox()
        self.addCleanup(lambda: quit_if_possible(oni_browser))
        self.browser = oni_browser
        self.create_pre_authenticated_session('oniciferous@example.com')

        # Edith goes to the home page and starts a list
        self.browser = edith_browser
        self.browser.get(self.live_server_url)
        self.add_list_item('Get help')

        # She notices a "Share this list" option
        share_box = self.browser.find_element_by_css_selector(
            'input[name="sharee"]'
        )
        self.assertEqual(
            share_box.get_attribute('placeholder'),
            'your-friend@example.com'
        )
```

The interesting feature to note about this section is the addCleanup function, whose documentation you can find online (*https://docs.python.org/3/library/ unittest.html#unittest.TestCase.addCleanup*). It can be used as an alternative to the tearDown function as a way of cleaning up resources used during the test. It's most useful when the resource is only allocated halfway through a test, so you don't have to spend time in tearDown figuring out what does or doesn't need cleaning up.

addCleanup is run after tearDown, which is why we need that try/except formulation for quit_if_possible; whichever of edith_browser and oni_browser is also assigned to self.browser at the point at which the test ends will already have been quit by the tearDown function.

We'll also need to move `create_pre_authenticated_session` from *test_my_lists.py* into *base.py*.

OK, let's see if that all works:

```
$ python manage.py test functional_tests.test_sharing
[...]
Traceback (most recent call last):
  File "...python-tdd-book/functional_tests/test_sharing.py", line 31, in
test_can_share_a_list_with_another_user
[...]
selenium.common.exceptions.NoSuchElementException: Message: Unable to locate
element: input[name="sharee"]
```

Great! It seems to have got through creating the two user sessions, and it gets onto an expected failure—there is no input for an email address of a person to share a list with on the page.

Let's do a commit at this point, because we've got at least a placeholder for our FT, we've got a useful modification of the `create_pre_authenticated_session` function, and we're about to embark on a bit of an FT refactor:

```
$ git add functional_tests
$ git commit -m "New FT for sharing, move session creation stuff to base"
```

The Page Pattern

Before we go any further, I want to show an alternative method for reducing duplication in your FTs, called "Page objects" (*http://bit.ly/2uWBvsM*).

We've already built several helper methods for our FTs, including `add_list_item`, which we've used here, but if we just keep adding more and more, it's going to get very crowded. I've worked on a base FT class that was over 1,500 lines long, and that got pretty unwieldy.

Page objects are an alternative which encourage us to store all the information and helper methods about the different types of pages on our site in a single place. Let's see how that might look for our site, starting with a class to represent any lists page:

```
from selenium.webdriver.common.keys import Keys
from .base import wait


class ListPage(object):

    def __init__(self, test):
        self.test = test   ❶


    def get_table_rows(self):   ❸
        return self.test.browser.find_elements_by_css_selector('#id_list_table tr')


    @wait
    def wait_for_row_in_list_table(self, item_text, item_number):   ❷
        expected_row_text = f'{item_number}: {item_text}'
        rows = self.get_table_rows()
        self.test.assertIn(expected_row_text, [row.text for row in rows])


    def get_item_input_box(self):   ❷
        return self.test.browser.find_element_by_id('id_text')


    def add_list_item(self, item_text):   ❷
        new_item_no = len(self.get_table_rows()) + 1
        self.get_item_input_box().send_keys(item_text)
        self.get_item_input_box().send_keys(Keys.ENTER)
        self.wait_for_row_in_list_table(item_text, new_item_no)
        return self   ❹
```

❶ It's initialised with an object that represents the current test. That gives us the ability to make assertions, access the browser instance via self.test.browser, and use the self.test.wait_for function.

❷ I've copied across some of the existing helper methods from *base.py*, but I've tweaked them slightly…

❸ For example, they make use of this new method.

❹ Returning self is just a convenience. It enables method chaining (*https://en.wiki pedia.org/wiki/Method_chaining*), which we'll see in action immediately.

Let's see how to use it in our test:

```
from .list_page import ListPage
[...]

        # Edith goes to the home page and starts a list
        self.browser = edith_browser
        self.browser.get(self.live_server_url)
        list_page = ListPage(self).add_list_item('Get help')
```

```
        # She notices a "Share this list" option
        share_box = list_page.get_share_box()
        self.assertEqual(
            share_box.get_attribute('placeholder'),
            'your-friend@example.com'
        )

        # She shares her list.
        # The page updates to say that it's shared with Oniciferous:
        list_page.share_list_with('oniciferous@example.com')
```

We add the following three functions to our `ListPage`:

```
    def get_share_box(self):
        return self.test.browser.find_element_by_css_selector(
            'input[name="sharee"]'
        )


    def get_shared_with_list(self):
        return self.test.browser.find_elements_by_css_selector(
            '.list-sharee'
        )


    def share_list_with(self, email):
        self.get_share_box().send_keys(email)
        self.get_share_box().send_keys(Keys.ENTER)
        self.test.wait_for(lambda: self.test.assertIn(
            email,
            [item.text for item in self.get_shared_with_list()]
        ))
```

The idea behind the Page pattern is that it should capture all the information about a particular page in your site, so that if, later, you want to go and make changes to that page—even just simple tweaks to its HTML layout, for example—you have a single place to go to adjust your functional tests, rather than having to dig through dozens of FTs.

The next step would be to pursue the FT refactor through our other tests. I'm not going to show that here, but it's something you could do, for practice, to get a feel for what the trade-offs between DRY and test readability are like…

Extend the FT to a Second User, and the "My Lists" Page

Let's spec out just a little more detail of what we want our sharing user story to be. Edith has seen on her list page that the list is now "shared with" Oniciferous, and then we can have Oni log in and see the list on his "My Lists" page, maybe in a section called "lists shared with me":

functional_tests/test_sharing.py (ch22l010)

```
from .my_lists_page import MyListsPage
[...]

        list_page.share_list_with('oniciferous@example.com')

        # Oniciferous now goes to the lists page with his browser
        self.browser = oni_browser
        MyListsPage(self).go_to_my_lists_page()

        # He sees Edith's list in there!
        self.browser.find_element_by_link_text('Get help').click()
```

That means another function in our `MyListsPage` class:

functional_tests/my_lists_page.py (ch22l011)

```
class MyListsPage(object):

    def __init__(self, test):
        self.test = test


    def go_to_my_lists_page(self):
        self.test.browser.get(self.test.live_server_url)
        self.test.browser.find_element_by_link_text('My lists').click()
        self.test.wait_for(lambda: self.test.assertEqual(
            self.test.browser.find_element_by_tag_name('h1').text,
            'My Lists'
        ))
        return self
```

Once again, this is a function that would be good to carry across into *test_my_lists.py*, along with maybe a `MyListsPage` object.

In the meantime, Oniciferous can also add things to the list:

functional_tests/test_sharing.py (ch22l012)

```
# On the list page, Oniciferous can see says that it's Edith's list
self.wait_for(lambda: self.assertEqual(
    list_page.get_list_owner(),
    'edith@example.com'
))

# He adds an item to the list
list_page.add_list_item('Hi Edith!')

# When Edith refreshes the page, she sees Oniciferous's addition
self.browser = edith_browser
self.browser.refresh()
list_page.wait_for_row_in_list_table('Hi Edith!', 2)
```

That's another addition to our `ListPage` object:

functional_tests/list_page.py (ch22l013)

```
class ListPage(object):
    [...]

    def get_list_owner(self):
        return self.test.browser.find_element_by_id('id_list_owner').text
```

It's long past time to run the FT and check if all of this works!

```
$ python manage.py test functional_tests.test_sharing

    share_box = list_page.get_share_box()
    [...]
selenium.common.exceptions.NoSuchElementException: Message: Unable to locate
element: input[name="sharee"]
```

That's the expected failure; we don't have an input for email addresses of people to share with. Let's do a commit:

```
$ git add functional_tests
$ git commit -m "Create Page objects for list pages, use in sharing FT"
```

An Exercise for the Reader

> I probably didn't really understand what I was doing until after having completed the "Exercise for the reader" in Chapter 25.
>
> —Iain H. (reader)

There's nothing that cements learning like taking the training wheels off, and getting something working on your own, so I hope you'll give this a go.

Here's an outline of the steps you could take:

1. We'll need a new section in *list.html*, with, at first, a form with an input box for an email address. That should get the FT one step further.

2. Next, we'll need a view for the form to submit to. Start by defining the URL in the template, maybe something like *lists/<list_id>/share*.

3. Then, our first unit test. It can be just enough to get a placeholder view in. We want the view to respond to POST requests, and it should respond with a redirect back to the list page, so the test could be called something like `ShareList Test.test_post_redirects_to_lists_page`.

4. We build out our placeholder view, as just a two-liner that finds a list and redirects to it.

5. We can then write a new unit test which creates a user and a list, does a POST with their email address, and checks that the user is added to `list_.shared_with.all()` (a similar ORM usage to "My Lists"). That `shared_with` attribute won't exist yet; we're going outside-in.

6. So before we can get this test to pass, we have to move down to the model layer. The next test, in *test_models.py*, can check that a list has a `shared_with.add` method, which can be called with a user's email address and then check the lists' `shared_with.all()` queryset, which will subsequently contain that user.

7. You'll then need a `ManyToManyField`. You'll probably see an error message about a clashing `related_name`, which you'll find a solution to if you look around the Django docs.

8. It will need a database migration.

9. That should get the model tests passing. Pop back up to fix the view test.

10. You may find the redirect view test fails, because it's not sending a valid POST request. You can either choose to ignore invalid inputs, or adjust the test to send a valid POST.

11. Then back up to the template level; on the "My Lists" page we'll want a `<ul>` with a `for` loop of the lists shared with the user. On the lists page, we also want to show who the list is shared with, as well as mention of who the list owner is. Look back at the FT for the correct classes and IDs to use. You could have brief unit tests for each of these if you like, as well.

12. You might find that spinning up the site with `runserver` will help you iron out any bugs, as well as fine-tune the layout and aesthetics. If you use a private browser session, you'll be able to log multiple users in.

By the end, you might end up with something that looks like Figure 25-1.

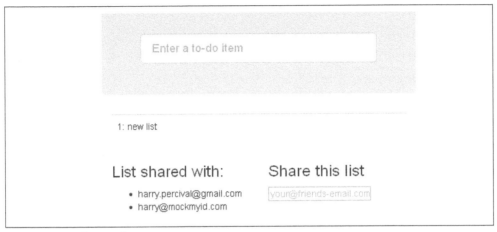

Figure 25-1. Sharing lists

The Page Pattern, and the Real Exercise for the Reader

Apply DRY to your functional tests

Once your FT suite starts to grow, you'll find that different tests will inevitably find themselves using similar parts of the UI. Try to avoid having constants, like the HTML IDs or classes of particular UI elements, duplicated between your FTs.

The Page pattern

Moving helper methods into a base `FunctionalTest` class can become unwieldy. Consider using individual Page objects to hold all the logic for dealing with particular parts of your site.

An exercise for the reader

I hope you've actually tried this out! Try to follow the outside-in method, and occasionally try things out manually if you get stuck. The real exercise for the reader, of course, is to apply TDD to your next project. I hope you'll enjoy it!

In the next chapter, we'll wrap up with a discussion of testing "best practices."

Fast Tests, Slow Tests, and Hot Lava

> The database is Hot Lava!
>
> —Casey Kinsey (*https://www.youtube.com/watch?v=bsmFVb8guMU*)

Right up until Chapter 23, almost all of the "unit" tests in the book should perhaps have been called *integrated* tests, because they either rely on the database or use the Django Test Client, which does too much magic with the middleware layers that sit between requests, responses, and view functions.

There is an argument that a true unit test should always be isolated, because it's meant to test a single unit of software. If it touches the database, it can't be a unit test. The database is hot lava!

Some TDD veterans say you should strive to write "pure", isolated unit tests wherever possible, instead of writing integrated tests. It's one of the ongoing (occasionally heated) debates in the testing community.

Being merely a young whippersnapper myself, I'm only partway towards all the subtleties of the argument. But in this chapter, I'd like to talk about why people feel strongly about it, and try to give you some idea of when you can get away with muddling through with integrated tests (which I confess I do a lot of!), and when it's worth striving for more "pure" unit tests.

Terminology: Different Types of Test

Isolated tests ("pure" unit tests) vs. integrated tests
> The primary purpose of a unit test should be to verify the correctness of the logic of your application. An *isolated* test is one that tests exactly one chunk of code, and whose success or failure does not depend on any other external code. This is what I call a "pure" unit test: a test for a single function, for example, written in

---

such a way that only that function can make it fail. If the function depends on another system, and breaking that system breaks our test, we have an *integrated* test. That system could be an external system, like a database, but it could also be another function which we don't control. In either case, if breaking the system makes our test fail, our test is not properly isolated; it is not a "pure" unit test. That's not necessarily a bad thing, but it may mean the test is doing two jobs at once.

Integration tests
An integration test checks that the code you control is integrated correctly with some external system which you don't control. *Integration* tests are typically also *integrated* tests.

System tests
If an integration test checks the integration with one external system, a system test checks the integration of multiple systems in your application—for example, checking that we've wired up our database, static files, and server config together in such a way that they all work.

Functional tests and acceptance tests
An acceptance test is meant to test that our system works from the point of view of the user ("would the user accept this behaviour?"). It's hard to write an acceptance test that's not a full-stack, end-to-end test. We've been using our functional tests to play the role of both acceptance tests and system tests.

If you'll forgive the pretentious philosophical terminology, I'd like to structure our discussion of these issues like a Hegelian dialectic:

- The Thesis: the case for "pure", fast unit tests.
- The Antithesis: some of the risks associated with a (naive) pure unit testing approach.
- The Synthesis: a discussion of best practices like "Ports and Adapters" or "Functional Core, Imperative Shell", and of just what it is that we want from our tests, anyway.

Thesis: Unit Tests Are Superfast and Good Besides That

One of the things you often hear about unit tests is that they're much faster. I don't think that's actually the primary benefit of unit tests, but it's worth exploring the theme of speed.

Faster Tests Mean Faster Development

Other things being equal, the faster your unit tests run, the better. To a lesser extent, the faster *all* your tests run, the better.

I've outlined the TDD test/code cycle in this book. You've started to get a feel for the TDD workflow, the way you flick between writing tiny amounts of code and running your tests. You end up running your unit tests several times a minute, and your functional tests several times a day.

So, on a very basic level, the longer they take, the more time you spend waiting for your tests, and that will slow down your development. But there's more to it than that.

The Holy Flow State

Thinking sociology for a moment, we programmers have our own culture, and our own tribal religion in a way. It has many congregations within it, such as the cult of TDD to which you are now initiated. There are the followers of vi and the heretics of emacs. But one thing we all agree on, one particular spiritual practice, our own transcendental meditation, is the holy flow state. That feeling of pure focus, of concentration, where hours pass like no time at all, where code flows naturally from our fingers, where problems are just tricky enough to be interesting but not so hard that they defeat us…

There is absolutely no hope of achieving flow if you spend your time waiting for a slow test suite to run. Anything longer than a few seconds and you're going to let your attention wander, you context-switch, and the flow state is gone. And the flow state is a fragile dream. Once it's gone, it takes at least 15 minutes to live again.

Slow Tests Don't Get Run as Often, Which Causes Bad Code

If your test suite is slow and ruins your concentration, the danger is that you'll start to avoid running your tests, which may lead to bugs getting through. Or, it may lead to our being shy of refactoring the code, since we know that any refactor will mean having to wait ages while all the tests run. In either case, bad code can be the result.

We're Fine Now, but Integrated Tests Get Slower Over Time

You might be thinking, OK, but our test suite has lots of integrated tests in it—over 50 of them, and it only takes 0.2 seconds to run.

But remember, we've got a very simple app. Once it starts to get more complex, as your database grows more and more tables and columns, integrated tests will get slower and slower. Having Django reset the database between each test will take longer and longer.

Don't Take It from Me

Gary Bernhardt, a man with far more experience of testing than me, put these points eloquently in a talk called Fast Test, Slow Test (*https://www.youtube.com/watch?v=RAxiiRPHS9k*). I encourage you to watch it.

And Unit Tests Drive Good Design

But perhaps more importantly than any of this, remember the lesson from Chapter 23. Going through the process of writing good, isolated unit tests can help us drive out better designs for our code, by forcing us to identify dependencies, and encouraging us towards a decoupled architecture in a way that integrated tests don't.

The Problems with "Pure" Unit Tests

All of this comes with a huge "but". Writing isolated united tests comes with its own hazards, particularly if, like you or me, we are not yet advanced TDD'ers.

Isolated Tests Can Be Harder to Read and Write

Cast your mind back to the first isolated unit test we wrote. Wasn't it ugly? Admittedly, things improved when we refactored things out into the forms, but imagine if we hadn't followed through? We'd have been left with a rather unreadable test in our codebase. And even the final version of the tests we ended up with contain some pretty mind-bending bits.

Isolated Tests Don't Automatically Test Integration

As we saw a little later on, isolated tests by their nature only test the unit under test, in isolation. They won't test the integration between your units.

This problem is well known, and there are ways of mitigating it. But, as we saw, those mitigations involve a fair bit of hard work on the part of the programmer—you need to remember to keep track of the interfaces between your units, to identify the implicit contract that each component needs to honour, and to write tests for those contracts as well as for the internal functionality of your unit.

Unit Tests Seldom Catch Unexpected Bugs

Unit tests will help you catch off-by-one errors and logic snafus, which are the kinds of bugs we know we introduce all the time, so in a way we are expecting them. But they don't warn you about some of the more unexpected bugs. They won't remind you when you forgot to create a database migration. They won't tell you when the middleware layer is doing some clever HTML-entity escaping that's interfering with the way your data is rendered…something like Donald Rumsfeld's unknown unknowns?

Mocky Tests Can Become Closely Tied to Implementation

And finally, mocky tests can become very tightly coupled with the implementation. If you choose to use `List.objects.create()` to build your objects but your mocks are expecting you to use `List()` and `.save()`, you'll get failing tests even though the actual effect of the code would be the same. If you're not careful, this can start to work against one of the supposed benefits of having tests, which was to encourage refactoring. You can find yourself having to change dozens of mocky tests and contract tests when you want to change an internal API.

Notice that this may be more of a problem when you're dealing with an API you don't control. You may remember the contortions we had to go through to test our form, mocking out two Django model classes and using `side_effect` to check on the state of the world. If you're writing code that's totally under your own control, you're likely to design your internal APIs so that they are cleaner and require fewer contortions to test.

But All These Problems Can Be Overcome

But, isolation advocates will come back and say, all that stuff can be mitigated; you just need to get better at writing isolated tests, and, remember the holy flow state? The holy flow state!

So do we have to choose one side or the other?

Synthesis: What Do We Want from Our Tests, Anyway?

Let's step back and have a think about what benefits we want our tests to deliver. Why are we writing them in the first place?

Correctness

We want our application to be free of bugs—both low-level logic errors, like off-by-one errors, and high-level bugs like the software not ultimately delivering what our users want. We want to find out if we ever introduce regressions which break something that used to work, and we want to find that out before our users see something broken. We expect our tests to tell us our application is correct.

Clean, Maintainable Code

We want our code to obey rules like YAGNI and DRY. We want code that clearly expresses its intentions, which is broken up into sensible components that have well-defined responsibilities and are easily understood. We expect our tests to give us the confidence to refactor our application constantly, so that we're never scared to try to improve its design, and we would also like it if they would actively help us to find the right design.

Productive Workflow

Finally, we want our tests to help enable a fast and productive workflow. We want them to help take some of the stress out of development, and we want them to protect us from stupid mistakes. We want them to help keep us in the "flow" state not just because we enjoy it, but because it's highly productive. We want our tests to give us feedback about our work as quickly as possible, so that we can try out new ideas and evolve them quickly. And we don't want to feel like our tests are more of a hindrance than a help when it comes to evolving our codebase.

Evaluate Your Tests Against the Benefits You Want from Them

I don't think there are any universal rules about how many tests you should write and what the correct balance between functional, integrated, and isolated tests should be. Circumstances vary between projects. But, by thinking about all of your tests and asking whether they are delivering the benefits you want, you can make some decisions.

Table 26-1. How do different types of test help us achieve our objectives?

Objective	Some considerations
Correctness	• Do I have enough functional tests to reassure myself that my application *really* works, from the point of view of the user?
	• Am I testing all the edge cases thoroughly? This feels like a job for low-level, isolated tests.
	• Do I have tests that check whether all my components fit together properly? Could some integrated tests do this, or are functional tests enough?
Clean, maintainable code	• Are my tests giving me the confidence to refactor my code, fearlessly and frequently?
	• Are my tests helping me to drive out a good design? If I have a lot of integrated tests and few isolated tests, are there any parts of my application where putting in the effort to write more isolated tests would give me better feedback about my design?

Objective	Some considerations
Productive workflow	• Are my feedback cycles as fast as I would like them? When do I get warned about bugs, and is there any practical way to make that happen sooner?
	• If I have a lot of high-level, functional tests that take a long time to run, and I have to wait overnight to get feedback about accidental regressions, is there some way I could write some faster tests, integrated tests perhaps, that would get me feedback quicker?
	• Can I run a subset of the full test suite when I need to?
	• Am I spending too much time waiting for tests to run, and thus less time in a productive flow state?

Architectural Solutions

There are also some architectural solutions that can help to get the most out of your test suite, and particularly that help avoid some of the disadvantages of isolated tests.

Mainly these involve trying to identify the boundaries of your system—the points at which your code interacts with external systems, like the database or the filesystem, or the internet, or the UI—and trying to keep them separate from the core business logic of your application.

Ports and Adapters/Hexagonal/Clean Architecture

Integrated tests are most useful at the *boundaries* of a system—at the points where our code integrates with external systems, like a database, filesystem, or UI components.

Similarly, it's at the boundaries that the downsides of test isolation and mocks are at their worst, because it's at the boundaries that you're most likely to be annoyed if your tests are tightly coupled to an implementation, or to need more reassurance that things are integrated properly.

Conversely, code at the *core* of our application—code that's purely concerned with our business domain and business rules, code that's entirely under our control—has less need for integrated tests, since we control and understand all of it.

So one way of getting what we want is to try to minimise the amount of our code that has to deal with boundaries. Then we test our core business logic with isolated tests and test our integration points with integrated tests.

Steve Freeman and Nat Pryce, in their book *Growing Object-Oriented Software, Guided by Tests*, call this approach "Ports and Adapters" (see Figure 26-1).

We actually started moving towards a ports and adapters architecture in Chapter 23, when we found that writing isolated unit tests was encouraging us to push ORM code out of the main application, and hide it in helper functions from the model layer.

This pattern is also sometimes known as the "clean architecture" or "hexagonal architecture". See "Further Reading" on page 477 for more info.

Functional Core, Imperative Shell

Gary Bernhardt pushes this further, recommending an architecture he calls "Functional Core, Imperative Shell", whereby the "shell" of the application, the place where interaction with boundaries happens, follows the imperative programming paradigm, and can be tested by integrated tests, acceptance tests, or even (gasp!) not at all, if it's kept minimal enough. But the core of the application is actually written following the functional programming paradigm (complete with the "no side effects" corollary), which actually allows fully isolated, "pure" unit tests, *entirely without mocks*.

Check out Gary's presentation titled "Boundaries" (*https://www.youtube.com/watch?v=eOYal8elnZk*) for more on this approach.

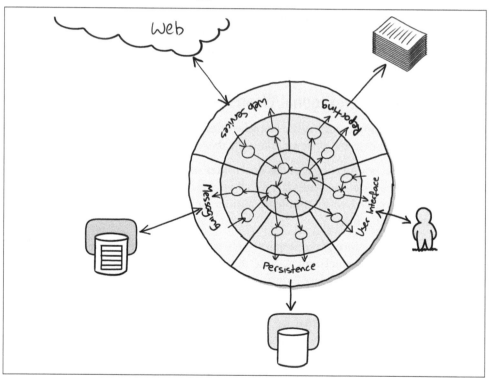

Figure 26-1. Ports and Adapters (diagram by Nat Pryce)

Conclusion

I've tried to give an overview of some of the more advanced considerations that come into the TDD process. Mastery of these topics is something that comes from long years of practice, and I'm not there yet, by any means. So I heartily encourage you to take everything I've said with a pinch of salt, to go out there, try various approaches, listen to what other people have to say too, and find out what works for you.

Here are some places to go for further reading.

Further Reading

Fast Test, Slow Test and Boundaries
> Gary Bernhardt's talks from Pycon 2012 (*https://www.youtube.com/watch?v=RAx iiRPHS9k*) and 2013 (*https://www.youtube.com/watch?v=eOYal8elnZk*). His screencasts (*http://www.destroyallsoftware.com*) are also well worth a look.

Ports and Adapters
> Steve Freeman and Nat Pryce wrote about this in their book. You can also catch a good discussion in this talk (*http://vimeo.com/83960706*). See also Uncle Bob's description of the clean architecture (*http://blog.8thlight.com/uncle-bob/ 2012/08/13/the-clean-architecture.html*), and Alistair Cockburn coining the term "hexagonal architecture" (*http://alistair.cockburn.us/Hexagonal+architecture*).

Hot Lava
> Casey Kinsey's memorable phrase (*https://www.youtube.com/watch? v=bsmFVb8guMU*) encouraging you to avoid touching the database, whenever you can.

Inverting the Pyramid
> The idea that projects end up with too great a ratio of slow, high-level tests to unit tests, and a visual metaphor for the effort to invert that ratio (*http://watirme lon.com/tag/testing-pyramid/*).

Integrated tests are a scam
> J.B. Rainsberger has a famous rant (*http://blog.thecodewhisperer.com/2010/10/16/ integrated-tests-are-a-scam/*) about the way integrated tests will ruin your life. Then check out a couple of follow-up posts, particularly this defence of acceptance tests (*http://www.jbrains.ca/permalink/using-integration-tests-mindfully-a-case-study*) (what I call functional tests), and this analysis of how slow tests kill productivity (*http://www.jbrains.ca/permalink/part-2-some-hidden-costs-of-integration-tests*).

The Test-Double testing wiki
> Justin Searls's online resource is a great source of definitions and discussions of testing pros and cons, and arrives at its own conclusions of the right way to do things: testing wiki (*https://github.com/testdouble/contributing-tests/wiki/Test-Driven-Development*).

A pragmatic view

Martin Fowler (author of *Refactoring*) presents a reasonably balanced, pragmatic approach (*http://martinfowler.com/bliki/UnitTest.html*).

On Getting the Balance Right Between Different Types of Test

Start out by being pragmatic

Spending a long time agonising about what kinds of test to write is a great way to prevaricate. Better to start by writing whichever type of test occurs to you first, and change it later if you need to. Learn by doing.

Focus on what you want from your tests

Your objectives are *correctness*, *good design*, and *fast feedback cycles*. Different types of test will help you achieve each of these in different measures. Table 26-1 has some good questions to ask yourself.

Architecture matters

Your architecture to some extent dictates the types of tests that you need. The more you can separate your business logic from your external dependencies, and the more modular your code, the closer you'll get to a nice balance between unit tests, integration tests and end-to-end tests.

Obey the Testing Goat!

Back to the Testing Goat.

Groan, I hear you say, *Harry, the Testing Goat stopped being funny about 17 chapters ago*. Bear with me, I'm going to use it to make a serious point.

Testing Is Hard

I think the reason the phrase "Obey the Testing Goat" first grabbed me when I saw it was that it really spoke to the fact that testing is hard—not hard to do in and of itself, but hard to *stick to*, and hard to keep doing.

It always feels easier to cut corners and skip a few tests. And it's doubly hard psychologically because the payoff is so disconnected from the point at which you put in the effort. A test you spend time writing now doesn't reward you immediately, it only helps much later—perhaps months later when it saves you from introducing a bug while refactoring, or catches a regression when you upgrade a dependency. Or, perhaps it pays you back in a way that's hard to measure, by encouraging you to write better designed code, but you convince yourself you could have written it just as elegantly without tests.

I myself started slipping when I was writing the test framework for this book (*https://github.com/hjwp/Book-TDD-Web-Dev-Python/tree/master/tests*). Being a quite complex beast, it has tests of its own, but I cut several corners, coverage isn't perfect, and I now regret it because it's turned out quite unwieldy and ugly (go on, I've open sourced it now, so you can all point and laugh).

Keep Your CI Builds Green

Another area that takes real hard work is continuous integration. You saw in Chapter 24 that strange and unpredictable bugs sometimes occur on CI. When you're looking at these and thinking "it works fine on my machine", there's a strong temptation to just ignore them…but, if you're not careful, you start to tolerate a failing test suite in CI, and pretty soon your CI build is actually useless, and it feels like too much work to get it going again. Don't fall into that trap. Persist, and you'll find the reason that your test is failing, and you'll find a way to lock it down and make it deterministic, and green, again.

Take Pride in Your Tests, as You Do in Your Code

One of the things that helps is to stop thinking of your tests as being an incidental add-on to the "real" code, and to start thinking of them as being a part of the finished product that you're building—a part that should be just as finely polished, just as aesthetically pleasing, and a part you can be justly proud of delivering…

So do it because the Testing Goat says so. Do it because you know the payoff will be worth it, even if it's not immediate. Do it out of a sense of duty, or professionalism, or OCD, or sheer bloody-mindedness. Do it because it's a good thing to practice. And, eventually, do it because it makes software development more fun.

Remember to Tip the Bar Staff

This book wouldn't have been possible without the backing of my publisher, the wonderful O'Reilly Media. If you're reading the free edition online, I hope you'll consider buying a real copy (*https://shop.oreilly.com/product/0636920051091.do*)…if you don't need one for yourself, then maybe as a gift for a friend?

Don't Be a Stranger!

I hope you enjoyed the book. Do get in touch and tell me what you thought!

Harry.

- @hjwp (*https://twitter.com/hjwp*)
- *obeythetestinggoat@gmail.com*

PythonAnywhere

This book is based on the assumption that you're running Python and coding on your own computer. Of course, that's not the only way to code Python these days; you could use an online platform like PythonAnywhere (which is where I work, incidentally).

It is possible to follow along with the book on PythonAnywhere, but it does require several tweaks and changes—you'll need to set up a web app instead of the test server, you'll need to use Xvfb to run the Functional Tests, and, once you get to the deployment chapters, you'll need to upgrade to a paying account. So, it is possible, but it might be easier to follow along on your own PC.

With that caveat, if you're still keen to give it a try, here are some details on what you need to do.

If you haven't already, you'll need to sign up for a PythonAnywhere account. A free one should be fine.

Then, start a *Bash Console* from the consoles page. That's where we'll do most of our work.

Running Firefox Selenium Sessions with Xvfb

The first thing is that PythonAnywhere is a console-only environment, so it doesn't have a display in which to pop up Firefox. But we can use a virtual display.

In Chapter 1, when we write our first ever test, you'll find things don't work as expected. The first test looks like this, and you can type it in using the PythonAnywhere editor just fine:

```
from selenium import webdriver
browser = webdriver.Firefox()
browser.get('http://localhost:8000')
assert 'Django' in browser.title
```

But when you try to run it (in a *Bash console*), you'll get an error:

```
(virtualenv)$ python functional_tests.py
Traceback (most recent call last):
File "tests.py", line 3, in <module>
browser = webdriver.Firefox()
[...]
selenium.common.exceptions.WebDriverException: Message: 'geckodriver' executable
needs to be in PATH.
```

Because PythonAnywhere is pinned to an older version of Firefox, we don't actually need Geckodriver. But we do need to switch back to Selenium 2 instead of Selenium 3:

```
(virtualenv) $ pip install "selenium<3"
Collecting selenium<3
Installing collected packages: selenium
  Found existing installation: selenium 3.4.3
    Uninstalling selenium-3.4.3:
      Successfully uninstalled selenium-3.4.3
Successfully installed selenium-2.53.6
```

Now we run into a second problem:

```
(virtualenv)$ python functional_tests.py
Traceback (most recent call last):
File "tests.py", line 3, in <module>
browser = webdriver.Firefox()
[...]
selenium.common.exceptions.WebDriverException: Message: The browser appears to
have exited before we could connect. If you specified a log_file in the
FirefoxBinary constructor, check it for details.
```

Firefox can't start because there's no display for it to run on, because PythonAnywhere is a server environment. The workaround is to use *Xvfb*, which stands for X Virtual Framebuffer. It will start up a "virtual" display, which Firefox can use even though the server doesn't have a real one (we use the same tool in Chapter 24 to run tests on a CI server).

The command xvfb-run will run the next command in Xvfb. Using that will give us our expected failure:

```
(virtualenv)$ xvfb-run -a python functional_tests.py
Traceback (most recent call last):
File "tests.py", line 11, in <module>
assert 'Django' in browser.title
AssertionError
```

So the lesson is to use `xvfb-run -a` whenever you need to run the functional tests.

Setting Up Django as a PythonAnywhere Web App

Shortly after that, we set up Django, using the `django-admin.py startproject` command. But, instead of using `manage.py runserver` to run the local development server, we'll set up our site as a real PythonAnywhere web app.

Go to the Web tab and hit the button to add a new web app. Choose "Manual configuration" and then "Python 3.4".

On the next screen, enter your virtualenv path (e.g., */home/yourusername/superlists/virtualenv*).

Finally, click through to the link to *edit your wsgi file* and find and uncomment the section for Django. Hit Save and then Reload to refresh your web app.

From now on, instead of running the test server from a console on `localhost:8000`, you can use the real URL of your PythonAnywhere web app:

```
browser.get('http://my-username.pythonanywhere.com')
```

 You'll need to remember to hit Reload whenever you make changes to the code, to update the site.

That should work better.[1] You'll need to keep using this pattern of pointing the FTs at the PythonAnywhere version of the site, and hitting Reload before each FT run, until Chapter 7, when we switch to using `LiveServerTestCase` and `self.live_server_url`.

Cleaning Up /tmp

Selenium and Xvfb tend to leave a lot of junk lying around in */tmp*, especially when they're not shut down tidily (that's why I included a `try`/`finally` earlier).

In fact they leave so much stuff lying around that they might max out your storage quota. So do a tidy-up in */tmp* every so often:

---

1 You *could* run the Django dev server from a console instead, but the problem is that PythonAnywhere consoles don't always run on the same server, so there's no guarantee that the console you're running your tests in is the same as the one you're running the server in. Plus, when it's running in the console, there's no easy way of visually inspecting how the site looks.

```
$ rm -rf /tmp/*
```

Screenshots

In Chapter 5, I suggest using a `time.sleep` to pause the FT as it runs, so that we can see what the Selenium browser is showing on screen. We can't do that on PythonAnywhere, because the browser runs in a virtual display. Instead, you can inspect the live site, or you could "take my word for it" regarding what you should see.

The best way of doing visual inspections of tests that run in a virtual display is to use screenshots. Take a look at Chapter 24 if you're curious—there's some example code in there.

The Deployment Chapter

When you hit Chapter 9, you'll have the choice of continuing to use PythonAnywhere, or of learning how to build a "real" server. I recommend the latter, because you'll get the most out of it.

If you really want to stick with PythonAnywhere, which is cheating really, you could sign up for a second PythonAnywhere account and use that as your staging site. Or you could add a second domain to your existing account. But most of the instructions in the chapter will be irrelevant (there's no need for Nginx or Gunicorn or domain sockets on PythonAnywhere).

One way or another, at this point, you'll probably need a paying account:

- If you want to run your staging site on a non-PythonAnywhere domain
- If you want to be able to run the FTs against a non-PythonAnywhere domain (because it won't be on our whitelist)
- Once you get to Chapter 11, if you want to run Fabric against a PythonAnywhere account (because you need SSH)

If you want to just "cheat", you could try running the FTs in "staging" mode against your existing web app, and just skip the Fabric stuff, although that's a big cop-out if you ask me. Hey, you can always upgrade your account and then cancel again straight away, and claim a refund under the 30-day guarantee. ;)

 If you are using PythonAnywhere to follow through with the book, I'd love to hear how you get on! Do send me an email at *obeythetestinggoat@gmail.com*.

Django Class-Based Views

This appendix follows on from Chapter 15, in which we implemented Django forms for validation and refactored our views. By the end of that chapter, our views were still using functions.

The new shiny in the Django world, however, is class-based views. In this appendix, we'll refactor our application to use them instead of view functions. More specifically, we'll have a go at using class-based *generic* views.

Class-Based Generic Views

There's a difference between class-based views and class-based *generic* views. Class-based views (CBVs) are just another way of defining view functions. They make few assumptions about what your views will do, and they offer one main advantage over view functions, which is that they can be subclassed. This comes, arguably, at the expense of being less readable than traditional function-based views. The main use case for *plain* class-based views is when you have several views that reuse the same logic. We want to obey the DRY principle. With function-based views, you would use helper functions or decorators. The theory is that using a class structure may give you a more elegant solution.

Class-based *generic* views (CBGVs) are class-based views that attempt to provide ready-made solutions to common use cases: fetching an object from the database and passing it to a template, fetching a list of objects, saving user input from a POST request using a `ModelForm`, and so on. These sound very much like our use cases, but as we'll soon see, the devil is in the details.

I should say at this point that I've not used either kind of class-based views much. I can definitely see the sense in them, and there are potentially many use cases in Django apps where CBGVs would fit in perfectly. However, as soon as your use case is slightly outside the basics—as soon as you have more than one model you want to use, for example—I find that using class-based views can (again, debatably) lead to code that's much harder to read than a classic view function.

Still, because we're forced to use several of the customisation options for class-based views, implementing them in this case can teach us a lot about how they work, and how we can unit test them.

My hope is that the same unit tests we use for function-based views should work just as well for class-based views. Let's see how we get on.

The Home Page as a FormView

Our home page just displays a form on a template:

lists/views.py

```python
def home_page(request):
    return render(request, 'home.html', {'form': ItemForm()})
```

Looking through the options (*https://docs.djangoproject.com/en/1.11/ref/class-based-views/*), Django has a generic view called `FormView`—let's see how that goes:

lists/views.py (ch31l001)

```python
from django.views.generic import FormView
[...]


class HomePageView(FormView):
    template_name = 'home.html'
    form_class = ItemForm
```

We tell it what template we want to use, and which form. Then, we just need to update *urls.py*, replacing the line that used to say `lists.views.home_page`:

superlists/urls.py (ch31l002)

```python
[...]
urlpatterns = [
    url(r'^$', list_views.HomePageView.as_view(), name='home'),
    url(r'^lists/', include(list_urls)),
]
```

And the tests all check out! That was easy...

```
$ python manage.py test lists
[...]

Ran 34 tests in 0.119s
OK
```

```
$ python manage.py test functional_tests
[...]
Ran 5 tests in 15.160s
OK
```

So far, so good. We've replaced a one-line view function with a two-line class, but it's still very readable. This would be a good time for a commit...

Using form_valid to Customise a CreateView

Next we have a crack at the view we use to create a brand new list, currently the new_list function. Here's what it looks like now:

lists/views.py

```python
def new_list(request):
    form = ItemForm(data=request.POST)
    if form.is_valid():
        list_ = List.objects.create()
        form.save(for_list=list_)
        return redirect(list_)
    else:
        return render(request, 'home.html', {"form": form})
```

Looking through the possible CBGVs, we probably want a CreateView, and we know we're using the ItemForm class, so let's see how we get on with them, and whether the tests will help us:

lists/views.py (ch31l003)

```python
from django.views.generic import FormView, CreateView
[...]

class NewListView(CreateView):
    form_class = ItemForm

def new_list(request):
    [...]
```

I'm going to leave the old view function in *views.py*, so that we can copy code across from it. We can delete it once everything is working. It's harmless as soon as we switch over the URL mappings, this time in:

lists/urls.py (ch31l004)

```python
[...]
urlpatterns = [
    url(r'^new$', views.NewListView.as_view(), name='new_list'),
    url(r'^(\d+)/$', views.view_list, name='view_list'),
]
```

Now running the tests gives six errors:

```
$ python manage.py test lists
[...]

ERROR: test_can_save_a_POST_request (lists.tests.test_views.NewListTest)
TypeError: save() missing 1 required positional argument: 'for_list'

ERROR: test_for_invalid_input_passes_form_to_template
(lists.tests.test_views.NewListTest)
django.core.exceptions.ImproperlyConfigured: TemplateResponseMixin requires
either a definition of 'template_name' or an implementation of
'get_template_names()'

ERROR: test_for_invalid_input_renders_home_template
(lists.tests.test_views.NewListTest)
django.core.exceptions.ImproperlyConfigured: TemplateResponseMixin requires
either a definition of 'template_name' or an implementation of
'get_template_names()'

ERROR: test_invalid_list_items_arent_saved (lists.tests.test_views.NewListTest)
django.core.exceptions.ImproperlyConfigured: TemplateResponseMixin requires
either a definition of 'template_name' or an implementation of
'get_template_names()'

ERROR: test_redirects_after_POST (lists.tests.test_views.NewListTest)
TypeError: save() missing 1 required positional argument: 'for_list'

ERROR: test_validation_errors_are_shown_on_home_page
(lists.tests.test_views.NewListTest)
django.core.exceptions.ImproperlyConfigured: TemplateResponseMixin requires
either a definition of 'template_name' or an implementation of
'get_template_names()'


FAILED (errors=6)
```

Let's start with the third—maybe we can just add the template?

lists/views.py (ch31l005)

```
class NewListView(CreateView):
    form_class = ItemForm
    template_name = 'home.html'
```

That gets us down to just two failures: we can see they're both happening in the generic view's `form_valid` function, and that's one of the ones that you can override to provide custom behaviour in a CBGV. As its name implies, it's run when the view has detected a valid form. We can just copy some of the code from our old view function, that used to live after `if form.is_valid()`::

```python
class NewListView(CreateView):
    template_name = 'home.html'
    form_class = ItemForm

    def form_valid(self, form):
        list_ = List.objects.create()
        form.save(for_list=list_)
        return redirect(list_)
```

That gets us a full pass!

```
$ python manage.py test lists
Ran 34 tests in 0.119s
OK
$ python manage.py test functional_tests
Ran 5 tests in 15.157s
OK
```

And we *could* even save two more lines, trying to obey "DRY", by using one of the main advantages of CBVs: inheritance!

```python
class NewListView(CreateView, HomePageView):

    def form_valid(self, form):
        list_ = List.objects.create()
        form.save(for_list=list_)
        return redirect(list_)
```

And all the tests would still pass:

```
OK
```

 This is not really good object-oriented practice. Inheritance implies an "is-a" relationship, and it's probably not meaningful to say that our new list view "is-a" home page view…so, probably best not to do this.

With or without that last step, how does it compare to the old version? I'd say that's not bad. We save some boilerplate code, and the view is still fairly legible. So far, I'd say we've got one point for CBGVs, and one draw.

A More Complex View to Handle Both Viewing and Adding to a List

This took me *several* attempts. And I have to say that, although the tests told me when I got it right, they didn't really help me to figure out the steps to get there…mostly it was just trial and error, hacking about in functions like `get_context_data`, `get_form_kwargs`, and so on.

One thing it did made me realise was the value of having lots of individual tests, each testing one thing. I went back and rewrote some of Chapters 10–12 as a result.

The Tests Guide Us, for a While

Here's how things might go. Start by thinking we want a `DetailView`, something that shows you the detail of an object:

lists/views.py (ch31l009)
```
from django.views.generic import FormView, CreateView, DetailView
[...]

class ViewAndAddToList(DetailView):
    model = List
```

And wiring it up in *urls.py*:

lists/urls.py (ch31l010)
```
url(r'^(\d+)/$', views.ViewAndAddToList.as_view(), name='view_list'),
```

That gives:
```
[...]
AttributeError: Generic detail view ViewAndAddToList must be called with either
an object pk or a slug.


FAILED (failures=5, errors=6)
```

Not totally obvious, but a bit of Googling around led me to understand that I needed to use a "named" regex capture group:

```
@@ -3,6 +3,6 @@ from lists import views

 urlpatterns = [
     url(r'^new$', views.NewListView.as_view(), name='new_list'),
-    url(r'^(\d+)/$', views.view_list, name='view_list'),
+    url(r'^(?P<pk>\d+)/$', views.ViewAndAddToList.as_view(), name='view_list')
 ]
```

The next set of errors had one that was fairly helpful:

```
[...]
django.template.exceptions.TemplateDoesNotExist: lists/list_detail.html

FAILED (failures=5, errors=6)
```

That's easily solved:

```
class ViewAndAddToList(DetailView):
    model = List
    template_name = 'list.html'
```

That takes us down five and two:

```
[...]
ERROR: test_displays_item_form (lists.tests.test_views.ListViewTest)
KeyError: 'form'

FAILED (failures=5, errors=2)
```

Until We're Left with Trial and Error

So I figured, our view doesn't just show us the detail of an object, it also allows us to create new ones. Let's make it both a `DetailView` *and* a `CreateView`, and maybe add the `form_class`:

```
class ViewAndAddToList(DetailView, CreateView):
    model = List
    template_name = 'list.html'
    form_class = ExistingListItemForm
```

But that gives us a lot of errors saying:

```
[...]
TypeError: __init__() missing 1 required positional argument: 'for_list'
```

And the `KeyError: 'form'` was still there too!

At this point the errors stopped being quite as helpful, and it was no longer obvious what to do next. I had to resort to trial and error. Still, the tests did at least tell me when I was getting things more right or more wrong.

My first attempts to use get_form_kwargs didn't really work, but I found that I could use get_form:

lists/views.py (ch31l014)

```python
def get_form(self):
    self.object = self.get_object()
    return self.form_class(for_list=self.object, data=self.request.POST)
```

But it would only work if I also assigned to self.object, as a side effect, along the way, which was a bit upsetting. Still, that takes us down to just three errors, but we're still apparently not quite there!

```
django.core.exceptions.ImproperlyConfigured: No URL to redirect to.  Either
provide a url or define a get_absolute_url method on the Model.
```

Back on Track

And for this final failure, the tests are being helpful again. It's quite easy to define a get_absolute_url on the Item class, such that items point to their parent list's page:

lists/models.py (ch31l015)

```python
class Item(models.Model):
    [...]

    def get_absolute_url(self):
        return reverse('view_list', args=[self.list.id])
```

Is That Your Final Answer?

We end up with a view class that looks like this:

lists/views.py

```python
class ViewAndAddToList(DetailView, CreateView):
    model = List
    template_name = 'list.html'
    form_class = ExistingListItemForm

    def get_form(self):
        self.object = self.get_object()
        return self.form_class(for_list=self.object, data=self.request.POST)
```

Compare Old and New

Let's see the old version for comparison?

lists/views.py

```python
def view_list(request, list_id):
    list_ = List.objects.get(id=list_id)
    form = ExistingListItemForm(for_list=list_)
    if request.method == 'POST':
        form = ExistingListItemForm(for_list=list_, data=request.POST)
        if form.is_valid():
            form.save()
            return redirect(list_)
    return render(request, 'list.html', {'list': list_, "form": form})
```

Well, it has reduced the number of lines of code from nine to seven. Still, I find the function-based version a little easier to understand, in that it has a little bit less magic —"explicit is better than implicit", as the Zen of Python would have it. I mean… `SingleObjectMixin`? What? And, more offensively, the whole thing falls apart if we don't assign to `self.object` inside `get_form`? Yuck.

Still, I guess some of it is in the eye of the beholder.

Best Practices for Unit Testing CBGVs?

As I was working through this, I felt like my "unit" tests were sometimes a little too high-level. This is no surprise, since tests for views that involve the Django Test Client are probably more properly called integrated tests.

They told me whether I was getting things right or wrong, but they didn't always offer enough clues on exactly how to fix things.

I occasionally wondered whether there might be some mileage in a test that was closer to the implementation—something like this:

lists/tests/test_views.py

```python
def test_cbv_gets_correct_object(self):
    our_list = List.objects.create()
    view = ViewAndAddToList()
    view.kwargs = dict(pk=our_list.id)
    self.assertEqual(view.get_object(), our_list)
```

But the problem is that it requires a lot of knowledge of the internals of Django CBVs to be able to do the right test setup for these kinds of tests. And you still end up getting very confused by the complex inheritance hierarchy.

Take-Home: Having Multiple, Isolated View Tests with Single Assertions Helps

One thing I definitely did conclude from this appendix was that having many short unit tests for views was much more helpful than having a few tests with a narrative series of assertions.

Consider this monolithic test:

lists/tests/test_views.py

```python
def test_validation_errors_sent_back_to_home_page_template(self):
    response = self.client.post('/lists/new', data={'text': ''})
    self.assertEqual(List.objects.all().count(), 0)
    self.assertEqual(Item.objects.all().count(), 0)
    self.assertTemplateUsed(response, 'home.html')
    expected_error = escape("You can't have an empty list item")
    self.assertContains(response, expected_error)
```

That is definitely less useful than having three individual tests, like this:

lists/tests/test_views.py

```python
def test_invalid_input_means_nothing_saved_to_db(self):
    self.post_invalid_input()
    self.assertEqual(List.objects.all().count(), 0)
    self.assertEqual(Item.objects.all().count(), 0)

def test_invalid_input_renders_list_template(self):
    response = self.post_invalid_input()
    self.assertTemplateUsed(response, 'list.html')

def test_invalid_input_renders_form_with_errors(self):
    response = self.post_invalid_input()
    self.assertIsinstance(response.context['form'], ExistingListItemForm)
    self.assertContains(response, escape(empty_list_error))
```

The reason is that, in the first case, an early failure means not all the assertions are checked. So, if the view was accidentally saving to the database on invalid POST, you would get an early fail, and so you wouldn't find out whether it was using the right template or rendering the form. The second formulation makes it much easier to pick out exactly what was or wasn't working.

Lessons Learned from CBGVs

Class-based generic views can do anything
> It might not always be clear what's going on, but you can do just about anything with class-based generic views.

Single-assertion unit tests help refactoring
> With each unit test providing individual guidance on what works and what doesn't, it's much easier to change the implementation of our views to using this fundamentally different paradigm.

Provisioning with Ansible

We used Fabric to automate deploying new versions of the source code to our servers. But provisioning a fresh server, and updating the Nginx and Gunicorn config files, was all left as a manual process.

This is the kind of job that's increasingly given to tools called "Configuration Management" or "Continuous Deployment" tools. Chef and Puppet were the first popular ones, and in the Python world there's Salt and Ansible.

Of all of these, Ansible is the easiest to get started with. We can get it working with just two files:

```
pip2 install --user ansible  # Python 2 sadly
```

An "inventory file" at *deploy_tools/inventory.ansible* defines what servers we can run against:

deploy_tools/inventory.ansible

```
[live]
superlists.ottg.eu ansible_become=yes ansible_ssh_user=elspeth

[staging]
superlists-staging.ottg.eu ansible_become=yes ansible_ssh_user=elspeth

[local]
localhost ansible_ssh_user=root ansible_ssh_port=6666 ansible_host=127.0.0.1
```

(The local entry is just an example, in my case a Virtualbox VM, with port forwarding for ports 22 and 80 set up.)

Installing System Packages and Nginx

Next the Ansible "playbook", which defines what to do on the server. This uses a syntax called YAML:

deploy_tools/provision.ansible.yaml

```
---

- hosts: all

  vars:
      host: "{{ inventory_hostname }}"

  tasks:

    - name: Deadsnakes PPA to get Python 3.6
      apt_repository:
        repo='ppa:deadsnakes/ppa'
    - name: make sure required packages are installed
      apt: pkg=nginx,git,python3.6,python3.6-venv state=present

    - name: allow long hostnames in nginx
      lineinfile:
        dest=/etc/nginx/nginx.conf
        regexp='(\s+)#? ?server_names_hash_bucket_size'
        backrefs=yes
        line='\1server_names_hash_bucket_size 64;'

    - name: add nginx config to sites-available
      template: src=./nginx.conf.j2 dest=/etc/nginx/sites-available/{{ host }}
      notify:
          - restart nginx

    - name: add symlink in nginx sites-enabled
      file:
          src=/etc/nginx/sites-available/{{ host }}
          dest=/etc/nginx/sites-enabled/{{ host }}
          state=link
      notify:
          - restart nginx
```

The `inventory_hostname` variable is the domain name of the server we're running against. I'm using the `vars` section to rename it to "host", just for convenience.

In this section, we install our required software using `apt`, tweak the Nginx config to allow long hostnames using a regular expression replacer, and then write the Nginx config file using a template. This is a modified version of the template file we saved into *deploy_tools/nginx.template.conf* in Chapter 9, but it now uses a specific templating syntax—Jinja2, which is actually a lot like the Django template syntax:

```
server {
    listen 80;
    server_name {{ host }};

    location /static {
        alias /home/{{ ansible_ssh_user }}/sites/{{ host }}/static;
    }

    location / {
        proxy_set_header Host {{ host }};
        proxy_pass http://unix:/tmp/{{ host }}.socket;
    }
}
```

Configuring Gunicorn, and Using Handlers to Restart Services

Here's the second half of our playbook:

```
- name: write gunicorn service script
  template:
      src=./gunicorn.service.j2
      dest=/etc/systemd/system/gunicorn-{{ host }}.service
  notify:
      - restart gunicorn

handlers:
  - name: restart nginx
    service:  name=nginx state=restarted

  - name: restart gunicorn
    systemd:
        name=gunicorn-{{ host }}
        daemon_reload=yes
        enabled=yes
        state=restarted
```

Once again we use a template for our Gunicorn config:

```
[Unit]
Description=Gunicorn server for {{ host }}

[Service]
User={{ ansible_ssh_user }}
WorkingDirectory=/home/{{ ansible_ssh_user }}/sites/{{ host }}/source
Restart=on-failure
ExecStart=/home/{{ ansible_ssh_user }}/sites/{{ host }}/virtualenv/bin/gunicorn \
    --bind unix:/tmp/{{ host }}.socket \
    --access-logfile ../access.log \
    --error-logfile ../error.log \
    superlists.wsgi:application

[Install]
WantedBy=multi-user.target
```

Then we have two "handlers" to restart Nginx and Gunicorn. Ansible is clever, so if it sees multiple steps all call the same handlers, it waits until the last one before calling it.

And that's it! The command to kick all these off is:

```
ansible-playbook -i inventory.ansible provision.ansible.yaml --limit=staging --ask-become-pass
```

Lots more info in the Ansible docs (*https://docs.ansible.com/*).

What to Do Next

I've just given a little taster of what's possible with Ansible. But the more you automate about your deployments, the more confidence you will have in them. Here are a few more things to look into.

Move Deployment out of Fabric and into Ansible

We've seen that Ansible can help with some aspects of provisioning, but it can also do pretty much all of our deployment for us. See if you can extend the playbook to do everything that we currently do in our Fabric deploy script, including notifying the restarts as required.

Use Vagrant to Spin Up a Local VM

Running tests against the staging site gives us the ultimate confidence that things are going to work when we go live, but we can also use a VM on our local machine.

Download Vagrant and Virtualbox, and see if you can get Vagrant to build a dev server on your own PC, using our Ansible playbook to deploy code to it. Rewire the FT runner to be able to test against the local VM.

Having a Vagrant config file is particularly helpful when working in a team—it helps new developers to spin up servers that look exactly like yours.

Testing Database Migrations

Django-migrations and its predecessor South have been around for ages, so it's not usually necessary to test database migrations. But it just so happens that we're introducing a dangerous type of migration—that is, one that introduces a new integrity constraint on our data. When I first ran the migration script against staging, I saw an error.

On larger projects, where you have sensitive data, you may want the additional confidence that comes from testing your migrations in a safe environment before applying them to production data, so this toy example will hopefully be a useful rehearsal.

Another common reason to want to test migrations is for speed—migrations often involve downtime, and sometimes, when they're applied to very large datasets, they can take time. It's good to know in advance how long that might be.

An Attempted Deploy to Staging

Here's what happened to me when I first tried to deploy our new validation constraints in Chapter 17:

```
$ cd deploy_tools
$ fab deploy:host=elspeth@superlists-staging.ottg.eu
[...]
Running migrations:
  Applying lists.0005_list_item_unique_together...Traceback (most recent call
last):
  File "/usr/local/lib/python3.6/dist-packages/django/db/backends/utils.py",
line 61, in execute
    return self.cursor.execute(sql, params)
  File
"/usr/local/lib/python3.6/dist-packages/django/db/backends/sqlite3/base.py",
line 475, in execute
    return Database.Cursor.execute(self, query, params)
sqlite3.IntegrityError: columns list_id, text are not unique
[...]
```

What happened was that some of the existing data in the database violated the integrity constraint, so the database was complaining when I tried to apply it.

In order to deal with this sort of problem, we'll need to build a "data migration". Let's first set up a local environment to test against.

Running a Test Migration Locally

We'll use a copy of the live database to test our migration against.

 Be very, very, very careful when using real data for testing. For example, you may have real customer email addresses in there, and you don't want to accidentally send them a bunch of test emails. Ask me how I know this.

Entering Problematic Data

Start a list with some duplicate items on your live site, as shown in Figure D-1.

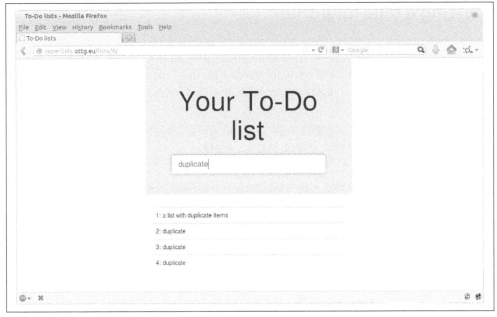

Figure D-1. A list with duplicate items

Copying Test Data from the Live Site

Copy the database down from live:

```
$ scp elspeth@superlists.ottg.eu:\
/home/elspeth/sites/superlists.ottg.eu/database/db.sqlite3 .
$ mv ../database/db.sqlite3 ../database/db.sqlite3.bak
$ mv db.sqlite3 ../database/db.sqlite3
```

Confirming the Error

We now have a local database that has not been migrated, and that contains some problematic data. We should see an error if we try to run `migrate`:

```
$ python manage.py migrate --migrate
python manage.py migrate
Operations to perform:
[...]
Running migrations:
[...]
  Applying lists.0005_list_item_unique_together...Traceback (most recent call
last):
[...]
    return Database.Cursor.execute(self, query, params)
sqlite3.IntegrityError: columns list_id, text are not unique
```

Inserting a Data Migration

Data migrations (*https://docs.djangoproject.com/en/1.11/topics/migrations/#data-migrations*) are a special type of migration that modifies data in the database rather than changing the schema. We need to create one that will run before we apply the integrity constraint, to preventively remove any duplicates. Here's how we can do that:

```
$ git rm lists/migrations/0005_list_item_unique_together.py
$ python manage.py makemigrations lists --empty
Migrations for 'lists':
  0005_auto_20140414_2325.py:
$ mv lists/migrations/0005_*.py lists/migrations/0005_remove_duplicates.py
```

Check out the Django docs on data migrations (*https://docs.djangoproject.com/en/1.11/topics/migrations/#data-migrations*) for more info, but here's how we add some instructions to change existing data:

lists/migrations/0005_remove_duplicates.py

```
# encoding: utf8
from django.db import models, migrations


def find_dupes(apps, schema_editor):
    List = apps.get_model("lists", "List")
    for list_ in List.objects.all():
        items = list_.item_set.all()
        texts = set()
        for ix, item in enumerate(items):
            if item.text in texts:
                item.text = '{} ({})'.format(item.text, ix)
                item.save()
            texts.add(item.text)


class Migration(migrations.Migration):

    dependencies = [
        ('lists', '0004_item_list'),
    ]

    operations = [
        migrations.RunPython(find_dupes),
    ]
```

Re-creating the Old Migration

We re-create the old migration using makemigrations, which will ensure it is now the sixth migration and has an explicit dependency on 0005, the data migration:

```
$ python manage.py makemigrations
Migrations for 'lists':
  0006_auto_20140415_0018.py:
    - Alter unique_together for item (1 constraints)
$ mv lists/migrations/0006_* lists/migrations/0006_unique_together.py
```

Testing the New Migrations Together

We're now ready to run our test against the live data:

```
$ cd deploy_tools
$ fab deploy:host=elspeth@superlists-staging.ottg.eu
[...]
```

We'll need to restart the live Gunicorn job too:

```
elspeth@server:$ sudo systemctl restart gunicorn-superlists.ottg.eu
```

And we can now run our FTs against staging:

```
$ STAGING_SERVER=superlists-staging.ottg.eu python manage.py test functional_tests
[...]
....
 ---------------------------------------------------------------------
Ran 4 tests in 17.308s

OK
```

Everything seems in order! Let's do it against live:

```
$ fab deploy --host=superlists.ottg.eu
[superlists.ottg.eu] Executing task 'deploy'
[...]
```

And that's a wrap. `git add lists/migrations`, `git commit`, and so on.

Conclusions

This exercise was primarily aimed at building a data migration and testing it against some real data. Inevitably, this is only a drop in the ocean of the possible testing you could do for a migration. You could imagine building automated tests to check that all your data was preserved, comparing the database contents before and after. You could write individual unit tests for the helper functions in a data migration. You could spend more time measuring the time taken for migrations, and experiment with ways to speed it up by, for example, breaking up migrations into more or fewer component steps.

Remember that this should be a relatively rare case. In my experience, I haven't felt the need to test 99% of the migrations I've worked on. But, should you ever feel the need on your project, I hope you've found a few pointers here to get started with.

On Testing Database Migrations

Be wary of migrations which introduce constraints

99% of migrations happen without a hitch, but be wary of any situations, like this one, where you are introducing a new constraint on columns that already exist.

Test migrations for speed

Once you have a larger project, you should think about testing how long your migrations are going to take. Database migrations typically involve downtime, as, depending on your database, the schema update operation may lock the table it's working on until it completes. It's a good idea to use your staging site to find out how long a migration will take.

Be extremely careful if using a dump of production data

In order to do so, you'll want fill your staging site's database with an amount of data that's commensurate to the size of your production data. Explaining how to do that is outside of the scope of this book, but I will say this: if you're tempted to just take a dump of your production database and load it into staging, be *very* careful. Production data contains real customer details, and I've personally been responsible for accidentally sending out a few hundred incorrect invoices after an automated process on my staging server started processing the copied production data I'd just loaded into it. Not a fun afternoon.

Behaviour-Driven Development (BDD)

Now I haven't used BDD "in anger," so I can't claim any sort of expertise, but I really like what I have seen of it, and I thought that you deserved at least a whirlwind tour. In this appendix, we'll take some of the tests we wrote in a "normal" FT, and convert them to using BDD tools.

What Is BDD?

BDD, *strictly* speaking, is a methodology rather than a toolset—it's the approach of testing your application by testing the behaviour that we expect it to display to a user (the Wikipedia entry (*https://en.wikipedia.org/wiki/Behavior-driven_development*) has quite a good overview). So, in some ways, the Selenium-based FTs that I've shown in the rest of the book *could* be called BDD.

But the term has become closely associated with a particular set of tools for doing BDD, most importantly the Gherkin syntax (*https://github.com/cucumber/cucumber/wiki/Gherkin*), which is a human-readable DSL for writing functional (or acceptance) tests. Gherkin originally came out of the Ruby world, where it's associated with a test runner called Cucumber (*http://cukes.info/*).

In the Python world, we have a couple of equivalent test running tools, Lettuce (*http://lettuce.it/*) and Behave (*http://pythonhosted.org/behave/*). Of these, only Behave was compatible with Python 3 at the time of writing, so that's what we'll use. We'll also use a plugin called behave-django (*https://pythonhosted.org/behave-django/*).

Basic Housekeeping

We make a directory for our BDD "features," add a *steps* directory (we'll find out what these are shortly!), and placeholder for our first feature:

```
$ mkdir -p features/steps
$ touch features/my_lists.feature
$ touch features/steps/my_lists.py
$ tree features
features
├── my_lists.feature
└── steps
    └── my_lists.py
```

We install behave-django, and add it to *settings.py*:

```
$ pip install behave-django
```

superlists/settings.py

```
--- a/superlists/settings.py
+++ b/superlists/settings.py
@@ -40,6 +40,7 @@ INSTALLED_APPS = [
     'lists',
     'accounts',
     'functional_tests',
+    'behave_django',
 ]
```

And then run python manage.py behave as a sanity check:

```
$ python manage.py behave
Creating test database for alias 'default'...
0 features passed, 0 failed, 0 skipped
0 scenarios passed, 0 failed, 0 skipped
0 steps passed, 0 failed, 0 skipped, 0 undefined
Took 0m0.000s
Destroying test database for alias 'default'...
```

Writing an FT as a "Feature" Using Gherkin Syntax

Up until now, we've been writing our FTs using human-readable comments that describe the new feature in terms of a user story, interspersed with the Selenium code required to execute each step in the story.

BDD enforces a distinction between those two—we write our human-readable story using a human-readable (if occasionally somewhat awkward) syntax called "Gherkin", and that is called the "Feature". Later, we'll map each line of Gherkin to a function that contains the Selenium code necessary to implement that "step."

Here's what a Feature for our new "My lists" page could look like:

features/my_lists.feature

```
Feature: My Lists
    As a logged-in user
    I want to be able to see all my lists in one page
    So that I can find them all after I've written them

    Scenario: Create two lists and see them on the My Lists page

        Given I am a logged-in user

        When I create a list with first item "Reticulate Splines"
            And I add an item "Immanentize Eschaton"
            And I create a list with first item "Buy milk"

        Then I will see a link to "My lists"

        When I click the link to "My lists"
        Then I will see a link to "Reticulate Splines"
        And I will see a link to "Buy milk"

        When I click the link to "Reticulate Splines"
        Then I will be on the "Reticulate Splines" list page
```

As-a /I want to/So that

At the top you'll notice the As-a/I want to/So that clause. This is optional, and it has no executable counterpart—it's just a slightly formalised way of capturing the "who and why?" aspects of a user story, gently encouraging the team to think about the justifications for each feature.

Given/When/Then

Given/When/Then is the real core of a BDD test. This trilobite formulation matches the setup/exercise/assert pattern we've seen in our unit tests, and it represents the setup and assumptions phase, an exercise/action phase, and a subsequent assertion/ observation phase. There's more info on the Cucumber wiki (*https://github.com/ cucumber/cucumber/wiki/Given-When-Then*).

Not Always a Perfect Fit!

As you can see, it's not always easy to shoe-horn a user story into exactly three steps! We can use the And clause to expand on a step, and I've added multiple When steps and subsequent Then's to illustrate further aspects of our "My lists" page.

Coding the Step Functions

We now build the counterpart to our Gherkin-syntax feature, which are the "step" functions that will actually implement them in code.

Generating Placeholder Steps

When we run behave, it helpfully tells us about all the steps we need to implement:

```
$ python manage.py behave
Feature: My Lists # features/my_lists.feature:1
  As a logged-in user
  I want to be able to see all my lists in one page
  So that I can find them all after I've written them
  Scenario: Create two lists and see them on the My Lists page  #
features/my_lists.feature:6
    Given I am a logged-in user                                  # None
    Given I am a logged-in user                                  # None
    When I create a list with first item "Reticulate Splines"    # None
    And I add an item "Immanentize Eschaton"                     # None
    And I create a list with first item "Buy milk"               # None
    Then I will see a link to "My lists"                         # None
    When I click the link to "My lists"                          # None
    Then I will see a link to "Reticulate Splines"               # None
    And I will see a link to "Buy milk"                          # None
    When I click the link to "Reticulate Splines"                # None
    Then I will be on the "Reticulate Splines" list page         # None


Failing scenarios:
  features/my_lists.feature:6  Create two lists and see them on the My Lists
page


0 features passed, 1 failed, 0 skipped
0 scenarios passed, 1 failed, 0 skipped
0 steps passed, 0 failed, 0 skipped, 10 undefined
Took 0m0.000s

You can implement step definitions for undefined steps with these snippets:

@given(u'I am a logged-in user')
def step_impl(context):
    raise NotImplementedError(u'STEP: Given I am a logged-in user')

@when(u'I create a list with first item "Reticulate Splines"')
def step_impl(context):
[...]
```

And you'll notice all this output is nicely coloured, as shown in Figure E-1.

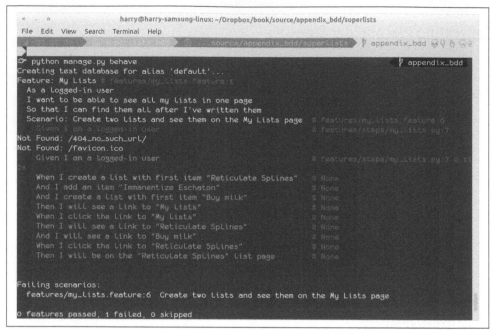

Figure E-1. Behave with coloured console ouptut

It's encouraging us to copy and paste these snippets, and use them as starting points to build our steps.

First Step Definition

Here's a first stab at making a step for our "Given I am a logged-in user" step. I started by stealing the code for `self.create_pre_authenticated_session` from *functional_tests/test_my_lists.py*, and adapting it slightly (removing the server-side version, for example, although it would be easy to re-add later).

```
from behave import given, when, then
from functional_tests.management.commands.create_session import \
    create_pre_authenticated_session
from django.conf import settings


@given('I am a logged-in user')
def given_i_am_logged_in(context):
    session_key = create_pre_authenticated_session(email='edith@example.com')
    ## to set a cookie we need to first visit the domain.
    ## 404 pages load the quickest!
    context.browser.get(context.get_url("/404_no_such_url/"))
    context.browser.add_cookie(dict(
        name=settings.SESSION_COOKIE_NAME,
        value=session_key,
        path='/',
    ))
```

The *context* variable needs a little explaining—it's a sort of global variable, in the sense that it's passed to each step that's executed, and it can be used to store information that we need to share between steps. Here we've assumed we'll be storing a browser object on it, and the `server_url`. We end up using it a lot like we used `self` when we were writing `unittest` FTs.

setUp and tearDown Equivalents in environment.py

Steps can make changes to state in the `context`, but the place to do preliminary set-up, the equivalent of `setUp`, is in a file called *environment.py*:

```
from selenium import webdriver


def before_all(context):
    context.browser = webdriver.Firefox()


def after_all(context):
    context.browser.quit()


def before_feature(context, feature):
    pass
```

Another Run

As a sanity check, we can do another run, to see if the new step works and that we really can start a browser:

```
$ python manage.py behave
[...]
1 step passed, 0 failed, 0 skipped, 9 undefined
```

The usual reams of output, but we can see that it seems to have made it through the first step; let's define the rest of them.

Capturing Parameters in Steps

We'll see how Behave allows you to capture parameters from step descriptions. Our next step says:

features/my_lists.feature

```
When I create a list with first item "Reticulate Splines"
```

And the autogenerated step definition looked like this:

features/steps/my_lists.py

```python
@given('I create a list with first item "Reticulate Splines"')
def step_impl(context):
    raise NotImplementedError(
        u'STEP: When I create a list with first item "Reticulate Splines"'
    )
```

We want to be able to create lists with arbitrary first items, so it would be nice to somehow capture whatever is between those quotes, and pass them in as an argument to a more generic function. That's a common requirement in BDD, and Behave has a nice syntax for it, reminiscent of the new-style Python string formatting syntax:

features/steps/my_lists.py (ch35l006)

```python
[...]

@when('I create a list with first item "{first_item_text}"')
def create_a_list(context, first_item_text):
    context.browser.get(context.get_url('/'))
    context.browser.find_element_by_id('id_text').send_keys(first_item_text)
    context.browser.find_element_by_id('id_text').send_keys(Keys.ENTER)
    wait_for_list_item(context, first_item_text)
```

Neat, huh?

 Capturing parameters for steps is one of the most powerful features of the BDD syntax.

As usual with Selenium tests, we will need an explicit wait. Let's re-use our @wait decorator from *base.py*:

```
from functional_tests.base import wait
[...]


@wait
def wait_for_list_item(context, item_text):
    context.test.assertIn(
        item_text,
        context.browser.find_element_by_css_selector('#id_list_table').text
    )
```

Similarly, we can add to an existing list, and see or click on links:

```
from selenium.webdriver.common.keys import Keys
[...]


@when('I add an item "{item_text}"')
def add_an_item(context, item_text):
    context.browser.find_element_by_id('id_text').send_keys(item_text)
    context.browser.find_element_by_id('id_text').send_keys(Keys.ENTER)
    wait_for_list_item(context, item_text)


@then('I will see a link to "{link_text}"')
@wait
def see_a_link(context, link_text):
    context.browser.find_element_by_link_text(link_text)


@when('I click the link to "{link_text}"')
def click_link(context, link_text):
    context.browser.find_element_by_link_text(link_text).click()
```

Notice we can even use our `@wait` decorator on steps themselves.

And finally the slightly more complex step that says I am on the page for a particular list:

```
@then('I will be on the "{first_item_text}" list page')
@wait
def on_list_page(context, first_item_text):
    first_row = context.browser.find_element_by_css_selector(
        '#id_list_table tr:first-child'
    )
    expected_row_text = '1: ' + first_item_text
    context.test.assertEqual(first_row.text, expected_row_text)
```

Now we can run it and see our first expected failure:

```
$ python manage.py behave

Feature: My Lists # features/my_lists.feature:1
  As a logged-in user
  I want to be able to see all my lists in one page
  So that I can find them all after I've written them
  Scenario: Create two lists and see them on the My Lists page  #
features/my_lists.feature:6
    Given I am a logged-in user                                 #
features/steps/my_lists.py:19
    When I create a list with first item "Reticulate Splines"   #
features/steps/my_lists.py:31
    And I add an item "Immanentize Eschaton"                    #
features/steps/my_lists.py:39
    And I create a list with first item "Buy milk"              #
features/steps/my_lists.py:31
    Then I will see a link to "My lists"                        #
functional_tests/base.py:12
      Traceback (most recent call last):
[...]
        File "features/steps/my_lists.py", line 49, in see_a_link
          context.browser.find_element_by_link_text(link_text)
[...]
      selenium.common.exceptions.NoSuchElementException: Message: Unable to
locate element: My lists

[...]

Failing scenarios:
  features/my_lists.feature:6  Create two lists and see them on the My Lists
page

0 features passed, 1 failed, 0 skipped
0 scenarios passed, 1 failed, 0 skipped
4 steps passed, 1 failed, 5 skipped, 0 undefined
```

You can see how the output really gives you a sense of how far through the "story" of the test we got: we manage to create our two lists successfully, but the "My lists" link does not appear.

Comparing the Inline-Style FT

I'm not going to run through the implementation of the feature, but you can see how the test will drive development just as well as the inline-style FT would have.

Let's have a look at it, for comparison:

```
def test_logged_in_users_lists_are_saved_as_my_lists(self):
    # Edith is a logged-in user
    self.create_pre_authenticated_session('edith@example.com')

    # She goes to the home page and starts a list
    self.browser.get(self.live_server_url)
    self.add_list_item('Reticulate splines')
    self.add_list_item('Immanentize eschaton')
    first_list_url = self.browser.current_url

    # She notices a "My lists" link, for the first time.
    self.browser.find_element_by_link_text('My lists').click()

    # She sees that her list is in there, named according to its
    # first list item
    self.wait_for(
        lambda: self.browser.find_element_by_link_text('Reticulate splines')
    )
    self.browser.find_element_by_link_text('Reticulate splines').click()
    self.wait_for(
        lambda: self.assertEqual(self.browser.current_url, first_list_url)
    )

    # She decides to start another list, just to see
    self.browser.get(self.live_server_url)
    self.add_list_item('Click cows')
    second_list_url = self.browser.current_url

    # Under "my lists", her new list appears
    self.browser.find_element_by_link_text('My lists').click()
    self.wait_for(
        lambda: self.browser.find_element_by_link_text('Click cows')
    )
    self.browser.find_element_by_link_text('Click cows').click()
    self.wait_for(
        lambda: self.assertEqual(self.browser.current_url, second_list_url)
    )

    # She logs out.  The "My lists" option disappears
    self.browser.find_element_by_link_text('Log out').click()
    self.wait_for(lambda: self.assertEqual(
        self.browser.find_elements_by_link_text('My lists'),
        []
    ))
```

It's not entirely an apples-to-apples comparison, but we can look at the number of lines of code in Table E-1.

Table E-1. Lines of code comparison

BDD	Standard FT
Feature file: 20 (3 optional)	test function body: 45
Steps file: 56 lines	helper functions: 23

The comparison isn't perfect, but you might say that the feature file and the body of a "standard FT" test function are equivalent in that they present the main "story" of a test, while the steps and helper functions represent the "hidden" implementation details. If you add them up, the total numbers are pretty similar, but notice that they're spread out differently: the BDD tests have made the story more concise, and pushed more work out into the hidden implementation details.

BDD Encourages Structured Test Code

This is the real appeal, for me: the BDD tool has *forced* us to structure our test code. In the inline-style FT, we're free to use as many lines as we want to implement a step, as described by its comment line. It's very hard to resist the urge to just copy-and-paste code from elsewhere, or just from earlier on in the test. You can see that, by this point in the book, I've built just a couple of helper functions (like `get_item_input_box`).

In contrast, the BDD syntax has immediately forced me to have a separate function for each step, so I've already built some very reusable code to:

- Start a new list
- Add an item to an existing list
- Click on a link with particular text
- Assert that I'm looking at a particular list's page

BDD really encourages you to write test code that seems to match well with the business domain, and to use a layer of abstraction between the story of your FT and its implementation in code.

The ultimate expression of this is that, theoretically, if you wanted to change programming languages, you could keep all your features in Gherkin syntax exactly as they are, and throw away the Python steps and replace them with steps implemented in another language.

The Page Pattern as an Alternative

In Chapter 25 of the book, I present an example of the "Page pattern", which is an object-oriented approach to structuring your Selenium tests. Here's a reminder of what it looks like:

functional_tests/test_sharing.py

```python
from .my_lists_page import MyListsPage
[...]

class SharingTest(FunctionalTest):

    def test_can_share_a_list_with_another_user(self):
        # [...]
        self.browser.get(self.live_server_url)
        list_page = ListPage(self).add_list_item('Get help')

        # She notices a "Share this list" option
        share_box = list_page.get_share_box()
        self.assertEqual(
            share_box.get_attribute('placeholder'),
            'your-friend@example.com'
        )

        # She shares her list.
        # The page updates to say that it's shared with Oniciferous:
        list_page.share_list_with('oniciferous@example.com')
```

And the Page class looks like this:

functional_tests/lists_pages.py

```python
class ListPage(object):

    def __init__(self, test):
        self.test = test


    def get_table_rows(self):
        return self.test.browser.find_elements_by_css_selector('#id_list_table tr')


    @wait
    def wait_for_row_in_list_table(self, item_text, item_number):
        row_text = '{}: {}'.format(item_number, item_text)
        rows = self.get_table_rows()
        self.test.assertIn(row_text, [row.text for row in rows])


    def get_item_input_box(self):
        return self.test.browser.find_element_by_id('id_text')
```

So it's definitely possible to implement a similar layer of abstraction, and a sort of DSL, in inline-style FTs, whether it's by using the Page pattern or whatever structure you prefer—but now it's a matter of self-discipline, rather than having a framework that pushes you towards it.

 In fact, you can actually use the Page pattern with BDD as well, as a resource for your steps to use when navigating the pages of your site.

BDD Might Be Less Expressive than Inline Comments

On the other hand, I can also see potential for the Gherkin syntax to feel somewhat restrictive. Compare how expressive and readable the inline-style comments are, with the slightly awkward BDD feature:

functional_tests/test_my_lists.py

```
# Edith is a logged-in user
# She goes to the home page and starts a list
# She notices a "My lists" link, for the first time.
# She sees that her list is in there, named according to its
# first list item
# She decides to start another list, just to see
# Under "my lists", her new list appears
# She logs out.  The "My lists" option disappears
[...]
```

That's much more readable and natural than our slightly forced Given/Then/When incantations, and, in a way, might encourage more user-centric thinking. (There is a syntax in Gherkin for including "comments" in a feature file, which would mitigate this somewhat, but I gather that it's not widely used.)

Will Nonprogrammers Write Tests?

I haven't touched on one of the original promises of BDD, which is that nonprogrammers—business or client representatives perhaps—might actually write the Gherkin syntax. I'm quite skeptical about whether this would actually work in the real world, but I don't think that detracts from the other potential benefits of BDD.

Some Tentative Conclusions

I've only dipped my toes into the BDD world, so I'm hesitant to draw any firm conclusions. I find the "forced" structuring of FTs into steps very appealing though—in that it looks like it has the potential to encourage a lot of reuse in your FT code, and that it neatly separates concerns between describing the story and implementing it, and that it forces us to think about things in terms of the business domain, rather than in terms of "what we need to do with Selenium."

But there's no free lunch. The Gherkin syntax is restrictive, compared to the total freedom offered by inline FT comments.

I also would like to see how BDD scales once you have not just one or two features, and four or five steps, but several dozen features and hundreds of lines of steps code.

Overall, I would say it's definitely worth investigating, and I will probably use BDD for my next personal project.

My thanks to Daniel Pope, Rachel Willmer, and Jared Contrascere for their feedback on this chapter.

BDD Conclusions

Encourages structured, reusable test code
> By separating concerns, breaking your FTs out into the human-readable, Gherkin syntax "feature" file and a separate implementation of steps functions, BDD has the potential to encourage more reusable and manageable test code.

It may come at the expense of readability
> The Gherkin syntax, for all its attempt to be human-readable, is ultimately a constraint on human language, and so it may not capture nuance and intention as well as inline comments do.

Try it! I will
> As I keep saying, I haven't used BDD on a real project, so you should take my words with a heavy pinch of salt, but I'd like to give it a hearty endorsement. I'm going to try it out on the next project I can, and I'd encourage you to do so as well.

Building a REST API: JSON, Ajax, and Mocking with JavaScript

Representational State Transfer (REST) is an approach to designing a web service to allow a user to retrieve and update information about "resources". It's become the dominant approach when designing APIs for use over the web.

We've built a working web app without needing an API so far. Why might we want one? One motivation might be to improve the user experience by making the site more dynamic. Rather than waiting for the page to refresh after each addition to a list, we can use JavaScript to fire off those requests asynchronously to our API, and give the user a more interactive feeling.

Perhaps more interestingly, once we've built an API, we can interact with our back-end application via other mechanisms than the browser. A mobile app might be one new candidate client application, another might be some sort of command-line application, or other developers might be able to build libraries and tools around your backend.

In this chapter we'll see how to build an API "by hand". In the next, I'll give an over-view of how to use a popular tool from the Django ecosystem called Django-Rest-Framework.

Our Approach for This Appendix

I won't convert the entirety of the app for now; we'll start by assuming we have an existing list. REST defines a relationship between URLs and the HTTP methods (GET and POST, but also the more funky ones like PUT and DELETE) which will guide us in our design.

The Wikipedia entry on REST (*http://bit.ly/2u6qeYw*) has a good overview. In brief:

- Our new URL structure will be */api/lists/{id}/*
- GET will give you details of a list (including all its items) in JSON format
- POST lets you add an item

We'll take the code from its state at the end of Chapter 25.

Choosing Our Test Approach

If we were building an API that was entirely agnostic about its clients, we might want to think about what levels to test it at. The equivalent of functional tests would perhaps spin up a real server (maybe using `LiveServerTestCase`) and interact with it using the `requests` library. We'd have to think carefully about how to set up fixtures (if we use the API itself, that introduces a lot of dependencies between tests) and what additional layer of lower-level/unit tests might be most useful to us. Or we might decide that a single layer of tests using the Django Test Client would be enough.

As it is, we're building an API in the context of a browser-based client side. We want to start using it on our production site, and have the app continue to provide the same functionality as it did before. So our functional tests will continue to serve the role of being the highest-level tests, and of checking the integration between our JavaScript and our API.

That leaves the Django Test Client as a natural place to site our lower-level tests. Let's start there.

Basic Piping

We start with a unit test that just checks that our new URL structure returns a 200 response to GET requests, and that it uses the JSON format (instead of HTML):

lists/tests/test_api.py

```python
import json
from django.test import TestCase

from lists.models import List, Item


class ListAPITest(TestCase):
    base_url = '/api/lists/{}/'  ❶

    def test_get_returns_json_200(self):
        list_ = List.objects.create()
        response = self.client.get(self.base_url.format(list_.id))
        self.assertEqual(response.status_code, 200)
        self.assertEqual(response['content-type'], 'application/json')
```

① Using a class-level constant for the URL under test is a new pattern we'll introduce for this appendix. It'll help us to remove duplication of hardcoded URLs. You could even use a call to `reverse` to reduce duplication even further.

First we wire up a couple of *urls* files:

superlists/urls.py

```python
from django.conf.urls import include, url
from accounts import urls as accounts_urls
from lists import views as list_views
from lists import api_urls
from lists import urls as list_urls

urlpatterns = [
    url(r'^$', list_views.home_page, name='home'),
    url(r'^lists/', include(list_urls)),
    url(r'^accounts/', include(accounts_urls)),
    url(r'^api/', include(api_urls)),
]
```

and:

lists/api_urls.py

```python
from django.conf.urls import url
from lists import api

urlpatterns = [
    url(r'^lists/(\d+)/$', api.list, name='api_list'),
]
```

And the actual core of our API can live in a file called *api.py*. Just three lines should be enough:

lists/api.py

```python
from django.http import HttpResponse

def list(request, list_id):
    return HttpResponse(content_type='application/json')
```

The tests should pass, and we have the basic piping together:

```
$ python manage.py test lists
[...]
.......................................................
 ----------------------------------------------------------------------
Ran 50 tests in 0.177s

OK
```

Actually Responding with Something

Our next step is to get our API to actually respond with some content—specifically, a JSON representation of our list items:

lists/tests/test_api.py (ch36l002)

```python
def test_get_returns_items_for_correct_list(self):
    other_list = List.objects.create()
    Item.objects.create(list=other_list, text='item 1')
    our_list = List.objects.create()
    item1 = Item.objects.create(list=our_list, text='item 1')
    item2 = Item.objects.create(list=our_list, text='item 2')
    response = self.client.get(self.base_url.format(our_list.id))
    self.assertEqual(
        json.loads(response.content.decode('utf8')),  ❶
        [
            {'id': item1.id, 'text': item1.text},
            {'id': item2.id, 'text': item2.text},
        ]
    )
```

❶ This is the main thing to notice about this test. We expect our response to be in JSON format; we use `json.loads()` because testing Python objects is easier than messing about with raw JSON strings.

And the implementation, conversely, uses `json.dumps()`:

lists/api.py

```python
import json
from django.http import HttpResponse
from lists.models import List, Item


def list(request, list_id):
    list_ = List.objects.get(id=list_id)
    item_dicts = [
        {'id': item.id, 'text': item.text}
        for item in list_.item_set.all()
    ]
    return HttpResponse(
        json.dumps(item_dicts),
        content_type='application/json'
    )
```

A nice opportunity to use a list comprehension!

Adding POST

The second thing we need from our API is the ability to add new items to our list by using a POST request. We'll start with the "happy path":

lists/tests/test_api.py (ch36l004)

```python
def test_POSTing_a_new_item(self):
    list_ = List.objects.create()
    response = self.client.post(
        self.base_url.format(list_.id),
        {'text': 'new item'},
    )
    self.assertEqual(response.status_code, 201)
    new_item = list_.item_set.get()
    self.assertEqual(new_item.text, 'new item')
```

And the implementation is similarly simple—basically the same as what we do in our normal view, but we return a 201 rather than a redirect:

lists/api.py (ch36l005)

```python
def list(request, list_id):
    list_ = List.objects.get(id=list_id)
    if request.method == 'POST':
        Item.objects.create(list=list_, text=request.POST['text'])
        return HttpResponse(status=201)
    item_dicts = [
        [...]
```

And that should get us started:

```
$ python manage.py test lists
[...]

Ran 52 tests in 0.177s

OK
```

 One of the fun things about building a REST API is that you get to use a few more of the full range of HTTP status codes (*https://en.wikipedia.org/wiki/List_of_HTTP_status_codes*).

Testing the Client-Side Ajax with Sinon.js

Don't even *think* of doing Ajax testing without a mocking library. Different test frameworks and tools have their own; *Sinon* is generic. It also provides JavaScript mocks, as we'll see…

Start by downloading it from its site, *http://sinonjs.org/*, and putting it into our *lists/ static/tests/* folder.

Then we can write our first Ajax test:

```html
<div id="qunit-fixture">
  <form>
    <input name="text" />
    <div class="has-error">Error text</div>
  </form>
  <table id="id_list_table">  ❶
  </table>
</div>

<script src="../jquery-3.1.1.min.js"></script>
<script src="../list.js"></script>
<script src="qunit-2.0.1.js"></script>
<script src="sinon-1.17.6.js"></script>  ❷

<script>
/* global sinon */

var server;
QUnit.testStart(function () {
  server = sinon.fakeServer.create();  ❸
});
QUnit.testDone(function () {
  server.restore();  ❸
});

QUnit.test("errors should be hidden on keypress", function (assert) {
[...]


QUnit.test("should get items by ajax on initialize", function (assert) {
  var url = '/getitems/';
  window.Superlists.initialize(url);

  assert.equal(server.requests.length, 1);  ❹
  var request = server.requests[0];
  assert.equal(request.url, url);
  assert.equal(request.method, 'GET');
});

</script>
```

❶ We add a new item to the fixture div to represent our list table.

❷ We import *sinon.js* (you'll need to download it and put it in the right folder).

❸ testStart and testDone are the QUnit equivalents of setUp and tearDown. We use them to tell Sinon to start up its Ajax testing tool, the fakeServer, and make it available via a globally scoped variable called server.

---

❹ That lets us make assertions about any Ajax requests that were made by our code. In this case, we test what URL the request went to, and what HTTP method it used.

To actually make our Ajax request, we'll use the jQuery Ajax helpers (*https:// api.jquery.com/jQuery.get/*), which are *much* easier than trying to use the low-level browser standard XMLHttpRequest objects:

lists/static/list.js

```
@@ -1,6 +1,10 @@
 window.Superlists = {};
-window.Superlists.initialize = function () {
+window.Superlists.initialize = function (url) {
    $('input[name="text"]').on('keypress', function () {
      $('.has-error').hide();
    });
+
+   $.get(url);
+
 };
+
```

That should get our test passing:

```
5 assertions of 5 passed, 0 failed.
1. errors should be hidden on keypress (1)
2. errors aren't hidden if there is no keypress (1)
3. should get items by ajax on initialize (3)
```

Well, we might be pinging out a GET request to the server, but what about actually *doing* something? How do we test the actual "async" part, where we deal with the (eventual) response?

Sinon and Testing the Asynchronous Part of Ajax

This is a major reason to love Sinon. `server.respond()` allows us to exactly control the flow of the asynchronous code.

```
QUnit.test("should fill in lists table from ajax response", function (assert) {
  var url = '/getitems/';
  var responseData = [
    {'id': 101, 'text': 'item 1 text'},
    {'id': 102, 'text': 'item 2 text'},
  ];
  server.respondWith('GET', url, [
    200, {"Content-Type": "application/json"}, JSON.stringify(responseData) ❶
  ]);
  window.Superlists.initialize(url); ❷

  server.respond(); ❸

  var rows = $('#id_list_table tr');  ❹
  assert.equal(rows.length, 2);
  var row1 = $('#id_list_table tr:first-child td');
  assert.equal(row1.text(), '1: item 1 text');
  var row2 = $('#id_list_table tr:last-child td');
  assert.equal(row2.text(), '2: item 2 text');
});
```

❶ We set up some response data for Sinon to use, telling it what status code, headers, and importantly what kind of response JSON we want to simulate coming from the server.

❷ Then we call the function under test.

❸ Here's the magic. *Then* we can call `server.respond()`, whenever we like, and that will kick off all the async part of the Ajax loop—that is, any callback we've assigned to deal with the response.

❹ Now we can quietly check whether our Ajax callback has actually populated our table with the new list rows…

The implementation might look something like this:

lists/static/list.js (ch36l010)

```
if (url) {
  $.get(url).done(function (response) {  ❶
    var rows = '';
    for (var i=0; i<response.length; i++) {  ❷
      var item = response[i];
      rows += '\n<tr><td>' + (i+1) + ': ' + item.text + '</td></tr>';
    }
    $('#id_list_table').html(rows);
  });
}
```

We're lucky because of the way jQuery registers its callbacks for Ajax when we use the .done() function. If you want to switch to the more standard JavaScript Promise .then() callback, we get one more "level" of async. QUnit does have a way of dealing with that. Check out the docs for the async (*http://api.qunitjs.com/async/*) function. Other test frameworks have something similar.

Wiring It All Up in the Template to See If It Really Works

We break it first, by removing the list table {% for %} loop from the *lists.html* template:

lists/templates/list.html

```
@@ -6,9 +6,6 @@

 {% block table %}
   <table id="id_list_table" class="table">
-    {% for item in list.item_set.all %}
-      <tr><td>{{ forloop.counter }}: {{ item.text }}</td></tr>
-    {% endfor %}
   </table>

   {% if list.owner %}
```

This will cause one of the unit tests to fail. It's OK to delete that test at this point.

Graceful Degradation and Progressive Enhancement

By removing the non-Ajax version of the lists page, I've removed the option of graceful degradation (*https://www.w3.org/wiki/Graceful_degradation_versus_progressive_enhancement*)—that is, keeping a version of the site that will still work without JavaScript.

This used to be an accessibility issue: "screen reader" browsers for visually impaired people used not to have JavaScript, so relying entirely on JS would exclude those users. That's not so much of an issue any more, as I understand it. But some users will block JavaScript for security reasons.

Another common problem is differing levels of JavaScript support in different browsers. This is a particular issue if you start adventuring off in the direction of "modern" frontend development and ES2015.

In short, it's always nice to have a non-JavaScript "backup". Particularly if you've built a site that works fine without it, don't throw away your working "plain old" HTML version too hastily. I'm just doing it because it's convenient for what I want to demonstrate.

That causes our basic FT to fail:

```
$ python manage.py test functional_tests.test_simple_list_creation
[...]
FAIL: test_can_start_a_list_for_one_user
[...]
  File "...python-tdd-book/functional_tests/test_simple_list_creation.py", line
32, in test_can_start_a_list_for_one_user
    self.wait_for_row_in_list_table('1: Buy peacock feathers')
[...]
AssertionError: '1: Buy peacock feathers' not found in []
[...]
FAIL: test_multiple_users_can_start_lists_at_different_urls

FAILED (failures=2)
```

Let's add a block called {% scripts %} to the base template, which we can selectively override later in our lists page:

lists/templates/base.html

```
<script src="/static/list.js"></script>

{% block scripts %}
  <script>
$(document).ready(function () {
  window.Superlists.initialize();
});
  </script>
{% endblock scripts %}

</body>
```

And now in *list.html* we add a slightly different call to `initialize`, with the correct URL:

lists/templates/list.html (ch36l016)

```
{% block scripts %}
  <script>
$(document).ready(function () {
  var url = "{% url 'api_list' list.id %}";
  window.Superlists.initialize(url);
});
  </script>
{% endblock scripts %}
```

And guess what? The test passes!

```
$ python manage.py test functional_tests.test_simple_list_creation
[...]
Ran 2 test in 11.730s

OK
```

That's a pretty good start!

Now if you run all the FTs you'll see we've got some failures in other FTs, so we'll have to deal with them. Also, we're using an old-fashioned POST from the form, with page refresh, so we're not at our trendy hipster single-page app yet. But we'll get there!

Implementing Ajax POST, Including the CSRF Token

First we give our list form an `id` so we can pick it up easily in our JS:

lists/templates/base.html

```
<h1>{% block header_text %}{% endblock %}</h1>
{% block list_form %}
  <form id="id_item_form" method="POST" action="{% block form_action %}{% endblock %}">
    {{ form.text }}
    [...]
```

Next tweak the fixture in our JS test to reflect that ID, as well as the CSRF token that's currently on the page:

lists/static/tests/tests.html

```
@@ -9,9 +9,14 @@
 <body>
   <div id="qunit"></div>
   <div id="qunit-fixture">
-     <form>
+     <form id="id_item_form">
        <input name="text" />
-       <div class="has-error">Error text</div>
+       <input type="hidden" name="csrfmiddlewaretoken" value="tokey" />
+       <div class="has-error">
+         <div class="help-block">
+           Error text
+         </div>
+       </div>
     </form>
```

And here's our test:

```
QUnit.test("should intercept form submit and do ajax post", function (assert) {
  var url = '/listitemsapi/';
  window.Superlists.initialize(url);

  $('#id_item_form input[name="text"]').val('user input');          ❶
  $('#id_item_form input[name="csrfmiddlewaretoken"]').val('tokeney');    ❶
  $('#id_item_form').submit();      ❶

  assert.equal(server.requests.length, 2);    ❷
  var request = server.requests[1];
  assert.equal(request.url, url);
  assert.equal(request.method, "POST");
  assert.equal(
    request.requestBody,
    'text=user+input&csrfmiddlewaretoken=tokeney'    ❸
  );
});
```

❶ We simulate the user filling in the form and hitting Submit.

❷ We now expect that there should be a second Ajax request (the first one is the GET for the list items table).

❸ We check our POST `requestBody`. As you can see, it's URL-encoded, which isn't the most easy value to test, but it's still just about readable.

And here's how we implement it:

```
[...]
  $('#id_list_table').html(rows);
});

var form = $('#id_item_form');
form.on('submit', function(event) {
  event.preventDefault();
  $.post(url, {
    'text': form.find('input[name="text"]').val(),
    'csrfmiddlewaretoken': form.find('input[name="csrfmiddlewaretoken"]').val(),
  });
});
```

That gets our JS tests passing but it breaks our FTs, because, although we're doing our POST all right, we're not updating the page after the POST to show the new list item:

```
$ python manage.py test functional_tests.test_simple_list_creation
[...]
AssertionError: '2: Use peacock feathers to make a fly' not found in ['1: Buy
peacock feathers']
```

Mocking in JavaScript

We want our client side to update the table of items after the Ajax POST completes. Essentially it'll do the same work as we do as soon as the page loads, retrieving the current list of items from the server, and filling in the item table.

Sounds like a helper function is in order!

lists/static/list.js

```javascript
window.Superlists = {};

window.Superlists.updateItems = function (url) {
  $.get(url).done(function (response) {
    var rows = '';
    for (var i=0; i<response.length; i++) {
      var item = response[i];
      rows += '\n<tr><td>' + (i+1) + ': ' + item.text + '</td></tr>';
    }
    $('#id_list_table').html(rows);
  });
};

window.Superlists.initialize = function (url) {
  $('input[name="text"]').on('keypress', function () {
    $('.has-error').hide();
  });

  if (url) {
    window.Superlists.updateItems(url);

    var form = $('#id_item_form');
    [...]
```

That was just a refactor; now we check that the JS tests all still pass:

```
12 assertions of 12 passed, 0 failed.
1. errors should be hidden on keypress (1)
2. errors aren't hidden if there is no keypress (1)
3. should get items by ajax on initialize (3)
4. should fill in lists table from ajax response (3)
5. should intercept form submit and do ajax post (4)
```

Now how to test that our Ajax POST calls `updateItems` on POST success? We don't want to dumbly duplicate the code that simulates a server response and checks the items table manually...how about a mock?

First we set up a thing called a "sandbox". It will keep track of all the mocks we create, and make sure to un-monkeypatch all the things that have been mocked after each test:

lists/static/tests/tests.html (ch36l023)

```
var server, sandbox;
QUnit.testStart(function () {
  server = sinon.fakeServer.create();
  sandbox = sinon.sandbox.create();
});
QUnit.testDone(function () {
  server.restore();
  sandbox.restore(); ❶
});
```

❶ This `.restore()` is the important part; it undoes all the mocking we've done in each test.

lists/static/tests/tests.html (ch36l024)

```
QUnit.test("should call updateItems after successful post", function (assert) {
  var url = '/listitemsapi/';
  window.Superlists.initialize(url); ❶
  var response = [
    201,
    {"Content-Type": "application/json"},
    JSON.stringify({}),
  ];
  server.respondWith('POST', url, response); ❶
  $('#id_item_form input[name="text"]').val('user input');
  $('#id_item_form input[name="csrfmiddlewaretoken"]').val('tokeney');
  $('#id_item_form').submit();

  sandbox.spy(window.Superlists, 'updateItems'); ❷
  server.respond(); ❷

  assert.equal(
    window.Superlists.updateItems.lastCall.args, ❸
    url
  );
});
```

❶ First important thing to notice: We only set up our server response *after* we do the initialize. We want this to be the response to the POST request that happens on form submit, not the response to the initial GET request. (Remember our lesson from Chapter 16? One of the most challenging things about JS testing is controlling the order of execution.)

❷ Similarly, we only start mocking our helper function *after* we know the first call for the initial GET has already happened. The `sandbox.spy` call is what does the job that `patch` does in Python tests. It replaces the given object with a mock version.

❸ Our `updateItems` function has now grown some mocky extra attributes, like `lastCall` and `lastCall.args`, which are like the Python mock's `call_args`.

To get it passing, we first make a deliberate mistake, to check that our tests really do test what we think they do:

lists/static/list.js

```javascript
$.post(url, {
  'text': form.find('input[name="text"]').val(),
  'csrfmiddlewaretoken': form.find('input[name="csrfmiddlewaretoken"]').val(),
}).done(function () {
  window.Superlists.updateItems();
});
```

Yep, we're almost there but not quite:

```
12 assertions of 13 passed, 1 failed.
[...]
6. should call updateItems after successful post (1, 0, 1)
     1. failed
         Expected: "/listitemsapi/"
         Result: []
         Diff: "/listitemsapi/"[]
         Source: file://...python-tdd-book/lists/static/tests/tests.html:124:15
```

And we fix it thusly:

lists/static/list.js

```javascript
}).done(function () {
  window.Superlists.updateItems(url);
});
```

And our FT passes! Or at least one of them does. The others have problems, and we'll come back to them shortly.

Finishing the Refactor: Getting the Tests to Match the Code

First, I'm not happy until we've seen through this refactor, and made our unit tests match the code a little more:

```
@@ -50,9 +50,19 @@ QUnit.testDone(function () {
 });


-QUnit.test("should get items by ajax on initialize", function (assert) {
+QUnit.test("should call updateItems on initialize", function (assert) {
   var url = '/getitems/';
+  sandbox.spy(window.Superlists, 'updateItems');
   window.Superlists.initialize(url);
+  assert.equal(
+    window.Superlists.updateItems.lastCall.args,
+    url
+  );
+});
+
+QUnit.test("updateItems should get correct url by ajax", function (assert) {
+  var url = '/getitems/';
+  window.Superlists.updateItems(url);

   assert.equal(server.requests.length, 1);
   var request = server.requests[0];
@@ -60,7 +70,7 @@ QUnit.test("should get items by ajax on initialize", function (assert) {
   assert.equal(request.method, 'GET');
 });

-QUnit.test("should fill in lists table from ajax response", function (assert) {
+QUnit.test("updateItems should fill in lists table from ajax response", function (assert) {
   var url = '/getitems/';
   var responseData = [
     {'id': 101, 'text': 'item 1 text'},
@@ -69,7 +79,7 @@ QUnit.test("should fill in lists table from ajax response", function [...]
   server.respondWith('GET', url, [
     200, {"Content-Type": "application/json"}, JSON.stringify(responseData)
   ]);
-  window.Superlists.initialize(url);
+  window.Superlists.updateItems(url);

   server.respond();
```

And that should give us a test run that looks like this instead:

```
14 assertions of 14 passed, 0 failed.
1. errors should be hidden on keypress (1)
2. errors aren't hidden if there is no keypress (1)
3. should call updateItems on initialize (1)
4. updateItems should get correct url by ajax (3)
5. updateItems should fill in lists table from ajax response (3)
6. should intercept form submit and do ajax post (4)
7. should call updateItems after successful post (1)
```

Data Validation: An Exercise for the Reader?

If you do a full test run, you should find two of the validation FTs are failing:

```
$ python manage.py test
[...]
ERROR: test_cannot_add_duplicate_items
(functional_tests.test_list_item_validation.ItemValidationTest)
[...]
ERROR: test_error_messages_are_cleared_on_input
(functional_tests.test_list_item_validation.ItemValidationTest)
[...]
selenium.common.exceptions.NoSuchElementException: Message: Unable to locate
element: .has-error
```

I won't spell this all out for you, but here's at least the unit tests you'll need:

lists/tests/test_api.py (ch36l027)

```python
from lists.forms import DUPLICATE_ITEM_ERROR, EMPTY_ITEM_ERROR
[...]
    def post_empty_input(self):
        list_ = List.objects.create()
        return self.client.post(
            self.base_url.format(list_.id),
            data={'text': ''}
        )


    def test_for_invalid_input_nothing_saved_to_db(self):
        self.post_empty_input()
        self.assertEqual(Item.objects.count(), 0)


    def test_for_invalid_input_returns_error_code(self):
        response = self.post_empty_input()
        self.assertEqual(response.status_code, 400)
        self.assertEqual(
            json.loads(response.content.decode('utf8')),
            {'error': EMPTY_ITEM_ERROR}
        )


    def test_duplicate_items_error(self):
        list_ = List.objects.create()
        self.client.post(
            self.base_url.format(list_.id), data={'text': 'thing'}
        )
        response = self.client.post(
            self.base_url.format(list_.id), data={'text': 'thing'}
        )
        self.assertEqual(response.status_code, 400)
        self.assertEqual(
            json.loads(response.content.decode('utf8')),
            {'error': DUPLICATE_ITEM_ERROR}
        )
```

And on the JS side:

lists/static/tests/tests.html (ch36l029-2)

```
QUnit.test("should display errors on post failure", function (assert) {
  var url = '/listitemsapi/';
  window.Superlists.initialize(url);
  server.respondWith('POST', url, [
    400,
    {"Content-Type": "application/json"},
    JSON.stringify({'error': 'something is amiss'})
  ]);
  $('.has-error').hide();

  $('#id_item_form').submit();
  server.respond(); // post

  assert.equal($('.has-error').is(':visible'), true);
  assert.equal($('.has-error .help-block').text(), 'something is amiss');
});

QUnit.test("should hide errors on post success", function (assert) {
    [...]
```

You'll also want some modifications to *base.html* to make it compatible with both displaying Django errors (which the home page still uses for now) and errors from JavaScript:

```
@@ -51,17 +51,21 @@
        <div class="col-md-6 col-md-offset-3 jumbotron">
          <div class="text-center">
            <h1>{% block header_text %}{% endblock %}</h1>
+
            {% block list_form %}
              <form id="id_item_form" method="POST" action="{% block [...]
                {{ form.text }}
                {% csrf_token %}
-               {% if form.errors %}
-                 <div class="form-group has-error">
-                   <div class="help-block">{{ form.text.errors }}</div>
+               <div class="form-group has-error">
+                 <div class="help-block">
+                   {% if form.errors %}
+                     {{ form.text.errors }}
+                   {% endif %}
+                 </div>
-               {% endif %}
+               </div>
              </form>
            {% endblock %}
+
          </div>
        </div>
      </div>
```

By the end you should get to a JS test run a bit like this:

```
20 assertions of 20 passed, 0 failed.
1. errors should be hidden on keypress (1)
2. errors aren't hidden if there is no keypress (1)
3. should call updateItems on initialize (1)
4. updateItems should get correct url by ajax (3)
5. updateItems should fill in lists table from ajax response (3)
6. should intercept form submit and do ajax post (4)
7. should call updateItems after successful post (1)
8. should not intercept form submit if no api url passed in (1)
9. should display errors on post failure (2)
10. should hide errors on post success (1)
11. should display generic error if no error json (2)
```

And a full test run should pass, including all the FTs:

```
$ python manage.py test
[...]
Ran 81 tests in 62.029s
OK
```

Laaaaaahvely.[1]

And there's your hand-rolled REST API with Django. If you need a hint finishing it off yourself, check out the repo (*https://github.com/hjwp/book-example/tree/appen dix_rest_api*).

But I would never suggest building a REST API in Django without at least checking out *Django-Rest-Framework*. Which is the topic of the next appendix! Read on, Macduff.

REST API Tips

Dedupe URLs
URLs are more important, in a way, to an API than they are to a browser-facing app. Try to reduce the amount of times you hardcode them in your tests.

Don't work with raw JSON strings
`json.loads` and `json.dumps` are your friend.

Always use an Ajax mocking library for your JS tests
Sinon is fine. Jasmine has its own, as does Angular.

Bear graceful degradation and progressive enhancement in mind
Especially if you're moving from a static site to a more JavaScript-driven one, consider keeping at least the core of your site's functionality working without JavaScript.

---

1 Put on your best cockney accent for this one.

Django-Rest-Framework

Having "rolled our own" REST API in the last appendix, it's time to take a look at Django-Rest-Framework (*http://www.django-rest-framework.org/*), which is a go-to choice for many Python/Django developers building APIs. Just as Django aims to give you all the basic tools that you'll need to build a database-driven website (an ORM, templates, and so on), so DRF aims to give you all the tools you need to build an API, and thus avoid you having to write boilerplate code over and over again.

Writing this appendix, one of the main things I struggled with was getting the exact same API that I'd just implemented manually to be replicated by DRF. Getting the same URL layout and the same JSON data structures I'd defined proved to be quite a challenge, and I felt like I was fighting the framework.

That's always a warning sign. The people who built Django-Rest-Framework are a lot smarter than I am, and they've seen a lot more REST APIs than I have, and if they're opinionated about the way that things "should" look, then maybe my time would be better spent seeing if I can adapt and work with their view of the world, rather than forcing my own preconceptions onto it.

"Don't fight the framework" is one of the great pieces of advice I've heard. Either go with the flow, or perhaps reassess whether you want to be using a framework at all.

We'll work from the API we had at the end of the last appendix, and see if we can rewrite it to use DRF.

Installation

A quick pip install gets us DRF. I'm just using the latest version, which was 3.5.4 at the time of writing:

```
$ pip install djangorestframework
```

And we add `rest_framework` to INSTALLED_APPS in *settings.py*:

superlists/settings.py

```python
INSTALLED_APPS = [
    #'django.contrib.admin',
    'django.contrib.auth',
    'django.contrib.contenttypes',
    'django.contrib.sessions',
    'django.contrib.messages',
    'django.contrib.staticfiles',
    'lists',
    'accounts',
    'functional_tests',
    'rest_framework',
]
```

Serializers (Well, ModelSerializers, Really)

The Django-Rest-Framework tutorial (*http://bit.ly/2t6T6eX*) is a pretty good resource to learn DRF. The first thing you'll come across is serializers, and specifically in our case, "ModelSerializers". They are DRF's way of converting from Django database models to JSON (or possibly other formats) that you can send over the wire:

lists/api.py (ch37l003)

```python
from lists.models import List, Item
[...]
from rest_framework import routers, serializers, viewsets


class ItemSerializer(serializers.ModelSerializer):

    class Meta:
        model = Item
        fields = ('id', 'text')


class ListSerializer(serializers.ModelSerializer):
    items = ItemSerializer(many=True, source='item_set')

    class Meta:
        model = List
        fields = ('id', 'items',)
```

Viewsets (Well, ModelViewsets, Really) and Routers

A ModelViewSet is DRF's way of defining all the different ways you can interact with the objects for a particular model via your API. Once you tell it which models you're interested in (via the `queryset` attribute) and how to serialize them (`serial izer_class`), it will then do the rest—automatically building views for you that will let you list, retrieve, update, and even delete objects.

Here's all we need to do for a ViewSet that'll be able to retrieve items for a particular list:

lists/api.py (ch37l004)

```python
class ListViewSet(viewsets.ModelViewSet):
    queryset = List.objects.all()
    serializer_class = ListSerializer


router = routers.SimpleRouter()
router.register(r'lists', ListViewSet)
```

A *router* is DRF's way of building URL configuration automatically, and mapping them to the functionality provided by the ViewSet.

At this point we can start pointing our *urls.py* at our new router, bypassing the old API code and seeing how our tests do with the new stuff:

superlists/urls.py (ch37l005)

```python
[...]
# from lists.api import urls as api_urls
from lists.api import router

urlpatterns = [
    url(r'^$', list_views.home_page, name='home'),
    url(r'^lists/', include(list_urls)),
    url(r'^accounts/', include(accounts_urls)),
    # url(r'^api/', include(api_urls)),
    url(r'^api/', include(router.urls)),
]
```

That makes loads of our tests fail:

```
$ python manage.py test lists
[...]
django.urls.exceptions.NoReverseMatch: Reverse for 'api_list' not found.
'api_list' is not a valid view function or pattern name.
[...]
AssertionError: 405 != 400
[...]
AssertionError: {'id': 2, 'items': [{'id': 2, 'text': 'item 1'}, {'id': 3,
'text': 'item 2'}]} != [{'id': 2, 'text': 'item 1'}, {'id': 3, 'text': 'item
2'}]


 -----------------------------------------------------------------
Ran 54 tests in 0.243s

FAILED (failures=4, errors=10)
```

Let's take a look at those 10 errors first, all saying they cannot reverse `api_list`. It's because the DRF router uses a different naming convention for URLs than the one we used when we coded it manually. You'll see from the tracebacks that they're happening when we render a template. It's *list.html*. We can fix that in just one place; `api_list` becomes `list-detail`:

lists/templates/list.html (ch37l006)

```
    <script>
$(document).ready(function () {
  var url = "{% url 'list-detail' list.id %}";
});
    </script>
```

That will get us down to just four failures:

```
$ python manage.py test lists
[...]
FAIL: test_POSTing_a_new_item (lists.tests.test_api.ListAPITest)
[...]
FAIL: test_duplicate_items_error (lists.tests.test_api.ListAPITest)
[...]
FAIL: test_for_invalid_input_returns_error_code
(lists.tests.test_api.ListAPITest)
[...]
FAIL: test_get_returns_items_for_correct_list
(lists.tests.test_api.ListAPITest)
[...]
FAILED (failures=4)
```

Let's DONT-ify all the validation tests for now, and save that complexity for later:

```
[...]
    def DONTtest_for_invalid_input_nothing_saved_to_db(self):
        [...]
    def DONTtest_for_invalid_input_returns_error_code(self):
        [...]
    def DONTtest_duplicate_items_error(self):
        [...]
```

And now we have just two failures:

```
FAIL: test_POSTing_a_new_item (lists.tests.test_api.ListAPITest)
[...]
    self.assertEqual(response.status_code, 201)
AssertionError: 405 != 201
[...]
FAIL: test_get_returns_items_for_correct_list
(lists.tests.test_api.ListAPITest)
[...]
AssertionError: {'id': 2, 'items': [{'id': 2, 'text': 'item 1'}, {'id': 3,
'text': 'item 2'}]} != [{'id': 2, 'text': 'item 1'}, {'id': 3, 'text': 'item
2'}]
[...]
FAILED (failures=2)
```

Let's take a look at that last one first.

DRF's default configuration does provide a slightly different data structure to the one we built by hand—doing a GET for a list gives you its ID, and then the list items are inside a key called "items". That means a slight modification to our unit test, before it gets back to passing:

```
@@ -23,10 +23,10 @@ class ListAPITest(TestCase):
         response = self.client.get(self.base_url.format(our_list.id))
         self.assertEqual(
             json.loads(response.content.decode('utf8')),
-            [
+            {'id': our_list.id, 'items': [
                 {'id': item1.id, 'text': item1.text},
                 {'id': item2.id, 'text': item2.text},
-            ]
+            ]}
         )
```

That's the GET for retrieving list items sorted (and, as we'll see later, we've got a bunch of other stuff for free too). How about adding new ones, using POST?

A Different URL for POST Item

This is the point at which I gave up on fighting the framework and just saw where DRF wanted to take me. Although it's possible, it's quite torturous to do a POST to the "lists" ViewSet in order to add an item to a list.

Instead, the simplest thing is to post to an item view, not a list view:

lists/api.py (ch37l009)

```python
class ItemViewSet(viewsets.ModelViewSet):
    serializer_class = ItemSerializer
    queryset = Item.objects.all()


[...]
router.register(r'items', ItemViewSet)
```

So that means we change the test slightly, moving all the POST tests out of the `ListAPITest` and into a new test class, `ItemsAPITest`:

lists/tests/test_api.py (ch37l010)

```python
@@ -1,3 +1,4 @@
 import json
+from django.core.urlresolvers import reverse
 from django.test import TestCase
 from lists.models import List, Item
@@ -31,9 +32,13 @@ class ListAPITest(TestCase):


+
+class ItemsAPITest(TestCase):
+    base_url = reverse('item-list')
+
     def test_POSTing_a_new_item(self):
         list_ = List.objects.create()
         response = self.client.post(
-            self.base_url.format(list_.id),
-            {'text': 'new item'},
+            self.base_url,
+            {'list': list_.id, 'text': 'new item'},
         )
         self.assertEqual(response.status_code, 201)
```

That will give us:

```
django.db.utils.IntegrityError: NOT NULL constraint failed: lists_item.list_id
```

Until we add the list ID to our serialization of items; otherwise, we don't know what list it's for:

```
class ItemSerializer(serializers.ModelSerializer):

    class Meta:
        model = Item
        fields = ('id', 'list', 'text')
```

And that causes another small associated test change:

```
@@ -25,8 +25,8 @@ class ListAPITest(TestCase):
        self.assertEqual(
            json.loads(response.content.decode('utf8')),
            {'id': our_list.id, 'items': [
-                {'id': item1.id, 'text': item1.text},
-                {'id': item2.id, 'text': item2.text},
+                {'id': item1.id, 'list': our_list.id, 'text': item1.text},
+                {'id': item2.id, 'list': our_list.id, 'text': item2.text},
            ]}
        )
```

Adapting the Client Side

Our API no longer returns a flat array of the items in a list. It returns an object, with a .items attribute that represents the items. That means a small tweak to our update Items function:

```
@@ -3,8 +3,8 @@ window.Superlists = {};
 window.Superlists.updateItems = function (url) {
   $.get(url).done(function (response) {
     var rows = '';
-    for (var i=0; i<response.length; i++) {
-      var item = response[i];
+    for (var i=0; i<response.items.length; i++) {
+      var item = response.items[i];
       rows += '\n<tr><td>' + (i+1) + ': ' + item.text + '</td></tr>';
     }
     $('#id_list_table').html(rows);
```

And because we're using different URLs for GETing lists and POSTing items, we tweak the initialize function slightly too. Rather than multiple arguments, we'll switch to using a params object containing the required config:

```
@@ -11,23 +11,24 @@ window.Superlists.updateItems = function (url) {
    });
  };

 -window.Superlists.initialize = function (url) {
 +window.Superlists.initialize = function (params) {
     $('input[name="text"]').on('keypress', function () {
       $('.has-error').hide();
     });

 -  if (url) {
 -    window.Superlists.updateItems(url);
 +  if (params) {
 +    window.Superlists.updateItems(params.listApiUrl);

     var form = $('#id_item_form');
     form.on('submit', function(event) {
       event.preventDefault();
 -      $.post(url, {
 +      $.post(params.itemsApiUrl, {
 +        'list': params.listId,
         'text': form.find('input[name="text"]').val(),
         'csrfmiddlewaretoken': form.find('input[name="csrfmiddlewaretoken"]').val(),
       }).done(function () {
         $('.has-error').hide();
 -        window.Superlists.updateItems(url);
 +        window.Superlists.updateItems(params.listApiUrl);
       }).fail(function (xhr) {
         $('.has-error').show();
         if (xhr.responseJSON && xhr.responseJSON.error) {
```

We reflect that in *list.html*:

```
$(document).ready(function () {
  window.Superlists.initialize({
    listApiUrl: "{% url 'list-detail' list.id %}",
    itemsApiUrl: "{% url 'item-list' %}",
    listId: {{ list.id }},
  });
});
```

And that's actually enough to get the basic FT working again:

```
$ python manage.py test functional_tests.test_simple_list_creation
[...]
Ran 2 tests in 15.635s

OK
```

There's a few more changes to do with error handling, which you can explore in the repo for this appendix (*https://github.com/hjwp/book-example/blob/appendix_Djan goRestFramework/lists/api.py*) if you're curious.

What Django-Rest-Framework Gives You

You may be wondering what the point of using this framework was.

Configuration Instead of Code

Well, the first advantage is that I've transformed my old procedural view function into a more declarative syntax:

lists/api.py

```python
def list(request, list_id):
    list_ = List.objects.get(id=list_id)
    if request.method == 'POST':
        form = ExistingListItemForm(for_list=list_, data=request.POST)
        if form.is_valid():
            form.save()
            return HttpResponse(status=201)
        else:
            return HttpResponse(
                json.dumps({'error': form.errors['text'][0]}),
                content_type='application/json',
                status=400
            )
    item_dicts = [
        {'id': item.id, 'text': item.text}
        for item in list_.item_set.all()
    ]
    return HttpResponse(
        json.dumps(item_dicts),
        content_type='application/json'
    )
```

If you compare this to the final DRF version, you'll notice that we are actually now entirely configured:

```python
class ItemSerializer(serializers.ModelSerializer):
    text = serializers.CharField(
        allow_blank=False, error_messages={'blank': EMPTY_ITEM_ERROR}
    )

    class Meta:
        model = Item
        fields = ('id', 'list', 'text')
        validators = [
            UniqueTogetherValidator(
                queryset=Item.objects.all(),
                fields=('list', 'text'),
                message=DUPLICATE_ITEM_ERROR
            )
        ]


class ListSerializer(serializers.ModelSerializer):
    items = ItemSerializer(many=True, source='item_set')

    class Meta:
        model = List
        fields = ('id', 'items',)


class ListViewSet(viewsets.ModelViewSet):
    queryset = List.objects.all()
    serializer_class = ListSerializer


class ItemViewSet(viewsets.ModelViewSet):
    serializer_class = ItemSerializer
    queryset = Item.objects.all()


router = routers.SimpleRouter()
router.register(r'lists', ListViewSet)
router.register(r'items', ItemViewSet)
```

Free Functionality

The second advantage is that, by using DRF's ModelSerializer, ViewSet, and routers, I've actually ended up with a much more extensive API than the one I'd rolled by hand.

- All the HTTP methods, GET, POST, PUT, PATCH, DELETE, and OPTIONS, now work, out of the box, for all list and items URLs.

- And a browsable/self-documenting version of the API is available at *http://localhost:8000/api/lists/* and *http://localhost:8000/api/items.* (Figure G-1; try it!)

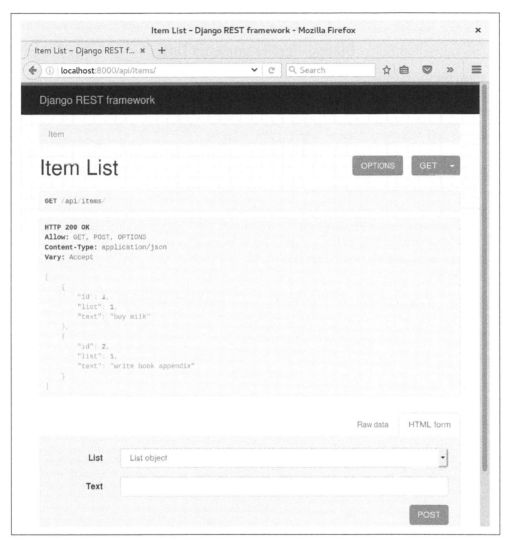

Figure G-1. A free browsable API for your users

There's more information in the DRF docs (*http://www.django-rest-framework.org/topics/documenting-your-api/#self-describing-apis*), but those are both seriously neat features to be able to offer the end users of your API.

In short, DRF is a great way of generating APIs, almost automatically, based on your existing models structure. If you're using Django, definitely check it out before you start hand-rolling your own API code.

Django-Rest-Framework Tips

Don't fight the framework
Going with the flow is often the best way to stay productive. That, or maybe don't use the framework. Or use it at a lower level.

Routers and ViewSets for the principle of least surprise
One of the advantages of DRF is that its generic tools like routers and ViewSets will give you a very predictable API, with sensible defaults for its endpoints, URL structure, and responses for different HTTP methods.

Check out the self-documenting, browsable version
Check out your API endpoints in a browser. DRF responds differently when it detects your API is being accessed by a "normal" web browser, and displays a very nice, self-documenting version of itself, which you can share with your users.

Cheat Sheet

By popular demand, this "cheat sheet" is loosely based on the little recap/summary boxes from the end of each chapter. The idea is to provide a few reminders, and links to the chapters where you can find out more to jog your memory. I hope you find it useful!

Initial Project Setup

- Start with a *User Story* and map it to a first *functional test*.
- Pick a test framework—`unittest` is fine, and options like `py.test`, `nose`, or `Green` can also offer some advantages.
- Run the functional test and see your first *expected failure*.
- Pick a web framework such as Django, and find out how to run *unit tests* against it.
- Create your first *unit test* to address the current FT failure, and see it fail.
- Do your *first commit* to a VCS like *Git*.

Relevant chapters: Chapter 1, Chapter 2, Chapter 3

The Basic TDD Workflow

- Double-loop TDD (Figure H-1)
- Red, Green, Refactor
- Triangulation
- The scratchpad

- "3 Strikes and Refactor"
- "Working State to Working State"
- "YAGNI"

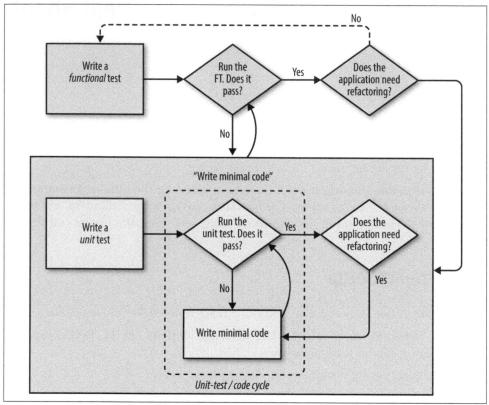

Figure H-1. The TDD process with functional and unit tests

Relevant chapters: Chapter 4, Chapter 5, Chapter 7

Moving Beyond Dev-Only Testing

- Start system testing early. Ensure your components work together: web server, static content, database.
- Build a staging environment to match your production environment, and run your FT suite against it.
- Automate your staging and production environments:
  — PaaS vs. VPS

— Fabric

— Configuration management (Chef, Puppet, Salt, Ansible)

— Vagrant

- Think through deployment pain points: the database, static files, dependencies, how to customise settings, and so on.

- Build a CI server as soon as possible, so that you don't have to rely on self-discipline to see the tests run.

Relevant chapters: Chapter 9, Chapter 11, Chapter 24, Appendix C

General Testing Best Practices

- Each test should test one thing.

- One test file per application code source file.

- Consider at least a placeholder test for every function and class, no matter how simple.

- "Don't test constants".

- Try to test behaviour rather than implementation.

- Try to think beyond the charmed path through the code, and think through edge cases and error cases.

Relevant chapters: Chapter 4, Chapter 13, Chapter 14

Selenium/Functional Testing Best Practices

- Use explicit rather than implicit waits, and the interaction/wait pattern.

- Avoid duplication of test code—helper methods in a base class and the Page pattern are possible solutions.

- Avoid double-testing functionality. If you have a test that covers a time-consuming process (e.g., login), consider ways of skipping it in other tests (but be aware of unexpected interactions between seemingly unrelated bits of functionality).

- Look into BDD tools as another way of structuring your FTs.

Relevant chapters: Chapter 21, Chapter 24, Chapter 25

Outside-In, Test Isolation Versus Integrated Tests, and Mocking

Remember the reasons we write tests in the first place:

- To ensure correctness and prevent regressions
- To help us to write clean, maintainable code
- To enable a fast, productive workflow

And with those objectives in mind, think of different types of tests, and the trade-offs between them:

Functional tests
- Provide the best guarantee that your application really works correctly, from the point of view of the user
- But: it's a slower feedback cycle
- And they don't necessarily help you write clean code

Integrated tests (reliant on, for example, the ORM or the Django Test Client)
- Are quick to write
- Are easy to understand
- Will warn you of any integration issues
- But: may not always drive good design (that's up to you!)
- And are usually slower than isolated tests

Isolated ("mocky") tests
- Involve the most hard work
- Can be harder to read and understand
- But: are the best ones for guiding you towards better design
- And run the fastest

If you do find yourself writing tests with lots of mocks, and they feel painful, remember *"listen to your tests"*—ugly, mocky tests may be trying to tell you that your code could be simplified.

Relevant chapters: Chapter 22, Chapter 23, Chapter 26

What to Do Next

Here I offer a few suggestions for things to investigate next, to develop your testing skills, and to apply them to some of the cool new technologies in web development (at the time of writing!).

I hope to turn each one of these into at least some sort of blog post, if not a future appendix to the book. I hope to also produce code examples for all of them, as time goes by. So do check out *http://www.obeythetestinggoat.com*, and see if there are any updates.

Or, why not try to beat me to it, and write your own blog post chronicling your attempt at any one of these?

I'm very happy to answer questions and provide tips and guidance on all these topics, so if you find yourself attempting one and getting stuck, please don't hesitate to get in touch at *obeythetestinggoat@gmail.com*!

Notifications—Both on the Site and by Email

It would be nice if users were notified when someone shares a list with them.

You can use django-notifications to show a message to users the next time they refresh the screen. You'll need two browsers in your FT for this.

And/or, you could send notifications by email. Investigate Django's email test capabilities. Then, decide this is so critical that you need real tests with real emails. Use the IMAPClient library to fetch actual emails from a test webmail account.

Switch to Postgres

SQLite is a wonderful little database, but it won't deal well once you have more than one web worker process fielding your site's requests. Postgres is everyone's favourite database these days, so find out how to install and configure it.

You'll need to figure out a place to store the usernames and passwords for your local, staging, and production Postgres servers. Since, for security, you probably don't want them in your code repository, look into ways of modifying your deploy scripts to pass them in at the command line. Environment variables are one popular solution for where to keep them…

Experiment with keeping your unit tests running with SQLite, and compare how much faster they are than running against Postgres. Set it up so that your local machine uses SQLite for testing, but your CI server uses Postgres.

Run Your Tests Against Different Browsers

Selenium supports all sorts of different browsers, including Chrome and Internet Exploder. Try them both out and see if your FT suite behaves any differently.

You should also check out a "headless" browser like PhantomJS.

In my experience, switching browsers tends to expose all sorts of race conditions in Selenium tests, and you will probably need to use the interaction/wait pattern a lot more (particularly for PhantomJS).

404 and 500 Tests

A professional site needs good-looking error pages. Testing a 404 page is easy, but you'll probably need a custom "raise an exception on purpose" view to test the 500 page.

The Django Admin Site

Imagine a story where a user emails you wanting to "claim" an anonymous list. Let's say we implement a manual solution to this, involving the site administrator manually changing the record using the Django admin site.

Find out how to switch on the admin site, and have a play with it. Write an FT that shows a normal, non–logged-in user creating a list, then have an admin user log in, go to the admin site, and assign the list to the user. The user can then see it in their "My Lists" page.

Write Some Security Tests

Expand on the login, my lists, and sharing tests—what do you need to write to assure yourself that users can only do what they're authorized to?

Test for Graceful Degradation

What would happen if Persona went down? Can we at least show an apologetic error message to our users?

- Tip: one way of simulating Persona being down is to hack your hosts file (at */etc/ hosts* or *c:\Windows\System32\drivers\etc*). Remember to revert it in the test `tear Down`!
- Think about the server side as well as the client side.

Caching and Performance Testing

Find out how to install and configure `memcached`. Find out how to use Apache's `ab` to run a performance test. How does it perform with and without caching? Can you write an automated test that will fail if caching is not enabled? What about the dreaded problem of cache invalidation? Can tests help you to make sure your cache invalidation logic is solid?

JavaScript MVC Frameworks

JavaScript libraries that let you implement a Model-View-Controller pattern on the client side are all the rage these days. To-do lists are one of the favourite demo applications for them, so it should be pretty easy to convert the site to being a single-page site, where all list additions happen in JavaScript.

Pick a framework—perhaps Backbone.js or Angular.js—and spike in an implementation. Each framework has its own preferences for how to write unit tests, so learn the one that goes along with it, and see how you like it.

Async and Websockets

Supposing two users are working on the same list at the same time. Wouldn't it be nice to see real-time updates, so if the other person adds an item to the list, you see it immediately? A persistent connection between client and server using websockets is the way to get this to work.

Check out one of the Python async web servers—Tornado, gevent, Twisted—and see if you can use it to implement dynamic notifications.

To test it, you'll need two browser instances (like we used for the list sharing tests), and check that notifications of the actions from one appear in the other, without needing to refresh the page…

Switch to Using py.test

py.test lets you write unit tests with less boilerplate. Try converting some of your unit tests to using *py.test*. You may need to use a plugin to get it to play nicely with Django.

Check Out coverage.py

Ned Batchelder's `coverage.py` will tell you what your *test coverage* is—what percentage of your code is covered by tests. Now, in theory, because we've been using rigorous TDD, we should always have 100% coverage. But it's nice to know for sure, and it's also a very useful tool for working on projects that didn't have tests from the beginning.

Client-Side Encryption

Here's a fun one: what if our users are paranoid about the NSA, and decide they no longer want to trust their lists to The Cloud? Can you build a JavaScript encryption system, where the user can enter a password to encypher their list item text before it gets sent to the server?

One way of testing it might be to have an "administrator" user that goes to the Django admin view to inspect users' lists, and checks that they are stored encrypted in the database.

Your Suggestion Here

What do you think I should put here? Suggestions, please!

Source Code Examples

All of the code examples I've used in the book are available in my repo (*https://github.com/hjwp/book-example/*) on GitHub. So, if you ever want to compare your code against mine, you can take a look at it there.

Each chapter has its own branch named after it, like so:

Chapter 1
    https://github.com/hjwp/book-example/tree/chapter_01

Be aware that each branch contains all of the commits for that chapter, so its state represents the code at the *end* of the chapter.

Full List of Links for Each Chapter

Chapter 1
    https://github.com/hjwp/book-example/tree/chapter_01

Chapter 2
    https://github.com/hjwp/book-example/tree/chapter_02_unittest

Chapter 3
    https://github.com/hjwp/book-example/tree/chapter_unit_test_first_view

Chapter 4
    https://github.com/hjwp/book-example/tree/chapter_philosophy_and_refactoring

Chapter 5
    https://github.com/hjwp/book-example/tree/chapter_post_and_database

Chapter 6
    https://github.com/hjwp/book-example/tree/chapter_explicit_waits_1

Chapter 7
   https://github.com/hjwp/book-example/tree/chapter_working_incrementally

Chapter 8
   https://github.com/hjwp/book-example/tree/chapter_prettification

Chapter 9
   https://github.com/hjwp/book-example/tree/chapter_manual_deployment

Chapter 10
   https://github.com/hjwp/book-example/tree/chapter_making_deployment_produc tion_ready

Chapter 11
   https://github.com/hjwp/book-example/tree/chapter_automate_deploy ment_with_fabric

Chapter 12
   https://github.com/hjwp/book-example/tree/chapter_organising_test_files

Chapter 13
   https://github.com/hjwp/book-example/tree/chapter_database_layer_validation

Chapter 14
   https://github.com/hjwp/book-example/tree/chapter_simple_form

Chapter 15
   https://github.com/hjwp/book-example/tree/chapter_advanced_forms

Chapter 16
   https://github.com/hjwp/book-example/tree/chapter_javascript

Chapter 17
   https://github.com/hjwp/book-example/tree/chapter_deploying_validation

Chapter 18
   https://github.com/hjwp/book-example/tree/chapter_spiking_custom_auth

Chapter 19
   https://github.com/hjwp/book-example/tree/chapter_mocking

Chapter 20
   https://github.com/hjwp/book-example/tree/chapter_fixtures_and_wait_decorator

Chapter 21
   https://github.com/hjwp/book-example/tree/chapter_server_side_debugging

Chapter 22
   https://github.com/hjwp/book-example/tree/chapter_outside_in

Chapter 23
> *https://github.com/hjwp/book-example/tree/chapter_purist_unit_tests*

Chapter 24
> *https://github.com/hjwp/book-example/tree/chapter_CI*

Chapter 25
> *https://github.com/hjwp/book-example/tree/chapter_page_pattern*

Appendix B
> *https://github.com/hjwp/book-example/tree/appendix_Django_Class-Based_Views*

Appendix E
> *https://github.com/hjwp/book-example/tree/appendix_bdd*

Appendix F
> *https://github.com/hjwp/book-example/tree/appendix_rest_api*

Appendix G
> *https://github.com/hjwp/book-example/tree/appendix_DjangoRestFramework*

Using Git to Check Your Progress

If you feel like developing your Git-Fu a little further, you can add my repo as a *remote*:

```
git remote add harry https://github.com/hjwp/book-example.git
git fetch harry
```

And then, to check your difference from the *end* of Chapter 4:

```
git diff harry/chapter_philosophy_and_refactoring
```

Git can handle multiple remotes, so you can still do this even if you're already pushing your code up to GitHub or Bitbucket.

Be aware that the precise order of, say, methods in a class may differ between your version and mine. It may make diffs hard to read.

Downloading a ZIP File for a Chapter

If, for whatever reason, you want to "start from scratch" for a chapter, or skip ahead,[1] and/or you're just not comfortable with Git, you can download a version of my code as a ZIP file, from URLs following this pattern:

---

[1] I don't recommend skipping ahead. I haven't designed the chapters to stand on their own; each relies on the previous ones, so it may be more confusing than anything else…

https://github.com/hjwp/book-example/archive/chapter_01.zip

https://github.com/hjwp/book-example/archive/chapter_philosophy_and_refactoring.zip

Don't Let it Become a Crutch!

Try not to sneak a peek at the answers unless you're really, really stuck. Like I said at the beginning of the last chapter, there's a lot of value in debugging errors all by yourself, and in real life, there's no "harrys repo" to check against and find all the answers.

Bibliography

[dip] Mark Pilgrim, *Dive Into Python*: *http://www.diveintopython.net/*

[lpthw] Zed A. Shaw, *Learn Python the Hard Way*: *http://learnpythonthehardway.org/*

[iwp] Al Sweigart, *Invent Your Own Computer Games with Python*: *http://inventwithpython.com*

[tddbe] Kent Beck, *Test Driven Development: By Example*, Addison-Wesley

[refactoring] Martin Fowler, *Refactoring*, Addison-Wesley

[seceng] Ross Anderson, *Security Engineering, Second Edition*, Addison-Wesley: *http://www.cl.cam.ac.uk/~rja14/book.html*

[jsgoodparts] Douglas Crockford, *JavaScript: The Good Parts* (*http://oreil.ly/SuXjXq*), O'Reilly

[twoscoops] Daniel Greenfeld and Audrey Roy, *Two Scoops of Django*, *http://twoscoopspress.com/products/two-scoops-of-django-1-6*

[mockfakestub] Emily Bache, *Mocks, Fakes and Stubs*, *https://leanpub.com/mocks-fakes-stubs*

[GOOSGBT] Steve Freeman and Nat Pryce, *Growing Object-Oriented Software Guided by Tests*, Addison-Wesley

Index

integrated development environments (IDEs), xxv
integrated tests
  architectural considerations, 475
  benefits and drawbacks of, 426, 438, 477
  vs. isolated, 435-437
  vs. unit tests, 67, 469
invalid input, 229
  (see also model-layer validation)
isolation, ensuring
  benefits and drawbacks of, 407, 438
  failed test example, 407
  forms layer, 418-422
  in functional tests, 83-87
  vs. integrated tests, 435-437
  layer interactions as contracts, 427-431
  using mocks for, 408-411
  models layer, 422-426
  refactoring ugly tests, 412
  removing redundant code, 432-435
  risks of mocking, 426
  view layer, 412-418
iterative development style, 55, 101

J

Jasmine, 299
JavaScript testing
  additional considerations for, 299
  additional resources, 283
  boilerplate and namespacing, 297
  functional test, 283
  in Jenkins with PhantomJS, 454-456
  jQuery and fixtures div, 287-291
  key challenges of, 293-297
  managing global state, 293, 300
  syntax errors, 299
  in the TDD cycle, 298
  test running libraries, 285-287, 300
  unit test, 291
Jenkins
  configuration, 440
  first build, 445
  installation, 439
  project setup, 444
  QUnit JavaScript tests with, 454-456
  timeout bumping, 453
  virtual display setup, 447-449
jQuery, 287-291
JSON fixtures, 370, 374

jumbotron class (Bootstrap), 146

L

lambda functions, 215
layout (see CSS; design and layout testing)
Lettuce, 509
Linux servers, 162
list comprehensions, 42
list items, 63, 76, 109-113, 207-213
LiveServerTestCase class, 84
loaddata command, 374
logging, 319, 376, 389
login process, skipping, 366
  (see also authentication)

M

MacOS, xxviii
mail.out box attribute, 329
Meta attributes, 268
meta-comments, 100
minimum viable applications, 96
mocks
  benefits and drawbacks of, 329, 426, 438
  de-spiking custom authentication, 343-350
  functional test for, 357
  isolating tests using, 401, 408-411
  logout link, 361
  manual, 330-333
  mock.return_value, 353
  mock_auth variable, 355
  practical application of, 359
  preparing for, 329
  Python Mock library, 334-343, 363
  reducing duplication with, 350-356, 364
model-layer validation
  benefits and drawbacks of, 224, 240
  POST requests processing, 231-237
  preventing duplicate items, 266
  removing hardcoded URLs, 237-240
  running full validation, 225
  self.assertRaises context manager, 224
  surfacing errors in the view, 226-231
Model-View-Controller (MVC) pattern, 25, 96
ModelForm class, 244
monkeypatching, 330-333, 363
multiple lists testing
  adding items to existing lists, 119-122
  incremental design implementation, 97
  iterative development style, 101

refactoring, 43-47, 49, 64-66, 106, 208, 219, 221, 412
regression, 82, 99-101
regular expressions, 125
Representational State Transfer (REST)
    additional resources, 525
    building a REST API, 526-545
    defined, 525
    inspiration gained from, 96
    tips for REST APIs, 545
requirements.txt, 165, 189
response.context, 127
reverse lookups, 128

S

scratchpad to-do list, 82
screenshots, 449-453, 457
scripts, building standalone, 382
secret values, 377
security issues and settings
    ALLOWED_HOSTS, 182
    Cross-Site Request Forgery, 57
    login systems, 363
    server security, 194
sed (stream editor), 203
Selenium
    best CI practices, 457
    installation, xxxi
    and JavaScript, 300
    and PythonAnywhere, 481
    testing user interactions with, 40-42
    upgrading, 88
self.assertRaises context manager, 224
self.browser.refresh(), 146
self.wait_for helper method, 218, 221, 370
send_mail function, 310-312
server provisioning, 160, 178
sessions, pre-creating, 366-370, 382
single-assertion unit tests, 495
small vs. big design, 95-97, 131
socket.error: [WinError 10054], 146
software requirements, xxv-xxx
spiking and de-spiking
    branching your VCS, 309
    de-spiking, 319-322, 343-350
    defined, 308, 328
    logging to stderr, 319
staging sites
    adapting functional tests for, 158-160

benefits of, 156, 173
catching final bugs with, 375-377
continuous integrations and, 457
domain names, 160
fixtures and, 389
local vs. staged sessions, 386
managing test databases, 382-387
manual code deployment, 163
manual server provisioning, 160
StaleElementException, 90
static files
    challenges of, 136, 156
    collecting for deployment, 149-152
    finding, 144
    serving with Nginx, 180, 194
    URL requests for, 144
StaticLiveServerTestCase, 145
stderr, 319
string representations, 269-271
style (see CSS; design and layout testing)
superlists, 6
system tests, 470
Systemd, 188

T

table styling (Bootstrap), 147
templates
    designing APIs using, 398
    Django template inheritance, 141
    inheritance hierarchy, 397
    passing variables to, 60
    saving for provisioning config files, 190-193
    separate list viewing templates, 107-108
    syntax, 60
    tags
        {% csrf_token %}, 58
        {% for … endfor %}, 76
        {% url %}, 237
    views layer and, 399
Test Client (Django), 47-49
test files
    organizing and refactoring, 221
    running single, 212
    splitting FTs into many, 209
    splitting unit tests into several, 219
test fixtures, 370, 374
test running libraries, 285
Test-Driven Development (TDD)

W

wait_for helper method, 221

wait_for_row_in_list_table helper method, 218, 370

wait_to_be_logged_in/out, 370

Windows

    Gunicorn support, 190

    tips, xxvii

with statements, 225

working state to working state, 118, 131

X

Xvfb, 481

Y

YAGNI (You ain't gonna need it!), 96, 131

About the Author

After an idyllic childhood spent playing with BASIC on French 8-bit computers like the Thomson T-07 whose keys go "boop" when you press them, Harry spent a few years being deeply unhappy with economics and management consultancy. Soon he rediscovered his true geek nature, and was lucky enough to fall in with a bunch of XP fanatics, working on the pioneering but sadly defunct Resolver One spreadsheet. He now works at PythonAnywhere LLP, and spreads the gospel of TDD worldwide at talks, workshops, and conferences, with all the passion and enthusiasm of a recent convert.

Colophon

The animal on the cover of *Test-Driven Development with Python* is a cashmere goat. Though all goats can produce a cashmere undercoat, only those goats selectively bred to produce cashmere in commercially viable amounts are typically considered "cashmere goats." Cashmere goats thus belong to the domestic goat species *Capra hircus*.

The exceptionally fine, soft hair of the undercoat of a cashmere goat grows alongside an outer coat of coarser hair as part of the goat's double fleece. The cashmere undercoat appears in winter to supplement the protection offered by the outer coat, called *guard hair*. The crimped quality of cashmere hair in the undercoat accounts for its lightweight yet effective insulation properties.

The name "cashmere" is derived from the Kashmir Valley region on the Indian subcontinent where the textile has been manufactured for thousands of years. A diminishing population of cashmere goats in modern Kashmir has led to the cessation of exports of cashmere fiber from the area. Most cashmere wool now originates in Afghanistan, Iran, Outer Mongolia, India, and—predominantly—China.

Cashmere goats grow hair of varying colors and color combinations. Both males and females have horns, which serve to keep the animals cool in summer and provide the goats' owners with effective handles during farming activities.

Many of the animals on O'Reilly covers are endangered; all of them are important to the world. To learn more about how you can help, go to *animals.oreilly.com*.

The cover image is from Wood's Animate Creation. The cover fonts are URW Typewriter and Guardian Sans. The text font is Adobe Minion Pro; the heading font is Adobe Myriad Condensed; and the code font is Dalton Maag's Ubuntu Mono.

Learn from experts.
Find the answers you need.

Sign up for a **10-day free trial** to get **unlimited access** to all of the content on Safari, including Learning Paths, interactive tutorials, and curated playlists that draw from thousands of ebooks and training videos on a wide range of topics, including data, design, DevOps, management, business—and much more.

Start your free trial at:

oreilly.com/safari

(No credit card required.)

Milton Keynes UK
Ingram Content Group UK Ltd.
UKHW020219131024
449553UK00004B/9